Number Three: Environmental History Series

MARTIN V. MELOSI, *General Editor*

VISION OR VILLAINY

VISION OR VILLAINY

Origins of the
Owens Valley-Los Angeles
Water Controversy

By
ABRAHAM HOFFMAN

Texas A&M University Press

COLLEGE STATION

Library of Congress Cataloging in Publication Data
Hoffman, Abraham.

Vision or villainy.

(Environmental history series ; no. 3)
Bibliography: p.
Includes index.
1. Los Angeles (Calif.)—Water-supply—History.
2. Water resources development—California—Owens
Valley—History. I. Title. II. Title: Owens Valley–Los
Angeles water controversy. III. Series.
HD4464.L7H64   333.91′009794′94   80–6111
ISBN 0–89096–112–3 cloth   AACR2
ISBN 0-89096-509-9 pbk.

Manufactured in the United States of America
Second printing, 1992

To John and LaRee Caughey
and
Everett and Anna Marie Hager

Contents

List of Illustrations

Preface

FOLLOWING the release of the motion picture *Chinatown* in 1974, a high-ranking official in the Los Angeles Department of Water and Power (DWP) attended a dinner party where he became embroiled in an argument concerning the film's historical accuracy. "It's all wrong," complained the official; "it's totally inaccurate." The other person then asked the official to be specific. Exactly which facts were incorrect? The DWP official emphatically replied, "There was never any incest involved."[1]

The story is probably apocryphal, but it perhaps best illustrates the general lack of understanding as to why the Owens Valley–Los Angeles water controversy continues without end. It is now in its eighth decade, and there is little hope that the issues can be satisfactorily resolved for all parties concerned. Incest may well be the only element missing from a controversy that already includes dynamiting, suicide, embezzlement, endless litigation, allegations of fraud, and doubt cast on the integrity of some of Los Angeles' most famous civic leaders.

The water controversy dates from 1905 and continues to this day. Its ramifications transcend the geographical boundaries of California, since it has raised questions concerning the rights of a rural region as against a growing metropolitan area, environmental issues, and governmental responsibilities on several levels. Complex

---

[1]"Water under the Bridge," *Los Angeles* 20 (January, 1975), 34–35.

questions involving industrial growth, suburban development, loss of agricultural land, and innumerable other calculations measure the limits of our quality of life. Such present-day problems, now recognized on a national scale, are mirrored in the events surrounding the growth of Los Angeles from an obscure western town to a major metropolitan area and in the penalties paid for that growth.

Today, except for the federal government, Los Angeles is the largest single landholder in Inyo County, California. Whatever promise of growth Inyo County's Owens Valley might have had was stunted, and it is only in recent years that the valley's descendants have enjoyed an irony of sorts as a result of the city's victory. Multilane highways have placed Owens Valley within easy reach of Southern California, and people from Los Angeles who never heard of the controversy (being transplanted Easterners or worshipers of the Mammoth ski slopes with no time for reading history books) willingly deposit their recreational savings in the coffers of Owens Valley motels, restaurants, service stations, and sporting goods stores. Owens Valley has the scenery; Los Angeles, the congestion and pollution.

The beginnings of the controversy involved considerable personal conflict. This has long since given way to an impersonal battle of court proceedings, injunctions, and environmental impact reports. Problems continue to arise over the Los Angeles Department of Water and Power's management of its land and water holdings in the valley. No longer at the boiling point, the controversy simmers on at both philosophical and practical levels. The idea of a city's acquiring a distant water supply at the expense of the region that loses it is inextricably mixed with the fact that Los Angeles did it.

Unfortunately, the history of the controversy is at best incompletely and at worst imperfectly remembered. The best accounts have relied on published records or interviews with people many years after the events they are asked to recall; the worst ones repeat earlier errors as facts for new generations to misinterpret. Surprisingly few sources have provided the basis for a retelling of the controversy, and some of these have not been critically appraised.[2] Additionally,

---

[2] On the historiography of the controversy see Abraham Hoffman, "Joseph Barlow Lippincott and the Owens Valley Controversy: Time for Revision," *Southern California Quarterly* 54 (Fall, 1972), 239–240.

conventional accounts of the controversy have focused on a city-versus-valley orientation, overlooking the presence of the federal government in the origins of the dispute. In a broader context, Owens Valley fell victim to policies set not by the City of Los Angeles but by Washington, D.C., acting in accordance with the philosophy of the Progressive movement in the first decade of the twentieth century. The views of President Theodore Roosevelt and his subordinates who worked in such agencies as the Geological Survey, the Reclamation Service, and the Bureau of Forestry were of major consequence in determining the future of Los Angeles and the fate of Inyo County.[3]

This book presents the history of the Owens Valley–Los Angeles water controversy with the added perspective of the federal government's involvement, particularly the role played by Reclamation Service Supervising Engineer Joseph B. Lippincott in the dispute. Lippincott, whose appearance in previous articles and books has been mainly limited to that of the villain who sold out the valley to the city, was a far more complex person than the caricatures of him have shown. To support this perspective, primary source materials—unpublished correspondence, reports, and manuscripts—many of them until now unused, have been utilized.

Two approaches have been used in writing this history of the controversy. One was, as much as possible, to place the people involved in the situation as they themselves saw it at the time—that is, without benefit of hindsight. The other was to call attention where appropriate to errors in the historical record that have appeared because some writers did use hindsight, excessively or unfairly, and later authors accepted such earlier work as factual. Overall, I have attempted to remain objective in presenting the controversy, backing off from portrayals of anyone as deep-dyed villains or virtuous heroes. Governmental representatives on whatever level—city, state, or federal—are too often shown as puppets of their institutions, incapable of personal soul-searching. If there is any partiality shown here, it is in the desire to redress the balance in a historical record that too often oversimplifies the complexity of the controversy,

[3]Abraham Hoffman, "Origins of a Controversy: The U.S. Reclamation Service and the Owens Valley–Los Angeles Water Dispute," *Arizona and the West* 19 (Winter, 1977), 334, 345–346.

usually at the expense of the city. Little expectation is held that this book can provide definitive answers to the questions raised about the causes and consequences of the controversy. But it is hoped that this study, grounded in documentation rather than assertion, may point to a pathway that others can follow with new footnotes on long-forgotten evidence.

The Owens Valley–Los Angeles water controversy breaks down into roughly three phases. The first phase is marked by the creation of the controversy, including the city's search for a new water supply following its struggle to recapture its water works operation from a private company; the federal government's surveys for possible reclamation projects as provided for by the Reclamation Act of 1902; and the desire of Owens Valley settlers to have such a project in their valley. The city's victory in obtaining lands riparian to the Owens River was followed by the construction of the aqueduct, along with land speculation in the San Fernando Valley adjacent to the city of Los Angeles. This phase approximately spans the years 1898 to 1915.

The second phase began in the early 1920's as Los Angeles attempted to increase the flow of water through the aqueduct and embarked on a policy of large-scale land purchases in Owens Valley. The valley people resisted, resorting on a number of occasions to dynamiting the aqueduct. Resistance ended when Inyo County bankers fighting the city were arrested and convicted of embezzlement. The tragedy was compounded with the failure of the St. Francis Dam, a storage reservoir for aqueduct water, resulting in the deaths of more than four hundred people. A state senate investigating committee censured Los Angeles for failure to honor obligations to the valley. This phase ran approximately from 1923 to 1940.

The final phase continues through to today—the city's economic dominance over the valley and the evolution of a new environmental philosophy that directly contrasts with the attitudes of the Progressive Era, when the phrase "the greatest good for the greatest number" was often repeated. Litigation continues to the present, as Inyo County claims that the withdrawal of Owens River water adversely affects the valley's environment.

Concurrent with these phases we find attempts by concerned people to write about the controversy. For the most part these authors were partial to one side or another, and their writings must be used with caution. An attempt is made here to place these writings and their authors in historical perspective.

No historical inquiry involving a lengthy period of research can be made without the help of many people, and the debts to be paid here through brief acknowledgment hardly compensate for the time given to me by librarians, colleagues, and interested individuals. Dr. Robert C. Post of the Smithsonian Institution made it possible for me to obtain manuscripts never before used in any study of the controversy. My debt to him simply cannot be overstated. The Los Angeles Public Library provided access to one-of-a-kind materials, including a major run of the long-forgotten Los Angeles *Graphic*. The late John Bruckman, head bibliographer at the library, recognized the importance of the Los Angeles *Gridiron* and preserved its copies by having them microfilmed. William French of the American Society of Civil Engineers kindly made available copies of the applications for membership of key participants in the water dispute; this and related material yielded important biographical information. Librarians at the Bancroft Library, Huntington Library, National Archives, Library of Congress, and Special Collections Department and Government and Public Affairs Department at the University of California, Los Angeles, assisted in the search for materials. Dr. William O. Hendricks, director of the Sherman Library, kept a constant eye out for materials. Gerald J. Giefer, director of the Water Resources Center Archives at the Berkeley campus of the University of California, made available important materials from the J. B. Lippincott and Andrae B. Nordskog collections. The Minnesota Historical Society provided important manuscript materials on Nordskog. Donald F. Hinrichs, librarian at the Los Angeles Department of Water and Power, was most helpful and cooperative, and the DWP allowed me free use of its photographic collection; my particular thanks go to Ed Gill and Ed Freudenburg for their assistance.

Research was facilitated at several points through institutional generosity. The Sourisseau Academy at San Jose State University provided a stipend for 1974 to 1976, which helped cover the cost of photocopying and the purchase of materials. My taking part in the National Endowment for the Humanities Summer Seminar in

1977 enabled me to spend additional time at the Bancroft Library. Professors W. Turrentine Jackson, the late Robert E. Levinson, Lawrence B. Lee, Leonard Leader, Norris Hundley, jr., Donald Pisani, Samuel H. Mayo, and Gene M. Gressley have all given constructive criticism and encouragement at one point or another. Dr. Martin Ridge, senior research associate at the Huntington Library, invited me to give a presentation of my research to a conference of California historians in 1978. They offered more suggestions and advice than I could reasonably incorporate, but their interest and criticisms were nonetheless appreciated.

Although the major participants have long since passed away, I was able to interview several people who knew or were related to them. My thanks to William Mulholland, nephew of his namesake; the late Paul F. Gemperle, who was at one time employed by the Lippincott engineering firm; the late Mrs. Gertrude Nordskog, widow of Andrae B. Nordskog; Robert Killion, executor of Mrs. Nordskog's estate; and Robert Nordskog, Andrae Nordskog's son. I have profited from correspondence with the late Carey McWilliams, Cedric Belfrage, Allen R. Ottley, Vernon M. Freeman, and Remi Nadeau, and from conversations with Catherine Mulholland, William Kahrl, and the late James Bassett.

In a conversation with Mrs. Gertrude Nordskog shortly before her death in 1971, I learned that Nordskog papers had been given to the Water Resources Center Archives, University of California at Berkeley, and the Minnesota Historical Society after her husband's death in 1962. The summaries, transcriptions, and letters utilized in the "Boulder Dam" manuscript research are at the Water Resources Center Archives. I am grateful for the help of Mr. Gerald Giefer, director of the Water Resources Center Archives, and Ms. Sue Holbert of the Minnesota Historical Society for permitting me to bring these two sets of materials together through photocopies.

Elements of my research have appeared in several publications cited in the bibliography. Professor Doyce B. Nunis, Jr., editor of *Southern California Quarterly*, has offered advice and encouragement, as have Professor Harwood P. Hinton, editor of *Arizona and the West*, and Dr. Norton B. Stern, editor of *Western States Jewish Historical Quarterly*. The Los Angeles Westerners Corral has been unusually patient and supportive. The members heard a presentation on the water controversy in 1976 and thought enough of it to nominate it for the Philip A. Danielson Award. The presentation received second prize in the 1977 competition. The Corral also accepted an article on the controversy for its *Brand Book No. 15.* Helpful Westerners include Glen Dawson, Ray Billington, Anthony Lehman, C. Woodrow Wilson, Ernest Marquez, Victor Plukas, and many others in the Corral.

A special word of thanks belongs to the recipients of the book's dedication. Mr. Everett Hager and his wife Anna Marie and Professor Emeritus John Caughey and his wife LaRee long ago recognized some possibilities in me that if nurtured might contribute something of value to the cause of history. I hope that this contribution will not be a disappointment to them.

Finally, a word of appreciation to my family for enduring restrictions on living space and leisure time and for sharing the frustrations and obstacles such a project as this one required. To my wife Susan and our sons Joshua and Gregory, I can only promise that any future projects will receive no more than equal time, not the lion's share of my waking thoughts.

A long roster of acknowledgments invariably calls for a disclaimer concerning possible errors of fact, interpretation, spelling, and syntax, and regret if people deserving credit were overlooked. I readily accept the responsibility.

List of Abbreviations

BL   Bancroft Library, University of California, Berkeley

DWP   Los Angeles Department of Water and Power

GPA   Government and Public Affairs Department, University of California, Los Angeles

HL   Huntington Library, San Marino, California

LAPL   Los Angeles Public Library

LC   Library of Congress, Washington, D.C.

MHS   Minnesota Historical Society, St. Paul, Minnesota

NPRC Status of Employees, Joseph Barlow Lippincott, National Personnel Records Center (Civilian Personnel Records), St. Louis, Missouri

RBR   Records of the Bureau of Reclamation, National Archives, Washington, D.C. All records from Record Group 115:

        OV-GCRW General correspondence re Right-of-Way Applications in Owens River Valley, General Administrative and Project Records

        OVPM   Owens Valley Project Miscellaneous, Project File 1902–1919

        OV-PR   Owens Valley, Preliminary Reports on General Plans, General Administrative and Project Records

SCD   Special Collections Department, University of California, Los Angeles

WFM   Western Federation of Miners

WRCA Water Resources Center Archives, University of California, Berkeley

VISION OR VILLAINY

1

Owens Valley and
the City of Los Angeles

"That action is best, which procures the *greatest Happiness* for the *greatest* Numbers . . . "—Francis Hutcheson, "Inquiry Concerning Moral Good and Evil" (1720)

SATURDAY, July 29, 1905, promised to usher in an active summer's weekend in the City of the Angels. The sky was cloudy in the morning, but the forecast was for the mid-70's and a typically clear day. Tourists hiking to the summit of Mount Wilson could easily see Catalina Island, twenty-six miles out in the Pacific Ocean. Below them stretched the Los Angeles basin, a plain dotted with orchards, scattered modest but growing cities, and such occasional oddities as ostrich farms and automobiles.

Los Angeles residents planning an evening at the theater found a variety of offerings scheduled for their pleasure. At the Grand Opera House the Ulrich Stock Company presented its final performance of *Lighthouse by the Sea*, and readied its suggestively titled production of *Queen of the White Slaves* for Sunday. The Orpheum—not the present downtown theater, but one located on Spring Street between Second and Third—featured a series of vaudeville acts. Morosco's Burbank Theater (destined in its last years to become a sleazy burlesque house) presented the final performances of *My Partner*, a story of mining days; meanwhile, the Belasco Theater continued the comedy *The Stubbornness of Geraldine*. Residents on fashionable Bunker Hill could descend with ease from Grand Avenue to Hill Street, taking the Angel's Flight funicular railway, now in its fourth year of operation. Theatergoers in outlying areas could ride into the city in the comfort of a Pacific Electric streetcar. Downtown Los Angeles offered a number of fine restaurants, ranging from Al Levy's Cafe to the Pacific Electric Grill, where diners could enjoy an eight-course French dinner for fifty cents.

Aside from cultural and culinary offerings, Los Angeles citizens had their choice of no fewer than five metropolitan newspapers, running the political spectrum from the archconservative *Times* to the liberal *Record*. The city's oldest paper, the *Express*, maintained an independent political position. William Randolph Hearst, the young journalism magnate, had started the *Examiner* in December, 1903, to compete with the *Times* for morning readers. This morning the *Times* and *Examiner* devoted their front pages to the pressing issue of the day: the Russo-Japanese War was winding down, and newspaper editorials speculated—in those days journalism being a more personal affair between editor and reader—on the success of the peace talks then under way at Portsmouth, New Hampshire, mediated by President Theodore Roosevelt.

As a rule the Los Angeles newspapers placed news of local interest on the front page of their second section. On July 29 the lead articles in the *Examiner* described mundane civic matters. The *Times*, by contrast, proclaimed in a major headline, "Titanic Project to Give City a River," and proceeded to present a most unusual report:

The Times announces this morning the most important movement for the development of Los Angeles in all the city's history—the closing of the preliminary negotiations securing 30,000 inches of water, or about ten times our present total supply, enough for a city of 2,000,000 people. In brief, the project is to bring this water to Los Angeles from Owens River in Inyo county, a distance of 240 miles at a cost of about $23,000,-000. Options on the water-bearing lands have been closed by the city's representatives and a series of bond issues will be asked of the voters. This new water supply, immense and unfailing, will make Los Angeles forge ahead by leaps and bounds and remove every specter of drought or doubt. With such an enormous stream of the purest mountain water pouring in here, Los Angeles will have one of the best supplies in the land, she will have water to sell to the San Fernando Valley and even to San Diego; she will have assured her future for a century. There is no doubt that the bonds will be forthcoming.[1]

[1] *Los Angeles Times*, July 29, 1905.

Column after column revealed details about a plan previously and totally unknown to almost everyone in Los Angeles. The scheme had been kept a secret, it was now revealed, because municipal enterprises invited land speculators who would charge high prices for necessary options. The city now owned—that is, had bought options on—some fifty miles of land bordering the Owens River. All the good citizens of Los Angeles would have to do to bring this source of sparkling "snow-fed" water to the city would be to vote some $25 million in bonds for the purchase of the lands and for the construction of an aqueduct second only to the Panama Canal in scope and ambition.

The story of how the options had been secured received attention as well. The *Times* credited former Mayor Fred Eaton for his "financial daring" in traveling through Owens Valley in the guise of a buyer of property for cattle ranches. According to the *Times*, Eaton had served as a willing dupe for the farmers and ranchers of Inyo County. They had sold him marginal land "that in reality was little else than a lava bed," with Eaton looking the other way as Owens Valley settlers dampened arid soil, "hoping to get a better price for it." Eaton had willingly accepted the asking price, had even paid several hundred dollars more when pressed for it. The settlers then departed with their profits, heading for the prospecting possibilities in the vicinity of the mining towns of Goldfield and Tonopah across the border in Nevada. The Los Angeles Board of Water Commissioners gladly accepted Eaton's options and voted to pay him for their cost; a bond issue, if approved by Los Angeles voters, would pay for the full purchase price of the properties. The *Times* did not doubt for an instant that the city would rise to this magnificent opportunity and give wholehearted support to the water board's plans.

Another article featured William Mulholland's bringing "the glad tidings" to the city (in actuality a *Times* reporter had telegraphed news of the closure of the final option deal from Inyo County). "Scorched and browned by the almost intolerable desert wind and sun Superintendent Mulholland returned yesterday afternoon from a daring nine days' automobile trip into the heart of the Owens River country, bearing the glad tidings that 'the last spike has been driven; the options are all secured; the deal by which Los

Angeles city becomes the owner of thirty thousand inches of the purest snow water has been nailed.' " Mulholland, the superintendent of the city's Water Department, heaped praise upon Eaton for his foresight in knowing of the potential liquid wealth in the Owens River and his early recognition of its value for Los Angeles. Mulholland claimed that as far back as 1892 Eaton had recognized the possibilities of the river. Somewhat slower in his own powers of prescience, Mulholland had not taken Eaton seriously until 1902, when the city had been, as to an extent it still was, suffering from a prolonged drought.

Other articles also lavished praise on the proposed project. Water had been the only ingredient lacking in the recipe for the continuing growth of Los Angeles. The city already had "a salubrious climate," fertile soil, and a growing population. Even the federal government, considered a possible rival to the city's plans, had the "good grace" to recognize "that the Owens River water would fulfill a greater mission in Los Angeles than if it were to be spread over acres of desert land that ordinarily would have come under its influence."

Photographs of the men principally responsible for creating the proposed project were prominently placed among the stories. There were portraits of Mulholland and Eaton, Mayor Owen McAleer, and City Attorney William B. Mathews. A group photograph of the Board of Water Commissioners featured the five men who had given their approval to Eaton's vision: John Fay, John Elliott, Moses Sherman, Fred Baker, and William Mead. All were prominent businessmen in the Los Angeles community. Fay and Elliott were bankers; Baker owned the Baker Iron Works, a major steel producer; Sherman had put electric streetcars on Los Angeles tracks and served as a director on numerous bank boards; and Mead was in real estate and finance. Rounding out the pantheon of civic heroes was a portrait of Joseph Barlow Lippincott, the United States Reclamation Service's supervising engineer for California. "It is the extreme good fortune of Los Angeles that Mr. Lippincott should have been the engineer in charge of the [federal government's] survey of these water lands," stated the *Times*. "Being a resident of Los Angeles, fully cognizant of the pressing need that confronted the city, he was quick to realize the fact that it was in Los Angeles that this water would afford the greatest good to the greatest number."

The *Times* broke faith with the other Los Angeles newspapers in releasing the sensational story. Enterprising reporters had caught wind of the plan several months earlier. In order to prevent land speculators from inflating the price of the needed Owens Valley properties, all the papers had agreed to keep the plan a secret. On Sunday, July 30, the *Examiner*, understandably angry over the *Times*'s jumping of the gun, informed its readers that it had kept faith with the pledge "when silence meant saving of millions to city." Mayor McAleer published a front-page statement to that effect, with the *Examiner* taking small consolation in the fact that it was scooped "because others held lightly their word of honor." Nevertheless, the *Examiner* featured numerous articles—now somewhat tardily—on the proposed aqueduct. The afternoon newspapers, which did not publish Sunday editions, had to wait until Monday, at which time they added their own embellishments.[2]

The citizens of Los Angeles were attracted to the proposals described in the newspaper articles, but while the news of the ambitious project came as a surprise, the story of a water shortage for the city was hardly a new one. For several years now, as the city's population had mushroomed beyond all expectation and belief, people familiar with the region's water resources had warned that the city's future depended on the acquisition of an adequate water supply. Existing sources simply could not, in a semiarid region, support a city that in the first half of the first decade of the twentieth century had already doubled its population. Many of these newcomers had never heard of Inyo County, much less the Owens River or the valley through which it ran. On the surface the proposal seemed a far-fetched, visionary scheme. But city leaders, men known for their expertise in solving water problems, endorsed the project and said it could be done—would have to be done if future growth was to be assured.

On hearing about the project, the object of Los Angeles' en-

[2]*Los Angeles Examiner*, July 30, 1905. Cf. *Los Angeles Herald* and *Los Angeles Evening Express*, July 31, 1905.

thusiastic plans displayed scant affection for a union of city dreams with Owens River water at the expense of Owens Valley. Farmers and ranchers in the valley, who expected their own region to grow by means of an anticipated federal reclamation project, were outraged at the idea that a city over two hundred miles away proposed to use their water. Willie A. Chalfant, editor of Bishop's *Inyo Register*, vented his hostility in unrestrained editorial anger. "Owens Valley is to be made the victim of the greatest water steal on record, if the plans of Los Angeles are carried into effect," he said. "The lands affected being bought by the promoters, in this crime against a county there may be nothing which cannot be supported by law; it will consist in taking from a valley's lands the streams which nature intended for them, and to a very large degree converting into waste places what should become a fertile and populous area, even though owned by Los Angeles people."[3]

Apart from Chalfant's understandable if almost ungrammatical outrage at the proposal, the news of the project as revealed by the *Times* suffered from distortions, inaccuracies, and omissions. Because of the initial impact of the project announcement, many of the errors in the news reports were accepted as truth in spite of later retractions and denials. The *Times*'s assertions of the project's providing surplus water for sale to San Diego and the San Fernando Valley were not only inaccurate but illegal. Eaton's "financial daring" was interpreted in Owens Valley as fraud and misrepresentation. Contrary to the *Times*'s assertion, the Reclamation Service had not surrendered its proposed reclamation project to the city. Lippincott, in the pivotal role of supervising a survey for a proposed federal reclamation project while allegedly helping the city get the water instead, denied all the credit given him by the *Times*. But he found his later career shadowed by accusations that ranged from poor judgment at the very least to involvement in a grand conspiracy to swindle Owens Valley's people and enrich Los Angeles speculators. Mulholland, enshrined in Los Angeles, with a junior high school, a highway, a reservoir, and a memorial named for him, became hated in Owens Valley as the personification of the extremes to which an

[3]*Inyo Register*, August 3, 1905.

for improvements. After considerable political debate and maneuvering, the Southern Pacific lost the contest, and San Pedro received the federal blessing. Several years later the harbor area was annexed to the City of Los Angeles through a long shoestring-like strip.

With the development of the city on the seaward side secured, Los Angeles in the 1890's considered its fresh-water problems. Located in a semiarid basin, Los Angeles for its first century had depended on the Los Angeles River for its domestic water needs. Increasing population and rival municipalities now presented new challenges. The city's ownership of the river became a matter of litigation. Disputes over riparian rights, appropriative rights, whether a municipality could sell its water outside its limits, and other questions kept the courts of the state busy at all levels. One major case settled whether the City of Los Angeles could exercise its pueblo water rights, which dated to the city's founding under Spanish rule. In *City of Los Angeles* v. *Pomeroy,* decided in 1899, the California Supreme Court ruled that the city's pueblo right predated any subsequent riparian rights along the river and that the river's subterranean flow also belonged to the city. The court decision adversely affected agriculture in the San Fernando Valley, twenty miles upriver from Los Angeles. This in effect made it inevitable for Los Angeles to become the dominant city on Southern California's coastal plain, since the only way other communities could obtain a water supply was either by finding one outside the watershed of the Los Angeles River or by surrendering to the City of Los Angeles through annexation.[6]

By the beginning of the twentieth century Los Angeles could be counted as one of America's great urban success stories. Within only a portion of the lifetimes of many of its residents the city had progressed from a scruffy backwater town of adobe buildings and vigilante violence to the beginnings of an important economic and commercial center. Oil, oranges, climate, and advertising had brought tremendous numbers of people to the region, and Los Angeles grew to dominance as the heart of Southern California. Reflecting on the

[6]Vincent Ostrom, *Water and Politics: A Study of Water Policies and Administration in the Development of Water Rights,* pp. 146–147; Wells A. Hutchins, *The California Law of Water Rights,* pp. 256–262; *Los Angeles Times,* June 4 and 5, 1899.

city's success, Charles Dwight Willard, a booster and local historian, said in 1901, "The southwestern region of the United States will support at least one great city, and all doubt as to where that city will be located is now at an end." He observed that the notion that Los Angeles "should someday become one of the great metropolitan centers of the nation is not a dream, but the natural outgrowth of existing conditions."[7]

But existing conditions also dictated that the city's growth might come to a sudden stop. The Los Angeles River could support the presence of only so many people. Anyone with a feasible idea for increasing the city's water resources—or the region's, for that matter—could gain an audience. Rainmakers, who were taken seriously in many circles, claimed they could bring water down from the heavens. Other people, less prone to confuse imagination with vision, investigated more earthly possibilities, including a river located nowhere near Los Angeles.

A Valley's Hopes

Two hundred and forty miles north of Los Angeles lies the Owens Valley, tucked behind the southern Sierras. It is a land of contrasts: from Mount Whitney, the highest point in the forty-eight contiguous states, one gazes east across Inyo County past Owens Valley to Death Valley, at 282 feet below sea level the lowest spot in the United States. Its source of life, the Owens River, flows from its headwaters in the Sierra Nevada Mountains south for 125 miles into Owens Lake. The river water is fresh; the lake is alkaline, containing, according to one Inyo County newspaper, enough bicarbonate of soda to supply the entire world.[8]

[7]Charles Dwight Willard, *The Herald's History of Los Angeles City*, p. 354; *Men of Achievement in the Great Southwest: A Story of Pioneer Struggles During Early Days in Los Angeles and Southern California*, chap. 10; "A Community that Exploits Itself," *World's Work* 7 (November, 1903), 4152–53; Arthur MacDonald Dole, "How Los Angeles Grows," *Sunset* 16 (December, 1905), 176–188; Bertha H. Smith, "The Making of Los Angeles," *Sunset* 19 (July, 1907), 237–254.

[8]*Inyo Independent*, March 17, 1893; E. C. LaRue and F. F. Henshaw, "Surface Water Supply of the United States, 1909: Part X, the Great Basin," U.S. Department of the Interior, Geological Survey, *Water-Supply and Irriga-*

The valley, river, and lake received their name from John C. Fremont, who in October, 1845, passed through the region on his third expedition. Richard Owens was one of Fremont's guides. In reviewing the discoveries made by his party Fremont stated, "To one of the lakes I gave Owens' name." Curiously, Owens never saw the landmarks named for him. Other members of the expedition were similarly honored.[9]

With the ambitions of most early arrivals to California centered on gold-seeking, few people paid attention to the Owens Valley region for a number of years. Problems surfaced in the 1850's with Indians. A military expedition organized in 1859 went through the valley, finding few hostiles but noting the area's physical attractions. When gold and silver were discovered in the region, a decade-long conflict with the Indians erupted. Throughout the 1860's the warfare continued on, off, and on again, with atrocities committed on both sides. Some sixty whites and two hundred Indians were killed. For the Indians it was a question of defending their domain; for the whites, of not having any room for Indians in their plans to use the resources the region offered.[10]

In the spring of 1865 several prospectors discovered silver at Cerro Gordo, "Fat Hill," northeast of Owens Lake. A minor rush resulted in the establishing of a mining camp, with freight and passenger transportation, and the production of silver and lead in bullion-bar form; later finds included gold and zinc. As much as $17 million in mineral riches was extracted from the Cerro Gordo mines, most of it brought down by way of Los Angeles to the small seaport of Wilmington and from there to San Francisco. The major transporter of bullion, Remi Nadeau, so dominated the freighting busi-

tion Paper 270, pp. 152–156; Russ Leadabrand, "Dry Lake, Dry Land," *Westways* 63 (February, 1971), 14–16, 54. Owens Lake is now dry.

[9]John C. Fremont, *Memoirs of My Life*, p. 455; J. M. Guinn, "Some Early History of Owens River Valley," Historical Society of Southern California, *Annual Publications* 10 (1917), 41–42; W. A. Chalfant, *The Story of Inyo*, p. 98. Chalfant's book remains the definitive account of Owens Valley's pioneer period. Unless otherwise noted, all references to *Story of Inyo* are to its second edition. J. M. Guinn also wrote a letter to the *Los Angeles Times*, September 7, 1905, explaining how the river and valley were named.

[10]Chalfant, *Story of Inyo*, pp. 228–229; W. A. Chalfant, "Charley's Butte," *Irrigation Age* 24 (December, 1908), 46–47.

ness that it was said that Los Angeles newspapers made the arrival of his wagons a leading story every week. For the small Southern California pueblo, the Nadeau wagons provided important business.[11]

Inyo County gained attention in 1872 as the location of a major earthquake whose epicenter was only a few miles from Owens Lake, near the small settlement of Lone Pine. At 2:25 A.M. on March 26 the earth convulsed, reducing stone and adobe buildings to ruins and wrecking strong frame structures. Modern estimates place the tremor at 8.3 on the Richter scale, making it the strongest earthquake in California's recorded history. At Lone Pine 23 of the town's 250 residents were killed, and only seven of fifty-nine buildings escaped damage. Aftershocks continued for months. Almost everyone lost a friend or relative. Other Owens Valley towns also suffered damage. The land itself was altered, with a new lake formed, crevasses opened, and miles of scarps. Indians in the region, with an oral tradition of a major earthquake centuries before, left in anticipation of a much worse one to come. People came up with various theories as to the cause of the earthquake, including shooting stars and electricity. Author Bret Harte was inspired by the quake to write a fictional story predicting the demise by the end of the nineteenth century of another California town—San Francisco. Everyone agreed that the Owens Valley earthquake would have caused much more destruction of life and property had it occurred in an area of greater population or, conversely, had there been greater settlement and population in Owens Valley.[12]

Schemes to end Owens Valley's isolation and expand the marketability of its products included such proposals as wagon roads and railroad connections. In the early 1870's Los Angeles feared losing the profitable Owens Valley ore business to some other trade

[11]Chalfant, *Story of Inyo*, chap. 26; W. A. Chalfant, "Cerro Gordo," *Historical Society of Southern California Quarterly* 22 (June, 1940), 55–59; Nadeau, *City-Makers*, chaps. 8 and 9. Author Nadeau is the great-great-grandson of freighter Nadeau.

[12]C. Mulholland, "The Owens Valley Earthquake of 1872," Historical Society of Southern California, *Annual Publications* 3 (1894), 27–32; Chalfant, *Story of Inyo*, chap. 24; Guinn, "Some Early History of Owens River Valley," pp. 46–47; Bret Harte, "The Ruins of San Francisco," *Out West* 24 (June, 1906), 542–543, reprint of a story written in 1872. A brief modern account of the 1872 earthquake is in Rick Ridgeway, "In Earth's Way," *Westways* 69 (May, 1977), 56–59.

center, possibly Bakersfield. Since Bakersfield expected to be reached by the Southern Pacific line before Los Angeles acquired a rail connection, the threat seemed real enough. Then Nevada's senator John P. Jones, who had made his fortune in the Comstock Lode, incorporated the Los Angeles and Independence Railroad in 1875, visualizing the movement of Inyo County ore by rail to a Pacific seaport— Santa Monica. As it happened, Jones owned considerable Santa Monica acreage which he proceeded to subdivide and auction off, which earned for him the title "father of Santa Monica." Rails were laid between Los Angeles and Santa Monica, and scheduled trains made the run daily. It quickly developed that land sales were far more successful and profitable than railroad plans. The Los Angeles and Independence Railroad, originally intended to run from a Santa Monica wharf east through Los Angeles and San Bernardino, over Cajon Pass, and all the way up to Owens Valley, never made it beyond Los Angeles. Undercut by the Southern Pacific and having encountered financial difficulties, Jones sold his railroad to the Southern Pacific in 1877. The Southern Pacific ended the ambitious plan; for good measure, the wharf was torn down in 1879. Some years later the Southern Pacific would change its mind about Santa Monica.[13]

Rail connections finally came to Owens Valley, but not from the direction of Los Angeles. In 1883, anticipating a decline in Comstock Lode production and an increase in the yield of Owens Valley mines, Nevada silver financiers underwrote the Carson & Colorado Railroad, a narrow-gauge line stretching from Carson City, Nevada, in the north to Keeler at Owens Lake in the south. A slump in the price of silver ended plans to extend the line south to the Colorado River. As San Francisco financier D. O. Mills observed when he inspected the new railroad, "Gentlemen, we either built it 300 miles too long or 300 years too soon." Eventually he sold the Carson & Colorado to the Southern Pacific, ironically just months before the gold strike at Tonopah, Nevada.[14]

[13]Franklyn Hoyt, "The Los Angeles and Independence Railroad," *Historical Society of Southern California Quarterly* 32 (December, 1950), 293–308; Chalfant, *Story of Inyo,* p. 310.

[14]Genny Schumacher, ed., *Deepest Valley: Guide to Owens Valley and Its Mountain Lakes, Roadsides, and Trails,* pp. 188–189; Chalfant, *Story of Inyo,* pp. 312–314.

By the 1890's enough history had passed—a generation—for one family in the Bishop area to throw a party for the old-timers living there. The oldest couple attending had come to Owens Valley in 1860. The guests included pioneers who had worked in the mines or had started ranches or farms. They had fought Indians, endured isolation, and to a great extent made themselves self-sufficient. Dreams of developing grand cities in the valley had vanished along with their names—Graham City, Owensville, San Carlos, Bend City. Kearsarge had been completely destroyed in 1864 by an avalanche. Other towns—Bishop, Independence, Laws, Lone Pine, Big Pine— proved more enduring. The mining pattern of boom-bust-boom continued in diminished degree at the southern end of the valley, while in the northern part of the region settlers found Bishop a slowly but steadily growing center for the surrounding farms and ranches. Adobe houses were replaced by frame buildings, settlers planted trees and flower gardens, and neighbors socialized. The region promised a slow and unspectacular growth in agriculture, coupled with mining for such less sensational minerals as zinc, asbestos, and borax.[15]

Then, with the new century, came a new opportunity for sudden prosperity. Gold was discovered in the desert of southwestern Nevada, and overnight the mining camp of Tonopah became a thriving— and hungry—city. Soon other strikes were publicized, and the Tonopah success was echoed by excitement at Goldfield, Bullfrog, Rhyolite, and other boom towns. Owens Valley recognized its geographic affinity to the new Nevada mining district. The Tonopah & Goldfield Railroad connected with the Carson & Colorado at Tonopah Junction, creating an easy route for Owens Valley agricultural products to arrive at Nevada cookstoves. Anticipating a prosperous future, Bishop incorporated in 1903—barely meeting minimum requirements—and voted bonds the following year for water and sewer systems. In March, 1902, the Inyo County Bank was established. The beginnings of a telephone system promised eventual direct com-

---

[15]Eleanor Pyle Thomas. "The History and Settlement of the Owens River Valley Region" (Master's thesis, University of Southern California, 1934), pp. 31–35; Schumacher, *Deepest Valley*, p. 191.

munication with the outside world. The river seemed ideal for power production.[16]

Much in the way of development, however, seemed beyond the reach of the valley's settlers. Water existed in abundance from the river, but in flood season lowland areas became swamps, ungraded roads were unfordable, and bridges washed out. At the same time and in direct contrast, most of the valley's acreage lacked adequate water. Control of the river's flow meant greater control of the environment, and that could mean new farms and more corn, wheat, butter, potatoes, apples, and livestock. The task seemed beyond the reach of even the most ambitious private enterprise effort. Providentially, an answer to this need appeared in June, 1902, with the passage of the Reclamation Act. The law authorized the secretary of the interior "to make examinations and surveys for, and to locate and construct . . . irrigation works for the storage, diversion, and development of water." A year later the first of the new Reclamation Service's engineers arrived. Expectation ran high that a federal reclamation project would enhance and enrich Owens Valley.[17]

Two Regions, One River

So it was that two regions, separated by hundred of miles, came to see their future mirrored in the clear waters of a generous mountain stream. For the valley, development of its most precious artery could mean establishing Owens Valley as an economic center for a long-isolated area made suddenly popular by a latter-day bonanza. For the city, a new and plentiful water source meant there would be no end to the growing influence of Los Angeles. Before the city could even think of achieving this goal, however, one problem remained that had to be solved in its own region. The City of Los Angeles, which owned the water of the Los Angeles River, did not own the method by which its citizens consumed it. The city's recapture of its own water from a private company would serve as a prelude for the greater controversy that followed.

---

[16]Chalfant, *Story of Inyo*, pp. 330–332; George L. Bossemeyer, "The Desert Mining Region of Southern Nevada Today," *Pacific Monthly* 15 (May, 1906), 455–458; Clara E. Douglas, "Those Nevada Bonanzas," *Sunset* 17 (September, 1906), 258–265.

[17]U.S., *Statutes at Large*, vol. 32, part 1, chap. 1093, p. 388.

2

Private versus Public Control
of the Los Angeles River

"The Los Angeles River was the greatest attraction. It was
a beautiful, limpid little stream. . . . so attractive to me that
it at once became something about which my whole life was
woven, I loved it so much."—William Mulholland (1929)

THEY came from all over the United States and from Europe, and
their ambitions were exceeded only by their accomplishments. They
had visions. They came to a town barely out of its frontier stage,
and within the lifetimes of most of them they helped, guided, and
made their town a city. Vision came at a costly price. High-pressure
real estate promotions precluded orderly planning. There was competition from other municipalities, and there was a challenge from
the powerful Southern Pacific Railroad, which decreed where the
region's chief seaport would be located. The municipalities lost, and
so did the Southern Pacific. Men of vision in the city of Los Angeles
used the bombing of the *Los Angeles Times* in 1910 as a symbol to
crush the labor movement and welcome businesses to an open-shop
town. Ambition knew no bounds.

Some Los Angeles men such as Stephen M. White, defender of
the free harbor concept, were recognized as heroes. Others were
controversial, if not in who they were, then in what they did. Charles
F. Lummis, the founder of the Southwest Museum, publisher of *Out
West*, sponsor of new poets and promoter of the sunshine land, and
Frank Wiggins, booster par excellence, founder of the Los Angeles
Chamber of Commerce, the man who advertised the virtues of Los
Angeles around the world, owner of a soup-straining moustache that,

like his advertisements, strained the imagination, were examples of this type. Some men were painted with a dark brush. These were men like *Times* publisher Harrison Gray Otis, dubbed the "Walrus of Moron-Land" by a writer unfriendly to Otis and city alike, and Griffith J. Griffith, a millionaire whose gifts to the city were rebuffed because while in an alcoholic rage he had shot his wife. She lived, and after his release from San Quentin, still a millionaire, he promoted parks and prison reform.

In 1900 the population of the city of Los Angeles was approximately 100,000. Within five years the number doubled. It was a large town on the threshold of becoming a major metropolitan area but still small enough so that everyone knew everyone. If you knew people and you knew real estate, you could get ahead. Fast. People got ahead. California was the golden state, and if San Francisco was its Pacific jewel, then at least Los Angeles offered new ways to opportunity. It was unfortunate for Los Angeles that while the ambitions of its most ardent boosters knew no bounds, the city's river did. Los Angeles could grow so far and no more, as there was only so much water to go around.

And so among the heroic, the controversial, and those stained with a dark brush, we find men of vision who merged all three categories. Men who linked their future with their adopted city's (there were few native-born Angelenos relative to the general population, a situation that continued for generations), and in doing so enjoyed the praise, endured the vilification, and waited only for history to judge the course of their actions.[1] Men who knew about water.

Lippincott's Arrival

Joseph Barlow Lippincott knew about water. He fulfilled all of the requirements: he came from somewhere else, he was highly trained, ambitious, and dedicated to the success of his city's and

---

[1]Good discussions of Los Angeles at the beginning of the twentieth century can be found in Richard G. Lillard, *Eden in Jeopardy—Man's Prodigal Meddling with His Environment: The Southern California Experience*; Remi Nadeau, *Los Angeles: From Mission to Modern City*; John D. Weaver, *El Pueblo Grande: A Nonfiction Book about Los Angeles*; Lynn Bowman, *Los Angeles: Epic of a City.* See also the many articles in *Out West*, 1901–1905.

his own aspirations. Born in Scranton, Pennsylvania, in 1864, Lippincott could trace his American ancestors on his father's side back to 1642. Despite the coincidence in initials, he was not or was at best very remotely related to the J. B. Lippincott Company of publishing fame. More immediately, his father, the Reverend Joshua Allan Lippincott, was a fairly prominent nineteenth-century educator, who during his son's boyhood taught mathematics at Dickinson College in Carlisle, just west of Harrisburg. The father picked up a few titles during his long career, a doctor of divinity from Franklin and Marshall College, a doctor of laws from the University of Michigan. In 1883 Reverend Lippincott accepted the chancellorship of the University of Kansas. Young Joseph, at that time attending Dickinson College, suddenly found himself a transfer student. Whereas education and religion occupied the attention of the father, engineering attracted the son. He earned his first dollar at age eighteen when he worked as axeman on a surveying party, for which he received $30 a month. He used part of his first paycheck to buy a clock for his mother.[2]

While a student at the University of Kansas, Lippincott contracted pneumonia. He went to Texas and regained his health working as a cowboy driving cattle to the Santa Fe Railroad. His health restored, Lippincott, a permanent convert to the outdoor life, returned to college and was graduated in 1887 with a B.S. in civil engineering. His first postcollege employment came with the Santa Fe Railroad, followed by work on several other rail lines. Lippincott's main tasks were construction of roadbeds and bridges. Then, in June, 1889, came an opportunity to work as a topographer for the Geological Survey. It was his introduction to government work,

[2]Biographical information on Lippincott comes from: Kenneth Q. Volk, "Joseph Barlow Lippincott," American Society of Civil Engineers, Transactions 108 (1943), 1543–50; National Cyclopaedia of American Biography, 36:413; "Joseph Barlow Lippincott," Civil Engineering 7 (January, 1937), 76–77; Los Angeles Tribune, October 14, 1911; Who's Who in California: A Biographical Directory, 1928–1929, p. 108; California Biography File, Los Angeles Public Library (library hereafter cited as LAPL). On Lippincott's father, see the National Cyclopaedia, 9:494, and Twentieth Century Biographical Dictionary of Notable Americans, vol. 6, no pagination. Within these biographical sketches there are occasional conflicts as to dates.

and it lasted four years. Among other tasks, the survey assigned him to make topographic maps covering an area from New Mexico to California, a sparsely settled, hostile region, only recently finished with the Apache wars. During this time Lippincott made his first acquaintance with the government's way of doing things. Wages were low, and yet from his meager pay he was expected to finance his operation. This included renting everything from mules to houses, tasks frustrated by the long delays between submission of vouchers and receipt of reimbursement funds. On one assignment, a reconnaissance survey in the unexplored Bitterroot Range between Idaho and Montana, Lippincott spent the summer surveying possible National Forest locations. His pack train included a small mule that carried his camera and photographic plates. Near the end of the reconnaissance the mule stopped short to view the scenery. The larger mules crowded it off the edge of the cliff, along with a summer's work of photographic plates and the camera. Lippincott climbed down, expecting to find an injured mule and smashed equipment. Both he and the mule were lucky. The mule had landed between two small pine trees, unhurt, upside down, and wedged in. None of the plates was broken.

While in government service, Lippincott married and grew a moustache. The moustache offered no competition for that sported by Frank Wiggins, whom Lippincott later came to know, but it was one of the better examples of its kind to be seen in the late nineteenth and early twentieth centuries. And one of the better examples of her kind was his bride, Josephine Cook of Kansas City, whom he married in April, 1890. Nine months later, on Christmas Day, Mrs. Lippincott presented her husband with a baby girl, whom they named Rose. Josephine accompanied her husband on his many peregrinations throughout the West, camping out in remote places. Rose's first crib was a soap box suspended from a tent pole.

During his service with the Geological Survey, Lippincott came into contact with many other young, ambitious, and dedicated engineers. One of the most dedicated was Arthur Powell Davis, nephew of John Wesley Powell of Colorado River fame. Powell was director of the Geological Survey. There was no question of nepotism, however, as Davis earned his position on his own merit. A topographer at the time, Davis received the assignment to do the first topographic maps in Southern California. He invited Lippincott to join him as his assistant. Sometime in late 1891, or possibly early 1892, Lippincott, his wife, and their baby daughter joined Davis in Southern California. Lippincott's first experience after arriving in Los Angeles was to leave the city, hiking deep into the San Gabriel Mountains on map-making expeditions. Mrs. Lippincott and baby Rose came along. In appreciation for her help in preparing mathematical tables, the topographers named a mountain for Lippincott's wife—Mount Josephine, elevation 5,558 feet.[3]

In June, 1892, Lippincott resigned from government service to take a position as assistant engineer in the Bear Valley Irrigation Company of Redlands. The company attempted to build a canal near the headwaters of the Santa Ana River. It went bankrupt, and in August, 1893, Lippincott was looking for new employment in Southern California, the land of opportunity. Together with Davis, he organized the Antelope Valley Water Company, designing storage works and distribution systems in the Piru Creek area of Ventura County. Unfortunately, the company's plans ran headlong into the Panic of 1893. "My good wife ran the camp for me, doing the cooking, and we lived throughout the winter in these mountains in a tent with a baby girl some two years of age," Lippincott recalled many years later. "At the time it did not appear to us that we were enduring any particular hardships, but looking back at it I often wonder how my wife stood for it."[4]

With the money gone, Lippincott retreated from the mountains to the city and opened an office in Los Angeles. In June, 1895, he accepted an appointment as resident hydrographer for California.

[3]J. B. Lippincott to V. M. Freeman, May 6, 1938, letter in the possession of V. M. Freeman, Santa Paula, California. The letter has been reproduced in Vernon M. Freeman, *People—Land—Water: The Santa Clara Valley and Oxnard Plain, Ventura County, California,* pp. 42–44. See also Walt Wheelock, *Southern California Peaks,* p. 15; John W. Robinson, *Trails of the Angeles,* p. 111; and Volk, "Joseph Barlow Lippincott," p. 1550.

[4]Quoted in Freeman, *People—Land—Water,* pp. 43–44. Lippincott's resignation is explained in J. W. Powell to Secretary of the Interior, December 11, 1893, file 23 Alpha. (pt. 1), Status of Employees, Joseph Barlow Lippincott, National Personnel Records Center (Civilian Personnel Records), St. Louis, Missouri (hereafter cited as NPRC).

The Hydrographic Branch of the Geological Survey needed someone with energy and ambition. Lippincott had both. California had virtually no stream-flow measurements for any of its rivers. Lippincott established gauging stations on the larger rivers and cajoled local people into serving as observers without pay, as funds were again meager. Lippincott knew that private rainfall records had been kept by many people, so he wrote to every postmaster in the state, asking that they request people whom they knew were keeping records to get in touch with him. It paid off. In a brief time Lippincott amassed a tremendous amount of information and acquired an intimate knowledge of California hydrography. He decided to specialize as a hydraulic engineer.

When Lippincott reentered government service in 1895, it was with the understanding that he be allowed to maintain a private practice. John Wesley Powell had permitted this, since wages were too low to expect anyone to remain for long without additional income. Lippincott's talents soon became well known in Southern California, and in a very short time he could forget the lean period of 1893 to 1894. His studies on California water supplies were published in the Geological Survey's *Annual Reports* for 1898, 1899, and 1900, and he began to prepare several studies for the *Water-Supply and Irrigation Papers* series. He also started writing articles for professional publications such as *Engineering News*. In the fall of 1897 he was invited to serve on a board of consulting engineers in connection with a lawsuit involving Los Angeles' pueblo water right against the City of San Fernando. New assignments brought new responsibilities and recognition. He joined the newly organized Engineers and Architects Association of Southern California in 1896, and, later on, the California Club, and the Los Angeles Country Club. *Land of Sunshine* magazine featured him prominently in an article, "Workers for the West," noting that he "aimed to make the results of his work of practical benefit to the community." By 1899 Lippincott—known to everyone as J. B.—felt assured enough of his position to apply for full membership in the prestigious American Society of Civil Engineers. He listed seven members as references, among them his friend Arthur Powell Davis and Fred Eaton, the mayor of Los Angeles. The application was accepted on December 28, 1899. Along with the twentieth century, Joseph Barlow Lippincott had arrived.[5]

Mulholland's Drive

While Lippincott's reputation grew because of his gathering of water data, William Mulholland won recognition because he worked *with* water. So many legends and encrustations have become attached to Mulholland's life as to make a balanced portrait an elusive goal. For example, one might note that on July 11, 1855, two months before Mulholland's birth in Belfast, Ireland, a major earthquake struck Southern California. According to Los Angeles resident Harris Newmark, who experienced the tremor, water in the town's *zanjas* ("ditches") "bubbled and splashed and overflowed."[6] There are those who would see the event as a portent of Mulholland's birth, but such hindsight violates the humble state of his origins.

Some versions of his life describe him as poorly educated and penniless when he arrived in California in 1877. Neither assertion is accurate. His father, Hugh Mulholland, had a position in the British government's postal service. Mulholland's mother died while he was young; his father remarried, and relations with his step-mother were cordial. Young Mulholland was educated in the national schools in Dublin—similar to American elementary schools—and he also attended Christian Brothers College, equivalent to American high school. At the age of fifteen, bitten by the desire to go to sea, Mulholland left home. He recalled many years later, "I had always wanted to travel, nurturing this desire since I was ten years old, and so, at my first opportunity, some four or five years

[5]Lippincott's membership application is in the offices of the American Society of Civil Engineers, New York City; Volk, "Joseph Barlow Lippincott," pp. 1544–1545; "Workers for the West," *Land of Sunshine* 15 (August–September, 1901), 185–186; *Los Angeles Times*, February 3, 1901. For a contemporary's estimate of Lippincott's abilities, see Harold Hedger, "Harold Hedger: Flood Control Engineer," Oral History Program, University of California, Los Angeles, p. 62. On the understanding giving Lippincott permission to continue in private work, see C. D. Walcott to Secretary of the Interior, May 24, 1899, file 23 Alpha. (pt. 1), NPRC.

[6]Harris Newmark, *Sixty Years in Southern California, 1853–1913*, p. 165.

later, I became an apprentice aboard the *Gleniffer*, owned by the Allen line, without the whole-hearted approval of my father."[7]

Mulholland worked as an apprentice seaman for four years, receiving little or no pay. During his seafaring years he crossed the Atlantic Ocean nineteen times, learned something of navigation, and enjoyed himself immensely. The novelty finally wore off, however, and in 1874 he sailed on the *Gleniffer* for the last time, disembarking in New York City on June 9. He went to Michigan, where he spent a couple of years working as a sailor on logging ships in the summer and working in lumber camps in wintertime. "It was doubtless the 'salt horse' which we were fed there which gave me such a taste for water," he later recalled. While working in the lumber camps he sustained a leg injury that almost resulted in amputation. He then spent several months as an itinerant mechanic's apprentice, repairing clocks and sharpening scissors.[8]

Following these jobs Mulholland journeyed to Pittsburgh, Pennsylvania, where his aunt and uncle operated a dry goods store. While clerking in the dry goods store, Mulholland indulged in a favorite pastime, reading. One book that caught his attention was Charles Nordhoff's best-seller, *California: For Health, Pleasure, and Residence*. Mr. and Mrs. Deakers, Mulholland's aunt and uncle, were quite taken with the idea of moving to California. Mrs. Deakers suffered from rheumatism, and the warmth and sunshine advertised by Nordhoff sounded most attractive. The Deakers determined to move to California. They advised William and his brother Hugh, who had joined him, to remain in Pittsburgh and find some business opportunity. On December 9, 1876, the Deakers left for California

---

[7]Quoted in Elisabeth Mathieu Spriggs, "The History of the Domestic Water Supply of Los Angeles" (Master's thesis, University of Southern Califorina, 1931), p. 64.

[8]Ibid., p. 65. See also Robert William Matson, *William Mulholland: A Forgotten Forefather*, p. 5; H. A. Van Norman, "William Mulholland," American Society of Civil Engineers, *Transactions* 101 (1936), 1604); Joseph B. Lippincott, "William Mulholland—Engineer, Pioneer, Raconteur," *Civil Engineering* 11 (February, 1941), 105–107, and (March, 1941), 161–164. All biographical sketches of Mulholland are subject to contradictions in names, dates, places, and events and must be used with caution. A typical example of a Mulholland panegyric is in Robert J. Burdette, *American Biography and Genealogy, California Edition*, 1:33, 35.

on board the *Crescent City*. A few hours later while on deck they ran into the Mulholland brothers, who on their own had decided to accompany the family.[9]

Mulholland's aunt and uncle and their family disappear from the biographical record at this point. On reaching Colón at the Isthmus of Panama, the Mulholland brothers decided to forego taking the train and paying the twenty-five-dollar fare. They walked the forty-seven miles from Colón to Balboa, William later declaring, "I would walk that far today to make twenty-five dollars." At Balboa the brothers found employment on a ship bound for Acapulco and from there on another ship to San Francisco, where they arrived in February, 1877. They then headed down the San Joaquin Valley, admiring firsthand what Nordhoff had described in prose. At Martinez they brought horses, then continued south through Bakersfield and on to Los Angeles—population, some 5,700. In 1929 Mulholland recalled his thoughts during this journey and his initial impressions of Los Angeles:

The world was my oyster and I was just opening it. . . . Los Angeles was a place after my own heart. It was the most attractive town I had ever seen. The people were hospitable. There was plenty to do and a fair compensation offered for whatever you did. In fact, the country had the same attraction for me that it had for the Indians who originally chose this spot as their place to live. The Los Angeles River was the greatest attraction. It was a beautiful, limpid little stream, with willows on its banks. . . . It was so attractive to me that it at once became something about which my whole scheme of life was woven, I loved it so much.[10]

For someone who had lived in Dublin, New York, and Pittsburgh, among other cities, to think of Los Angeles in 1877 as "the most attractive town I had ever seen" and the Los Angeles River as "so attractive" suggests either a faulty recollection of youthful enthusiasm or else a total lack of appreciation for architecture. Los Angeles in 1877 was scarcely out of its frontier phase. Tiburcio Vasquez, the notorious outlaw who had terrorized the region for years, was less than two years in his grave. The rail connection with the Southern Pacific had been made only the previous September

[9]Spriggs, "History of the Domestic Water Supply of Los Angeles," pp. 63, 65–66.
[10]Ibid., pp. 66–67.

and only after a hefty subsidy had been paid to prevent the rail-road's bypassing the scruffy little town. Prudent Beaudry, a prominent local citizen who had just finished a term as mayor of Los Angeles, had hesitated not a second in shooting a stray dog that was bothering his horse. The town still smarted from the lingering effects of the Panic of 1873, which, along with poor banking practice, had helped ruin the Temple and Workman Bank and had caused William Workman, another prominent citizen, to put a bullet in his brain. On the other hand, the Widney brothers—one a judge, the other a physician, and both inveterate promoter-specu-lators in Southern California real estate—continued to "boom" the town. People seemed willing to forget that a mob had murdered some twenty-odd Chinese back in October, 1871; from Calle de los Negros in Mexican days and Nigger Alley in the frontier period, the name of the street where the massacre occurred was changed to the respectably innocuous Los Angeles Street shortly after the arrival of the Mulholland brothers.[11]

All in all, the town showed promise, though not immediately for Hugh and William. William's first employment was not in Los Angeles but in the little village of Compton, where he dug artesian wells by hand drill. This job held little appeal (although it must be noted that Mulholland was again working in and around water), and before long the brothers were off to Arizona Territory on a prospecting expedition. Their gold-seeking efforts proved fruitless. After several months the Mulhollands returned to California, taking the first passenger train from Yuma to Los Angeles. During their prospecting trip the brothers may or may not have been chased by Apaches; an encounter may have taken place, growing in fierceness as Mulholland's legend grew.[12]

William Mulholland's return to Los Angeles in the spring of 1878 marked a commitment to his adopted city that proved enduring. His first employment efforts were humble enough to suit anyone

[11]Newmark, *Sixty Years*, p. 510; Remi Nadeau, *City-Makers: The Story of Southern California's First Boom, 1868–76*, p. 55.

[12]Lippincott, "William Mulholland," pp. 105–106; Van Norman, "William Mulholland," p. 1605; Matson, *William Mulholland*, p. 6; Edgar Lloyd Hampton, "An Irishman Moves West," *Success* 7 (August, 1923), 28, 79; Samuel T. Clover, *Constructive Californians: Men of Outstanding Ability Who Have Added Greatly to the Golden State's Prestige*, p. 131.

starting up the ladder in the era of Horatio Alger stories. The Los Angeles City Water Company gave him a job as a ditch tender at a salary of $1.50 a day. As a former Spanish/Mexican pueblo with a small population, Los Angeles satisfied its water needs by use of a *Zanja Madre*, or Mother Ditch, which ran from the Los Angeles River near what is now Griffith Park to a reservoir in the Elysian Hills, now best known for Dodger Stadium. From the reservoir a system of pipes and ditches brought water to city homes. The system was privately owned. The water company had obtained a thirty-year lease from the city to supply the city's own water to its residents; the company supplied the pipes and maintained the ditches. In exchange for the lucrative franchise, the company constructed a fountain in the plaza on Main Street.

Mulholland's job was to keep the ditch clear of weeds, brush, and other debris. Although he had the advantage of working in the nineteenth century, and thus avoided such modern debris as metal shopping carts, polyethelene bags, aerosol cans, and the like, the job required his presence at the ditch twenty-four hours a day. For four years he lived in a one-room shack at what is now the intersection of Riverside Drive and Los Feliz Boulevard.

One famous story described an early encounter between Mulholland and William Perry, president of the water company. Perry saw Mulholland shoveling out weeds and dirt from the *Zanja Madre*. Impressed by Mulholland's energy, the president, perhaps too abruptly, asked him who he was and what he was doing. Unaware of Perry's identity, Mulholland retorted, "It's none of your damn business!" After Perry left, Mulholland learned the identity of his questioner. He went to the company office to get his pay, figuring he was fired. He wasn't. Perry recognized a good worker when he saw one. He promoted Mulholland to foreman of the ditch gang.[13]

Over the next few years Mulholland rose rapidly in the ranks of the Los Angeles City Water Company. In 1881 he moved out of the shack to another cabin, this one in the Elysian Hills. Out of a salary of $65 a month Mulholland bought more than a thousand small trees and planted them around the Buena Vista Reservoir in the Elysian Hills, after first nurturing them in salmon cans filled with

---

[13]Van Norman, "William Mulholland," p. 1605; Matson, *William Mulholland*, pp. 8–9; Lippincott, "William Mulholland," p. 106.

dirt. In his spare time he read books on mathematics, hydraulic engineering, and geology. He spoke with surveyors and engineers. For light reading he read the classics, chiefly Shakespeare, and memorized his favorite passages. He also enjoyed poetry and opera. Years later a friendship was formed with the Lippincotts. Josephine Lippincott knew a number of songs from *The Mikado*. Mulholland once surprised her by joining in. Not only did he know Gilbert and Sullivan's operas, he also knew Sir Arthur Sullivan, who for a time had lived in Los Angeles. However, Mulholland also was known for his use of colorful swear words. Soon Mulholland came to epitomize the self-educated man. His abilities received an ultimate accolade from the water company in November, 1886, when he was promoted to superintendent at $500 a month. No more ditch digging or one-room cabins. He took a suite of rooms at the Marchessault Building. Ranchers and land developers came to him to discuss their water problems.[14]

In 1890, at age thirty-five, Mulholland married Lily Ferguson, a native of Port Huron, Michigan, whose family had moved to Los Angeles. Unlike Mulholland, who became very much a public figure, Lily Mulholland remained in the background, filling the role of wife and mother to their five children. By the mid-1890's the Mulhollands were gaining in social prominence. Mulholland became a charter member of the Engineers and Architects Association of Southern California. He joined the California Club, the Sunset Club, and the Celtic Club. Membership in the American Society of Civil Engineers came later, in 1907; among his references were J. B. Lippincott and Fred Eaton.[15]

By 1898 Mulholland enjoyed a growing reputation as a capable administrator and an expert on the city's water system. However, the Los Angeles City Water Company did not share the esteem

[14]Lippincott, "William Mulholland," p. 107; Spriggs, "History of the Domestic Water Supply of Los Angeles," p. 69; Matson, *William Mulholland*, pp. 7–8; J. Gregg Layne, *Water and Power for a Great City: A History of the Department of Water and Power of the City of Los Angeles to December, 1950*, p. 55. According to Layne, Mulholland was not the first choice for the job of superintendent.

[15]Spriggs, "History of the Domestic Water Supply of Los Angeles," p. 72; Lippincott, "William Mulholland," p. 164; *Los Angeles Times*, February 3, 1901.

accorded its star employee. The year 1898 marked the thirtieth year of the company's operation of the water system franchise, and the years had not worn well. During the period of litigation in which the city negotiated for the purchase of the company's properties, Mulholland occupied an anomalous position. He found that his employers, seeing the end of the franchise, had no desire in the last years to improve equipment or service. This was despite the city's rapid growth following the boom of the 1880's. Mulholland may have been an employee of the company, but the city found his expertise invaluable in determining an exact inventory of pipes, hydrants, valves, and other equipment.

Los Angeles employed a special board of engineers to investigate the company's holdings and present its findings to the arbitrators handling the negotiations. The board found the company records inadequate. Mulholland asked, "What is it you want to know?" One of the engineers replied, "The thing we want is a complete list showing the length of pipe, its size, character, and age. We also want to know the number of gate valves and all about them, as well as fire hydrants and all other structures connected with the water system." Mulholland proceeded to delineate, entirely from memory, the size, kind, and age of all the pipes laid in the streets of Los Angeles, along with hydrants and gate valves, pointing out all the locations on a large-scale city map. The engineers admired the feat of memory but decided to test Mulholland's statement with actual inspection. They indicated two hundred locations, drawing red circles on the map, where they wanted to see the pipe. Mulholland, pleased at the opportunity to display his powers of memory, ordered the pipe dug up. He was right in every instance. The board then accepted the entire inventory based on Mulholland's memory.[16]

When Los Angeles finally took over the operation of the waterworks, there was only one logical candidate for the post of chief engineer. Mulholland enthusiastically succeeded himself and was transformed from private employee to public servant. Everyone looked forward to his capable operation of the municipal water system. The one-time ditch tender, through luck and pluck, was now

[16]Lippincott, "William Mulholland," p. 161.

in a position of major responsibility in a rapidly growing city. The fact still remained that he had risen to that position without benefit of formal education beyond a limited time in high school. If anyone might challenge him on this, and once in awhile someone did, he had a ready answer as to the preparation he had received to face life: "I learned the Ten Commandments and had my mother's blessing."[17]

Eaton's Influence

In contrast to Lippincott and Mulholland, Frederick Eaton was that rarity of rarities in late-nineteenth-century Los Angeles—not only a Californian, but a native to the city in which he lived. Born on September 23, 1855, Eaton was two weeks younger than Mulholland, but preceded him in the advantages of location and influence, not to mention contact with Los Angeles River water. His father, Benjamin Eaton, was a Harvard graduate bitten by the gold bug in 1849. He rode to California on horseback from St. Joseph, Missouri. At the same time, his wife and infant daughter traveled west via the Panama route. The family reunited in Stockton, where the golden dream quickly died. After a brief attempt at publishing a newspaper, Eaton settled in Los Angeles, where he practiced law. He was soon elected district attorney, was a founder of the Pasadena Colony (which became the City of Pasadena), and generally did well through the wise purchase of real estate. His son Fred (few ever called him Frederick) was born on Fort Moore Hill in an adobe building that also served as the city jail (the site is now the headquarters of the Los Angeles Unified School District). Young Fred experienced firsthand the vigilante justice of Los Angeles in its "Queen of the Cow Counties" era. "One of my earliest recollections is of seeing the bodies of four men who had been hanged by the Vigilantes on Spring Street," recalled Eaton. "I ran home in terror, and was unable to get over my fright for several days."[18]

[17]Ibid., p. 107.

[18]Quoted in Mary Timpe Smith, "Growing Up with the City," *Los Angeles Times Sunday Magazine*, October 19, 1930, p. 5. Other biographical information is in *Illustrated History of Los Angeles County, California*, pp. 462–463; J. M. Guinn, *Historical and Biographical Record of Southern Cali-*

Fred attended what passed for school in Los Angeles until age thirteen. He early exhibited a talent for drawing, which inadvertently ended his formal education. The schoolmaster assigned him the task of teaching drawing to the other pupils. Meanwhile, the Los Angeles City Water Company was beginning its operation of the city's waterworks. Included in the arrangement was the company's responsibility to construct a fountain in the plaza while the city improved the area. Charles Miles, the superintendent of the company, learned of Fred's drawing talent and invited the boy to come to his office and draw a plan for the plaza. Thirteen-year-old Fred did so, creating an elaborate but well-drawn design. The city, which had earlier agreed to spend $2,500 on plaza beautification, reduced the sum to $300. Of this amount Fred was to receive $100. He never did.[19] Apparently no one considered this a portent for future negotiations between Fred Eaton and the City of Los Angeles.

At the age of fifteen Fred began an apprenticeship with the Los Angeles City Water Company that resulted in a rapid rise in responsibility. Five years later, in 1875, he became the company's general superintendent. Just prior to this, at age nineteen, Eaton had married Helen Burdick, like himself a native of Los Angeles. Recognizing his lack of professional training—apart from a brief stint at Santa Clara College, he had no higher education—Eaton began to study civil engineering in earnest. Over the next thirteen years he applied himself to the subject, combining practical training with intensive study. In 1884, after thirteen years as superintendent, Eaton resigned the position, which was to be filled by Mulholland several years later. He went into private practice as a civil engineer, examining how various eastern cities supplied water to their residents. He designed irrigation works for private companies. Then, in 1886, he ran for the office of city engineer of Los Angeles and was elected. He took office in January, 1887. Later in the year he ap-

fornia, p. 404; J. B. Lippincott, "Frederick Eaton," American Society of Civil Engineers, Transactions 100 (1935), 1645–47; John S. McGroarty, ed., History of Los Angeles County, 3:482–485; Los Angeles Examiner, March 13, 1934. The records conflict as to dates and events and must be used with caution.

[19]Smith, "Growing Up with the City," p. 5.

plied for membership in the American Society of Civil Engineers and was accepted as a full member.[20]

As city engineer, Eaton designed a sewer system for Los Angeles that for its time was both advanced and efficient. With the great boom in land speculation that made the mid-1880's so famous, every municipality envisioned itself as an incipient metropolis. On the strength of his accomplishments and capabilities Eaton was re-elected to another term as city engineer. During this time he designed the original plans for Central Park (now Pershing Square), Elysian Park, Westlake (now MacArthur) Park, and Eastlake (now Lincoln) Park. For a time he served as chief engineer of the Consolidated Electric Railway as Los Angeles entered the streetcar era. New opportunities abounded. He designed a new $140,000 business block to be owned by his wife and mother-in-law. And his interest in water continued.[21]

In the summer of 1892 Fred Eaton made his first trip to Inyo County, where he saw Owens Valley for the first time. He was there to explore some sort of colony and irrigation project proposed by a man named Frank Austin. Eaton felt the idea was not feasible because of the lack of transportation. But he marveled at the waters of the Owens River and at the snow in the High Sierras. Somewhere in the back of his mind an idea was conceived, to germinate some thirteen years before becoming reality.[22]

Eaton was quite taken with the Owens Valley country. When his family became ill soon after his return and their doctor advised a trip to the mountains, Eaton at once thought of Inyo County. "I have just come from such mountains as you have never dreamed of," he said to his wife. The family took a train to Mojave. From

[20]*Illustrated History of Los Angeles County*, p. 463; McGroarty, *History of Los Angeles County*, 3:483; Guinn, *Historical and Biographical Record*, p. 404; Eaton's application for membership, American Society of Civil Engineers, New York City office. Eaton also served briefly in 1885 as a surveyor for the City of Los Angeles.

[21]California Biography File, LAPL; *Illustrated History*, p. 463.

[22]Smith, "Growing Up with the City," p. 16, mentions Frank Austin. In one of history's odd coincidences Frank Austin, who invited Eaton to make the trip, was the older brother of Stafford Wallace Austin, the land register at Independence in 1905 (T. M. Pearce, *Mary Hunter Austin*, p. 31, and see below, chap. 4).

there to the small town of Independence they traveled in a three-seater wagon drawn by four horses, making fifty miles a day and camping out at night. The family recovered its health. They returned to Los Angeles, the thought of the Owens River pouring wasted into Owens Lake never quite leaving Eaton's mind. In a conversation with Mulholland that later assumed legendary status, Eaton described the Owens Valley region and its bounteous supply of water. Mulholland laughed at the idea that Los Angeles might need more water than the town's own river provided. "We have enough water here in the river to supply the city for the next fifty years," Mulholland said. To which Eaton replied, "You are wrong. I was born here and have seen dry years—years that you know nothing about. Wait and see."[23]

During the 1890's Eaton assumed the role of a prominent and successful citizen in a growing city. He was a charter member of the Los Angeles Athletic Club, a charter member of the Native Sons of the Golden West, and a member of other clubs and organizations. He joined the California Club in 1900. He agreed to serve as a reference when Lippincott applied for membership in the American Society of Civil Engineers, and he did the same for Mulholland several years later. Like Mulholland, Eaton neatly fit the category of self-made man. One last local pinnacle remained, and on December 15, 1898, Eaton reached it, as the citizens of Los Angeles elected him their mayor.[24]

Eaton's term of office was a time of great advances for Los Angeles. The population approached 100,000, and more people were arriving daily. Two hundred proud citizens owned automobiles, and an organization called the Automobile Club of Southern California

[23]Smith, "Growing Up with the City," p. 16; Remi Nadeau, *The Water Seekers*, pp. 11–12; *Los Angeles Times*, July 29, 1905. Virtually all accounts of the Owens Valley–Los Angeles water dispute make much of Eaton's first glimpse of the river. However, the degree to which a "plan" formed in his mind has never been assessed. J. Gregg Layne interviewed J. H. Campbell, a boyhood friend of Eaton's, in 1947. Campbell recalled a camping trip to Owens Valley in 1880 on which Judge Eaton took his sons Fred and George, Campbell, and another boy (Layne, *Water and Power*, p. 99). No other available source mentions this trip. Eaton would have been twenty-five years old at the time and married.

[24]California Biography File, LAPL; *Los Angeles Times*, February 3, 1901.

was being formed. Congress approved funds for harbor development at San Pedro, ending Collis Huntington's Southern Pacific plans for a Santa Monica harbor. Collis and his nephew, Henry E. Huntington, had other irons in the fire anyway, as they commenced the construction of interurban electric streetcars, moving in on such competitors as Moses H. Sherman and Eli P. Clark.[25] But the biggest issue of Eaton's term centered on the Los Angeles City Water Company.

Public Water, Private Control

For thirty years the Los Angeles City Water Company had enjoyed a most lucrative franchise. As a small town with a population under 5,000 in the 1860's, Los Angeles had awarded leases to private companies to supply water to its residents rather than undertaking the expense of municipal operation. Indeed, many in the town viewed municipal ownership of the water works as an invitation to political corruption. The first leases were for limited periods of time, and the leaseholders' efforts to create an efficient waterworks system met with mixed results. By 1868 the short history of the leasing system included a development of a small reservoir in the plaza, an earth-fill dam and a forty-foot waterwheel that raised the water from the river, and wooden pipes made from pine logs. As Harris Newmark wryly observed, the pipes "were continuously bursting, causing springs of water that made their way to the surface of the streets." Criticism of the system led to the sensational suicide of Damien Marchessault, one of the leaseholders and twice mayor of Los Angeles, in the common council room on January 20, 1868.[26]

In 1868 the three men who had taken over the existing lease requested renegotiation of its terms. In return for a system of twelve miles of iron pipes, replacement of the wooden pipes, construction of new reservoirs and ditches, and erection of a plaza fountain,

[25]Spencer Crump, *Ride the Big Red Cars: How Trolleys Helped Build Southern California,* chaps. 11–14; Los Angeles Municipal Arts Department, *Mayors of Los Angeles,* p. 51.

[26]Newmark, *Sixty Years,* pp. 350, 366; Vincent Ostrom, *Water and Politics: A Study of Water Policies and Administration in the Development of Los Angeles,* pp. 40–42.

John S. Griffin, Prudent Beaudry, and Solomon Lazard asked for a fifty-year lease, the city to provide land for reservoirs and rights of way over city land, and other amenities. Their proposal was turned down. A second proposal became mixed up with local politics but was accepted. Under the terms of this new agreement, a lease was granted for thirty years, the leaseholder to make essentially the same improvements as the first proposal had called for. The city would receive $1,500 a year in consideration for the lease. No more than ten miner's inches of water was to be taken from the river without prior agreement from the city. From these negotiations was born the Los Angeles City Water Company.[27]

Over the next three decades a number of interesting events occurred surrounding the company's arrangement with the city. The company fulfilled its construction obligations; iron pipes replaced the wooden ones, a teenage Fred Eaton designed the plaza within which the fountain was constructed, and a generally reliable system of water distribution was established. But there were flaws. In 1870 the annual rental of the lease was lowered from $1,500 a year to $400 as the council decided to avoid litigation over payment of water fund warrants.

Far more serious than this financial loss was the question of where the Los Angeles City Water Company was obtaining its water. Under the 1868 agreement the company was to develop its own water supply from Crystal Springs, a swampy area with a high water table near the Los Angeles River by what is now Griffith Park. This was the reason for the company's limitation of 10 miner's inches of allowable diversion from the river. The springs, however, yielded much less water than anticipated. The company then proceeded to dig a secret tunnel to the river and tap its flow. When the existence of the tunnel was revealed, the city faced a most unusual problem. Since the company was supplying domestic water and since there was no other available system, the city could do little about this liquid embezzlement. By 1898 up to 1,500 miner's inches of water came from the company, although its maximum diversion allowance was 10 inches. For consumers rates were high—some said far too high, possibly netting between 60 to 90 percent profit for the company.

[27]Layne, *Water and Power,* pp. 37–42; Ostrom, *Water and Politics,* pp. 42–44.

The company's pipes were also a target for complaint. Many were only two inches in diameter, yielding low water pressure and inadequate protection against fire.[28]

The Los Angeles City Water Company also devised several schemes in the best tradition of nineteenth-century private enterprise. In 1886 the company formed a new corporation, the Crystal Springs Land and Water Company, in an effort to establish a separate claim to the first company's headworks and the water supply. The second company then contended that it was not covered by the provisions of the 1868 lease, since it did not exist at the time the lease was made. The existence of this company, which consisted of the same directors and shareholders as the Los Angeles City Water Company, was not revealed for several years. To further complicate matters, the owners of the company could not in any sense be considered villains. In fact, they included some of the most upright citizens of the community, people who appreciated a profitable venture and wished to continue it indefinitely, certainly beyond the expiration of the lease in 1898. They included Isaias W. Hellman, president of the Farmers and Merchants Bank; Herman W. Hellman, Isaias' brother, who was also a prominent banker; Emeline Childs, widow of Ozro W. Childs, a gold rush pioneer, successful businessman, and civic leader; William H. Perry, a leading businessman (furniture, lumberyard, beehives), and sometime member of the city council; Harris Newmark, Boyle Workman, Andrew Glassell, and Stephen H. Mott, all important business and civic leaders; Cameron Thom, a former mayor of Los Angeles; and others of similar stature. Representing their interests was Senator Stephen M. White, the hero of the free-harbor contest.[29]

Los Angeles residents now generally favored a municipal takeover of the waterworks, and in the months preceding the expiration of the lease Los Angeles newspapers carried an ongoing discussion of the issue. Although the newspapers all favored municipal opera-

[28]Layne, *Water and Power*, pp. 45–46. Ironically, a system for fire protection was one of the reasons for the lease idea ("Los Angeles Water Supply Question," *Municipal Engineering* 13 [September, 1897], 150).

[29]Morrison I. Swift, "Public Purchase of the Los Angeles Water System," *Public Ownership Review* 2 (August–September, 1898), 52–53; C. P. Dorland, "The Los Angeles River—Its History and Ownership," Historical Society of Southern California, *Annual Publications* 3 (1893), 35.

tion, the opposing view was given fair treatment as well—an unusual editorial procedure for the era, possibly due to the prominence of the company's stockholders. One of the frankest rebuttals to the idea of municipal operation appeared in the *Times* when the paper interviewed a number of citizens for their opinions shortly before the lease expired. Maurice H. Newmark expressed the old fear of political graft:

It is a dangerous experiment to increase the number of public offices. When public utilities are managed by the government, as in the case of the post office, the results seem to be for the best interests of the people. But municipalities don't do things the way that the Federal government does. On account of the danger of official corruption, I am opposed to municipal ownership. If you are going to have the city run the water plant, why don't you have it run the gas works, the flour mills and the butcher shops. Not every man takes baths, but everybody eats bread. I may take a one-sided view of the situation, as my father owns stock in the water company.[30]

The movement for the city's takeover of the domestic waterworks began in January, 1897, with the city facing the immediate question whether to buy out the company or build its own system. By far the simpler solution was to purchase the company's operation, and negotiations soon began. On February 25 the city council sent a letter to the Los Angeles City Water Company asking for a conference "for the purpose of taking up . . . the question of the purchase of the plant of the Los Angeles City Water Company by this municipality."[31] The company's reply was noncommittal. Neither side had yet mentioned a possible purchase price. J. Henry Dockweiler, the city engineer, prepared a survey of the waterworks, which he submitted to the city council on July 26. Dockweiler suggested the city purchase the system; to build its own could take up to twelve years. The city council then offered $1,190,655 for the waterworks. The company replied. Its asking price, $3 million.[32]

At this point the complication of the Crystal Springs Land and Water Company was introduced, with the claim that the city did not own the water handled by the Crystal Springs company—a defiance of the city's pueblo water right. The city decided to wait until a

[30]*Los Angeles Times*, July 19, 1898.
[31]Quoted in Layne, *Water and Power*, p. 58.
[32]Ibid., pp. 57–58; Ostrom, *Water and Politics*, p. 47.

pending court action dealing with the pueblo right question at the state supreme court level (*City of Los Angeles* v. *Pomeroy*, on whether the pueblo right applied to the subterranean flow of the Los Angeles River) was resolved. The city again offered to reopen negotiations in December. The company continued to reply evasively.[33]

With the lease moving into the final six months of its life, something had to happen. Nothing did, at least, not until June, 1898, barely a month before the expiration date. The company again offered its works, breaking down the figure differently. It was now $2 million for the Los Angeles City Water Company, $1 million for the Crystal Springs Land and Water Company (which stubbornly maintained that its water came from a subterranean source independent of the Los Angeles River). The sum total, however, remained the same. So did the stockholders of the two companies. The city responded with an offer of $1.3 million, an offer the company found unacceptable. July 21 came and went. On July 23 the city council appointed an arbitrator to begin the arduous task of negotiating the purchase of the pipes to carry its own water.[34]

During the months that followed, the city ran a gauntlet of alternate proposals, injunctions, lawsuits over water rates and water rights, stalemate with the water company, and endless delays. Although the company soon picked its arbitrator as the 1868 lease provided, both arbitrators then delayed on their mutual choice of a third person until the end of October. Some fascinating side issues also emerged. A proposal called the Kessler proposition was presented to the city council, calling for a new lease arrangement. Kessler and Company, a New York firm, wanted a fifty-year lease, for which a number of promises about service and operation were made. To this proposal the *Times* responded, "The experience which we have had with private control of this great public utility has not been such as to make the prospect of a continuance of private control very attractive." The proposal was referred to the council's Water Supply Committee.[35] Beyond the Kessler proposition citizens

[33]Layne, *Water and Power*, p. 59.

[34]*Los Angeles Times*, June 15 and 17, July 22 and 24, 1898; Layne, *Water and Power*, p. 60.

[35]*Los Angeles Times*, July 12 and 16, October 26, 1898; Layne, *Water and Power*, p. 65; Swift, "Public Purchase," p. 54.

heard of the Merrill proposition, the Burbank plan, and other schemes.

The political parties found the idea of a "water company ring" as tempting an issue as the agitation on the state level against a "railroad machine." The Republicans pronounced strongly against the water company, the Democrats somewhat less so, a factor in the election of Republican Fred Eaton over incumbent Democrat Meredith Snyder on December 15, 1898.[36]

The three arbitrators, after a slow beginning, spent the first part of 1899 investigating and evaluating. Mulholland, superintendent of the water company, spent a total of six full weeks in giving testimony. The arbitrators inspected pipes taken from selected excavations, appraised real estate, and held daily sessions, all in an effort to determine a fair value for the waterworks. Finally, on May 12, the arbitrators submitted their findings. They voted, two to one, for a value of $1,183,591.42, giving a clear victory to the city since its board of consulting engineers (who, it will be recalled, had found Mulholland most cooperative and his memory most remarkable) had claimed the value at around $1.4 million. Dissent came from the company-chosen arbitrator who persisted in holding to the $3.0 million price.[37]

Amid protests from Senator White and supporters of the water company that the board of arbitration's award was unacceptable—and, indeed, legally invalid—because there had not been unanimous consent, some good news for the city was announced. The state supreme court had found in the city's favor in the *Pomeroy* case; in its essence, this meant that Los Angeles' pueblo right included the subsurface flow of the Los Angeles River. For the water company litigation, the *Pomeroy* decision undercut the Crystal Springs company's contention that its source was independent of the river's streamflow. But settlement between city and company over the value of the company's property still remained in dispute.[38]

Determined to settle the dispute with his old employer, Mayor

[36]*Los Angeles Times*, July 17 and December 16, 1898.

[37]Ibid., May 13, 1899; Layne, *Water and Power*, p. 66; Spriggs, "History of the Domestic Water Supply of Los Angeles," pp. 53–54.

[38]*Los Angeles Times*, June 4, 5, and 16, 1899; Fred Eaton, "The Water Controversy at Los Angeles," *California Municipalities* 1 (November, 1899), 104–105; *City of Los Angeles v. A. E. Pomeroy*, 124 Cal. 597 (1899).

Eaton now called for a city bond election. The city council agreed but decided, in convoluted fashion, that to send out notice of a special election might be construed as official support of the bonds. With one exception the councilmen took the position that since everyone knew about the coming election, it would be a waste of taxpayers' money to send out notices about it. The local political parties, however, came to the rescue. Eaton, as the city's ranking Republican, sent a letter to David W. Edelman, chairman of the Democratic City Council Committee, urging both parties to work for the common goal of getting out the vote on August 23, the date of the special election. Observed the *Times*, "This is no party issue, but one in which all public-spirited citizens should be deeply interested."[39]

Eaton organized a Citizens' Committee of One Hundred, a nonpartisan group of leading citizens, to push for passage of the bonds. The bond issue of $2 million was to buy out the company at the arbitration-set price and also to improve and modernize the system. The Committee of One Hundred met on Friday, August 17, a week before the election, to plan its strategy. One large city map was marked off into the sixteen election precincts especially set up by the city council. Then sixteen maps were prepared, one for each precinct, to show the polling places. These maps would be reproduced in sufficient quantities to help voters find their new polling places. J. B. Lippincott volunteered to prepare the maps and distribute them at the committee's meeting the next evening. Mayor Eaton provided his outer office for the use of the Committee of One Hundred's executive committee.[40]

At the August 18 committee meeting Lippincott carried out his promise by presenting 40,000 precinct maps. Chairmen were elected for each precinct; an address to the public was adopted and ordered printed in large quantities. Each precinct committee drew up lists of campaign workers to distribute literature. Several committees reported on their work. The finance committee laid plans to canvass the city for funds, while the committee on public meetings

[39]*Los Angeles Times*, August 15, 1899.

[40]Ibid., August 18, 1899. In the same issue, Lippincott published a letter comparing municipal and private ownership. See also *Los Angeles Record*, August 18, 1899.

arranged for a mass meeting at Hazard's Pavilion on Monday evening. Meanwhile, the Republican and Democratic Central Committees declared themselves in favor of the water bonds.[41]

As election day neared, newspapers granted space to both factions to make their final arguments. Each side cited statistics proving that its service would provide good water at less cost than the other's. In addition, paid advertisements were placed. The water company warned that if the city took over the waterworks more bond issues would be needed in the future to pay for additional construction expenses.[42]

On Monday evening the Committee of One Hundred held its mass meeting. Among the speakers were Eaton and Lippincott. The turnout was disappointing, as only "several hundred" people came to Hazard's Pavilion. Nevertheless, the *Times* reporter optimistically speculated, "The emptiness of the seats was not ascribed . . . to lack of interest in the subject under discussion, but was considered, rather, as an indication that the people of the city, generally, deem themselves already sufficiently informed on the water question and are merely waiting for a chance to declare their wishes in the matter at the polls."

Election day came on Wednesday, August 23, and the will of the people went overwhelmingly in favor of the bonds' passage—7,189 voted for the bonds, 973 against, a seven-to-one margin. The successful outcome was credited to the work of the Committee of One Hundred.[43]

Unfortunately, the water bonds immediately became tangled in a series of new lawsuits. By November five suits had been filed against the city on various aspects of the water question. As his term of office entered its second year, Eaton grew increasingly frustrated over the stalemate. Lawsuits ranged from technicalities in the bond election to the reduction of water rates. The bond issue so

[41]*Los Angeles Times*, August 19, 1899; *Los Angeles Record*, August 19, 1899.

[42]*Los Angeles Times*, August 21 and 22, 1899; *Los Angeles Record*, August 21, 1899.

[43]*Los Angeles Times*, August 22, 1899; Lippincott to William Henry Knight, August 21, 1899, Box 87, Knight Collection, Special Collections Department, University of California, Los Angeles (hereafter cited as SCD); *Los Angeles Times*, August 24, 1899.

energetically campaigned for was never sold because of the litigation against it. During this time the Los Angeles City Water Company, perhaps recognizing what was probably inevitable, gave minimum attention to maintenance and none at all to improvement of the water system. To add to the legal confusion, the city at first accepted the annual rental payment on the expired lease and then, recognizing its error, returned it. Other problems also presented themselves. Southern California was in a dry cycle, and without any company efforts to build up water reserves, the water table became ominously low.[44]

The Democrats recaptured control of the mayor's office with the election once again of Meredith Snyder in December, 1900. Snyder was now fully committed to ending the water company dispute. His continual pressure on the city council finally brought forth a plea from its finance committee that the stalemate be ended and negotiations renewed. This brought some response from the water company, which expressed a willingness to settle, since the Crystal Springs claim, in the face of the *Pomeroy* decision, could no longer stand up in court. The city offered $2 million in full settlement, subject to passage of another bond issue. Litigation was to be suspended immediately.[45]

Mulholland, respected by both sides for his honesty, paid a visit to Isaias Hellman, the major stockholder in the water company, at his summer home at Lake Tahoe in mid-July, 1901. Hellman heard Mulholland's views on the proposed settlement. The public, said Mulholland, was pretty well fed up with the drawn-out dispute, and a settlement could well be reached that would give the company less than what the city now offered. Hellman accepted Mulholland's suggestions, did his own thinking on the matter, and agreed to accept the city's offer on July 29, 1901.[46]

Within two weeks the city council passed an ordinance scheduling a new bond election for August 28; the previously voted bonds,

[44]*Los Angeles Times*, November 18, 1899, and January 7, 1901; Ostrom, *Water and Politics*, pp. 47–48; Layne, *Water and Power*, pp. 67–68.

[45]Layne, *Water and Power*, p. 68; Ostrom, *Water and Politics*, pp. 42–48; Boyle Workman, *The City that Grew*, p. 295.

[46]Spriggs, "History of the Domestic Water Supply of Los Angeles," p. 58; Ostrom, *Water and Politics*, p. 129.

still unsold, were invalidated. Election day finished the long controversy. The bonds were approved 6,284 to 1,267, a five to one ratio, much more than the two-thirds required for passage. The city was now once again in the domestic water business.[47]

Under New Management

Los Angeles lost no time in moving toward the takeover of the water company properties. There was little ceremony involved in the changeover. Following the marketing of the bonds on February 3, 1902, the city council passed an ordinance, approved by Mayor Snyder, creating a municipal Board of Water Commissioners. On February 5 Snyder, accompanied by the six city council members, walked from the city hall over to the water company building at Alameda and Marchessault Streets. He called the workers there to attention and announced that, on behalf of the City of Los Angeles, he was taking possession of the waterworks. Current water company employees would be retained by the city and paid their regular salary. With that, Snyder and the councilmen returned to city hall. A week later the first Board of Water Commissioners was organized.

Snyder intended to avoid petty politics in the naming of the board. A list of twenty-one citizens was drawn up by the Los Angeles Chamber of Commerce; of these, seven were picked to be on the new board. James C. Kays, the city-appointed arbitrator in the long negotiations, resigned his appointment immediately, having had his fill of water issues. The new water board carried some slight resemblance to the old company's board of directors. John M. Elliott and J. C. Drake, who had been water company directors, were among those who accepted the new responsibility. All of those appointed were prominent citizens. For the Water Department staff, all thirty of the old company employees were retained and placed on civil service; Mulholland accepted the appointment as superintendent.

A city charter amendment soon changed the composition of the Board of Water Commissioners. Effective February 5, 1903, the board consisted of five members appointed by the mayor, serving

[47]Layne, *Water and Power*, p. 68.

staggered terms. Elliott and L. A. Grant from the old board were appointed to the new one. This new board exercised expanded financial powers to meet the new challenges and take care of neglected problems.[48]

Mulholland immediately set about making changes and improvements. There was much to be done, and under Mulholland's leadership much was soon accomplished—increased water storage facilities, meters, rate reductions, new water pipes, and other construction and repair work. Major problems faced the city. From the time Fred Eaton had drawn his design for the plaza until the beginning of the twentieth century, Los Angeles' population had multiplied twenty times over. The water table was seriously depleted. A prolonged dry spell taxed available reserves. Having learned its lesson from the water company experience, the city intended never again to alienate its control of the river. An amendment to the city charter, adopted in 1903, summed up the whole controversy. "The said city shall not convey, lease, or otherwise dispose of its rights in the waters of said River Los Angeles, or any part thereof, or grant, or lease to any corporation or person, any part or privilege to use, manage, or control the said waters, or any part thereof, for any purpose, public or private," it read; "No other water or water right now or hereafter owned by said city shall be conveyed, leased, or otherwise disposed of, without the assent of two-thirds of the qualified electors of said city voting upon such prohibition at an election. . . ."[49]

Los Angeles emerged from its long war with the water company to find itself at a developmental crossroad. The attractions of Southern California—its climate, oranges, and growth potential—continued to be proclaimed by the Los Angeles Chamber of Commerce, the All Year Club, and other booster-minded organizations. New interurban railways made Los Angeles the hub of an ever-spreading network of new communities. Most of the newcomers who came to take part in the city's rush to metropolitan status had little idea of the difficulties the city faced in putting together a

[48]Ibid., pp. 69, 74; Ostrom, *Water and Politics*, pp. 90–91, 92.

[49]"Water, Water Rights, and Waterworks," *California Statutes, 1903*, chap. 6, article 18, section 191, p. 562.

workable water system, providing for the needs of its thirsty citizens, and in figuring out where an adequate and dependable supply of water might come from. Some men of vision declared that the city's future would be dramatic and influential, overlooking the region's dependence on a finite water source. Other men were only too aware of the possible limitations. J. B. Lippincott, who in the fall of 1902 returned to government service full time as supervising engineer for California in the new United States Reclamation Service, knew that water was the crucial key to settlement of arid regions. William Mulholland, the respected "Chief" of the city's new water department, grew increasingly concerned as he watched Los Angeles bulge at the seams with new people looking for new opportunities while his adopted land of sunshine endured a prolonged period of drought. And Fred Eaton never forgot the sparkling water of the Owens River, two hundred and forty miles to the north.[50]

[50]Nadeau, *Water Seekers*, pp. 12–13.

3

The Reclamation Service and the Owens Valley Project

"The policy of the National Government should be to aid irrigation in the several States and Territories in such manner as will enable the people in the local communities to help themselves . . ."—Theodore Roosevelt, Annual Message to Congress, 1901

ON June 17, 1902, some four months after the City of Los Angeles regained control of its waterworks system, the United States Congress passed the National Reclamation Act. Its passage marked the end of a long campaign to irrigate the arid regions of the West—and the beginning of debate and controversy over how the act's provisions should be applied. Composed of such diverse elements as naive idealism, practical politics, greed, and business sense, there was something in the act for everyone. It would develop marginal land for cultivation through irrigation, enabling thousands of people back East to leave crowded city slums and regain pride of self in a twentieth century hearkening to America's pioneer experience. It would create a government agency to do for the West what private enterprise had failed to do and what had not been needed in the eastern half of the country, where inland waterways were both plentiful and navigable. It would pay for itself, as settlers would pay back into a reclamation fund the cost of the irrigation improvements. It would herald the commitment of a progressive era to help as many people as possible help themselves.[1]

---

[1]U.S., *Statutes at Large*, vol. 32, part 1, chap. 1093, pp. 388–390; John T. Ganoe, "The Origin of a National Reclamation Policy," *Mississippi Valley Historical Review* 18 (June, 1931), 34–52.

The act was not without its compromises, loopholes, and omissions. The number of projects in a western state or territory depended on the sale of public lands within that state or territory. The more sales, the more projects, whether or not the project was really needed. No one seemed to notice that unqualified people with inadequate capital and no farming experience could obtain reclamation land. In such fashion did the Progressive Era pay homage to the famous "agrarian myth," wherein any aspiring American could assertedly become a yeoman farmer. The act also gave the secretary of the interior broad discretionary powers in determining which projects were approved, how large the farm units might be, how much in reclamation-fund expenditures would be allocated, and other considerations. The requirement that settlers on reclamation projects repay the cost of the project gave rise to fraud and defalcation.[2]

Despite the shortcomings, many of which were not foreseen at the time of the act's passage, the Reclamation Act—or Newlands Act, after its sponsor, Representative Francis Newlands of Nevada—received acceptance and praise from many western settlers, conservationists, and politicians. The operative slogan of the era, as mentioned, was "the greatest good to the greatest number," or some variation of it. Everyone proclaimed it, subordinates echoing their superiors in endorsing the utilitarian philosophy. "Our aim should be not simply to reclaim the largest area of land and provide homes for the largest number of people," said President Theodore Roosevelt in his annual message to Congress in 1901, "but to create for this new industry the best possible social and industrial conditions."[3]

---

[2]Gene M. Gressley, "Arthur Powell Davis, Reclamation, and the West," *Agricultural History* 42 (July, 1968), 249–251; Leahmae Brown, "The Development of National Policy with Respect to Water Resources" (Ph.D. diss., University of Illinois, 1937), pp. 91–92. Mary Ellen Glass, "The Newlands Reclamation Project: Years of Innocence, 1903–1907," *Journal of the West* 7 (January, 1968), 55–63, provides an example of early Reclamation Service fallibility in its failure to conduct soil analyses on the Truckee-Carson project, with adverse results to settlers there.

[3]Theodore Roosevelt, *Works*, 17:125; Gifford Pinchot, *The Fight for Conservation*, p. 48; M. Nelson McGeary, *Gifford Pinchot: Forester-Politician*, pp. 74, 123–124.

Roosevelt, with the aid of like-minded progressives, made the Reclamation Act a reality six months later.

The Reclamation Service was the instrument by which the irrigation crusaders—men like George H. Maxwell and William E. Smythe, who had for years lobbied, written, and preached of the need for irrigating arid lands—were to see their goals implemented. Shortly after the passage of the Newlands Act, Secretary of the Interior Ethan A. Hitchcock created the Reclamation Service as a division within the Geological Survey. Personnel came from the survey's Hydrographic Branch, which had spent years investigating the water supply of arid regions. Frederick Haynes Newell, head of the Hydrographic Branch, was appointed chief engineer of the Reclamation Service. Newell reported to Charles D. Walcott, director of the Geological Survey, who in turn was responsible to Hitchcock.[4]

Newell's career epitomized that of the engineer who dedicated himself to government service. A native of Pennsylvania, Newell was forty years old when he became the chief engineer. His background included a degree in mining engineering from Massachusetts Institute of Technology. In October, 1888, he began government service as an assistant engineer in the Geological Survey under the redoubtable John Wesley Powell. He became chief of the Hydrographic Branch in 1890 and held that key position for thirteen years. As chief hydrographer, Newell was in an influential position to assist in the drafting of the Reclamation Act. Along with George Maxwell, president of the National Irrigation Association, and Chief Forester Gifford Pinchot, Newell helped Newlands draft successive pieces of legislation, finally putting through the act of 1902 with the help of President Roosevelt. His application for membership in the American Society of Civil Engineers was endorsed by no less than ten

[4]Betty Mae Kleinman, "Organization of the United States Bureau of Reclamation" (Master's thesis, University of California, 1946), p. 13; Lawrence B. Lee, "William Ellsworth Smythe and the Irrigation Movement: A Reconsideration," *Pacific Historical Review* 41 (August, 1972), 310–311; idem, "Environmental Implications of Governmental Reclamation in California," *Agricultural History* 49 (January, 1975), 226–227; Andrew Hudanick, Jr., "George Hebard Maxwell: Reclamation's Militant Evangelist," *Journal of the West* 14 (July, 1975), 115–117; Martin E. Carlson, "William E. Smythe: Irrigation Crusader," *Journal of the West* 7 (January, 1968), 41–47.

engineers, among them J. B. Lippincott and Arthur Powell Davis. Newell was recognized as a person of high integrity, high ideals, and dedication to his profession.[5] As the chief engineer of the new Reclamation Service, Newell cast about for engineers who shared similar ideals. For his chief assistant he found someone of like temperament, Arthur Powell Davis.

Like Newell, Davis had chosen to make his career in government service. Born in 1861 in Decatur, Illinois, Davis belonged to the generation of engineers who tackled so many of the technological challenges of the early twentieth century. Newell was a year younger and Lippincott three years younger than Davis, whose boyhood years were spent in Kansas, where his father served as a congressman. In 1882 Davis became an assistant topographer in the Geological Survey, under the tutelage of his uncle, John Wesley Powell. He finished college—the Corcoran Scientific School of Columbian University, now George Washington University—in 1888 and assumed additional responsibilities in the survey. In 1894 he joined the Hydrographic Branch, having spent a year out West instructing assistants in establishing gauging stations and doing hydrographic work. One of his assistants, as noted earlier, was Lippincott, with whom he tried a brief fling at a private irrigation project. Davis qualified for associate membership in the American Society of Civil Engineers in 1893 and was elevated to full membership in 1899, several months before his friend Lippincott achieved the same status. As a hydrographer Davis accepted a wide variety of assignments that added to his expertise, including surveys of proposed Panama and Nicaragua canal routes and surveys for irrigation projects on Arizona Indian reservations. When Newell tapped him for the position of assistant chief engineer, Davis brought along valuable Geological Survey expertise to help launch the new division.[6]

[5]Allen B. McDaniel, "Frederick Haynes Newell," American Society of Civil Engineers, Transactions 98 (1933), 1597–1600; Newell's application for membership, American Society of Civil Engineers, New York City office; Dictionary of American Biography, 7:456–457.

[6]Charles A. Bissell and F. E. Weymouth, "Arthur Powell Davis," American Society of Civil Engineers, Transactions 100 (1935), 1582–91; Davis' application for membership, American Society of Civil Engineers, New York City office; Dictionary of American Biography, 11, Supplement One, 224–226.

Newell also brought over engineers from other branches of the survey—men like Cyrus Babb and Nelson Darton, whose professional records included long service with the federal government. Most of the engineers, however, had taken on a variety of assignments on all levels of government, as well as in positions with private companies. Newell found it necessary to persuade some of them to return to government service. In the case of Lippincott, who had developed a successful and lucrative private practice while doing per diem work for Powell, Newell had to agree to permit Lippincott to finish his consultation work on current assignments. Lippincott promised to discharge these obligations as soon as possible, in the meantime transferring the work to a partner not connected with government service. Lippincott then became supervising engineer for California, third in the Reclamation Service hierarchy behind Newell and Davis.[7]

A Possible Project

The initial work of the Reclamation Service involved conducting surveys of locations in the western states and territories for possible irrigation projects. Engineers were assigned to each state and territory to conduct the surveys, building on data gathered by the Geological Survey, in many cases by the Reclamation Service engineers themselves in previous assignments.[8]

A number of likely sites existed in California for federal reclamation projects, including the Colorado River near Yuma, the Klamath River at the Oregon-California border, the Sacramento Valley, and the Kings River in the San Joaquin Valley. "In short," reported Newell while preliminary surveys were under way, "in California the number of possible projects and their range is so great that much time and thought must be given to the work in order that each possible project should get adequate consideration." He observed that some of the possible projects were "of such great

[7]F. H. Newell, comp., "Proceedings of the First Conference of Engineers of the Reclamation Service," U.S. Department of the Interior, Geological Survey, *Water-Supply and Irrigation Paper No. 93,* pp. 315–351.

[8]Ibid., pp. 16–19; U.S. Department of the Interior, Geological Survey, *Second Annual Report of the Reclamation Service, 1902–3,* pp. 41–42.

magnitude and others are so involved that immediate decision is impossible, and some time must be taken to obtain the essential facts."[9]

One proposed project that received early mention was in Owens Valley. On April 29, 1903, Newell wrote Lippincott about it. "Have you ever considered the advisability of an examination of Owens River Valley and the desirability of segregating public lands," he asked. "If you think this is a good plan, I wish you would send a suitable man . . . and have a reconnaissance quietly made, with the idea of withdrawing lands pending survey."[10]

In response to this request, Lippincott sent word to one of the assistant engineers in his employ, Jacob C. Clausen, to do a brief reconnaissance of the Owens Valley region and to report back to him on its possibilities. Clausen, a native Californian, was twenty-seven years old and a graduate of the University of California. After college he had done survey work for several private companies, locating canals and designing headgates. Lippincott found him a promising young engineer and in February, 1902, hired him to do hydrographic work for the Geological Survey. The following year Clausen began working for the Reclamation Service; the Owens Valley survey was his first major assignment. Clausen went to Inyo County and by early July completed his inspection of the area. "Have finished reconnaissance large reservoir site, all patents for dam site," he wired Lippincott; "Private parties have all water, sixty thousand public, fifty thousand private land irrigable."[11]

Lippincott reported to Newell that the region seemed favorable for an irrigation project but that private power interests were also checking on the area's possibilities. "We, of course, are interested in irrigation and I suggested that possibly we both could accomplish what we were after without mutual interference," said Lippincott. "I suggested that I would consult with you on the subject and if you were willing that I would discuss the situation with [Clausen]

[9]*Second Annual Report of the Reclamation Service*, p. 55.

[10]Newell to Lippincott, April 29, 1903, file 527/03, Owens Valley, Preliminary Reports on General Plans, General Administrative and Project Records, Records of the Bureau of Reclamation, Record Group 115, National Archives (hereafter cited as OV-PR, RBR).

[11]Telegram from Clausen to Lippincott, undated, quoted in Lippincott to Newell, July 6, 1903, ibid.

after my return and before we actually made our withdrawals or blocked any one else's proceeding up there." He asked for advice on whether to follow a policy of withdrawal first and then consultation or of delaying withdrawal of lands until the power companies made their needs known. Newell replied that the decisions were Lippincott's; three thousand miles' distance prevented him from considering such questions properly. "If there is an opportunity for Government reclamation on a large scale," said Newell, "I think that we should not let this opportunity go by."[12]

Lippincott then made a personal visit to the valley and concurred with Clausen's initial impressions. "The Valley is large, and contains much high grade public land," he found. As for the Owens Valley settlers, "They are anxious to have public construction of works." There was some concern over private projects for irrigation and electricity that could prevent construction of a comprehensive system of storage reservoirs and canals. "It is my judgment," said Lippincott, "that all the remaining public lands in Owens Valley should be withdrawn pending further examination."[13]

Clarifying Goals

In September, 1903, Newell called a meeting of Reclamation Service engineers at Ogden, Utah, concurrent with the Eleventh National Irrigation Congress. During the first year of the Reclamation Service's existence some confusion had arisen as to procedures and methods of operation. Newell also felt the service lacked clearly defined goals. At the meeting the engineers became acquainted with newer employees, met the delegates to the National Irrigation Congress, and held sessions on organization, methods of work, and other procedural matters. Twenty-five engineers—supervising, consulting, and district men—attended the conference, which ran September 15–18. Gifford Pinchot, chief forester of the United States, Utah's Senator Reed Smoot, California's Governor George C. Pardee, and other dignitaries addressed both meetings.

New regulations governed the Geological Survey, and one pur-

---

[12]Lippincott to Newell, July 6, 1903 and Newell to Lippincott, July 20, 1903, ibid.

[13]Lippincott to Newell, August 6, 1903, ibid.

pose of the meeting was to clarify organization responsibilities. The Reclamation Service held the status of a division within the Hydrographic Branch of the Geological Survey, itself a bureau within the Department of the Interior. The service was charged with surveying and constructing irrigation works for reclaiming lands in thirteen states and three territories, using funds drawn from the sale of public lands. "The engineers of the Reclamation Service are, in effect, the advisers of the Secretary of the Interior in the great work of reclaiming the arid lands of the West," Newell informed his audience. "They are to obtain facts as to the cost and advisability of various projects and to submit these with recommendations for the construction of certain selected works."[14]

Newell addressed his engineers on topics ranging from making five copies of contracts to checking "to the last cent" vouchers for tents, stoves, groceries, and other supplies and equipment. Meeting each morning at 8 A.M. and also attending National Irrigation Congress sessions, the engineers spent long days and evenings absorbing all the information. Newell also remarked on the high standards and expectations for the service, insisting on full dedication from his men. "It has been found wise to require that each man connected with the Geological Survey or its branches shall devote all of his energies to the work for which he is engaged and to abstain from any other occupation for which he will receive remuneration," said Newell. "In short, his entire time and energies should be devoted to advancing the work on which he is engaged."[15]

Engineers were also called upon to deliver reports on preliminary surveys then under way. Lippincott discussed the Colorado River, going into its historical background and the possibilities for land that could be irrigated by it. Since nothing had been done for Owens Valley beyond Clausen's brief reconnaissance and his own brief visit, Lippincott made no mention of the region. On Friday afternoon both conferences ended, and the Reclamation Service engineers returned home, full of plans for new projects and better informed on how to go about them.

[14]Newell, "Proceedings of First Conference," pp. 21–22.
[15]Ibid., p. 25.

A Project's Possibilities

Immediately following the Ogden conference, Lippincott informed Newell that his office would commence a full-scale survey of Owens River possibilities. "We are proceeding with the investigation of the Owens Valley project for the reclamation of arid lands, both public and private, in this section," he stated. "For this purpose a very large reservoir site is being surveyed by one party and a Hydrographer is engaged with a view to determining existing water rights and excess flood waters. . . . Mr. J. C. Clausen is in charge of this work and Mr. R. S. Hawley is his Hydrographer. I submit herewith estimate which Mr. Clausen has prepared to cover the cost of this investigation to July, 1904."[16]

For the next few months, while Clausen was out in the field, Lippincott supervised developments not only in Owens Valley but also on other possible projects within his jurisdiction. These included a dam on the Colorado River near Yuma, an irrigation project on the Klamath River at the Oregon-California border, and a complicated project on the Sacramento River. On December 1, Lippincott reported to Governor Pardee on the surveys being taken in California. "The Owens Valley project I think is a good one, but our knowledge of the available water supply is hardly sufficient to justify a heavy expenditure of funds at present there," he said. "We are keeping records of all canal diversions, as well as the flow of the river, and by next summer we will be able to have fairly intelligent ideas on the subject."[17]

One immediate concern for the Reclamation Service was the location for a major storage reservoir. The most feasible site for it, Long Valley, was already largely in private hands—the hands of Thomas B. Rickey, a major landholder in the eastern Sierra region. Harry Holgate, a Reclamation Service legal clerk stationed at Independence, reported to Lippincott that Rickey had probably committed fraud in obtaining some of his properties and others might be "legal" but not "legitimate." As Holgate put it, "Legal would

[16]Lippincott to Newell, September 24, 1903, file 527/03, OV-PR, RBR.

[17]Lippincott to Pardee, December 1, 1903, Pardee Papers, Bancroft Library, University of California, Berkeley (library hereafter cited as BL).

be a better adjective than legitimate, since many were forced to sell to Rickey after being coerced and hounded for months and sometimes years, by Rickey and his men." Rickey's corporation, the Rickey Land and Cattle Company, held 22,380 acres in Inyo and Mono Counties. The only way to restore acreage fraudulently obtained by Rickey—and Holgate held little doubt that thousands of acres of land had been taken that way—would be by court proceedings setting aside patents on grounds of fraud. Holgate also passed along the word that Rickey was amenable to the idea of selling some of his Owens Valley land and cattle holdings, possibly to the Miller and Lux firm. In any event, in order to create a feasible reclamation project in Owens Valley, Rickey's land manipulations would have to be dealt with somehow. Meanwhile, the Reclamation Service would continue posting water notices on public lands and obtaining cessions of water rights from ranchers and farmers.[18]

With survey work well under way, an old irritation surfaced to face Lippincott and Newell. As a prominent and successful civil engineer, Lippincott had returned to government service in 1902 with a personal understanding between himself and Newell concerning the continuation of work in the private sector. Newell frowned on the practice—he had stated so clearly at the Ogden meeting—but had looked the other way in order to secure the services of Lippincott, whose talents and abilities he much appreciated. In June, 1904, Newell had approved a salary raise for Lippincott, possibly with the implicit suggestion that Lippincott should completely end all ties with private work. Aware of his delicate position, Lippincott responded with a lengthy explanation of his relationship with his partner, O. K. Parker. "My arrangement with Mr. Parker is that he shall take entire charge of my private work, that he shall

---

[18]Holgate to Lippincott, December 5, 1903, file 63–B, General Correspondence re Right-of-Way Applications in Owens River Valley, General Administrative and Project Records, Records of the Bureau of Reclamation, Record Group 115, National Archives (hereafter cited as OV-GCRW, RBR). In the same records see also Holgate to Newell, December 7, 1903; C. D. Walcott to Commissioner of the General Land Office, March 3, 1904, Assistant Commissioner, General Land Office, to Walcott, March 14, 1904; Newell to Lippincott, March 17, 1904; and Newell to Holgate, March 17, 1904. Long Valley, now the site of Crowley Lake, is located in southern Mono County.

take the salary of $125.00 a month which I guarantee to him out of the profits, and the remaining net profits are to be equally divided." His share of the net profits for the present year would be over $2,000.

Lippincott defended this apparent conflict of interest on two grounds: first, that the private work was done only with public agencies and, second, that through his firm he was able to train bright young engineers he could then hire for the Reclamation Service as the need arose. In view of the controversy that would explode over this issue, Lippincott's defense deserves quotation at length:

I have declined all work that in any way would in my judgment interfere or complicate my public service, including work in court, with the exception of one case which I became involved in over two years ago, and which is now done with. As you know, we are building a water works for Santa Barbara, have built and are operating a water works in San Pedro, have drawn all the plans and specifications for both a sewer and water works in Bishop, and are connected with a municipal water works proposition in Pasadena. In practically every instance I have accepted employment from the people as distinct from corporation employment.

Lippincott went so far as to claim that his private office had been "a source of strength and assistance" to the Geological Survey, "rather than a disadvantage." Among the engineers he claimed to have hired who were then placed in government service were a number of qualified young men, among them Homer Hamlin, Jacob C. Clausen, and J. Frank Danforth.[19] "The firm has now quite a force of men and in case of emergency I always put them at the disposal of the Survey," stated Lippincott. "On the other hand, there is no private work done in the Survey office for individuals." Lippincott reminded Newell that he had started working for the Geological Survey on a per diem basis, and that he accepted a regular assignment "with the idea that I could spend a few days each

[19]Lippincott's judgment was not infallible. On October 5, J. Frank Danforth was arrested in a drunken brawl; the following month he absconded with Geological Survey funds (*Los Angeles Times*, October 6, 1904, and *Los Angeles Examiner*, November 7, 1904). "Wine, Cards, Women Cause of Downfall," read one headline.

month on private work." When Newell had suggested eliminating private work from the survey office completely, Lippincott had done so, moving such work to his private firm.

Lippincott then indicated his motives for continuing the private sector connection, and in doing so he revealed some interesting information about his acquaintance with and the ambitions of Harrison Gray Otis, the publisher of the *Los Angeles Times*:

I learned from my father that a man in public life almost inevitably has his years of service numbered. That enemies of one sort or another will accumulate without any more common basis of agreement than that of mutual apathy to him, and that when their numbers are sufficient it is best for him to go. I must confess that I have been more or less desirous to sufficiently hold my private practice so that if such a day did arrive I would not be helpless. In this connection I was informed by a friend who is in the East that Heber[20] and Otis were planning "to take my scalp" because I had to a certain extent opposed them. I again learned yesterday that our friend General Otis is ambitious to become Secretary of the Interior. How long would I last with Otis Secretary of the Interior? . . . In closing, I wish to again state that I thank you not only for this recent favor, but for many other favors now extending through a period of nine years, and to say that my greatest desire is to be able to serve you in the best way possible. If you still insist on my dropping my private work entirely, please notify me again.[21]

Enclosed with the letter to Newell was an editorial Lippincott had read in the *Engineering Record* supporting outside employment for government engineers.[22] Apparently impressed by Lippincott's eloquent statement, Newell delayed bringing the matter up again until the following spring.

A Camping Trip and Its Consequences

Clausen's survey work was well in progress by midsummer, 1904, and Lippincott decided to take some vacation time for a

[20]Probably Anthony H. Heber, a partner in the California Development Company in the Imperial Valley (see Remi Nadeau, *The Water Seekers*, p. 146).

[21]Lippincott to Newell, July 25, 1904, Newell Papers, Library of Congress, Washington, D.C. (library hereafter cited as LC).

[22]"The Technical Staff in the Employ of the United States Government," *Engineering Record* 50 (July 9, 1904), 37

camping and fishing trip to Yosemite. The outing would generate some questions about just where he did place his professional obligations, but it started innocently enough as a recreational affair. Lippincott took along his wife, teenage daughter Rose, and three-year-old son, and he also invited a number of friends and their families to accompany them. Included were Fred Eaton, noted artist-illustrator Fernand Lungren, and several guests. They journeyed up from Yosemite Valley to Tuolumne Meadows, where Lungren sketched the aspen groves, crossed 10,600-foot-high Tioga Pass, and descended to Mono Lake. There were several lakes in the area that offered excellent fishing. Then Lippincott, along with his daughter, Eaton, Lungren, and a few others, decided to go down into Owens Valley and obtain supplies at Bishop. Several other people joined them on the way, including Thomas Means, the Reclamation Service official conducting soil experiments in the area, and Jacob Clausen. On their tour through the area Clausen pointed out places of interest to the party and spoke of the irrigation possibilities of the region. Lippincott wondered about volcanic lava beneath the possible reservoir site at Long Valley and made a mental note to follow up on the request he had made earlier for a steam drill. Riding along with the others, Fred Eaton took a long and practiced look at Long Valley. During the trip the party met a number of Owens Valley residents who later recalled that Eaton and Lippincott seemed to be good friends.[23]

By September 13 Lippincott was back at the Reclamation

[23]Abraham Hoffman, "Origins of a Controversy: The U.S. Reclamation Service and the Owens Valley–Los Angeles Water Dispute," *Arizona and the West* 19 (Winter, 1977), 337–338; Nadeau, *Water Seekers*, p. 14; S. F. O'Fallon to Thomas Ryan, October 5, 1905, file 23 Alpha. (pt. 3), pp. 4–6, NPRC. The O'Fallon report contains important sworn testimony by Eaton, Lippincott, packer James W. Sherwin, and forest ranger Gus G. Goodale. On the request for the drill, see Lippincott to Newell, April 30, 1904; telegram from Lippincott to Hydrographer, September 1, 1904; and telegram from Morris Bien to A. P. Davis, September 2, 1904, all in file 527/04, OV-PR, RBR. Lippincott's telegram places him in Bishop on September 1. W. A. Chalfant, *The Story of Inyo*, p. 341, quoting Clausen, erroneously places the camping trip in August, 1903. Clausen corrected this error as a slip of his memory in a letter to Remi Nadeau, February 19, 1949, a copy of which Nadeau kindly made available to me. See also John A. Berger, *Fernand Lungren: A Biography*, pp. 137–139, for another version of the camping trip.

Service headquarters in Los Angeles, catching up on his mail. Governor Pardee was concerned over possible use of Lake Tahoe in the Truckee project which was not in Lippincott's jurisdiction. Thomas Means reported in with an account of his inspection of Owens Valley and a general recommendation that it merited a reclamation project.[24]

Then Lippincott learned that Eaton's interest in Owens Valley went far beyond that of a vacationer. Soon after returning to Los Angeles from Yosemite, Eaton called on William Mulholland. Mulholland, of course, was only too aware of Los Angeles' water needs. The city had just spent another hot, dry summer with water consumption far exceeding the Los Angeles River's capacity. Storage reservoirs were also at dangerously low points. Eaton urged Mulholland to accompany him to Owens Valley, and the two made a hasty trip there. Eaton showed Mulholland the area, including the proposed reservoir site. Mulholland, who some years earlier had scoffed at the idea of an aqueduct to such a remote place, was duly impressed with the Owens River streamflow.

Lippincott had been informed by either Eaton or Mulholland, or both, that this trip would be made and that Los Angeles in its desperation might well seek a new water source from the Owens River. Concerned over this development, Lippincott wrote Newell on September 17:

The City of Los Angeles . . . realizes that they must look elsewhere for an additional water supply, and I find that they are looking towards the Owens River for a solution. This will involve a conduit line 200 miles long and over. I learn that they already have had their engineers looking over the situation. We have already made extensive withdrawals in this section, filed on the water rights, and control the dam site at the principal reservoir. I believe that the City of Los Angeles should properly endeavor to bring in a new source of supply, rather than assist in depleting the supplies that are already failing in this immediate section; also that the City will need more water, and that the domestic use of water is the highest use to which it can be put. It will put us in rather an embarrassing position, however, with reference to the Owens Valley Project. That matter has not at all come to a head, but I wish to inform you confidentially of what is under consideration.[25]

[24]Lippincott to Pardee, September 13, 1904, Pardee Papers, BL; Means to Lippincott, September 14, 1904, file 527/04, OV-PR, RBR.

[25]Lippincott to Newell, September 17, 1904, file 23 Alpha. (pt. 3),

Lippincott, as a friend of both Eaton and Mulholland, agreed to keep the strictest confidentiality about the plans. His letter to Newell was written in that vein. Lippincott now arranged with Newell to meet in November with Eaton and Mulholland to define exactly the city's plans in the valley.

Meanwhile, the farmers and ranchers of Owens Valley were totally unaware of Eaton's—and now Mulholland's—scheme. So, for that matter, was the City of Los Angeles except possibly for the Board of Water Commissioners. In their enthusiastic support of the federal reclamation project, several hundred Owens Valley residents sent petitions to the Department of the Interior urging construction of the project. Newell responded warmly to the petitions, stating that it was "important to know the sentiment of the local people on such a question," and that "the Department appreciates the trouble you have taken to express yourself." The valley people did not think it was trouble at all. Visions of an expanding economy in the valley, with Inyo farms, ranches, and businesses supplying goods and services to the boom towns of southwestern Nevada, danced in their minds. "The rapid upbuilding of those camps gave a fresh impetus to mining throughout the region, an advance in which Inyo districts shared," wrote W. A. Chalfant in his history of Inyo County. "Far more important in effect was the creation of nearby cash markets which demanded the best efforts of the agricultural lands of Owens Valley."[26]

Newell, however, was growing increasingly cost conscious over

NPRC. Cf. Nadeau, *Water Seekers*, pp. 13–15. This letter marks the earliest known written acknowledgement by Lippincott of Eaton's plans. Nadeau is imprecise in placing the Eaton-Mulholland trip in September. For them to be in Owens Valley on September 24 (Nadeau, p. 15) means that Lippincott, writing to Newell on September 17, must have known about Eaton's idea before Eaton and Mulholland left for Owens Valley. The *Los Angeles Times*, January 1, 1914, stated that Eaton and Mulholland spent four weeks in Owens Valley. The Board of Water Commissioners granted Mulholland a leave of absence on September 13, 1905. Eaton and Mulholland probably left on September 14, 15, or 16.

[26]Petition from Owens Valley residents to Secretary of the Interior, received November 30, 1904, and Newell to George Watterson, December 6, 1904, file 527-A, Owens Valley Project Miscellaneous, Project File 1902–1919, Records of the Bureau of Reclamation, Record Group 115, National Archives, Washington, D.C. (hereafter cited as OVPM, RBR); Chalfant, *Story of Inyo*, p. 330.

Reclamation Service expenditures. On November 1, shortly before his trip to Los Angeles to meet with Lippincott and the Eaton group, he issued a confidential circular letter to his engineers warning that the funds were insufficient for the construction of all the contemplated projects. He cautioned his engineers "to consider carefully the relative merits of all the known projects, with a view to uniting in recommendations as to which projects should be pushed forward." He counseled that the matter should not be discussed until the secretary of the interior made public which projects would receive appropriations. A set of standards would have to be used to determine whether a proposed project would be approved. The standards included "relative feasibility and benefit to the country as a whole" and the judgment of a project's merit relative to other proposed projects within a state, not in comparison with projects in other states. This was made necessary by the provision in the Reclamation Act requiring 51 percent of a state's or territory's appropriated funds to be spent within that state. Also, the whole intent of the law was to recycle the money: people benefiting from a project were expected to pay back into the fund so that money might then be used for new projects. "No project shall be considered as feasible which is experimental in character," warned Newell, "or in which the return of the funds is not guaranteed in the most effective manner."[27]

To be sure, Lippincott had other possibilities to investigate besides the Owens River. Survey work continued on the Yuma and Klamath projects, with engineers also gathering data on Clear Lake, the Kings River, and other locations. Each area seemed to have its share of partisans and opponents demanding their arguments be heard. To awaken public awareness of the need for such projects, Lippincott and Newell began writing articles for popular consumption describing the efforts of the Reclamation Service. Other engineers did the same.[28]

[27]U.S. Geological Survey, Reclamation Service, circular letter (confidential), November 1, 1904, file 23 Alpha. (pt. 2), NPRC.

[28]Lippincott to Pardee, November 20, 1904, Pardee Papers, BL. Examples of articles include Joseph B. Lippincott, "The Reclamation Service in California," *Forestry and Irrigation* 10 (April, 1904), 162–169; idem, "The

Early in November Clausen submitted his report on the Owens Valley's feasibility as a reclamation project. "This report is based on investigations made by the United States Reclamation Service under the supervision of Mr. J. B. Lippincott, Supervising Engineer for the State of California," read his introduction. "In June, 1903, the writer was detailed to make a reconnaissance of the valley to determine the amount of arid public and private lands and the possibilities of their reclamation. As a result of this reconnaissance . . . the lands lying in Long Valley, Mono County covering a possible reservoir site were withdrawn for reservoir purposes and in a short time followed the withdrawal of all public lands in the Owens Valley, pending further investigations subject now only to the homestead law as affected by the Reclamation Act." In seventy-two pages Clausen described such features as hydrography, topography, existing irrigation systems and methods, and the possible use of Long Valley, above Owens Valley, as the location of a major reservoir.[29]

Clausen's findings were generally positive. Long Valley presented an ideal location for a 140-foot dam that could store 260,000 acre-feet of water; a network of canals could be built to irrigate the extensive arid lands in the area. Clausen found that the lands in Owens and Long valleys varied from first-class farmland to alkaline soils to swamplands. He recommended that the Reclamation Service secure control of the total water supply of the valley, and that valley residents form an association to negotiate with those holding private rights there. "This association should carry on negotiations with the separate holdings, formulate a plan of consolidation whereby the private rights pass into the hands of the Government on acceptable terms so that the plans of Reclamation Service may be completed unhampered by any existing claims."[30]

Clausen probably expected that, like other Reclamation Service surveys, his would be published in the *Water-Supply and Irri-*

Yuma Project," *Out West* 20 (June, 1904), 505–518; F. H. Newell, "The Reclamation Service," *Popular Science Monthly* 66 (December, 1904), 107–116; idem, "Work of the Reclamation Service in California," *Forestry and Irrigation* 11 (August, 1905), 346–347.

[29]J. C. Clausen, "Report on the Owens Valley, California," November, 1904, pp. 1–10, file 527/04, OV-PR, RBR.

[30]Ibid., pp. 50–51, 72.

gation Paper series. Lippincott's massive *California Hydrography* had been published as part of that series in 1903, and Willis T. Lee's *Geology and Water Resources of Owens Valley, California,* containing information gathered in the 1904 season and utilized by Clausen in his own report, would be published in 1906. Many similar reports appeared in the series. Lippincott, however, found a more immediate use for Clausen's report.[31]

At the meeting of Lippincott, Newell, and the Los Angeles men on November 22, Lippincott had copies of Clausen's report with him. Present at the meeting were Lippincott, Newell, Mulholland, Eaton, and William B. Mathews, the city attorney for Los Angeles, who would later have a long and controversial career as attorney for the Los Angeles Department of Water and Power. Although no record was kept of this important meeting, testimony from at least two of the participants is available. Mulholland requested that the Reclamation Service provide him with data on the stream measurements gathered in the Owens River survey—in other words, Clausen's report—in order to evaluate the importance of the stream as a water source. Mulholland recalled that "the subject was gone into as fully as lack of both time and information would permit." According to Lippincott, "I declined to furnish any information to the city concerning the Owens Valley at all until the subject had been passed on by the Chief Engineer [Newell], and his decision was to the effect that this would be only an ordinary and customary courtesy." Mulholland recalled, "Mr. Newell was particularly insistent in his inquiries with regard to the scheme being solely a public one, and received the most solemn assurance we could give that no private or corporate interest was in any way involved in its consummation."[32]

Newell apparently did not inquire as to just what credentials the men had to indicate they were speaking on behalf of the City of Los Angeles. He knew Mulholland to be the chief engineer of the city's water department, and Mathews was introduced to him; but how Eaton presented himself remains unknown, a crucial question in view of later developments. Eaton had originally envisioned the aqueduct as a joint private and municipal enterprise, a position

[31]Clausen's report was never published.
[32]O'Fallon to Ryan, October 5, 1905, file 23 Alpha. (pt. 3), pp. 7, 10, NPRC.

Mulholland and Mathews found unacceptable. By the time of the meeting with the Reclamation Service men he probably had been persuaded to act in favor of a wholly municipal venture.

Eaton's original intention was that of a public-private joint venture, with the city paying for the construction of the aqueduct, Eaton paying for the land and water rights. The water—up to 10,000 miner's inches—would be transported to Los Angeles over the aqueduct without charge. Eaton would be permitted to send surplus water down the aqueduct for his own commercial use, paying a toll to the city for the privilege. This plan and modifications of it met with resistance from Mulholland, who knew that only a municipal project owning and controlling all facets of the aqueduct would be acceptable to the Reclamation Service, the city, and Los Angeles voters. Eaton acceded to Mulholland's view and by the November 22 meeting, when the two men along with Mathews met with Lippincott and Newell, they were united in presenting a municipal plan to the Reclamation Service officials.[33]

The arguments of the Los Angeles men at last convinced Newell of the city's need for an additional water supply and their desire to include the Owens River as one possible option among several. "After considerable discussion it was then decided that the city should be given the benefit of the data that had been collected by the Reclamation Service concerning the Owens Valley," recalled Lippincott, "and that the Reclamation Service was not justified in taking any definite stand on the matter until future developments should determine what was the wisest course to pursue for the greatest public benefit." Lippincott insisted that the stream records were "considered public, and ordinarily subject to inspection." Since Clausen's report was still in typescript and in fact was never published—indeed, on the cover of the copy in the Reclamation Service

[33]Nadeau, *Water Seekers*, pp. 15–16. Crucial points in the controversy are the questions of just when Eaton began taking up options in the Owens Valley, when Mulholland converted Eaton to a wholly municipal view, and when Eaton commenced taking options on behalf of the city. Only the third of these questions can be answered with certainty: in early March, 1905 (see below, note 37). Eaton's earlier appearances in Owens Valley, noted by Chalfant and cited by subsequent authors, are often blurred with his 1905 trips. It is possible that Eaton bought options in the fall of 1904 in line with his original scheme, but these purchases were never recorded.

office was the inscription "do not publish"—Lippincott's interpretation of the report's availability is questionable. Lippincott also observed, "Absolutely no data whatsoever concerning the Owens Valley had ever been furnished to the City of Los Angeles" prior to November 22. Mulholland accepted the Clausen report with thanks, and the history of Owens Valley was forever changed. "He then gave us a report concerning the stream measurements of the Owens River and its tributaries," recalled Mulholland, "which I understand has since been published and distributed." Mulholland understood incorrectly. "This was the full extent of the assistance the Water Department of this City received from the Reclamation Department [sic]."[34]

Lippincott and Newell regarded their action as a convenience in helping Los Angeles determine which way was best for locating and obtaining additional water resources. Eaton and Mulholland, however, looked at it quite another way. The statistics they received provided additional hard evidence for clinching their proposal with the Los Angeles Board of Water Commissioners.

In fact, the Reclamation Service men were misled, for Mulholland was perfectly aware that the Owens River was the best choice, the only choice. He had said as much a week before the meeting with Newell, when he had delivered to the Engineers and Architects Association of Southern California an address entitled "The Water Supply of Southern California." Mulholland reviewed the available and potential water sources for the city. In tribute to Frank Wiggins' Chamber of Commerce activities in attracting people to Los Angeles, Mulholland at one point wryly suggested, "It is a question of either getting more water or killing Wiggins, for it is not to be expected that the present rush to this country will cease until he is dead." But the general tone of his address was somber. To grow, Los Angeles needed water, and all current schemes to get it were self-defeating, since they usually involved legal squabbles with other municipalities or lowering of the water table. All current schemes, that is, save one. Mulholland dropped a hint about Eaton's plans, saying "desperate diseases require desperate remedies, and the public must be prepared for somewhat of a shock at the enor-

[34]O'Fallon to Ryan, October 5, 1905, file 23 Alpha. (pt. 3), pp. 7, 9–10, 51, NPRC.

mous expenditure that will be required to bring a remote but reliable supply of water to this country."

Mulholland did not wish to elaborate on this hint. "For very obvious reasons it would not be well at the present time to disclose the plans of the various projects in contemplation, most of them being in the formative stage as yet." There was reason for optimism, he assured his audience. He simply wanted them to know "the facts as they exist to the end that preparation may be made to calmly and wisely consider them, and to give notice to the public that the officers appointed to look after the interests of the Water Department of this City are cognizant of the importance of this subject and are not supinely letting valuable time go by in which to prepare for the coming emergency."[35] With that, Mulholland declared a policy that the Department of Water and Power would follow for many decades.

What remained for Eaton and Mulholland was to translate their vision into reality. But Los Angeles had to have more than a scheme some would consider far-fetched in the extreme. The city needed a plan that was tangible, not visionary. The following spring Eaton determined to go to Owens Valley, buy up key water rights on the Owens River, and sell portions of them to the city, retaining certain elements for himself. One major prospect was Thomas B. Rickey, whom Eaton had heard was willing to sell his Long Valley ranch property. By this means Eaton could undercut the Reclamation Service's plans for a federal project, though not necessarily cause its abandonment.

Conflict of Interest

At this point there occurred a merging of events that has forever remained a cornerstone of the Owens Valley–Los Angeles water controversy. Of crucial importance is the role played by J. B.

[35]William Mulholland, "The Water Supply of Southern California," Engineers and Architects Association of Southern California, *Proceedings* **2** (1907), 120, 122–123. The evidence is not certain, but Lippincott was probably out of town at the time of this speech, on his way to the Twelfth National Irrigation Congress meeting at El Paso. However, he may have been aware of the context of the speech (see telegram from Lippincott to Pardee, November 11, 1904, and Lippincott to Pardee, November 20, 1904, Pardee Papers, BL; also *Los Angeles Examiner*, November 20, 1904).

Lippincott in his position as supervising engineer for the Reclamation Service. "Though an enthusiastic reclamationist, he was first of all a citizen of the ambitious city of Los Angeles," observed Remi Nadeau in his study of the controversy.[36] Lippincott was more than a citizen. He had served and was serving in several positions of civic and professional responsibility for the city. His work on behalf of Los Angeles to make its water department a municipal one has been noted. In 1904 he had accepted an appointment to the city's Civil Service Commission, somehow fitting the responsibility in with the other claims on his time. Now he had to live with a growing dilemma. One of his potential reclamation projects, favorably reported upon by his staff, conflicted with an unprecedented scheme that could affect his adopted city's future.

Lippincott's doubts were reflected in his letter to Newell on February 10, 1905, which was ostensibly concerned with drilling for bedrock at the Long Valley dam site. Eaton's plans, however, presented the real problem. "There is some possibility of our not constructing the Owens Valley project, but of our stepping aside in favor of the city of Los Angeles," said Lippincott. But at this time Eaton had yet to travel to Owens Valley to buy up options on behalf of the city.[37] Financial considerations also needed to be dealt with. "If we do yield to the City of Los Angeles, it seems to me that

[36]Nadeau, *Water Seekers*, p. 17.

[37]Ibid., p. 16. Considerable confusion exists on this issue. Chalfant, *Story of Inyo*, p. 341, asserts that Eaton began buying up options in the fall of 1904 and continued the following spring. The earliest recorded date of an option taken up by Eaton is March 25, 1905 (O'Fallon to Ryan, October 5, 1905, file 23 Alpha, [pt. 3], p. 17, NPRC). Nadeau, *Water Seekers*, p. 16, claims the Rickey sale occurred on March 22. The dates do not conflict because O'Fallon was unable to determine the date of the Rickey sale, other than to state it was probably the first option secured by Eaton. However, Mulholland himself in August, 1905, claimed that Eaton had obtained an option on the Rickey property a full year earlier and was negotiating for the purchase of the ranch prior to the Eaton-Mulholland visit to Owens Valley in September, 1904 (see Mulholland, "The Straight of the Owens River Deal," *Graphic* 23 [August 5, 1905], 4). It is possible that Mulholland himself was confused as to just when Eaton began his negotiations. Morrow Mayo, *Los Angeles*, p. 226, is at error, since maps Eaton used were first seen by Austin in 1905, not 1904. Subsequent accounts relying on Mayo have further garbled the details.

[Los Angeles] should pay for the cost of this work of sounding at the dam site," said Lippincott. "If we do the work, and pay the bills on our vouchers, will it be possible for the city of Los Angeles at some later date—say six months from now, to refund the money to the Reclamation Service so that we can use it elsewhere?" Lippincott expressed a concern, later more than justified, about the possibility of a financial irregularity. Finally, he speculated on the "strong possibility that we may build the Owens Valley project at some later date."[38]

Newell's response indicated the chief engineer was also concerned with possible ramifications. "If at a later date this work should be turned over to the City of Los Angeles," he said, "I think it would be wise to have an understanding to the effect that a reasonable amount of money should be placed at the disposal of the engineers of the Reclamation Service to be expended in work in California as an equivalent for the work which may have been done and which will result largely to the benefit of the City of Los Angeles." In other words, two top officials were aware that their agency was expending limited funds for work that might ultimately benefit Los Angeles, with no present agreement on repaying the Reclamation Service. "Just how this can be done is not at present plain," said Newell, "but I think that the money could be deposited to the account of some trustee, to be drawn upon as proper vouchers are presented."[39]

Several days later Lippincott forever blurred the interests of the Reclamation Service with those of Los Angeles, creating a storm of controversy and bitterness still unsettled. It started innocently enough. Early in 1905 the Colorado River created an emergency when it left its course and poured into the Salton Sink. Lippincott was suddenly "compelled by urgent necessity" to move his engineering crews from the Owens Valley area to the lower Colorado River. Despite his earlier claims of furnishing men for the Reclamation Service "in case of emergency," he was for the moment short of personnel. As he had no engineer available to report "on certain

[38]Lippincott to Newell, February 10, 1905, file 63-B, OV-GCRW, RBR.
[39]Newell to Lippincott, February 17, 1905, ibid.

power applications that are coming up in the Owens Valley," Lippincott asked his friend Fred Eaton, who he knew was going up to the
valley, to check on the applications when he got there.[40]

A week later Lippincott received a baffling request from Washington, D.C., concerning a telegram Eaton had sent to Reclamation
Service headquarters. Rickey had submitted a power application to
the Reclamation Service, which in turn sent the application to Eaton,
who then sent the telegram. Arthur Powell Davis, acting in the
absence of Newell, wanted to know what was going on. On March
10 Lippincott clearly stated what he had done. "The only authority
that I gave Mr. Eaton to report on the Rickey application for a
power plant was a request that he particularly inform me as to who
was making the application," he explained, "what they expected to
do with the power and whether in his judgment there would be any
interference, due to the granting of this application, with the plans
of the Reclamation Service or the City."[41]

Unfortunately, Lippincott had already muddied up the waters
of the Owens River situation. Four days earlier, he had accepted
new private work for the Lippincott & Parker firm. It had been
Newell's expectation and understanding that Lippincott would grad-
ually divest himself of past private commitments. The end result
would be Lippincott's full-time attention to the Reclamation Service. But on March 6 the Los Angeles Board of Water Commissioners voted unanimously to engage Lippincott as a consulting engineer, along with Mulholland, to compile a report on water data, for
the tidy sum of $2,500—two-thirds as much as Lippincott earned
from the Reclamation Service in an entire year.[42]

To modern eyes Lippincott's acceptance of the assignment is

[40]Lippincott to Eaton, March 3, 1905, file 23 Alpha. (pt. 2), NPRC.

[41]Lippincott to Davis, March 10, 1905, file 63-B, OV-GCRW, RBR.
This letter, which Andrae Nordskog must certainly have seen while doing
his research in 1928, was omitted from his "Boulder Dam in the Light of the
Owens Valley Fraud" manuscript (Nordskog Collection, Minnesota Historical
Society, St. Paul, Minnesota) and his *Communication to the California
Legislature* pamphlet (see below, chap. 7). Lippincott's mention of the city
shows that not only Newell but also Davis was aware of Los Angeles' plans.

[42]"Regular Meeting of the Board of Commissioners of the Water Department of the City of Los Angeles," March 6, 1905, copy in file 23 Alpha.
(pt. 2), NPRC.

such a clear conflict of interest as to render justifications of it irrelevant. Lippincott felt it obligatory to explain his action to Newell, which he did on March 9. "As you know, I have been connected with the study of the problems relative to the water supply of the City of Los Angeles for the last ten years," he said. "The local situation you are familiar with. It is recognized now that the City of Los Angeles will have to get an additional water supply. A number of schemes have been presented to the city, which have little value. The Water Commissioners want a definite report on these." To help compile the report, the commissioners requested Lippincott's services as a consulting engineer to aid Mulholland in the report's preparation. Lippincott had pleaded lack of time to the commissioners—interesting to note, he did not plead conflict of interest—but they overcame his protests by insisting his expertise was vitally needed. "I feel that it is a *public duty which I ought to perform* and that I can be of material assistance to this community in the way in which they request," Lippincott explained to Newell. "Mr. Mulholland informs me that he will furnish all the engineering and clerical work necessary for the compilation of the data under the general direction of himself and myself, and that it is only the expression of my judgment on these subjects that he wants."

Lippincott outlined the city's plans to Newell. Fred Eaton was to obtain options on as much irrigated property in Owens Valley as possible, "quickly and quietly." The project would be a wholly municipal enterprise, with all necessary water rights, canals, conduits, and facilities to be paid for and owned by Los Angeles. Eaton would retain certain land titles, but all water rights would be transferred to the city.

"It seems to me that under all the circumstances this is a reasonable and desirable business proposition to the city and one best calculated to serve its interests," claimed Lippincott. He cited the support of some of "the most public spirited and honorable men" in Los Angeles, who had approved of the plan. "I request that I be permitted to advise with Mr. Mulholland on these questions," he concluded. "This may take perhaps two to four days a month of my time for a few months."[43]

[43]Lippincott to Newell, March 9, 1905, Newell Papers, LC (emphasis in original).

Davis passed Lippincott's March 10 letter on to Newell, and Newell responded to both communications on March 18. His reaction to Eaton's involvement was short and to the point: "I fail to understand in what capacity he is acting in connection with the Department that he should be called upon for such report. Please advise me upon this subject."[44]

Lippincott's other letter demanded much more than a tacit permission from Newell to engage in outside work. It struck to the heart of a situation that had existed between Newell and Lippincott for almost three years and was now so blatant it could not be expected to fade away, as Newell had hoped in the past. Lippincott's letter had been marked "Personal and Confidential." Newell replied in kind, carefully composing a four-page typewritten letter that stopped short of demanding Lippincott cease the outside consultation work. The letter spelled out the anguish of a superior attempting to convince a subordinate of bad judgment when both are highly trained, professional men as well as friends. Newell wrote:

You state that you feel it is a public duty which you should perform. There is unquestionably a public duty; but in your present position I think that you have a far higher public duty, and one which is of such character that everything else must give way to it; that is, in pushing forward one or two great projects upon whose success rests, not merely the development of certain areas in California, but the reputation of a great work for the entire West. You already have in hand problems so momentous and far-reaching that all are agreed that your entire time and thought is none too much to give, and distractions elsewhere can not but serve to be a source of danger.

Newell expressed concern that the federal reclamation project in Owens Valley would be jeopardized "through cooperations with private parties," and he cautioned Lippincott that the Reclamation Service was an agency "where everything is new and there is no record of substantial past achievements to fall back upon." He felt that Lippincott was exposing himself to misunderstanding and misinterpretation by his attitude and actions.

More to the point was the issue of whether any outside work was justifiable. "I have been very uneasy about the outside connec-

[44]Newell to Lippincott, March 18, 1905, file 63-B, OV-GCRW, RBR. Lippincott provided further information to Newell on March 29, 1905 (ibid.).

tions of one or two of our most prominent men," he stated, "and hardly a week passes but that some man asks for special favors or consideration on the ground that Mr. Lippincott is a member of a firm with outside practice, and that if Mr. Lippincott can do thus and so, he should be given equivalent or greater consideration." Newell had tried to explain to such people that Lippincott was in the process of closing up his private affairs, with current Reclamation Service time so important that no time was left over for outside work. "Nevertheless, there is among your colleagues an undercurrent of what can not be called criticism, but a feeling, expressed by an occasional phrase or gesture, that your private work tends to delay or distract your attention from the Government work."

Newell further pointed out that some of Lippincott's associates "have had the feeling" that Lippincott might have rendered better service had he not been called away on several occasions by personal matters. "I merely recite these impressions, not to have them corrected, but simply to illustrate the fact that it will never be possible for us to explain or clear the minds of other persons of conceptions that the Government business is being jeopardized by complications with other matters," Newell said. "The only safe plan, in my opinion, is for our principal men to completely abstain from everything which resembles private practice."[45]

The exchange of correspondence continued into the following month. Both men wrote lengthy letters, each attempting to convince the other of his position. "I fear that you do not fully appreciate the extent to which I have withdrawn from private work," declared Lippincott. "I have not done to exceed four days private work in the last six months." He claimed to have turned down thousands of dollars, necessitating personal sacrifices. The Board of Water Commissioners had offered him a rare and generous opportunity for work that would not take more than ten days' effort, argued Lippincott. The city's water plans were crucial to its future. Lippincott indicated his desire to remain with the Reclamation Service and certainly to see the completion of the Yuma and Klamath projects.

But Newell, insisted Lippincott, wanted too much. "Your requirements are that I should avoid investments in localities where

[45]Newell to Lippincott, March 18, 1905, Newell Papers, LC.

we are doing business, where we know there will be great increases in real estate values," he said. "This I have done. In private work this is probably the largest source of income. You ask me now to cut out *all* private work." For this Lippincott would receive a diminished salary that, "taken together with my social position, I am unable to save anything from." Lippincott argued that his private work had always been secondary and that he had given of his time to government service "irrespective of office hours or holidays."

Lippincott could feel the pressure to make a final decision between full-time government service and his lucrative outside opportunities, but he still sought some sort of accommodation from Newell. "I have always been enthusiastic, loyal, and *frank* to you and the Service," he said. "If however, I am prevented from doing *any* private work which will enable me to provide for the future, you are making the retention of my position in the Service extremely difficult." He conceded that his engineering firm, Lippincott & Parker, was the most embarrassing feature of his private work, but he reminded Newell that when he joined the Reclamation Service they had agreed he could continue it and that on that understanding Parker had accepted Lippincott's offer of partnership. Lippincott concluded with a request for information on possible future government salary policies and a hope that Newell would consider all the facts he had presented before making a decision, inasmuch as he had already spent some time in helping prepare the Los Angeles report.[46]

Newell, however, already had enough of Reclamation Service engineers' accepting dual employment. At the second conference of Service personnel, held in El Paso in April, Newell urged all government engineers immediately to discontinue private employment.[47] At the end of the month he again wrote Lippincott, citing unnamed complaints against him and other engineers who persisted in the practice. "There are a large number of engineers struggling for work and recognition, and if they believe that any man connected with the number from securing work they will continue to make trouble,"

[46]Lippincott to Newell, April 6, 1905, ibid. (emphasis in original).

[47]F. H. Newell, comp., "Proceedings of Second Conference of Engineers of the Reclamation Service," U.S. Department of the Interior, Geological Survey, *Water-Supply and Irrigation Paper No. 146*, p. 235.

warned Newell. "The most glaring evidence to many of them seems to be the fact that in visiting our offices in Los Angeles the first thing that strikes their eyes in getting out of the elevator is the sign of 'Lippincott & Parker.' While this in itself may be trivial, it makes a great impression on men who are seeking to find fault."[48]

On receiving Newell's letter Lippincott penned yet another justification, taking the offensive as he demanded to know which unknown parties had criticized him. He still insisted that his outside work, done solely for municipalities, was of positive value to the Reclamation Service.[49]

Arthur Powell Davis, Newell's assistant chief engineer and a strong opponent of outside employment for Reclamation Service personnel, placed professional obligations above personal friendship in this problem. He urged Newell to press the issue with Lippincott:

It is over two years since Mr. Lippincott promised you in my presence to give up his private work as soon as you required it, and on another occasion promised to give it up as soon as you would make his salary $4,000 or more. He has now been receiving additional salary nearly a year, and instead of attempting to free himself from outside entanglements is industriously increasing them.

Davis recommended David C. Henny as a possible successor to Lippincott as supervising engineer. In fact, he recommended that Lippincott be asked to submit his resignation.[50]

Lippincott continued to procrastinate over the general issue of ending private work; however, in the specific area of the Los Angeles assignment, he went ahead with Mulholland and compiled the report for the Board of Water Commissioners. Aware of Eaton's and Mulholland's interest in the Owens River—and, in fact, aware that Eaton's purchase of options was for the city's interest—he must also have been aware that his gathering together of data on Southern California water resources was not so much a discussion of what was available as a compilation of what the city might consider as less desirable options to the Owens River. Mulholland knew this too.

---

[48]Newell to Lippincott, April 25, 1905, Newell Papers, LC. His letter was marked "Personal and Confidential."

[49]Lippincott to Newell, May 3, 1905, ibid.

[50]Davis to Newell, May 1, 1905, ibid.

The report, some 145 pages long, pointedly excluded the Owens River. Its essentially pessimistic tone found little water available in Southern California to provide for the future growth of Los Angeles. On May 22 Lippincott and Mulholland submitted the report to the Los Angeles Board of Water Commissioners. Lippincott was then excused from the meeting so that he was not present when Mulholland made his recommendation for the Owens River as the best source. If morality were subject to technicalities, then Lippincott might, on a technicality, declare his conscience clear insofar as a conflict between a federal Owens Valley project and Los Angeles' plans for Owens River water were concerned.[51]

Newell expressed his regret at Lippincott's acceptance of the Los Angeles assignment, commenting "that my views as given in conversation on the subject have apparently not been taken in the spirit in which they were intended. . . . The Reclamation Service and its men are constantly subject to attack and expect to be at all times. In my opinion, it is better for you to know and anticipate the character of the attacks than to be taken unawares," he went on. "I am as far as possible guarding against these and accumulating data in the official files to meet future investigations." Then, again, the heart of the matter: "It has been my impression of earlier conversations that it was your intention to draw out absolutely from private business, until at least some one of the great irrigation works was successfully concluded. If you ask my advice, or invite suggestions, I must of necessity advise you to keep out of entanglements such as that of the city of Los Angeles until the Yuma and Klamath Projects are on their feet. My feeling is that the amount you receive from the city of Los Angeles will not compensate you for the future difficulties."[52]

But Lippincott was no longer seeking advice; having already written the Los Angeles report, he was now attempting to justify his actions. On May 26 he wrote to Newell reviewing his consultation work for the City of Santa Barbara, which had been going on for several years and which, he believed, had not interfered with his Reclamation Service duties. He described the growth of the

    [51]O'Fallon to Ryan, October 5, 1905, file 23 Alpha. (pt. 3). pp. 14, 20, NPRC.
    [52]Newell to Lippincott, May 17, 1905, ibid.

Southern California region and the critical need for new sources of water. And he indicated his own qualifications for the report the Los Angeles water commissioners wanted of him. "I have now lived in this section for fifteen years, and have made during that entire period a detailed study of all the available water supplies within a radius of two hundred miles of this town," he said.

The water commissioners were exceedingly anxious for me to make this report to them and I have prepared a report on all the available supplies, with the exception of Owens Valley. This is not in the nature of employment by them for continuous service, but rather the presentation of a report based on data which I had previously collected. I have compiled this work outside of my regular office hours. This report has not yet been presented.

Here Lippincott either was misleading Newell or else inadvertently misdated his letter. On May 22, four days prior to the date of this letter, the water commissioners had accepted the Mulholland–Lippincott report and, having filed it as documentation of inadequate local supplies, were now proceeding with the plans for obtaining Owens River water. Lippincott was aware of the plans, for he described them candidly to Newell. "The present indications are that the City will endeavor to obtain a supply from the lower half of Owens Valley, including streams flowing directly into Owens Lake," he said. Most of the currently irrigated farms were in the northern half of Owens Valley, while the lands in the southern half of the valley were marginal in agricultural value. Almost all of the land expected to benefit from the proposed federal reclamation project was in the northern half of the valley. Although Los Angeles would control the Long Valley reservoir site area, actual purchase was not expected for a number of years. Lippincott claimed that the water needed by Los Angeles would come from the lower half of the valley. The benefits were many. "It will relieve the threatened water famine in our town, and put under cultivation a large area of surrounding country, where water will be more valuable than in any other portion of the United States," he claimed, unabashedly ignoring the possible illegality involved in using the water for agricultural instead of domestic purposes. Still, he argued, "The return waters from these districts will tend to replenish the ground water of the coastal plain, which is now shrinking, and the public good that will result from such a course is simply incalculable." Finally, in contrast to the adverse reactions predicted by Newell, Lippincott insisted "that a connection with this enterprise on the part of the Reclamation Service or its members will be considered as a marked public service."[53]

Other letters followed in the same vein. Newell asked Lippincott to submit an application for a leave of absence, giving as a reason the need to prepare the report for the city and justifying the report. In another letter, Newell requested a letter describing Lippincott's relationship with the Lippincott & Parker firm "and the points where it is related directly or indirectly to your work as a Government engineer."[54] Another Newell letter suggested that Los Angeles might contact the secretary of the interior and describe the city's plans to him instead of having a government employee help with the plans. To do otherwise would leave the Reclamation Service "open to the very serious charge of utilizing public information and experience acquired in public employment for private gain."[55]

On June 30 Lippincott sent the two letters to Newell, as Newell had wanted. The first one explained the city's request for his assistance and asked for permission to write the report (which actually had been submitted some six weeks earlier) and to act as a consulting engineer for the city as the need arose. The second letter briefly reviewed the history of the Lippincott & Parker firm and also succinctly presented Lippincott's justification for private work:

From 1895 to 1902 I was connected with the Hydrographic Branch of the U.S. Geological Survey on a per diem basis, devoting only a portion of my time to this work. In the fall of 1902 I was requested by the Chief Engineer to accept a regular commission with the Reclamation Service. At that time I stated that the value of my private business was such that I could ill afford to sacrifice it entirely, particularly because the com-

[53]Lippincott to Newell, May 26, 1905, ibid. On Lippincott's Santa Barbara work, see James W. Eckman, "The Search for Water in the South Coastal Area of Santa Barbara County" (Master's thesis, University of California, Los Angeles, 1967), pp. 22–29. This thesis, minus notes, was published in Santa Barbara Historical Society, Noticias 13 (Summer, 1967), 1–16. See also Owen H. O'Neill, ed., History of Santa Barbara County, State of California: Its People and Its Resources, p. 311.

[54]Newell to Lippincott, May 27, 1905, Newell Papers, LC.

[55]Newell to Lippincott, June 3, 1905, file 23 Alpha. (pt. 2), NPRC.

pensation that could be offered by the Reclamation Service was so much less than the value of my private business. It was finally understood that if I would completely separate my private business and permit my partner to do all of the private work, simply exercising a general supervision over it, that I would be permitted to remain in the firm, and also to accept a regular commission under the Reclamation Service. In the fall of 1902 I took the regular Civil Service examination, and received an appointment.[56]

Lippincott's repeated attempts to justify himself illustrate the complexities of his position. Essentially the long and numerous letters between Lippincott and Newell were arguing apples and oranges. Lippincott insisted he could devote full time to Reclamation Service duties. He justified his spare time or outside private work because it was concerned with municipalities, simply another level of government service. Newell tried in every way he could to convince Lippincott that whether the outside work was on the city, county, state, or national level was irrelevant; to work for the city on a potential water supply from the same area as a proposed federal reclamation project courted conflict-of-interest charges and rendered the Reclamation Service vulnerable to scandal.

Los Angeles Makes Its Move

Debate over permission to continue outside work and to prepare a report that had already been written and submitted soon seemed superfluous. Many things had transpired in Owens Valley since early March, 1905. Fred Eaton had gone there at Lippincott's request to secure information on certain power applications. He also went there with the intention of buying options at strategic locations from Owens Valley ranchers and farmers and if possible to purchase 20,000 acres of Long Valley and Owens Valley land from Thomas B. Rickey. Eaton first stopped at the General Land Office in Independence and requested permission to "look up" the applications. The land register, Stafford Wallace Austin, asked Eaton if he represented the Reclamation Service. Eaton replied that he had a letter from Lippincott authorizing him to report on the applications, but

[56]Lippincott to Newell, June 30, 1905 (two separate letters), ibid.; cover letter to Newell, June 30, 1905, Newell Papers, LC.

apparently Austin did not ask him to present the letter. This was the first of several visits by Eaton to the Independence Land Office.

On March 16 Eaton reported to Lippincott on several right-of-way applicants for water power development in Owens Valley—the Nevada Power, Mining and Milling Company, whose plans did not seem to interfere with a federal project; Frank V. Drake, who seemed to be attempting to tie up desirable power sites for speculative purposes; and the Owens River Power Company, whose applications might interfere, interestingly enough, with any proposals for Long Valley.[57]

Eaton's next contact was with Rickey, who lived in Carson City, Nevada. Rickey's Inyo and Mono County ranch properties, valuable in their own right, were crucial to the city's water plans. Rickey himself was unaware of Eaton's intention to turn over parts of his property and water rights to the City of Los Angeles. After some hard bargaining Rickey sold Eaton a two-month option on the ranchlands, along with 4,000 head of cattle, for $450,000. Eaton paid him $100 to bind the deal.[58]

Eaton then made a tour of the valley, picking up numerous properties on short options, then renewing them and buying new options. He also paid more visits to the General Land Office, where Austin and Richard Fysh, the receiver at the office, noticed he had Reclamation Service maps in his possession. Eaton asked Fysh to make tracings of them; Austin observed that Jacob C. Clausen had drawn the maps during his 1904 survey work. Eaton also asked Fysh to mail the maps to Lippincott, which Fysh did. On another visit, Austin observed Eaton looking over the plat maps showing the Reclamation Service withdrawals for the Owens River project. Ac-

[57]O'Fallon to Ryan, October 5, 1905, file 23 Alpha. (pt. 3), p. 25, NPRC.

[58]Nadeau, *Water Seekers*, p. 16. Portions of the controversy resemble a Chinese puzzle box. Rickey had financial interests in the Nevada Power and Milling Company, on which Eaton reported favorably to Lippincott (see O'Fallon to Ryan, October 5, 1905, file 23 Alpha. [pt. 3], p. 25, NPRC). Lippincott wrote to Clausen on March 20 asking him to comment on Eaton's report. Clausen strongly objected to Eaton's estimate of the Nevada Power Mining and Milling Company's plans. Unlike Eaton, Clausen believed that all reclamation-project water should be stored during the nonirrigating season (Lippincott to Clausen, March 20, 1905, and Clausen to Lippincott, March 24, 1905, file 23 Alpha. [pt. 2], NPRC).

cording to Austin, Eaton made some remarks concerning the withdrawals that suggested his involvement in Reclamation Service activity.

There were other aspects of Eaton's trips that helped confuse Owens Valley residents about the exact nature of Eaton's connection with the Reclamation Service. When word got around that Rickey, an opponent of the reclamation project, had sold his property to Eaton, who was checking on certain matters for the Reclamation Service, the implication was strong that Eaton's efforts were on behalf of the government. Eaton did not deny the implication; neither, however, did he directly misrepresent himself. He left others to draw their own erroneous conclusions as to what he was doing.

Other elements added to the confusion. Eaton employed a man named E. R. Bartlett, who either was or recently had been in the Geological Survey's geological branch, to do some survey work for him. Owens Valley residents assumed he was doing work on the reclamation project; Eaton did not correct the misimpression. About this time the firm of Lippincott & Parker ran a survey line at the Long Valley reservoir site. George Shuey, an engineer employed by the firm to assist in the surveying, at first thought he was working for the federal government, but camp gossip surmised otherwise. Shuey never was certain who was providing the funds for his paycheck. Eaton signed hotel registers for a group of friends he said were cattle buyers. The so-called cattle buyers turned out to be Los Angeles city officials.[59]

With important options secured, the stage was now set for Eaton to make a formal proposal to the Los Angeles Board of Water Commissioners. This was done on May 22, immediately after the Mulholland-Lippincott report was accepted. With Lippincott safely out of the room, Mulholland could proceed with his proposal for an aqueduct of some 250 miles at a cost of $23,000,-000. Eaton, who at first had hoped to benefit from ownership of the land and water rights, had been induced by Mulholland to sell at cost to the city those parts of his property needed for the aqueduct.

[59]O'Fallon to Ryan, October 5, 1905, file 23 Alpha. (pt. 3), pp. 25–26, 31–35, NPRC; Nadeau, *Water Seekers*, p. 16; deposition of George Shuey, September 16, 1905, file 23 Alpha. (pt. 3), NPRC.

The water commissioners then voted unanimously to purchase Eaton's options.[60]

Word reached Newell almost immediately. "It is reported that the Owens Valley Project may be abandoned as a reclamation project in favor of water supply for the city of Los Angeles," he wrote Lippincott on May 24. "The matter is apparently one of public discussion, and in view of this fact early action should be taken by the board of engineers to definitely consider what recommendations should be made to the Secretary." Newell called for a meeting of engineers to determine the fate of the Owens Valley project. After some delay, a meeting was scheduled for late July.[61]

The city, meanwhile, was prepared to be generous. Los Angeles offered $50,000 to the Reclamation Service to cover expenses for work done on property the city had acquired. Also, in appreciation of Newell's cooperation the previous November when Clausen's report had been given to Mulholland, the water board voted unanimously to write to Newell "acknowledging such assistance and reporting progress to date, as that department [sic] is holding in abeyance some. work it had designed to carry out in that valley, pending our action." The idea was Mulholland's. He dictated a letter of appreciation to Newell, "perhaps somewhat effusively," as he later conceded.

Fully recognizing the valuable assistance rendered the City of Los Angeles by the U.S. Geological Survey Department through your intercession, in its efforts to obtain an additional water supply from Owens River Valley, we deem it necessary in order to show our good faith in the matter to keep you informed of the progress being made by us to that end, so that it may be shown that we are not uselessly hampering the work already begun in that Valley by the Reclamation branch under your direction.[62]

Newell was probably less dismayed by the confusion over

[60]Nadeau, *Water Seekers*, p. 17: "Regular Meeting of the Board of Commissioners of the Water Department of the City of Los Angeles," May 22, 1905, copy in file 23 Alpha. (pt. 2), NPRC.

[61]Newell to Lippincott, May 24, 1905, and Newell to Davis, June 21, 1905, file 63-B, OV-GCRW, RBR.

[62]"Regular Meeting of the Board of Commissioners of the Water Department of the City of Los Angeles," May 29, June 5, and June 6, copies in file 23 Alpha. (pt. 2), NPRC; O'Fallon to Ryan, October 5. 1905, ibid., p. 8.

bureaucratic nomenclature than he was mystified by the contents of the letter, which he did not see until September 11 because of an extended trip west. Mulholland seemed to believe that he, Newell, had endorsed the city's scheme as far back as November. By the time Newell read it, the letter was already a controversial item, one that over the years would continue to resurface as evidence of perfidy cited by Owens Valley residents and anticity polemicists.[63]

By July the city's plans had become one of the worst-kept secrets in California. Los Angeles newspaper reporters, suspicions raised by the absence of the city officials who went to the valley posing as cattle buyers, were sworn to secrecy. Land promoters not connected with the municipal water enterprise caught wind of the plan. Owens Valley land began to increase in price.[64]

Meanwhile Stafford Austin and Richard Fysh, the employees in the General Land Office in Independence, had become increasingly suspicious as to Eaton's comings and goings. By July 12 they had heard enough of the growing rumors about a Los Angeles scheme to buy the Owens River that they wrote to the commissioner of the U.S. General Land Office, W. A. Richards, to express their concerns. In so doing they fired the first shot in the long war that would ensue between city and valley:

We consider it the duty of this office to call your attention to certain events which have taken place in this district relating to the success of the Owens River reclamation project. . . .

Within the last two months a prominent business man of Los Angeles, Mr. Fred Eaton, claiming in certain matters to be the representative of J. B. Lippincott . . . has purchased land and water rights in Owens River Valley to the extent of about $1,000,000. These purchases include all the patented lands within the government's withdrawal for reservoir purposes, and also riparian and other rights along

---

[63]Andrae B. Nordskog, *Communication to the California Legislature Relating to the Owens Valley Water Situation,* p. 17; Chalfant, *Story of Inyo,* p. 345; Davis to Secretary of the Interior, September 13, 1905, file 63-B, OV-GCRW, RBR. "This letter was received at this office after Mr. Newell's departure for the West and he did not see it until September 11," stated Davis. "The whole matter is something of a mystery to him, as he has had practically nothing to do with the matter, and so far as rendering assistance to the city of Los Angeles, cannot recall other than correspondence and transmission of printed [*sic*] documents or of results of river measurements made public from time to time."

[64]Nadeau, *Water Seekers,* pp. 18–19.

Owens River for over fifty miles. This purchaser now practically controls the waters of the river. The well-known personal friendship between the purchaser and Engineer J. B. Lippincott made it easy for these
valuable rights to be secured, as it was generally understood that they
were to be used for the benefit of the government project.

Austin and Fysh reported "a rapidly growing conviction" among
Owens Valley residents that Eaton "has secured this large supply
of water in order to take it to Southern California to be used for the
City of Los Angeles," having obtained government information
that, "if made public at all, ought surely to be given first to the
people of this district who are most nearly concerned in it." They
noted that prospective homesteaders in growing numbers were
asking about the city's intentions. Previous to such inquiries Austin
and Fysh had "no reason to doubt that Mr. Eaton was acting in
good faith for the engineer in charge, and that the water rights were
for the government."

At this point the ambiguity of Eaton's actions still puzzled
Owens Valley residents. "So profound is the conviction now that
Mr. Eaton is acting in his own interests that people are preparing
to put every obstacle in his way," the land office officials stated.
"If it can be shown, however, that he is acting for the government
they are ready to assist him in acquiring these water rights, as they
are very generously disposed toward the government project." Austin
and Fysh warned that abandonment of the reclamation project
could destroy the valley's future prospects and cause severe losses
to its people. "Such an abandonment at this time will make it appear
that the expensive surveys and measurements of the past two years
have all been made in the interests of a band of Los Angeles
speculators, and it will result in bringing our reclamation service into
disrepute."

Despite the obviously severe implications of their statements,
Austin and Fysh insisted they were not making "any charges whatever, but are simply advising you of the important events which
have taken place here in order that the proper authorities may be
placed on their guard in case these purchases are antagonistic to
the government project."[65]

[65]Austin and Fysh to W. A. Richards, July 12, 1905, file 63-B, OV-
GCRW, RBR. This letter, written two weeks before the *Times* "scoop" of

Austin and Fysh's letter moved around within the Department of the Interior until it landed on the desk of Arthur Powell Davis. Alarmed at the obvious conflict of interest, Davis circulated copies to Lippincott, Newell, and D. C. Henny and W. H. Sanders, two of the engineers who would compose the consulting board to hear on the project.[66]

As the scheduled date neared for the meeting of the board of engineers appointed to consider the Owens Valley reclamation project, skirmishes erupted. Wilfred Watterson, a leading Inyo County banker, spotted Los Angeles City Clerk Harry J. Lelande just after Lelande mailed an important ranch property deed. Watterson forced Lelande to disrobe as he searched in vain for the deed.[67]

Lippincott, informed in no uncertain terms of accusations against him stemming from Eaton's allegedly misrepresenting himself as a government agent, urged Eaton by telegram and letter to deny government affiliation. "I understand that it has been unadvisable heretofore for you to let the people of Owens Valley know really what you were doing," he acknowledged, "but I trust that the time has arrived when you can soon explain the situation to them and relieve me of the misconception I am placed in." Eaton promptly replied, also by both telegram and letter. He flatly stated that the impression he was connected with the Reclamation Service was erroneous. When he visited Austin, he "did not present myself to him as your agent but simply said I was requested by you to obtain the necessary information to enable me to judge as to their effect on the Gov. plans and report to you, which I did." In fact, he had just seen Austin and told him as much. Eaton assured Lippincott he had never represented himself as a government official and always denied having any connection with the Reclamation Service. As to

---

July 29, was not reproduced by Nordskog in his *Communication*, although he almost certainly had access to it.

    [66]Telegrams from Davis to Newell and Davis to Henny, July 28, 1905, reproducing text of Austin and Fysh letter of July 12, 1905; Davis to Sanders, July 28, 1905; and Davis to Lippincott, July 28, 1905, all in file 63-B, OV-GCRW, RBR; Lippincott to F. [*sic*] C. Smith, July 28, 1905, file 23 Alpha. (pt. 2), NPRC. Lippincott had seen a copy of the Austin and Fysh letter before Davis sent him one. See also Davis to Newell, July 29, 1905, file 63-B, OV-GCRW, RBR.

    [67]Nadeau, *Water Seekers*, p. 19.

his method of purchasing options, he observed, "I have been called an 'easy' here, but not a fool, which I would certainly have been in going around booming property I desired to buy." Finally, he promised to publish a public statement in the *Inyo Independent* "which will no doubt set the public to wondering what it is all about, as no one but the Land Office man ever dreamed I was acting otherwise than in a private capacity."[68]

A Crucial Meeting

The meeting of the consulting board for the reclamation project took place in San Francisco on July 27 and 28. Jacob Clausen began the session by reading selected portions of his 1904 report and answering questions from the board of engineers concerning various details about the project. Clausen was committed to the Owens Valley project on both a professional and a personal level. Having worked for over a year doing surveys for the project makes his professional position understandable; on the personal level, he had fallen in love with Elizabeth Watterson, a sister of the Watterson bankers of Inyo County.[69]

During the proceedings W. H. Sanders revealed that while traveling through Owens Valley to gain information on the proposed project he had met Austin. The land register had told him about Eaton's misrepresenting himself, whereupon Sanders had wired Davis wanting to know if Eaton did in fact have the right to say what Austin claimed he was saying. Davis had sent him word that Eaton did not represent the Reclamation Service, and Austin had sent Davis a copy of his and Fysh's July 12 letter. At Lippincott's request the Austin-Fysh letter was read into the record. The board

[68]Telegram from Lippincott to Eaton, July 26, 1905; Lippincott to Eaton, July 27, 1905; telegram from Eaton to Lippincott, July 29, 1905; Eaton to Lippincott, July 29, 1905, all in file 23 Alpha. (pt. 2), NPRC. Eaton's second telegram read: "Wired you this morning seen Austin since impression only his own." His denial appeared in the *Inyo Independent*, August 4, 1905.

[69]Nadeau, *Water Seekers*, pp. 19–20; Chalfant, *Story of Inyo*, p. 347; letters from Inyo County Clerk to the author, September 1 and 29, 1972, verifying the marriage of J. C. Clausen and Elizabeth Watterson on November 27, 1906; transcript of testimony. July 27, 1905, pp. 1–13, file 63-B, OV-GCRW, RBR.

gave the letter full consideration before reaching its conclusions about the future of the Owens Valley project.[70]

Lippincott praised Clausen's presentation in support of the project as being "exceedingly satisfactory." He commented, "It has been conducted energetically, intelligently and economically and the general results of the work are accepted as correct and conclusive as far as I am concerned." He believed a feasible project existed for the valley, one "worth careful consideration." However, there were complicating factors now involved in the proposal, and he proceeded to describe them.

Lippincott had prepared an eight-page statement assessing the value of the Owens Valley project. Most of it, however, was concerned with the needs of the City of Los Angeles and the feasibility of a gravity-flow aqueduct from the valley to the city. The initial reconnaissance surveys, done between the summer of 1903 and the fall of 1904, were done in good faith, "before the necessities of the City of Los Angeles were known." Lippincott noted that the city, once accepting the idea of an aqueduct from a remote water source, could hardly be expected to advertise openly for land and water rights in the valley. The November, 1904, meeting had resulted in the Reclamation Service's providing data on stream measurements to the city and an understanding that the service would wait and see what would develop with the city's plans before taking a definite position on the project. At this time Los Angeles controlled fifty miles of the lower part of the Owens River and most of the land around the Long Valley reservoir site, plus several canal systems. Because the Reclamation Service lacked adequate funds to construct the Owens Valley project at present, an estimated $2.3 million, because such funds as were available could be used to greater benefit on other Reclamation Service projects in the state, because "greater public benefit would undoubtedly accrue from the application of the water of Owens River for domestic uses in and around the City of Los Angeles," and because Los Angeles controlled the reservoir site and fifty miles of riparian land, making it impossible

---

[70]Davis to Newell, July 28, 1905, and Henny to Davis, July 31, 1905, file 63-B, OV-GCRW, RBR. Davis' letter to Newell included the text of the telegrams. For some reason Taylor did not get one. See also transcript of testimony, July 28, 1905, pp. 13–14, file 63-B, OV-GCRW, RBR.

anyway for the Reclamation Service to build a reclamation project even if it wanted to, Lippincott concluded that the best and most important use of the Owens River would be "a domestic and suburban use." He also recommended that Los Angeles refund all Reclamation Service expenditures to the service and that the secretary of the interior decline right-of-way applications over public lands in the route of the proposed aqueduct.[71]

Having heard the various arguments concerning the project, the three engineers prepared a report detailing their findings. They looked favorably upon a federal reclamation project in Owens Valley, but—and it was a big *but*—there were legal complications, not only from the City of Los Angeles but from filings made by the Owens River Water and Power Company. The feasibility of the project was not disputed, but the city's fait accompli rendered continuing federal efforts problematical. If the door to a federal project was not yet locked, it was definitely closing.[72]

The arrival of Davis' July 28 telegrams to Henny, Sanders, and Lippincott threw the meeting into some confusion. The report had already been compiled, the recommendations given. Henny notified Davis that Austin's letter had nonetheless been discussed after Sanders had presented it to the board. The consulting board now prepared a second, "special" report, with copies to Newell and Davis, in response to Davis' telegrams and Austin and Fysh's statements.[73]

The special report broke the Austin-Fysh letter down into eleven statements, with comments on each one. The first statement, describing the preliminary work of the Reclamation Service in the

[71]"Statement by J. B. Lippincott concerning the Owens Valley Project," July 26, 1905, file 23 Alpha. (pt. 3), NPRC; transcript of testimony, July 27, 1905, pp. 14, 17, file 63-B, OV-GCRW, RBR. Newell later criticized Henny and Sanders for permitting the stenographic report to be made, "as it furnishes material to a pettifogging opponent to weave an elaborate argument on some phrase or word taken from this context" (Newell to Sanders and Henny, November 8, 1905, file 63-B, OV-GCRW, RBR). Newell's fear became reality a quarter-century later when Andrae Nordskog quoted from Newell's letter (not the testimony) as an example of an attempt to hush up the proceedings (see Nordskog, *Communication*, p. 21).

[72]Sanders, Henny, and Taylor to Newell, July 28, 1905, file 63-B, OV-GCRW, RBR.

[73]Telegram from Henny to Davis, July 28, 1905, ibid.

valley, was accepted as correct. The second, asserting that Eaton had claimed to be Lippincott's representative, was taken as "probably true in a general way, although conclusive proof . . . is lacking." The third statement, that Eaton "now practically controls the waters of the River," the engineers considered uncertain because of legal complexities. The fourth point dealt with the mistaken understanding of Eaton's intentions, with the valley people's thinking he was working for the government as a result of his relationship with Lippincott. The board believed this allegation "a plausible one." The engineers agreed with the fifth statement, which noted the growing belief of the valley people that their water was going to Los Angeles. They considered as unauthenticated the sixth statement, which charged the government with bad faith in providing the city with secret information. The seventh statement expressed hope that the facts of the matter would not be withheld from the public, a point the board left to the Reclamation Service headquarters in Washington, D.C., to answer. The eighth statement naively held the hope that Eaton might yet be a government agent after all. The board emphatically denied this. It conceded as "probably true," however, the ninth statement, the fear that if the Reclamation Service abandoned the Owens Valley project "it will leave the Los Angeles parties in full control of the water and reservoir site and in a position to destroy future prospects of the valley and inflict severe loss upon all settlers and property owners." The tenth statement warned of the damage to the Reclamation Service's reputation resulting from these events, a point on which the board concurred. Finally, the last statement noted that no charges were being made, but the writers were "simply advising you of important events which have taken place." To this the board declared flatly, "We consider purchases made by Mr. Eaton antagonistic to the interests of the Owens Valley Project, and the Reclamation Service."[74]

Meanwhile, events took a sudden and dramatic turn. On the same day that the board delivered its first report, Mulholland re-

[74]Sanders, Henny, and Taylor to Davis (with cover letter from Henny), July 31, 1905, and identical letter to Newell, July 31, 1905, ibid. Omitted from the original Austin and Fysh letter was a postscript quoting an article by Lippincott in the July, 1905, issue of *Out West*, based on a paper he delivered to a water congress meeting on March 15.

turned to Los Angeles with the news that the final land-buying trip was completed. "The last spike is driven," he announced to the water commissioners, "the options are all secured." A *Los Angeles Times* reporter who had accompanied him on the trip telegraphed the news from Independence. Harrison Gray Otis, publisher of the *Times*, decided to scoop the rival *Examiner* and on Saturday morning, July 29, released the word: "Titanic Project to Give City a River."[75]

Lippincott, in San Francisco, received a copy of the *Times* by late Saturday afternoon. Among the many articles printed by the *Times* was one—"Good Grace of Government"—that gave to Lippincott a considerable amount of unwanted praise. "Without Mr. Lippincott's interest and cooperation, it is declared that the plan never would have gone through," the article claimed. Sitting at a writing desk in the St. Francis Hotel, Lippincott reflected on his role in the affair now that the city's plans had been made public. "I have never told anyone that the Govt. had withdrawn from Owens Valley," he informed Newell, "but I have stated that I thought they ought to under the circumstances as a matter of best public policy."[76]

But the time for such fine distinctions was now over. As the Board of Water Commissioners voted unanimously to hold a special bond election to vote $1.5 million towards the acquisition of Owens Valley "lands, water rights and other property necessary to provide the city with a source of water supply in the Owens River Valley," citizens in the city and the valley speculated on where it would all lead. Between the pessimism of land register Austin and the ebullient optimism of the *Los Angeles Times* there ran a spectrum of speculation, concern, and hope for the best. Reporting on the city's purchase of valley water rights, the *Times* proclaimed, "Everybody in the valley has money, and everyone is happy."[77] The *Times* could not have been more wrong.

[75]Nadeau, *Water Seekers*, p. 20; *Los Angeles Times*, July 29, 1905.

[76]Telegram from Lippincott to Davis, July 29, 1905, and Lippincott to Newell (enclosing *Los Angeles Times* clipping from July 29), July 29, 1905, file 63-B, OV-GCRW, RBR.

[77]"Regular Meeting of the Board of Commissioners of the Water Department of the City of Los Angeles," July 31, 1905, copy in file 23 Alpha. (pt. 2), NPRC; *Los Angeles Times*, July 29, 1905.

4

City Speculations, Valley Accusations, and Government Investigations

"The constant purpose of the government in connection with the Reclamation Service has been to use the water resources of the public lands for the ultimate greatest good of the greatest number. . . ."—Theodore Roosevelt, Annual Message to Congress, 1907

ONCE the Los Angeles Board of Water Commissioners committed itself to a water source some 240 miles away, the city set about testing the support of its citizens for the project. A bond election was set for September 7, and advocates of the project launched a five-week campaign to inform and educate the city's voters of the need for Owens River water. Angelenos followed the various arguments in the newspapers and had a fine time reading the vitriolic editorials, particularly those of the *Times* and the *Examiner*. Virtually no one opposed the idea of a plentiful water supply. The method of achieving the goal, however, and in some degree the supply's location (some diehards favored looking to Ventura County) seemed fitting topics for debate. The most avid supporters, including the *Times*, the *Express*, Mulholland and the Board of Water Commissioners, and the Los Angeles Municipal League, urged that action be taken as quickly as possible toward the construction of an aqueduct. Other positions, notably those taken by the *Examiner* and to a lesser extent by the literary weekly *Graphic*, urged a full investigation of details and cautioned against rash moves. The *Examiner* went a step further and called for an investigation of possible pecuniary motives that might be behind Harrison Gray Otis' desire for quick approval of the project. It all made for a lively campaign.

Throughout the debate William Mulholland commanded the respect of all factions. His enthusiasm for the water project was tempered by his knowledge of both technical and managerial details. People took his word as gospel, a fitting tribute to his expertise, since his arguments seemed blessed with logic and common sense. If his view of Owens Valley was a bit harsh—it was later said he believed the entire population of the valley could be hanged and still leave plenty of unused trees—his analysis of the aqueduct idea was precise to the penny. He cautioned that when the initial announcement of the project was made, "much matter crept into the accounts given by the daily press that was either positively inaccurate or so ambiguous in expression as to be very wide of an exact statement of the facts." Contrary to rumor, the Board of Water Commissioners had not hurried into approval of the project on insufficient information. The search for a new water source had gone on for several years. Eaton had brought the idea of Owens River water to him; the feasibility of a gravity-flow aqueduct from Inyo County had been carefully investigated. Alternative sources "sink into insignificance" when compared with the Owens River. The deal with Fred Eaton had been straightforward: the city obtained Long Valley and an easement for a reservoir, while Eaton retained certain lands not needed by the city and the Rickey ranch cattle. Eaton, it appeared, was going into the cattle business in a big way. The options obtained by Eaton acting as the city's agent were of course turned over by him to the city. Mulholland believed the arrangement was one "which all fair minded people must regard as an extremely advantageous one for the city."[1]

Mulholland also issued an open invitation to anyone who wished to examine the scope of his research. "If there are any people in Los Angeles who think we have gone into this proposition like a lot of schoolboys, with a whoop and a hurrah," he announced, "they should come in here and look over a few of the maps we have made during the last year."[2]

[1]William Mulholland, "The Straight of the Owens River Deal," *Graphic* 23 (August 5, 1905), 4–5.
[2]*Los Angeles Examiner*, August 3, 1905.

During the debate rumors flew about the quality of the water, its quantity, the possible quantity available from other sources, and Eaton's margin of profit in the deal. Dr. Adelbert Fenyes, a Pasadena physician, returned from a trip to Owens Valley and announced that Owens River water contained typhoid germs, with typhoid endemic in the valley all year round, especially in Bishop. Mulholland retorted that Bishop suffered from typhoid fever because the town lacked sewers; people there used cesspools. In any event, the town was now installing a sewer system, none of which had anything to do with the river. Mulholland pronounced the river water "the purest water that can be found, as it comes direct from the melting snows on the mountains. If there are typhoid germs in it somebody has thrown them in—that's the only way they could get there."[3]

Some dissidents claimed that Piru and Alamos creeks in Ventura County could provide 4,000 inches of water over a distance of fifty-seven miles for only $3.3 million. Other schemes included the Mojave River and the Kern River; all such ideas were dismissed by supporters of the use of Owens River. "That proposition of paying money to bring Piru Creek here is the most absurd one that I have heard since the quest of water started," declared Water Board President John Fay. "Why, there is not enough water in Piru Creek in the summer time to water a cow."[4]

As for Eaton's profit, the ex-mayor frankly stated that his arrangement with the city did mean a moderate profit for himself. At an informal reception held by him at the California Club, he admitted that his original intention had been to take the Owens River rights, form a company, and sell water and power to Los Angeles. However, City Attorney William Mathews and Mulholland had convinced him to make the project a municipal enterprise. Eaton failed to mention exactly when his conversion took place but said he seriously intended to go into the cattle business, utilizing the lands not needed by the city. His feelings about the aqueduct project merged altruism with boosterism. "This is not the greatest thing that could be done to build up Los Angeles," he said, "but in my

[3]Ibid.; *Los Angeles Herald*, August 4, 1905.

[4]*Los Angeles Times*, August 3, 1905; *Los Angeles Examiner*, August 2, 1905; *Los Angeles Herald*, August 2, 1905.

opinion it is the one thing that is absolutely necessary if the city is to continue to grow and prosper as it has during the past few years."[5]

On Monday, August 7, the Board of Water Commissioners formally presented its aqueduct plans to the city council and requested that an ordinance be adopted declaring it a necessity to increase the city's water supply. The council went into a committee of the whole on Wednesday to deliberate the matter while pressures mounted to reach a quick decision. Some council members still pleaded a lack of familiarity with details. Mulholland provided reams of statistics and additional information on the river's stream flow, the length of the proposed aqueduct, the elevation of the proposed aqueduct's intake at the river, and numerous other items. After hearing the presentations, the city council voted seven to one to adopt the necessary ordinances and call for a bond election. The first official step by the city was at last taken.[6]

Over the next month supporters of the aqueduct campaigned energetically for the bond passage. There were those who doubted the feasibility of the plan or the city's ability to pay for it. These people were dubbed "knockers" as opposed to the "boosters" who favored the aqueduct. A "campaign of intelligence" was outlined. Several city council members asked Mulholland and Eaton to join them for a trip to Owens Valley to see the river for themselves. The idea met with suspicion from city budget watchers; had they gone, Owens Valley would have given them a hostile welcome. More speculation surfaced about the feasibility of the aqueduct. It was said that summer cloudbursts could cause rock slides that would destroy the aqueduct unless it was placed entirely underground, an expensive proposition. Stories of typhoid fever continued to circulate. Aqueduct supporters denied the stories and explained again and again how the aqueduct could be built safely. The *Times* remained in the forefront of the propagandizers for the aqueduct

[5]*Los Angeles Times, Los Angeles Herald,* and *Los Angeles Examiner,* all August 5, 1905. The *Los Angeles Examiner,* August 29, 1905, printed Eaton's contract; the *Los Angeles Times,* August 30, 1905, belittled the *Examiner's* negative interpretation.
[6]*Los Angeles Examiner,* August 10, 1905.

project, dismissing complaints about its breach of faith with other Los Angeles papers over the agreement to keep the news a secret. "The *Times* published the news first and best, and with ample authority . . . and, moreover, published it without any breach of faith whatever; and there you are!"[7]

After some additional delay the city council formally set the bond election date for September 7. Mulholland helped end the council's indecisiveness—the pleas for more information before reaching a decision on the project—by putting his reputation on the line. "I have been in my present position as superintendent of the water works almost thirty years and am not in the habit of deceiving the people," he told the council on August 14. "I have never done it yet. For five months I have examined the Owens River and valley and it looks better to me each time I go back." He noted that the city could save $45,000 if the bonds were issued immediately, and that $50,000 was due on the options by October 1, so "immediate action is necessary." The council then adopted the resolution for the bond election on a seven-to-one vote.[8]

The next three weeks witnessed a major propaganda barrage by the city's newspapers, with the *Examiner* still reserving judgment on the motives of some of the aqueduct's proponents. In addition, public forums were addressed by city leaders who urged everyone to vote for the bonds. "From my own observation and from what I have learned in the Owens River Valley and from what I have learned with the gentlemen who were with me in showing me this country, I believe this project is absolutely feasible," Water Commissioner John M. Elliott told a Municipal League meeting; "I think that it will come within the limit of the appropriation asked for

[7]*Los Angeles Times*, August 12, 1905; *Los Angeles Examiner*, August 11, 1905. Anthony Cifarelli, "The Owens River Aqueduct and the Los Angeles *Times*: A Study in Early Twentieth Century Business Ethics and Journalism" (Master's thesis, University of California, Los Angeles, 1969), is a thorough study of the conduct of the *Times* and its publisher, Harrison Gray Otis, during the bond elections of 1905 and 1907.

[8]*Los Angeles Herald*, August 14 and 31, 1905; *Los Angeles Examiner*, August 22, 1905. Eaton had inserted a discount provision into the options, provided the option was taken up by January 1, 1906. The collected savings to the city would amount to $45,000 (*Los Angeles Herald*, August 28, 1905).

rather than outside of it." Mayor Owen McAleer, after visiting the valley and drinking Owens River water, enthusiastically signed the ordinance scheduling the election.[9]

On August 22 a change in the course of the aqueduct's history was narrowly averted when a block fell off a derrick at the city's new filtration gallery, narrowly missing Mulholland who was inspecting the facility. The workman standing next to him was fatally injured. "I guess that it was the other man that was called," Mulholland observed. "My time had not come."[10]

As election day neared, aqueduct supporters stressed in increasingly strident tones the urgency of passing the bonds. Mulholland, known for his epigrams, was quoted as saying, "If Los Angeles doesn't get this water, she won't need it,"[11] a phrase often quoted and since made legendary. He also used variations of the sentiment during the campaign. A member of the Carpenters' Union informed Mulholland of his union's opposition to the plan, stating that his men wanted more information and perhaps investigation of less costly possibilities. "My answer to him," said Mulholland, "was that if they didn't vote for it, or if the Owens River plan was not adopted, there would be no Carpenters' Union here in a very short time because there would be no work." The *Examiner* took exception to this position. "To refuse the information and to hold a threat over the heads of the people is hardly a satisfactory answer," declared an editorial. "Mr. Mulholland talks like a Czar, not like a salaried employee of the city." However, Mulholland did arrange to speak to the union's members on the issue. Despite such reservations, few prominent citizens could be found who actively opposed the project. The *Herald* canvassed the business community and found only one man who disapproved of the plan, and it developed that he himself had offered a plan that was rejected.[12]

At the end of August Los Angeles thermometers topped 100 degrees, and warnings of an imminent water famine were once again

[9]John M. Elliott, "Why Bonds Must Be Voted Speedily," *Graphic* 23 (August 19, 1905), 6; *Los Angeles Herald*, August 22, 1905.

[10]*Los Angeles Times*, August 23, 1905.

[11]Quoted in Charles F. Lummis, "In the Lion's Den," *Out West* 23 (September, 1905), 280.

[12]*Los Angeles Examiner*, August 28 and 30, 1905; *Los Angeles Herald*, August 29, 1905.

proclaimed. City reservoir levels dropped alarmingly as 15 million gallons of water were used in a five-day period. "Whenever a hot spell like this comes, the [Los Angeles] river is in itself entirely insufficient for the needs of the city," warned Mulholland. "This illustrates better than anything else could the absolute necessity for securing a source of water supply elsewhere. We must have it."[13]

In the final days before the election, publicity about the aqueduct reached peak levels. A committee with representatives from the Chamber of Commerce, the Municipal League, and the Merchants and Manufacturers Association returned from Owens Valley with renewed support for Mulholland and the project. Construction of the aqueduct promised to bring five thousand jobs to California; everyone from carpenters to muleskinners would find a place on the payroll. The *Examiner* made a final plea on September 2 for more time and less haste in approving the project. Then, on the next day, the newspaper reversed its editorial policy, coming around to support the project with only minimal reservations. "And the one thing the 'Examiner' has stood for and urged for many months remains—THE CITY MUST HAVE WATER."[14]

John Fay, president of the Water Board, assured the *Examiner* and all concerned persons of his own commitment to a successful project. "It is the intention of the Board that independent experts of the highest professional standing shall be employed, at once, to

[13]*Los Angeles Herald*, August 31, 1905; Remi Nadeau, *The Water Seekers*, p. 25. William L. Kahrl, "The Politics of California Water: Owens Valley and the Los Angeles Aqueduct, 1900–1927, Part I," *California Historical Quarterly* 55 (Spring, 1976), 8, 10, cites statistics that tend to disprove the existence of a drought period that stretched back to the 1890's, as do David Blake Chatfield and Bruce M. Bertram, "Water Rights of the City of Los Angeles: Power-Politics and the Courts," *San Fernando Valley Law Review* 6 (Spring, 1978), 181, n. 114. However, these statistics cite average annual rainfall and do not, except for a brief statement by Kahrl, measure the rainfall of particular storms and when they occurred during the year. Kahrl asserts that the drought "seems to have originated with Mulholland in the election of 1905," but no contemporary of Mulholland disputed the contention, although other antiaqueduct arguments were presented.

[14]*Los Angeles Examiner*, September 1–3, 1905; *Los Angeles Times*, September 2, 1905; *Los Angeles Herald*, September 3, 1905; "Another Use for Owens River," *Graphic* 23 (September 9, 1905), 9. Kahrl, "Politics of California Water," p. 12, suggests the change in *Examiner* editorial policy may have been due to William Randolph Hearst's political ambitions.

make a critical examination into and report upon the whole project of bringing a supply of water from the Owens River Valley to this city," he said. "And until a report of this character is received, favorable to such project, it will be the policy of the Water Board that no greater part of the money derived from the sale of the bonds shall be expended than shall be necessary to preserve and protect the interests of the city."[15]

The outcome of the election surprised no one. Voters were asked to indicate *Yes* or *No* to the question: "Shall the City of Los Angeles incur a bonded debt of $1,500,000 for the purpose of acquiring lands, water-rights, rights-of-way and other property, and constructing ditches, canals, tunnels, and other water works, necessary to provide said City with a water supply in the Owens River Valley, in the County of Inyo, California?" The question was approved with a vote of 10,693 in favor to 754 votes opposed, a fourteen-to-one majority. The *Examiner* called it a "light" vote compared with other recent municipal elections, placing the blame for the small turnout—less than half the total cast at the last special election—on "silent" voters who were protesting the short time allowed for consideration of the project.[16] The *Times*, on the other hand, proclaimed the results a major victory for the project, going so far as to publish a verse, whose author mercifully remains anonymous:

> Mulholland was a gentleman
>   Of credit and renown,
> A water expert eke was he
>   Of famous Angel Town.
> He measured Owens River and
>   He told us what 'twould cost;
> We've brought the snowy water—but
>   For the knockers what a frost!
> Fred Eaton was an engineer
>   Who knew a stream or two
> And Lippincott could figure out
>   The proper thing to do;
> "No, no," said Papa Lowenthal,
>   "They're criminals and guys!"
> The votes have now been counted and
>   The city has gone wise.

[15]*Los Angeles Examiner*, September 3, 1905.
[16]Ibid., September 7–8, 1905.

So let us say, oh, long live Fay,
And Sherman, long live he!
To all our faithful Water Board
Great praise and glory be![17]

The *Graphic* compared the aqueduct project to the San Pedro Harbor improvement and proposals to reclaim the Colorado Desert, citing all three as major factors contributing to the potential greatness of the city. The magazine predicted that "many of us will live to see Los Angeles the great commercial and industrial center of the New Southwest, with a population of a million citizens."[18] Before such accomplishments could be attained, however, the city still had to overcome numerous challenges and obstacles. An independent board of engineers, satisfactory to all factions, had to be chosen to judge the feasibility of Mulholland's plans. Owens Valley residents, angry at what they considered the theft of their water, appealed to the federal government to implement the reclamation project, while at the same time the city lobbied for permission to take the aqueduct across public lands. The initial steps also marked the beginning of a bitter war over water.

Austin's Accusations

In the days following the Board of Engineers conference at San Francisco, criticism mounted in intensity against the taking of Owens Valley water. Chief among the leaders in the valley's opposition to the "titanic project" was Stafford Wallace Austin, the Independence land register who had complained of Eaton's alleged misrepresentation. Austin now sought to move beyond the bureaucracy of the Department of the Interior and to reach the widest possible audience. His letter of July 12 had been directed to the commissioner of the General Land Office. With the *Times* publicity echoing throughout California, he now addressed his complaints to none less than President Theodore Roosevelt, writing to him on August 4. "I am register of the United States General Land Office at this place," he stated. "In behalf of the people of this district

[17]*Los Angeles Times*, September 8, 1905. Henry Lowenthal was editor of the *Examiner*.

[18]"Three Great Projects," *Graphic* 23 (September 16, 1905), 4.

and of the Government which I have served for nearly eight years I wish to protest against the proposed abandonment of the Owens River Project by the Reclamation Service."

Austin noted that there would be no cause for complaint if the project had been found unworkable, but such was not the case. All reports about the project were favorable, yet it was being sacrificed to the interests of Los Angeles. Austin enclosed clippings from Los Angeles newspapers, including the *Times* article crediting Lippincott with turning the project over to the city. He condemned Lippincott in the harshest terms:

Mr. Lippincott while drawing a large salary from the Government was employed by the City of Los Angeles to assist in securing this water for the city. He agreed to turn down this project at the critical moment when the Los Angeles men had secured other rights here which they wanted. With his connivance Mr. Fred Eaton came into the valley and purchased all the patented land within the Government's reservoir site and riparian rights along the Owens River. Mr. Eaton was known to be the intimate friend of Mr. Lippincott, they had looked over the project together, and Mr. Eaton had maps in his possession belonging to the Reclamation Service and was acting as Mr. Lippincott's representative in reporting on power applications referred to the Service. As these matters came before this office, I am stating what I know to be true.

Austin went on to accuse Lippincott and Eaton of deliberately deceiving the people of the valley, who in their innocence "could not believe that a plan to rob the valley of its water and turn down the Government's irrigation project was being carried out with the consent of the Supervising Engineer." He argued that the proposed reclamation project would benefit the valley and the neighboring part of Nevada and that, while Los Angeles could obtain its extra water from some other sources, "our district will remain arid and unsettled for all time if this water is taken away." Despite the city's claims, Austin pointed out that the government still retained control of key land locations. Finally, he appealed, "in justice, therefore, to the people here, in the interest of fairness and of the honor of the Reclamation Service," that Roosevelt not abandon the federal project, "but if feasible, carry it out in accordance with the spirit of the Act of June 17, 1902."[19]

[19]Austin to Roosevelt, August 4, 1905, file 63-B, OV-GCRW, RBR. A copy is in the Pardee Papers, BL.

Austin's letter reverberated through the offices of the Department of the Interior, its accusations of corruption and dishonesty threatening a departmental scandal that was all the more shocking since it was directed from an employee in one bureau against someone in another bureau. Roosevelt referred the Austin letter to the secretary of the interior; in Hitchcock's absence Acting Secretary Thomas Ryan took action, appointing Special Inspector S. F. O'Fallon to conduct an investigation into Austin's accusations. Ryan provided O'Fallon with the relevant correspondence, including Austin's letter and the board of engineers' reports of July 28 and 31. "The Department wishes to impress upon your mind that it wants the exact facts in this matter, so that it may be enabled to do exact justice to all parties concerned," stated Ryan. If the charges against Lippincott were sustained, he should be dismissed from government service, with the same penalty for Austin if the charges were false. O'Fallon was ordered to inspect the records at the land office and to interview Owens Valley residents who had sold options to Eaton, Reclamation Service employees, and the principal people involved, including Eaton, Mulholland, Lippincott, and Austin. Austin should provide evidence of his accusations. If possible, O'Fallon should try to determine if the rights the city had acquired rendered the federal project impracticable even if it was feasible. "When you have completed your examination, which you are urged to expedite with all the speed possible or consistent with thorough investigation of the matters in question, you will submit your report thereon to the Department, with your conclusions and such recommendations as you may deem advisable in the premises," ordered Ryan. O'Fallon received permission to employ stenographic aid in obtaining depositions. "The Department relies upon your judgment, sagacity and discretion to get to the bottom of this matter."[20]

The Austin Family

The instigator of the investigation, Stafford Wallace Austin, appears in most accounts of the Owens Valley–Los Angeles controversy as a one-dimensional figure, a loyal public official who

[20]Ryan to O'Fallon, August 31, 1905, file 23 Alpha. (pt. 2), NPRC. A copy is in Newell Papers, LC.

challenged what he believed to be corrupt actions. It comes somewhat as a surprise, therefore, to find quite a different context for
his appearance and other facets to his personality. Stafford Austin
was the husband of Mary Austin, the poet and novelist, who by
1905 had gained some literary attention through her contributions
to *Out West, Overland Monthly,* and other magazines, as well as
from the publication of her book *Land of Little Rain,* now considered a classic. Stafford's brother, Frank Austin, was the man
who had invited Fred Eaton to inspect the Owens Valley's possibilities for an irrigation-colonization project back in 1892. The
project had failed for lack of capital, a typical fate for private irrigation schemes in late nineteenth-century California. In one of history's incredible coincidences, Stafford met Eaton in 1905, possibly
for the first time and possibly without making any connection to his
brother's earlier acquaintance with Eaton. Since little documentation
is available, one can only speculate on the deeper levels of an Eaton-
Austin relationship, of the possible resentment Austin may have
had toward a man whose success contrasted with his own lack of
accomplishment.

   Mary Austin's biographers hold essentially negative views of
her husband. Helen McKnight Doyle, who knew Mary personally
in Bishop, depicted Wallace (as he was known to friends) as "a
very absent-minded but extremely intellectual man," someone who
crossed a ditch by wading through the water instead of taking a
nearby bridge.[21] After the failure of Frank's irrigation company,
Stafford tried a series of speculative ventures, none of which succeeded. In 1897 he became county superintendent of schools at
Lone Pine, resigning shortly afterward to take the position of register at the U.S. Land Office in Independence. The job was a poorly
paid one, a fact resented by his wife, who came to see him as one
of a number of Inyo County speculators awaiting the brass ring.
"He had a dream of himself pleasantly and remuneratively employed," recalled Mary, "but between that dream and the present
inadequately paid and not very rewarding situation there was a
hiatus always about to be bridged by his 'getting into something.'

   [21]Helen McKnight Doyle, *Mary Austin: Woman of Genius,* pp. 127,
192–195; T. M. Pearce, *Mary Hunter Austin,* pp. 31–33.

This was an attitude prevailing among men of Inyo; one on which they constantly reassured one another. *Something* was due to happen soon."[22]

When the unexpected happened, and the city captured the valley's water, Mary loyally supported her husband's crusade. She contributed an article to the *San Francisco Chronicle* describing Lippincott's perfidy and Los Angeles' devious maneuverings. Austin's moment of heroism in Owens Valley peaked, then faded. Although the *Inyo Register* praised him as "one of the greatest actors and movers in the defense of the valley, and to whom there is probably a greater debt of appreciation owing on this man than to any other man in the county," Austin failed to be elected to the state assembly in November, 1906, around the same time his marriage finally succumbed to the many tensions placed upon it. Mary Austin retreated from Inyo County to Carmel and her literary career, and Stafford Wallace Austin passed into obscurity.[23]

Friendship under Strain

Joseph Barlow Lippincott found himself in the center of a growing clamor over his decisions about where Owens River water should go. On one side were the Owens Valley residents, led by Austin, accusing him of conflict of interest, duplicity, and fraud. Willie Chalfant, editor of the *Inyo Register*, found a nickname for him: Judas B. Lippincott.[24] On the other side, the Reclamation Service was on the receiving end of demands for investigation and accountability to which, ultimately, Lippincott would have to respond. Somewhere on the sidelines the *Los Angeles Times*, having done its initial damage, continued to damn him with unwanted praise.

Perhaps the most crushing experience for Lippincott was the

[22]Mary Austin, *Earth Horizon: Autobiography*, p. 284, emphasis in original. T. M. Pearce interviewed W. A. Chalfant in 1939. Chalfant observed: "Stafford W. Austin is a fine man. Mrs. Austin doesn't treat him as well as she might in that book she wrote about her life in Bishop" (T. M. Pearce, *The Beloved House*, p. 94).

[23]*Inyo Register*, November 1 and 8, 1906; *San Francisco Chronicle*, September 3, 1905; Doyle, *Mary Austin*, pp. 218–219.

[24]*Inyo Register*, August 10, 1905; *Los Angeles Times*, August 13, 1905.

response of Arthur Powell Davis. During Newell's absence on a trip west (he would not return to Washington, D.C., until September 4), Davis assumed the position of acting chief engineer. He was immediately inundated with correspondence inquiring about Owens Valley project developments, accusing Lippincott of assorted crimes, and memos referred down from the president himself. From Senator George Perkins of California and from Congressman Sylvester C. Smith, whose Eighth Congressional District included Inyo County, down to the semiliterate scrawl of P. R. Lehmann, a Geological Survey rodman at Independence, everyone wanted to know the status of the Owens Valley project and whether Lippincott was going to be investigated, charged, arrested, dismissed, or whatever. A disillusioned Jacob Clausen, considered innocent by Inyo County protestors, joined them in urging retention of the project.[25]

George Watterson of the powerful Inyo County banking and merchandising family wired the secretary of the interior: "Circumstances point to irregularities in Owens Valley reclamation project. Please withhold final action pending asked for investigation." The telegram went from the secretary of the interior to the director of the Geological Survey to the Reclamation Service, ending up on Davis' desk.[26] Many other people sent newspaper clippings, particularly the *Times*'s "Good Grace of Government" article.

Of particular concern was a letter from David Henny, who had not been satisfied with the odd turn of developments in the hearing—the arrival of the Austin-Fysh letter and the news of Los Angeles' involvement in Owens Valley. "In considering the Owens Valley Project," Henny reported to Davis several days after the San Francisco meeting, "it will be apparent to you that we have confined ourselves to the subject matter in hand, and that we did not consider that Mr. Lippincott's connection with the project and with the City

[25]P. R. Lehmann to Department of the Interior, August 2, 1905; Senator George Perkins to C. D. Walcott, August 9, 1905; Acting Director, Geological Survey, to Secretary of the Interior, August 14, 1905; Acting Director, Geological Survey, to P. R. Lehmann, August 17, 1905, all in file 63-B, OV-GCRW, RBR.

[26]Telegram from Watterson to Secretary of the Interior, August 6, 1905; referral to Director of Geological Survey, August 7, 1905; telegram from Davis to Watterson, August 7, 1905; Davis to Watterson, August 7, 1905, all in ibid.

of Los Angeles was under investigation." Nevertheless, the two topics were closely allied, and to Henny's mind "Mr. Lippincott has allowed the U.S. Geological Survey and the U.S. Reclamation Service to be made use of for the private purposes of the City of Los Angeles." Henny also mentioned an unrelated matter about Lippincott's role in a proposed San Joaquin project which seemed to involve another conflict of interest. He concluded his personal letter with a handwritten postscript: "I have little doubt regarding an attractive offer likely to be made to Lippincott by the City of L.A. possibly as a reward for past services. . . . All these connections and alliances I think are vicious and must bring disrepute upon the Service."[27]

The information and inquiries, coming from so many sources and building on what Davis already knew of Lippincott's connection with Los Angeles, resulted in Davis' making up his mind to censure his old friend. He did so on August 7, stunning Lippincott with his blunt frankness. Lippincott had written Davis on August 8, explaining again his relationship with Eaton. Eaton had obtained his options "without my knowledge or the knowledge of any one else, so far as I know, in the Reclamation Service. After he had proceeded at some length with his work I became aware of his plans. Mr. Eaton is a personal friend of mine, whom I have known for many years and whom I respect as a man of high integrity and of marked engineering ability."[28]

Now Lippincott received the letter from Davis, which crossed his own in the mail—a letter that severely condemned his actions. He held off replying until September 5, by which time circumstances made it necessary for him to prepare a series of lengthy letters justifying what he had done. His letter to Davis, marked "Personal," was one of the briefer ones, only seven double-spaced typewritten pages. "I think that I never have received so severe a letter in my life as this one," he said. "It hurts me very deeply because I am perfectly aware of the fact that you write it as a frank and honest expression of opinion." Lippincott believed that Davis, in his effort to be impartial, had become overly severe. Since receiving Davis' letter he had gone to Portland where he had seen Newell at the

---

[27]Henny to Davis, August 2, 1905, ibid.
[28]Lippincott to Davis, August 8, 1905, file 23 Alpha. (pt. 2), NPRC.

National Irrigation Congress meeting. He had discussed his actions with Newell, Governor Pardee, Gifford Pinchot, and both California senators and had found them in agreement with his belief that the Owens Valley project was not financially justifiable. He reviewed the arrangement by which he had retained a private practice while in government service. His partnership with O. K. Parker was terminated as of September 1. Allegations of his writing a report on Owens Valley for the City of Los Angeles were untrue. Important Los Angeles citizens—bankers, judges, and businessmen—had asked him for his expertise, which he had given in the form of informal meetings at his home. "They have turned to me and asked me to aid in a solution of their water problem, and I consider that I have a public duty to perform for the city which I live in, in helping them to solve this problem." Lippincott conceded, "I perhaps was somewhat insubordinate in persisting in this work, but I did it believing that it was a duty that I ought to perform, and an important public service." He regretted embarrassment to the service for his actions, "but my conscience is perfectly clear." On his being paid generous fees for his consultation work, which actually took little time compared to the money, Lippincott argued that his firm name had developed a "commercial value."

Lippincott concluded by noting that he wished to remain with the Reclamation Service. "Your letter, however, makes it exceedingly hard for me to remain and to retain my self respect. If you still feel that I am a source of embarrassment, and am disloyal to the Service, you ought not to have me on it, and I do not want to remain." Finally, a conciliatory note: "I wish again to say that while your letter is exceedingly severe, and I believe unjustly so, that I know you have written it with no unfriendly feeling towards me. Whatever the results may be I certainly wish to express the hope that our long friendship now approaching some fifteen years will be more than able to withstand the shock of this correspondence."[29]

Davis continued the dialogue, replying on September 13. In the meantime he had written to Newell criticizing Lippincott for keeping untidy financial accounts and for the failure to give up pri-

[29]Lippincott to Davis, September 5, 1905, Newell Papers, LC. Davis' letter of August 7 could not be located, but its content emerges rather clearly from Lippincott's reply to it.

vate work. "So many things have come to my attention during the past summer," he had informed Newell, "that I am convinced that Mr. Lippincott is so blind to the public interest and so biased by private and selfish considerations that it will be impossible to secure loyal service from him; and I believe the only safe way for the Reclamation Service is to encourage him to devote his time to private practise [*sic*] and give up his connection with the Reclamation Service, except possibly in a consulting capacity on a per diam [*sic*] basis."[30] Now Davis replied to Lippincott's anguished letter, but in a more conciliatory tone. "I do not think that I accused you of being wilfully disloyal and certainly did not intend this," he said. On Lippincott's statement that he would not want to remain with the service if he were thought to be disloyal and a source of embarrassment, Davis stated, "I do not feel this way at all but have merely pointed out that your course is inconsistent with the interests of the service and have tried to disuade [*sic*] you from it." He still thought that outside work had no place for government employees. "If you give up your outside connection you will have no more loyal friend in the service than I," but if Lippincott wanted to continue the outside work, then Davis thought he should resign, "and I can not see for the life of me how anyone can come to a different conclusion." The difficulties of the exchange were made clear in Davis' final paragraph:

I have always regarded you as one of my eldest and best friends and no one has ever been held in higher esteem, and if we can get over the present difficulty safely to the service I am in favor of doing so in the manner most favorable to your interests consistent with those of the service and certainly hope with you, "that our old friendship now approaching some 15 years will be more than able to stand the shock of this correspondence."[31]

The exchange of letters between Davis and Lippincott illustrated the tensions faced by the Reclamation Service as angry Owens Valley residents communicated their outrage both directly and through their government representatives, or at least those representatives who were partial to the valley's interests. A citizens' committee formed at a mass meeting petitioned the secretary

[30]Davis to Newell, August 24, 1905, file 63-B, OV-GCRW, RBR.
[31]Davis to Lippincott, September 13, 1905, Newell Papers, LC.

of the interior for a thorough investigation into the conduct of the
Reclamation Service men responsible for the Owens Valley project.[32]
On August 23, Register Austin sent another letter to President
Roosevelt, this one a six-page review of how the Reclamation Ser-
vice had come to the valley, had withdrawn lands from entry, and
had led the citizens of the valley to believe that a federal reclamation
project was planned for the area. Eaton was a "secret agent" for
Los Angeles, who acted with the connivance of Lippincott. Owens
Valley did not object to the city's plans for an aqueduct; what the
valley wanted was for the reclamation project to proceed as planned.
If the project was to be abandoned, then the rights taken over by
the government should be returned to the valley so that a private
enterprise effort could be made to reclaim the arid lands. The letter
was presented in the form of a petition, signed by Inyo County's
district attorney, assessor, tax collector, clerk, and other officials.[33]

Thomas Ryan, acting secretary in the absence of Hitchcock,
responded to the Owens Valley communications at the end of
August. Besides appointing O'Fallon to investigate the charges, as
noted above, Ryan requested Austin to provide concrete evidence of
his accusations. He also informed Director Walcott of the Geological
Survey that as of that time, as far as he knew, the Reclamation
Service had yet to commit itself to construction of an Owens Valley
project. All things being equal—water storage, bedrock investigations, and water rights all having been evaluated—would the secretary of the interior still be justified in authorizing the project, in
spite of the presence of Los Angeles? Who had first informed
Newell of the city's interest, and when, and how much information
had Newell received? What knowledge did Lippincott have of the
city's intentions? Ryan requested "an early reply" from the Reclamation Service personnel involved.[34]

Lippincott, by now quite alarmed at the amount of misinforma-
tion being circulated concerning the actions of the Reclamation

[32]George A. Clark et al. to Secretary of the Interior, August 9, 1905,
file 63-B, OV-GCRW, RBR.

[33]S. W. Austin et al. to Roosevelt, August 23, 1905, file 23 Alpha.
(pt. 2), NPRC. A copy is in Pardee Papers, BL.

[34]Ryan to Austin, and Ryan to Director of Geological Survey (three
separate letters), all August 30, 1905, and telegram from Davis to Newell,
August 31, 1905, all in file 63-B, OV-GCRW, RBR.

Service and himself in what had become the "Owens Valley affair," attempted to correct the record as best he could. "In Los Angeles my effort has been to stop the papers here throwing boquets [*sic*] at me and at the Reclamation Service," he declared. The editor of the *Graphic* stoutly defended Lippincott as a man whose motives had been grossly misunderstood by both friends and anatagonists. It seemed, however, that no one was interested in fine distinctions when the general situation itself had become so murky. The main impression prevalent was that the Reclamation Service had withdrawn from the Owens Valley project in favor of Los Angeles. Although the city certainly had acquired a dominating presence in the valley, and although Lippincott had recommended discontinuance of the proposed project, federal involvement had yet to be ended. In fact, the Geological Survey believed that the river provided enough water both for the city's domestic needs and the valley's irrigation requirements.[35]

In response to the numerous departmental inquiries that were now being circulated among Reclamation Service personnel, Lippincott submitted a report to Newell on September 5, the same day as his response to Davis' accusations. His report attempted to answer questions raised by Acting Secretary Ryan, who in turn had been queried by Congressman Smith and others. To the question of who had first alerted Newell to the city's interest in Owens Valley, Lippincott noted it was he, in his letter of September 17, 1904, and in the meeting on November 22, who had done so. In recalling the meeting, Lippincott's memory proved faulty in at least one important detail: he believed that Eaton in November, 1904, was already "negotiating for certain properties for the City of Los Angeles in the Owens Valley." But Lippincott was incorrect in surmising that Eaton was buying options for Los Angeles, for as Lippincott himself noted, "At that time it was not determined that the City would undertake bringing water to Los Angeles from Owens Valley, and the whole matter was decidedly in the preliminary stages, both on the

[35]"Justice to Lippincott," *Graphic* 23 (September 23, 1905), 10–13; Acting Director, Geological Survey, to Secretary of the Interior, September 1, 1905, and Lippincott to Newell, September 28, 1905, both in file 63-B, OV-GCRW, RBR. Lippincott to Newell, September 28, 1905, Newell Papers, LC, is a slightly different version of the letter in the 63-B file.

part of the City and the Reclamation Service, neither one having decided to construct but both making investigations for the construction of public works." If Eaton therefore was buying up options in the fall of 1904, they were for his own speculation, not the city's. In any event, no option purchases by Eaton were formally recorded until March, 1905.[36]

Lippincott admitted that it was on his recommendation that Los Angeles had received Clausen's report. "I think that the whole responsibility and onus, if any, of giving this data should rest on me," he stated, "as I was the Supervising Engineer in charge of the work in California, and had recommended this course to the Chief Engineer, who was not as familiar with the situation as I was myself." In reference to the June 5 letter from the Los Angeles Board of Water Commissioners, thanking Newell for his help (a letter that Newell, arriving in Washington, D.C., on September 4, would not read until a week later), Lippincott expressed his irritation at the city's misdirected gratitude. "I must say . . . that in this communication, and in a great many other statements that have been made of late, the City has assumed that the Reclamation Service has been doing much more for them than they really have."

On the question of Lippincott's favoring the desires of the city, he insisted that his view supporting domestic use rather than irrigation was consistent with the policy that domestic needs took precedence as "the highest public use"; this, coupled with the factors of cost and relative feasibility to other projects, placed Owens Valley on a lesser priority than such projects as those being undertaken at Yuma and Klamath. Lippincott further asserted that he and Eaton were not involved in any conspiracy and that the Owens Valley residents had "jumped at conclusions." "I do not hesitate at all, however, to say that in my opinion the greatest public service will be rendered by using the water of Owens River in Southern California for domestic purposes in and around the City of Los Angeles." Finally, Lippincott stated that he would welcome a departmental investigation of his conduct should it be decided that one should

    [36]See O'Fallon to Ryan, October 5, 1905, file 23 Alpha. (pt. 3), pp. 17, 30, NPRC.

be made.[37] He shortly thereafter learned that the Department of the Interior was indeed conducting an investigation.

During this period Lippincott had not made any public statement about his position in the dispute, but the appearance of Mary Austin's article in the *San Francisco Chronicle*, along with the news that Stafford Austin had written to a number of prominent people, upset him considerably. On September 8 he notified Newell of his concern over Stafford Austin's accusations, which he termed "false and slanderous." Since both he and Austin worked for the Department of the Interior, the accusations "emanating from an officer of one branch of the Interior Department against other branches of that Department are improper; and I wish also to request that I either have the protection of the Department against these attacks or that Mr. Austin prove the statements which he has made."[38] Inaccuracies also entered the record due to Mrs. Austin's article, such as her statement that Lippincott had been censured at the July 28 meeting.

Lippincott proceeded to deny Austin's charges and defended his actions, first to his colleagues and superiors in the government and to his friends, and then publicly. "I firmly and conscientiously believe that I have acted for the greatest benefit of the greatest number, and for the best upbuilding of this section of the country," he said. During September his letters grew lengthy and repetitive. Several letters went to Newell, restating his belief that Austin's charges were absurd. On September 11 he wrote to Governor Pardee expressing his concern that the accusations, if accepted, could result in his dismissal from the service. Pardee wrote a letter on his behalf to Newell. Lippincott wrote an eleven-page letter to his friend Fernand Lungren in response to Lungren's request for clarification over the Owens Valley matter. On October 2 he sent Governor

[37]Lippincott to Newell, September 5, 1905, file 23 Alpha. (pt. 2), NPRC. The next day Lippincott sent another letter to Newell, explaining his actions in doing the report for the Los Angeles Board of Water Commissioners as a logical outgrowth of ten years' consultations "in connection with its municipal water works" (Lippincott to Newell, September 6, 1905, ibid.).

[38]Lippincott to Newell, September 8 and 18, 1905, ibid.; *San Francisco Chronicle*, September 3, 1905. A copy of the September 8 letter is in Pardee Papers, BL.

Pardee and Secretary of the Interior Hitchcock each a fourteen-page letter and then sent other letters to Newell.[39] Newell finally politely advised him "to write a very concise, specific letter to me covering the principal points, flatly contradicting the assertions made, making no admissions or qualified statements which can be misconstrued, and not entering into lengthy explanations."[40] Despite this advice, Lippincott continued to go into painstaking detail. On September 23 he issued to the Los Angeles and San Francisco news-papers a statement that received widespread attention. He also heard a rumor that Austin was involved in speculation with arid lands that would benefit from a federal project, lands the city was not interested in buying. Lippincott considered suing Austin for criminal libel. Complaints from Owens Valley, however, were still being made and publicized.[41]

Unwanted Gratitude

Newell soon found he had troubles of his own concerning the affair. When he returned from his extended trip west, he found the

[39]Lippincott to Newell, September 5, 6, 7, 8, 12, and 19, 1905, and Lippincott to Hitchcock, October 2, 1905, both in file 23 Alpha. (pt. 2), NPRC; Lippincott to Pardee, September 11 and 21, and October 2, 1905; Pardee to Newell, September 15, 1905; Pardee to Lippincott, September 16, 1905; Newell to Pardee, September 22, 1905, all in Pardee Papers, BL; Lippincott to Lungren, September 19, 1905, Lungren Papers, Huntington Library, San Marino, California (library hereafter cited as HL). The letter to Lungren is reproduced in Abraham Hoffman, "Joseph Barlow Lippincott and the Owens Valley Controversy: Time for Revision," *Southern California Quarterly* 54 (Fall, 1972), 245–251.

[40]Newell to Lippincott, September 26, 1905, file 23 Alpha. (pt. 2), NPRC.

[41]*Los Angeles Examiner, San Francisco Chronicle,* and *San Francisco Examiner,* all September 24, 1905. See also editorial in *San Francisco Chronicle,* September 19, 1905. Examples of Owens Valley complaints can be seen in Mrs. A. Matlick of Bishop to President of U.S., September 11, 1905, file 23 Alpha. (pt. 2), NPRC; E. S. Bigelow of Poleta, Inyo County, to Pardee, September 10, 1905, and Pardee to Bigelow, September 15, 1905, Pardee Papers, BL. Other relevant correspondence includes Lippincott to Newell, September 30, 1905, file 63-B, OV-GCRW, RBR; Pardee to Lippincott, September 30, 1905; Pardee to McAleer, September 30, 1905; Pardee to Austin, September 30, 1905; and Austin to Pardee, September 24, 1905, all in Pardee Papers, BL.

Reclamation Service headquarters in an uproar over the Owens Valley dispute. Davis had attempted to keep him posted on the latest developments, but events had moved much faster than the mail.

One such matter concerned the letter that Mulholland had so "effusively" written to Newell on June 5 thanking him for his help. The Owens River Water & Power Company, a private firm based in San Francisco, had applied to the Reclamation Service for permission to run power lines and to construct a power plant on the Owens River to serve the Nevada boom towns. This application was one of those Eaton had reported on to Lippincott. Following the application's rejection, the company claimed Reclamation Service partiality toward Los Angeles. Company attorneys inspected Los Angeles Water Commission minutes and found mention of the letter to Newell. The attorneys demanded to see it. James Vroman, the commission's secretary, stated he no longer had a copy of the letter; he had given it to City Attorney William Mathews who in turn had sent the copy on to Newell. Mathews informed Newell, "As it appears that the letter is one mainly of a personal nature, and I do not know what use the attorneys mentioned would make of it, I thought it best to send the copy to you, and if they see fit to apply to you for a copy you may act in the matter as you deem proper."[42]

The use contemplated by the attorneys for the Owens River Water & Power Company was obvious enough, even if not to Mathews. In seeking reconsideration of its application, the company hoped to use the letter to show that Newell had displayed favoritism to the City of Los Angeles. On September 7, the day after Mathews sent his carbon copy to Newell, Lippincott sent his own warning to the chief engineer. "I do not think there is anything in the letter that is of much importance," noted Lippincott, "but the Commissioners took the ground that they did not care to have their private correspondence with you placed in the hands of unfriendly attorneys."[43]

Newell had been unaware of the Water Commission's letter and did not see it until his return to Washington, D.C., three months

[42]Mathews to Newell, September 6, 1905, file 63-B, OV-GCRW, RBR.
[43]Lippincott to Newell, September 7, 1905, file 23 Alpha. (pt. 2), NPRC.

after it was written. He now found himself deeply involved in Lippincott's controversy. Anxious to keep the record clear, he sent
Mathews' letter and a copy of the commission letter to the director
of the Geological Survey, who forwarded it to the secretary of the
interior. "The whole matter is something of a mystery to [Newell],"
it was noted, "as he has had practically nothing to do with the
matter, and so far as rendering assistance to the city of Los Angeles,
cannot recall other than correspondence and transmission of printed
documents or of results of river measurements made public from
time to time."[44]

Despite Newell's disclaimers, the issue stirred some controversy
in Los Angeles, where the power company's attorneys sought a
writ of mandate against Vroman, who insisted the letter was no
longer in the commission's possession. A superior court judge denied
the attorneys' request, while Los Angeles newspapers had a field
day with the "secret," "mysterious," "closely guarded" letter.[45]

Other Owens Valley problems also required Newell's attention.
There were departmental demands for facts and evidence to replace
accusations and assertions. Newell communicated with Mayor Owen
McAleer of Los Angeles, requesting information on the city's claims
to Owens River water and valley land and on the city's future
plans. McAleer promised that a "definite statement" would be
prepared and sent "as soon as possible." Senator Frank Flint of
California, acting as a friend of the city, expressed to the secretary
of the interior his desire that Los Angeles' water needs be given fair
consideration. Register Austin, in contrast, continued to protest
against any possibility of the government's abandoning the project.
The Reclamation Service, in consequence of Lippincott's commitments to two masters, thus found itself in the center of a storm of
ever-increasing velocity.[46]

[44]Acting Director, Geological Survey, to Secretary of the Interior. Sep-
tember 13, 1905, file 63-B, OV-GCRW, RBR.
[45]*Los Angeles Times*, September 16, 1905; *Los Angeles Examiner*,
September 16, 19, and 21, 1905.
[46]Board of Water Commissioners to Flint, September 22, 1905, and
Flint to Secretary of the Interior, September 28, 1905, file 23 Alpha. (pt. 2),
NPRC; Lippincott to Newell, September 29, 1905, and Pardee to Newell,
September 30, 1905, enclosing copy of Austin to Pardee, September 24, 1905,

Lippincott under Fire

On October 5 Special Inspector O'Fallon completed his investigation and submitted his report to Acting Secretary Ryan. In the course of his duties he had traveled throughout California, examining documents and correspondence and taking depositions from the principal people involved, as well as interviewing residents in both city and valley. The end result was a fifty-seven-page report to Ryan, which encompassed the history of the federal reclamation project in Owens Valley, its feasibility, and the move by the city to stake its claim to Owens River water.[47]

Utilizing the evidence he had gathered, O'Fallon retraced the course of events in Owens Valley and in the city's search for a new water source. "Just when the City Authorities turned their attention to the Owens Valley is somewhat difficult to determine," he stated, "but probably some time during the summer or fall of 1904." O'Fallon, relying on statements submitted by Lippincott, Eaton, and other participants and observers, thought this point important "quite fully for the reason that the people of the Owens Valley regard it as important, and it is one of their principal complaints against Mr. Lippincott that he and Mr. Eaton visited the Long Valley reservoir site together." He reviewed the charge that Lippincott had planned to turn data over to the city from the very beginning of the federal surveys, an accusation that he noted Lippincott absolutely denied. The matter of the Water Commission June 5 letter to Newell was given full attention, as was Eaton's method of securing options on Owens Valley land and water rights. The city's employment of Lippincott to write a report while he was working full time for the

---

file 63-B, OV-GCRW, RBR. Austin conceded and corrected a point raised in his letter of August 4, stating now that the government had in fact not surrendered the project to the city.

[47]O'Fallon to Ryan, October 5, 1905, file 23 Alpha. (pt. 3), NPRC. A copy of this fifty-seven-page letter is also in Newell Papers, LC. The NPRC file also includes a number of depositions, sworn statements, and letters bearing on O'Fallon's investigation, many of which are appended to his report as exhibits and from which he frequently quotes. Lippincott's statement is also found appended to Lippincott to Newell, October 4, 1905, file 63-B, OV-GCRW, RBR. Occasional obvious typographical errors are corrected when quoting from O'Fallon's report.

Reclamation Service was traced, with lengthy excerpts from statements given by Mulholland and Fay.[48]

O'Fallon maintained a critical view of the complexities and nuances to be found in the investigation. Despite the brevity of time for his research and his lack of staff assistance, he nonetheless clearly perceived how the controversy had developed. His view of Lippincott's report for the city, which the supervising engineer had so laboriously attempted to justify to Newell, cut to the heart of the issue. "It seems that it was the purpose of the Board of Water Commissioners in obtaining a report from Mr. Lippincott to give the sanction of his authority to that position," O'Fallon noted. The Board of Water Commissioners used the report as a basis for justifying their refusal to consider any other possibilities in Southern California for an additional source of water supply. "This report," said O'Fallon, "would also be valuable as an answer to the objections that were likely to be put forward by promoters and other interested parties in the election which was shortly afterward to be called for the purpose of voting bonds in order to carry out the Owens Valley project."[49]

After tracing the chronology of events in a factual manner and with generous quotations from affidavits, depositions, statements, and letters he had gathered, O'Fallon proceeded to analyze the evidence and to draw conclusions. He admitted the difficulty of doing so: "The matter has got into such a condition that it will be quite hard to arrive at a determination of it without seeming injustice to some of the parties interested." O'Fallon found that the city's methods had left much to be desired. "It is to be regretted that the authorities of the City, after having made an investigation and come to the conclusion that the Owens River was an available source of supply and that it was feasible to conduct the water to the City of Los Angeles, that they did not at once present their claims to the Secretary of the Interior so that the question might have been determined on its merits in the beginning," he stated. "Instead of doing so, however, they proceeded into the valley secretly and secured

[48]O'Fallon to Ryan, October 5, 1905. file 23 Alpha. (pt. 3). pp. 3, 6–15 passim, NPRC.
[49]Ibid., p. 17.

options on land and water rights that possibly renders the Government project infeasible."[50]

As to the city's need for water, O'Fallon observed that the demand was made by the city in terms of its asserted potential growth rather than present requirements. He sounded a prescient note by predicting the city would eventually purchase most if not all of the valley, a circumstance he believed preferable to the piecemeal destruction of valley property rights.[51]

O'Fallon concluded his report with a summary and an eight-point recommendation. In the matter of collusion between Lippincott and Eaton as of the August, 1904, camping trip, O'Fallon stated, "I think the people of the valley were justified in their belief when they submitted this charge, and it was peculiarly unfortunate that this visit should have occurred in that locality, and yet under the evidence Mr. Lippincott should not be blamed if his own and Mr. Eaton's statements are true." The second point dealt with Lippincott's dual employment, and O'Fallon found it "highly improper" for Lippincott to have worked for the city. "His action in this matter injures the reputation of the Reclamation Service and places him in an equivocal position," observed the special inspector, "and when he now advises the Department that the Owens Valley Reclamation project be abandoned in favor of the City of Los Angeles, it has the appearance of coming from a paid representative of the City." Lippincott should have notified Mulholland and Eaton, even with their intentions given to him in confidence, that such intentions conflicted with government plans for a reclamation project. O'Fallon believed that the city would not have "spent a dollar" had it not known that Lippincott favored its plans and "at the proper time would recommend the abandonment of the Government project." Therefore Lippincott's conduct, in O'Fallon's opinion, merited "the severest condemnation."[52]

Lippincott's request that Eaton obtain information on right-of-way applications constituted the third point. O'Fallon felt the request would have been an ordinary action under other circumstances,

[50]Ibid., p. 37.
[51]Ibid., p. 45.
[52]Ibid., pp. 47–49.

but in this instance it was "certainly ill advised and calculated to bring the Reclamation Service into disrepute." He observed, "It seems almost farcical to have the promoter of a scheme that was antagonistic to the Government project reporting on other applications that they should be refused on account of interference with the plans of the Reclamation Service."

The fourth point dealt with Lippincott's providing government data to Los Angeles while Owens Valley was still under investigation as a proposed reclamation project. O'Fallon noted that to his knowledge the Clausen report had never been published. He left judgment as to whether providing the report was improper or not to his superiors. On the other hand, he definitely considered the government assistance rendered Eaton in his peregrinations around the valley "certainly improper and ill advised." This assistance, which included photographing Owens River tributaries and measuring stream flows, was done at government expense but to the eventual benefit of the city. The fifth point, on the survey of the Long Valley reservoir site by the Lippincott & Parker firm for the city's benefit, "was highly improper and deserves the severest condemnation." O'Fallon stated, "If Mr. Lippincott desired to retain a partnership while he was acting in an official capacity the partner certainly ought not to be employed in enterprises that were inimical and antagonistic to the enterprises that were under his control as a public official."[53]

On at least one point Lippincott was absolved of blame—the accusation that he directly assisted Eaton in securing options. Moreover, no proof existed that Eaton had deliberately misrepresented himself as a government official. "A combination of circumstances, however, did confuse and mislead the people of the valley." They were known to be friends; Eaton had Reclamation Service maps; Eaton used the services of government employees. All of this combined "to lead the people into the belief that Mr. Eaton, in some way, was secretly carrying out the purposes of the Reclamation Service in obtaining options on these lands and water rights."[54]

The seventh point considered the Austin-Fysh complaints. O'Fallon obtained depositions from both men and praised their

[53]Ibid., pp. 50–53.
[54]Ibid., pp. 53–54.

honesty and ability. Although their charges were "somewhat hysterical" in tone, and while he did not concur in all their conclusions, O'Fallon did find "that their conduct has been justified," and influenced by "a desire that the full facts be brought to the attention of the President and Department in this matter."[55]

The final point summarized all the findings. O'Fallon considered the entire affair most unfortunate, one that could have been prevented had Lippincott recognized his primary obligation was to the Reclamation Service. The future of an Owens Valley project was complicated by limited funds and the city's purchases. However, O'Fallon found no excuse for Lippincott's recommendation that the project should be abandoned, since there was no evidence that construction was unfeasible. "After considering the whole matter, I can arrive at no other conclusion than that Supervising Engineer Lippincott's action in the matter is indefensible, and for the good of the Reclamation Service he should be separated from it," O'Fallon stated. "He is no doubt a capable official and could have rendered valuable aid to the Reclamation Service, but his conduct in this matter has been such as, in my opinion, would destroy his usefulness as a public official."[56]

As an investigator, O'Fallon had no authority to back up his recommendations; actual dismissal of Lippincott would have to come as the result of a hearing. In the meantime endorsements and condemnations of Lippincott continued in equal measure. The Inyo County Board of Supervisors petitioned Secretary Hitchcock to "prosecute, with all due and reasonable diligence" the investigation into the affair, and the Owens Valley Water Protective Association acted in similar fashion. Lippincott's supporters also kept busy. The Los Angeles Chamber of Commerce sent Hitchcock a resolution commending Lippincott for conduct "eminently proper and in no wise detrimental or prejudicial to said United States Reclamation Service," while Governor Pardee also declared his support of the supervising engineer.[57]

[55]Ibid., p. 55.

[56]Ibid., pp. 56–57.

[57]William D. Dehy to Hitchcock, October 6, 1905; Owens Valley Water Protective Association to President of the United States, October 11, 1905; Los Angeles Chamber of Commerce to Hitchcock, October 6, 1905, all in

One interested effort on Lippincott's behalf came from Fred Eaton in an attempt to discredit Stafford Austin. He announced that Austin himself had filed a claim on Owens River riparian land on August 27, possibly with the intention of profiting from its sale following the government's construction of the reclamation project. Austin hotly protested the accusation, stating he had turned over the claim to the Owens Valley Water Protective Association "simply as a protective measure for our property owners."[58] Adding further complications to the affair were attorneys representing the Owens River Water & Power Company. They had come to Washington, D.C., where they were demanding presentation of the "missing" June 5 letter, personally attacking Lippincott, and, in Newell's words, making themselves "thoroughly obnoxious." To determine the legitimacy of the power company's claim, Newell requested the assistance of Albert E. Chandler, a Reclamation Service engineer experienced in land and legal matters, who until now had not been involved in the Owens Valley controversy and could be trusted to make an impartial investigation.[59]

Further Investigations

By the end of October Secretary Hitchcock had seen enough contradictory correspondence to stir him to action against what was

file 23 Alpha. (pt. 3), NPRC; Pardee to Newell, September 30, 1905, and Newell to Pardee, October 7, 1905, file 63-B, OV-GCRW, RBR; Lippincott to Newell, October 13, 1905, Newell Papers, LC; "Statement of the People of Owens Valley in Relation to the Proposed Diversion of the Waters of Owens River to the City of Los Angeles"; Pardee to Lippincott, October 31, 1905; and Lippincott to Pardee, November 9, 1905, all in Pardee Papers, BL.

[58]*Los Angeles Herald*, October 21, 1905; *San Francisco Chronicle*, October 21, 1905; *Los Angeles Times*, October 21, 1905. The *Times* article also claimed that I. H. Mulholland (no relation to William), although opposed to the city's plans, engaged in an altercation with Austin over the accuracy of Mary Austin's articles. Austin, according to the *Times*, received a black eye. Austin made no mention of this in his letter to Hitchcock, October 24, 1905, file 23 Alpha. (pt. 3), NPRC. See also Owens Valley Water Protective Association to Hitchcock, October 28, 1905; Lippincott to Newell, November 2, 1905; Lippincott to Pardee, November 4, 1905; and Walcott to Hitchcock, November 9, 1905 (two letters), all in file 63-B, OV-GCRW, RBR. Lippincott's letters enclosed clippings of the *Times* article.

[59]Newell to Lippincott, October 25, 1905, and Newell to A. E. Chandler, October 25, 1905 (two letters), file 63-B, OV-GCRW, RBR.

developing into an unwanted scandal. He requested Geological Survey Director Walcott to provide all correspondence bearing on the accusations leveled against the Reclamation Service. On November 6 Walcott did so, enclosing letters between Newell and Lippincott covering the entire year, newspaper clippings, and telegrams, having copies made where necessary if originals could not be submitted.[60]

Hitchcock's call for information prompted Newell to admonish Lippincott concerning what had by now become a voluminous collection of lengthy letters. "I think you could with great advantage to yourself and to the work read over your letters after dictation and carefully trim them down to the essential facts," advised Newell. Moreover, Lippincott should "try to omit references to previous correspondence, unless you accompany your report with copies of the correspondence. Otherwise you set up an endless chain." Newell illustrated the confusion that could easily occur: Lippincott would refer in one letter to another letter, the department would request the earlier letter, only to find that it mentioned still another letter, "and so on until our clerks are forced to haul over literally tons of old correspondence, one letter drawing out another." Newell urged Lippincott to avoid this problem by simply stating facts, eliminating the need for searching through the files for verification. "What we need above all are short, concise statements, clearly and impersonally given, omitting all side issues and personal allusions, or phrases which are not perfectly clear to any intelligent man."[61]

Chandler soon submitted his reports to Newell, who passed them up to Walcott. The Geological Survey director in turn prepared a formal report for Hitchcock. Chandler's findings were much more temperate in tone than O'Fallon's critical report had been. In the first place, Austin's private water filing on behalf of the Owens Valley Water Protective Association had been performed under a misunderstanding. Unless implementation of the filing was begun within sixty days of its being posted, it lapsed. The Austin filing therefore was of no value other than as an indication of Austin's "enthusiasm," as Chandler put it.[62]

[60]Hitchcock to Walcott, November 1, 1905, and Walcott to Hitchcock, November 6, 1905, file 23 Alpha. (pt. 3), NPRC.

[61]Newell to Lippincott, November 8, 1905, file 63-B, OV-GCRW, RBR.

[62]Chandler to Newell, November 10, 1905 (two letters), ibid.

Second, the Owens River Water & Power Company's claims would not be valid unless the company actually completed its construction of reservoir, tunnels, canals, and other projects and began using Owens River water. Even then, the claims might not be valid anyway because of imperfections in the land titles. The third element in Chandler's investigation concerned Los Angeles. Chandler believed the city's plans superior to the intentions of the power company since Los Angeles evinced every intention of constructing the aqueduct.[63]

Walcott consolidated Chandler's reports and submitted them to the secretary of the interior on December 9. He supported Chandler's negative conclusions on the power company's water rights claims. As to the city's plans, the method by which water rights had been acquired seemed less important than the fact that the city had them. With funds limited, the Reclamation Service could not proceed with an Owens Valley project anyway. Therefore, all circumstances considered, Walcott recommended that "further action in regard to the reclamation project in the Owens Valley be suspended."[64]

While Hitchcock digested the mass of information submitted to him, valley supporters conducted an aggressive lobbying campaign. The Owens River Water & Power Company retained local attorneys who approached congressmen, senators, and Interior Department officials and loudly criticized the actions of Los Angeles and the Reclamation Service. The Owens Valley Water Protective Association mailed several pamphlets in large quanties to members of Congress. These actions prompted Newell to inform Lippincott that without a lobbyist in Washington, Los Angeles' chances of congressional approval for important elements of its plans could be jeopardized.[65]

Los Angeles soon retaliated. The city council adopted a resolution urging Hitchcock to abandon a federal reclamation project and

[63]Chandler to Newell, November 16, 22 (three letters), and 25, 1905, ibid.

[64]Walcott to Hitchcock, December 9, 1905, file 23 Alpha. (pt. 3), NPRC. A similar report with slight modifications in wording is in file 63-B, OV-GCRW, RBR.

[65]Newell to Lippincott, November 21, 1905, Newell Papers, LC.

to deny any pending or future applications for right-of-way over government lands pertaining to Owens River water "upon the ground that the same would be incompatible with the public interests." In the months to follow additional resolutions were passed, the Chamber of Commerce sent lobbyists, and Mulholland and Mathews went to the nation's capital to press the city's case. Also, whereas Owens Valley had the backing of Representative Sylvester C. Smith, whose district included Inyo County, Los Angeles had the active support of Senator Frank P. Flint, a prominent western Republican leader.[66]

Hitchcock delayed making any decision concerning the Owens Valley project, the charges against Lippincott, or Los Angeles' plans, meanwhile requesting the opinion of Charles E. Grunsky, a prominent civil engineer who had previously acted for him in an advisory capacity. Grunsky was a widely respected engineer, whose views carried considerable influence with the secretary of the interior. On January 4, 1906, Grunsky presented Hitchcock with his recommendations on whether the Owens River could furnish enough water for the needs of Los Angeles and whether such a project could coexist with a federal project in the same region. Grunsky weighed all the arguments and, like Chandler, ignored the means by which the city's position had been achieved in favor of examining the engineering aspects of the question. His conclusion: "the irrigation project which has been under investigation in Owens Valley cannot be carried out if Los Angeles takes water from the valley for municipal use. . . . An irrigation project for Owens Valley if Los Angeles constructs the works under contemplation, including the reservoir at Long Valley, and if Los Angeles refuses cooperation, is practically out of the question."[67]

While Hitchcock continued to hold the Owens Valley project in a state of suspension, he did reach a decision on Lippincott's actions in the controversy. Lippincott had found a staunch friend in Governor George Pardee of California. Twice president of the Na-

[66]City Clerk H. J. Lelande to Hitchcock, December 13, 1905, file 23 Alpha. (pt. 3), NPRC, and a copy in file 63-B, OV-GCRW, RBR; *Los Angeles Times*, February 5, 1906; Nadeau, *Water Seekers*, p. 26.

[67]C. E. Grunsky to Hitchcock, January 4, 1906, file 63-B, OV-GCRW, RBR.

tional Irrigation Congress and an advocate of government reclamation, Pardee sympathized with his friend's difficulties. He went so far as to intercede actively on Lippincott's behalf, writing letters to Hitchcock and to California's senators. Senator Flint, an otherwise strong backer of the city's aqueduct plan, declined to assist because Lippincott had taken a fee from the city while working for the government. Flint considered Lippincott "honest, capable, and a very valuable officer of the Reclamation Service," but, as he had already informed Lippincott, he could not in good conscience speak on his behalf. Pardee's own letter to Hitchcock, however, strongly pleaded Lippincott's case. Lippincott went to Washington, D.C., early in February and had an interview with Hitchcock shortly after the secretary read Pardee's letter. "It went to the right spot at the right time," recalled Lippincott, "and he accepted my presentation of the case." O'Fallon's report and Davis' opinion notwithstanding, poor judgment in a complex issue was an inadequate basis for dismissal. Hitchcock insisted, however, that all private work must end once and for all.[68]

As the year 1906 progressed, Los Angeles and its supporters moved closer and closer to making the aqueduct a reality. One after another, obstacles were removed. To the disappointment of the Owens River Water & Power Company and the residents of Owens Valley, Hitchcock seemed to be allowing the federal project to die a slow death. John Laskey, representing the power company in Washington, D.C., continued to press for an acceptance of his client's position, but the Geological Survey rebuffed his requests. Recognizing the definite possibility of the abandonment of the project, the Owens Valley Water Protective Association, led by W. A. Chalfant, suggested a compromise to the Reclamation Service: a storage reservoir in the area of Fish Slough at the northern limit of Owens

[68]Pardee to Flint, February 2, 1906, and Pardee to Perkins, February 2, 1906, Pardee Papers, BL. An outline of charges and defenses in Lippincott's handwriting, dated February 1, in the Pardee Papers, suggests that Lippincott provided Pardee with the information needed for the letters. Pardee's letter to Hitchcock, also dated February 2, could not be located; however, internal evidence indicates it was substantially similar to the letters to Flint and Perkins. See also Flint to Pardee, February 8 and 21, 1906; Newell to Pardee, February 20, 1906; and Lippincott to Pardee, February 11 and 15, 1906, Pardee Papers, BL.

Valley, which might benefit both city and valley. Such questions would no longer be handled by Lippincott. He gratefully allowed Arthur Powell Davis to turn over any further matters concerning Owens Valley to someone else. Davis appointed L. H. Taylor to look into such possibilities as the Fish Slough compromise.[69]

But the city was not yet finished in its securing of Owens River water. Having vanquished the Reclamation Service, Los Angeles now sought even greater control over its adopted river. Beyond domestic use, that higher purpose to which Lippincott had philosophically surrendered, there were other purposes to which the river might be put for the city's benefit—irrigation, for example. Irrigation? Why would a city need water for irrigation? The answer to this question quickly became clear enough to Owens Valley residents. The river would provide for the city's potential growth. For the present, however, its surplus waters could be used profitably for the same purpose as in a federal reclamation project—only instead of Owens Valley benefiting from irrigation, the recipient would be the city's next-door neighbor, the San Fernando Valley.

The Syndicate Scheme

William Mulholland could and did provide many common-sense reasons for the proposed aqueduct to stop at the northern end of the San Fernando Valley rather than proceed all the way into the actual city limits of Los Angeles, which in 1905 encompassed a much smaller area than the metropolis of the future would. The San Fernando Valley constituted a vast underground reservoir which could store Owens River water, raising the water table in the process. In addition, the terminus of the aqueduct marked a location where power-plant construction was feasible. The Owens River would bring not only water to the thirsty city but also electricity.[70]

Prior to Eaton's conversion of Mulholland to the Owens River

[69]John Laskey to Walcott, February 8, 1906; Walcott to Laskey, February 10, 1906; Chalfant (for the Owens Valley Water Protective Association) to Hitchcock, February 3 and 9, 1906; Lippincott to Davis, February 20, 1906; Davis to Lippincott, February 28, 1906; Davis to Taylor, February 28, and March 6, 1906, all in file 63-B, OV-GCRW, RBR.

[70]Charles Amadon Moody, "Los Angeles and the Owens River," *Out West* 23 (October, 1905), 419, 441.

as a water source, some real estate speculators had viewed the San Fernando Valley as a likely area for future development. By 1903 Leslie C. Brand, president of the Title Guarantee and Trust Company, was already involved in the expansion of the city of Glendale in the eastern part of the valley. He and his associate, Henry E. Huntington, the head of the Pacific Electric Railway, planned to extend streetcar lines into the city of San Fernando and beyond into the valley, in much the same fashion as Huntington's other successes in combining real estate developments and public transportation systems.[71]

In October, 1903, Brand obtained a three-year option on some 16,200 acres in the northern part of the San Fernando Valley from George K. Porter, son of one of the founders of the city of San Fernando. Brand's land syndicate included Huntington, Edward H. Harriman, president of the Union Pacific and Southern Pacific Railroads, Joseph F. Sartori, president of the Security Bank, Harrison Gray Otis, publisher of the *Times*, Edwin T. Earl, publisher of the *Express*, and other prominent businessmen. Their risk was minimal, considering the rapid growth of Southern California and Huntington's successful Pacific Electric lines. In November, 1904, however, came the opportunity to maximize profits. A week after Lippincott and Newell met with Eaton, Mulholland, and Mathews, the Brand syndicate incorporated as the San Fernando Mission Land Company, with one thousand shares at $100 each going to ten investors—a capitalization of $1 million. On March 23, 1905, the day after the Water Commission approved Mulholland's presentation for Owens River water, the company took up the Porter Ranch options. Four months later came the news of the titanic project.[72]

The coincidences surrounding the formation of the land syndicate and the Eaton-Mulholland plans for the Owens River have ever since tantalized historians and conspiracy-theory devotees alike. Was it, most favorably, a highly successful business venture, or was it a most unsavory conspiracy to sell San Fernando Valley property by defrauding Owens Valley citizens of their water? Absence of documentation has prevented definite conclusions concerning the intentions of the syndicate. The conspiracy theory generally suffers from

[71]Frank Bies, "Glendale's Brand," *Westways* 70 (May, 1978), 40–41.
[72]*Los Angeles Examiner*, August 24, 1905.

the errors of its supporters in their poor retracing of the historical record. On the other hand, the best that may be said for the conduct of the land syndicate is that inside information about the Eaton-Mulholland plan prompted the purchase of the Porter property. The worst of it included possible conflict of interest, a problem that bothered those guilty of it much less than has been noted in Lippincott's soul-searching over his allegiances. Moses H. Sherman, a member of the Board of Water Commissioners, soon became involved in the San Fernando Mission Land Company. While no written evidence has been found linking Sherman the water commissioner to Sherman the land speculator, the conclusion seems inescapable that he used his position as a public servant to benefit his private interests.[73]

Other members of the land syndicate also abused their public responsibilities. Harrison Gray Otis and Edwin T. Earl, mortal enemies when in journalistic combat, found coexistence possible as directors of the San Fernando Mission Land Company. Both men, but especially Otis, used the editorial pages of their newspapers to campaign aggressively for approval of the aqueduct bonds. In so doing Otis turned the *Times* into a propaganda sheet for his own economic benefit.[74]

Otis' involvement in the land company came to the attention of the *Examiner* during the bond campaign. After reporting the news of the incorporation of the company and its anticipated profit from the sale of San Fernando Valley land, the newspaper speculated on why Otis and Earl belonged to the syndicate. The *Examiner* suggested, without offering proof, that they had exchanged their newspapers' support for land company stocks.[75] Otis probably laughed at the accusation, for no such exchange was necessary. It

[73]Nadeau, *Water Seekers*, pp. 24–25; Carey McWilliams, *Southern California Country: An Island on the Land*, p. 187. The *Los Angeles Times*, August 28, 1905, provides Sherman's view on the aqueduct project. Eaton and Mulholland, it should be noted, did not personally profit from and were not involved in the San Fernando Valley land schemes.

[74]Cifarelli, "Owens River Aqueduct and the Los Angeles *Times*," pp. 123–127; Richard C. Miller, "Otis and His *Times*: The Career of Harrison Gray Otis of Los Angeles" (Ph.D. diss., University of California, Berkeley, 1961), pp. 272–280.

[75]*Los Angeles Examiner*, August 24, 25, 27, and 28, 1905.

just happened that in this instance his interests and those of the city coincided, and he therefore saw nothing wrong in endorsing a project that would also happen to enrich his already considerable fortune. Meanwhile he defended his position in typical Otis fashion, moving to the direct offensive. "Sheer ignorance and petty envy might have accounted for the first furtive attacks made by Hearst's megalomaniac hired man [*Examiner* editor Lowenthal] upon the Owens River project, but the most abysmal ignorance could not persist in the face of the reiterated statements of fact which have been published, and it is now clear that the lying of the *Examiner* is deliberate, calculated, and for a sinister purpose," ran Otis' invective. "The latest editorial yawp of the Yellow Freak is a delerium of mendacity and malice. It is so full of lies direct, lies by implication and lies by suppression that twice the space occupied by the mouthings of the Impossible Dolt would be required to expose them in all their venomous enormity."[76] The newspaper war lasted until William Randolph Hearst overruled his editor, Henry Lowenthal, on September 3, and the *Examiner* thereafter editorially supported the aqueduct project.

As the election date for the bond question approached, the San Fernando Mission Land Company unabashedly advertised the values to be obtained in purchasing valley property. "Pacoima will feel the first benefits of the Owens River water and every purchaser investing now will reap the fruits of his wisdom in gratifying profits," ran a typical ad.[77] Presumably, the investors in the San Fernando Mission Land Company reaped just such fruits.

Roosevelt and the Right-of-Way

With the water of the Owens River sure to come to Los Angeles, certain complicating questions arose concerning its delivery. In order to generate electric power, a continuous flow of water would have to come through the aqueduct. Once the underground basin of the San Fernando Valley and the several contemplated

---

[76]*Los Angeles Times*, August 29, 1905.
[77]*Los Angeles Examiner*, September 5, 1905.

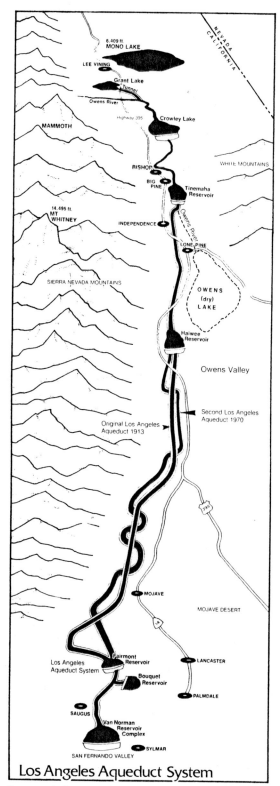

Los Angeles Aqueduct System

By permission of Mike Farewell and courtesy of

Mount McGee in Long Valley, north of Owens Valley. *Courtesy of Los Angeles Department of Water and Power.*

Owens River. *Courtesy of Historical Collections, Security Pacific National Bank.*

reservoirs were filled, however, what was to be done with the surplus? The city would suffer an embarrassment of riches since domestic use could not begin to utilize the amount the aqueduct would send to the city. And not to use the river could endanger the city's title to the water so carefully acquired.

Mulholland quickly realized that in order to make best use of the water the city would have to have the right to sell it not only for domestic use but for irrigation. Such use, however, was the same as that intended by Owens Valley residents. "The people of Owens Valley are willing to concede to the city whatever supply of water is actually needed for domestic and municipal use," declared W. A. Chalfant, "but are not willing that a supply for outside irrigation should be taken from our own lands for the benefit of outside Los Angeles tracts."[78]

Congressman Sylvester Smith sought to preserve the valley's rights through a compromise proposal. He would not oppose the city's receiving Owens River water for domestic consumption if the Reclamation Service might construct a possibly more modest reclamation project in the valley for irrigation purposes. The city hardly considered this a compromise. Even as Smith moved in this direction, Mulholland and Mathews began their campaign to capture the river for irrigation as well. Rumors flew thick and fast concerning the city's intentions. Governor Pardee, having defended Lippincott's conduct in the dispute, found it necessary to write to Mayor McAleer about this latest development. "The people of the Owens Valley are said to be entirely content to see Los Angeles take such water as she may need for domestic and municipal purposes," he said, "but they assert that the taking of water from Owens River for the purpose of irrigating Los Angeles lands will leave them without the water which is absolutely essential to the maintenance of their own section of the State." Pardee was also under the impression that the federal reclamation project had already been abandoned, although he was unclear on the reasons why. To Chalfant, Pardee reported, "There have been so many conflicting charges and countercharges concerning the attitude of Los Angeles toward the Owens River

[78]Chalfant to Pardee, March 17, 1906, Pardee Papers, BL.

matter, that I am free to say I do not feel that I understand exactly what the situation is."[79]

Although the governor of California may have been confused, Los Angeles officials knew full well what the stakes were for the city. On May 13 Mulholland and Mathews submitted to the Department of the Interior the city's request for a right-of-way for canal and conduit construction across public lands in the Owens Valley. Early in June Senator Flint introduced a bill to grant Los Angeles a right-of-way for the aqueduct across public lands for the entire route. The Senate passed the bill quickly and with little opposition, but its counterpart version in the House, where it was sponsored by Congressman James McLachlan, ran into trouble. Congressman Smith succeeded in putting the bill into the hands of the Public Lands Committee, on which he served and which referred it to the Department of the Interior. While Los Angeles Chamber of Commerce representatives lobbied desperately with House committee members, Smith approached Hitchcock with an amendment to the bill that would prohibit irrigation use by the city.[80]

Concern over these developments sent Mulholland and Mathews to Washington, D.C., and a meeting with Smith and Flint was held in Flint's office on June 21. The city officials agreed to concede the point on irrigation if Smith would support the actual right-of-way bill. Smith accepted the compromise and joined the Los Angeles forces in urging Hitchcock to approve the bill. Hitchcock did so, and the bill was sent back to the House committee.

Senator Flint then tried an end run. He called on President Roosevelt on June 23 and argued the necessity for protecting the city's water rights by including the right for irrigation use. The water was essential for the city's growth over the next half-century. Roosevelt accepted Flint's arguments and called a meeting of the officials involved—omitting Smith from his summons.

[79]Pardee to McAleer, March 14, 1906; Pardee to Newell, March 14, 1906; Pardee to Chalfant, March 14, 1906; Newell to Pardee, March 20, 1906, all in Pardee Papers, BL. Pardee wrote several times to McAleer, but the mayor failed to reply (see Pardee to Chalfant, March 27, 1906, Pardee Papers, BL). A copy of Pardee to Newell, March 14, 1906, is in file 63-B, OV-GCRW, RBR.

[80]Los Angeles Times, May 14, 1906; Los Angeles Record, July 4, 1906; Nadeau, Water Seekers, pp. 26–27.

On June 25 Roosevelt, Flint, Hitchcock, Walcott, and Pinchot met to discuss the issue further. Hitchcock pointed out that certain investors in San Fernando Valley real estate would profit greatly from an irrigation provision that favored the city. Pinchot, on the other hand, endorsed the city's original position. Roosevelt weighed the arguments. Some private investors would benefit from the city's project; at the same time, a private power company in Owens Valley opposed the bill. This last detail tended to place the progressive-oriented president in the city's camp. Roosevelt then made up his mind. To formalize the decision, he dictated a letter to Hitchcock in everyone's presence. "The question is whether the city of Los Angeles should be prohibited from using the water it will obtain under this bill for irrigation purposes," said Roosevelt. "Your feeling is that it should be so prohibited because the passage of the bill without the prohibition might establish a monopoly in the municipality of Los Angeles as regards irrigation, by permitting the municipality of use of the surplus of the water thus acquired, beyond the amount actually used for drinking purposes, for some irrigation scheme."

Roosevelt noted Senator Flint's explanation that Los Angeles would have to draw the full amount of water from the river, even though much of it was not presently needed, in order to retain its right of use. He conceded that other users could make use of the water, "yet it is a hundred or a thousand fold more important to the State and more valuable to the people as a whole if used by the city than if used by the people of Owens Valley." As to the definition of domestic use, Roosevelt accepted Flint's point that, if broadly defined, domestic use could easily include people's gardens and "little plots of land." To narrow the definition and exclude this use "would so nearly destroy the value of the bill as to make it an open question whether the city either could or would go on with the project." Neither Walcott nor Pinchot saw any objection to this kind of irrigation as long as it followed drinking, washing, fire fighting, and other domestic priorities. "They feel that no monopoly in an offensive sense is created by municipal ownership of the water as obtained under this bill, and that as a matter of fact to attempt to deprive the city of Los Angeles of the right to use the water for irrigation would mean that for many years no use whatever could be made by it of the surplus water beyond that required for drinking and similar purposes."

Roosevelt acknowledged the opposition of the "few" Owens Valley settlers whose position "must unfortunately be disregarded in view of the infinitely greater interest to be served by putting the water in Los Angeles." Interestingly enough, the president considered the opposition of private power companies to the city's plans to be of greater significance than the views of the small number of farmers. "Their opposition seems to me to afford one of the strongest arguments for passing the law, inasmuch as it ought not to be within the power of private individuals to control such a necessary of life as against the municipality itself." The president concluded the letter by recommending "that the bill be approved, with the prohibition against the use of the water by the municipality for irrigation struck out. I request, however, that there be put in the bill a prohibition against the City of Los Angeles ever selling or letting to any corporation or individual except the municipality, the right for that corporation or that individual itself to sell or sublet the water given to it or him by the city for irrigation purposes."

Upon completing the letter, Roosevelt read it aloud and proclaimed, "I now find that everyone agrees to it—you, Mr. Secretary, as well as Senator Flint, Director Walcott, and Mr. Pinchot, and therefore I subscribe to it with a far more satisfied heart than when I started to dictate this letter."[81]

Roosevelt's endorsement of the city's right to use the river for irrigation was sent to the House Public Lands Committee at the very moment the bill was under consideration. Smith immediately realized the city had outmaneuvered him, and he bitterly deferred to Roosevelt's authority. On June 26 the House approved the bill. Smith wrote an irate letter to Roosevelt protesting the decision:

I regret that I was not permitted to state the case from the standpoint of my constituents, the people of Inyo County, though I hasten to acquit you and all others of any intentional discourtesy or oversight.

[81] Roosevelt to Hitchcock, June 25, 1906, file 63-B, OV-GCRW, RBR. The text of this letter, with a few minor word changes, is in Elting E. Morison, ed., *The Letters of Theodore Roosevelt*, 5:315–316. Smith's account of the meetings is in *Inyo Register*, July 12, 1906. Roosevelt's statement was appended to the letter as a postscript.

In the line of what I conceive to be my duty toward the people of Inyo, I take the liberty of laying before you the following view of the case.

Smith admitted that Los Angeles had the right to increase its water supply and to provide for future growth. He agreed that Owens River water should be put to the beneficial use of irrigating arid lands. But which arid lands—the privately owned lands near Los Angeles, or the government land in Inyo County? Smith argued that the government's rights to Owens River water preceded the city's claims. The city hoped the federal reclamation project would be abandoned, giving Los Angeles the opportunity to sell its surplus water to farms in Los Angeles County. The congressman regretted that the federal and city governments had failed to unite on the logical idea of storing water at the head of Owens Valley, at the Long Valley location, a solution that would provide enough water for everyone.[82]

Theodore Roosevelt angrily responded to Smith's complaints, lecturing the congressman on how he should have defended his amendment and his constituency, if such a defense were actually needed:

I have just received your letter. You say that you regret that you "were not permitted to state the case from the standpoint of your constituents," and then you add that you "hasten to acquit" me "and all others of any intentional discourtesy or oversight." This seems to show on your part that you thought there was discourtesy or oversight shown you, although not intentionally. In view of this statement by you I desire to state in return that you have been guilty of laches [sic] and of failure in your duty both to your constituents and to the Department in not laying before the Department and myself any information as to why we should not approve of the bill; if you think there was a "discourtesy" in not hearing you. Senator Flint has been to me again and again on the bill, and it has been a matter of common notoriety that he and others of the California delegation have had this bill before the Department of the Interior and have been to me about it. It was clearly your duty to take the trouble to come before the Department and if necessary before me, any time to present your case instead of waiting until your colleagues of California had thrashed the matter all over and action had been taken, and then writing me such a letter as you have written me. Of course we cannot divine what men wish to be heard. Your letter is all the more extraordinary in view of the fact that, as I understand it, the bill is now

[82]Smith to Roosevelt, June 25, 1906, file 63-B, OV-GCRW, RBR.

before the House and that we are simply waiting for whatever action the body of which you are a member may take. I have referred your letter for comment to the Chief of the Reclamation Service.[83]

The bill—"An Act Authorizing and directing the Secretary of the Interior to sell to the city of Los Angeles, California, certain public lands in California; and granting rights in, over, and through the Sierra Forest Reserve, the Santa Barbara Forest Reserve, and the San Gabriel Timber Land Reserve, California, to the city of Los Angeles, California"—became law on June 30, 1906. It provided the city with rights-of-way over public lands in three California counties for the construction of ditches, tunnels, conduits, and whatever else was necessary for the building of the aqueduct. If the secretary of the interior formally abandoned the Owens Valley project, Los Angeles would reimburse the reclamation fund to the limit of $14,000 for surveys, river measurements, and other expenses. In return the city would receive maps, notes, and other data from the Reclamation Service. The city was given five years to begin construction of the aqueduct.[84]

Los Angeles officials were jubilant. Mayor McAleer wired Flint and McLachlan, "On behalf of the city of Los Angeles and vicinity, I desire to thank you and our other representatives for your grand and conscientious work in connection with the Owens river conduit bill." Mulholland and Mathews returned to Los Angeles and a hero's welcome. The water superintendent characteristically returned to his desk and the countless details demanding his attention but still found time to give the press his version of the political infighting. "Congressman Smith was like a thorn in our sides from the outset," he said. "He tried to play a foxy game. He wanted to throw every obstacle in our path, and at the same time make us believe that he was in sympathy with our cause. But we were on to him." Mulholland had been granted one interview with the president. "He treated me very cordially," recalled Mulholland. "He was wholly in sympathy with us, and we would never have gotten the bill through this session if it had not been for him."

[83]Roosevelt to Smith, June 26, 1906, ibid.

[84]U.S., *Statutes at Large*, vol. 34 (part 1), chap. 3926, pp. 801–803; *Los Angeles Examiner*, June 27, 1906; "Owens River Champions," *Graphic* 25 (July 7, 1906), 17.

City Attorney Mathews described meeting Roosevelt after the passage of the bill. Roosevelt had been in an ebullient mood. "We thanked him for his assistance, and he said very simply that he was there to do his duty," said Mathews. "We didn't have long to speak with him, but he assured us that he was entirely in sympathy with our water project. He promised to do what he could to keep the lands which we shall want from being filed and entered upon until we have staked out our course."[85]

The course to be followed was not without its pitfalls. Ahead lay approval of the city's plans by an independent board of engineers, the mapping of the aqueduct route, and the voters' approval of $23 million in bonds for the actual construction of the aqueduct. The city, however, could rejoice about the Roosevelt administration's support for its plans. Meanwhile, the people of Owens Valley, though disappointed, still held out some hope for a federal project. "Notwithstanding the talk of the Los Angeles press, our prediction as to reclamation of Owens Valley lands by some means still holds," stated the *Inyo Register*.[86] But the hold proved tenuous, then non-existent. A year later, on July 3, 1907, at the request of the City of Los Angeles in view of its imminent construction of the aqueduct, the Department of the Interior formally abandoned the idea of a federal reclamation project in Owens Valley.[87]

[85]*Los Angeles Record*, July 4, 1906; *Los Angeles Examiner*, June 27, 1906.

[86]*Inyo Register*, July 5, 1906. Smith issued a statement on the Owens River situation, published in the *Bakersfield Echo*, July 13, 1906, and reprinted in the *Inyo Register*, July 26, 1906.

[87]Gates, Thayer, and Rankin (attorneys for the City of Los Angeles) to U.S. Reclamation Service, June 29, 1907; Morris Bien to Secretary of the Interior, July 2, 1907; Acting Secretary of the Interior George Woodruff to Gates, Thayer, and Rankin, July 31, 1907, all in file 63-B, OV-GCRW, RBR.

5

An Aqueduct for Los Angeles

"There it is—take it."—William Mulholland, at the opening of the Owens Valley–Los Angeles Aqueduct, November 5, 1913

JOSEPH BARLOW LIPPINCOTT emerged from his February 10, 1906, meeting with Secretary of the Interior Hitchcock with his job intact, but with a warning to avoid dual employment in the future. He had dissolved his partnership with O. K. Parker in September, 1905, endured the condemnation of the O'Fallon report, and regretted the rupture in his long friendship with Davis. Through it all he steadfastly maintained that he had done what he believed was right. "Looking back over that affair I can see where I made mistakes which no one regrets more than I," he wrote to Newell in April, 1906, "but I really endeavored at the time to do what I thought to be a public duty & assumed the risk in doing it."[1]

The legacy of the affair, however, proved negative. Various unsettled problems still affected Newell, a circumstance Lippincott regretted. If, observed Lippincott, the best way to solve such problems would be for him to resign, he would willingly do so. "Please do not think I am saying this in a bitter way for I am not," he assured Newell. "I would continue to assist you in the future if I could in any event." Newell expressed the hope that Lippincott might oversee the Yuma and Klamath projects until they were well established, at which point Lippincott could decide whether he thereafter wished a full-time career in government service.[2]

[1]Lippincott to Newell, April 11, 1906, Newell Papers, LC.
[2]Lippincott to Newell, April 20, 1906, and Newell to Lippincott, April 27, 1906, ibid.

Events soon intervened that prompted Lippincott to make a much earlier decision than anticipated. During the first half of 1906 he spent considerable time on location at the Yuma and Klamath projects, with little time available for home and family. Because these projects were located on California's borders, Newell believed it might be more practical to shift the supervision of the projects to Phoenix and Portland. Having lived in Los Angeles for some fifteen years, Lippincott expressed great reluctance at the idea of uprooting his family.[3]

A new opportunity then presented itself to Lippincott. Mulholland, who in addition to his duties as water superintendent would be in charge of the aqueduct construction project, asked Lippincott to serve as his assistant chief engineer. The salary, naturally, would be a generous one, and he could continue to regard Los Angeles as his home city when not in the field. The decision was not a difficult one to make. "In view of the many able men in the Reclamation Service and their present complete organization," he informed Governor Pardee, "I am inclined to believe that I can be of greater public service in connection with the Owens Valley Project than I can with the Reclamation Service." The Owens Valley project to which he referred was, of course, the city's project, not the federal government's now-defunct proposal. Lippincott intended to resign as of July 1, but he was compelled to delay the effective date to July 31 as he wrapped up his affairs.[4]

Lippincott's new position (which changed his annual salary from $4,200 as a Reclamation Service engineer to $6,000 as a starting city employee) prompted the *Inyo Register* to observe sarcastically, "We would refer . . . to the files of the *Times* of last fall for reasons why the city should not be niggardly in providing for J. B., for did not that paper give him a large share of the credit for fixing up Owens river matters?"[5] Such criticism was to be ex-

[3]"No Longer Headquarters," *Graphic* 25 (November 3, 1906), 21–22.

[4]Lippincott to Pardee, June 26, 1906, and Pardee to Lippincott, July 3, 1906, Pardee Papers, BL; Lippincott to Newell, August 31, 1906, and Ryan to Lippincott, September 8, 1906, file 23 Alpha. (pt. 1), NPRC.

[5]*Inyo Register*, July 19, 1906 (the weekly paper's date of July 17 is a typographical error). "Are Government Officials Playing Fair? Some Facts about the Owens River Valley Condition," *Irrigation Age* 24 (December, 1908), 41, reported Lippincott's salary at $10,000, which suggests that the sum grew in the retelling.

pected, but it did not prevent Lippincott from posing for a photograph, in the company of Eaton and Mulholland, in the *Los Angeles Times* less than a week after his resignation went into effect. The weekly Los Angeles *Graphic*, whose editor had defended Lippincott's position on numerous occasions, evaluated his pivotal role in the affair. "Mr. Lippincott retires with the highest credentials from the Federal service and with a full vindication over the venomous charges brought against him by those who were interested in misrepresenting his recommendations to the Government concerning Owens River and the great assistance he rendered Los Angeles," the magazine stated, with more enthusiasm than accuracy. "Mr. Lippincott's services as Superintendent Mulholland's coadjutor will be invaluable."[6] Lippincott was already hard at work on his new job, touring the proposed aqueduct line and computing the cost of materials and labor.

More Federal Assistance

Among the many obstacles between the city's plan and its implementation was the need for continuing protection of the project by the federal government. Fortunately for the city the federal government, having given its blessing once, now found it easy to continue to do so. When the federal reclamation project was formally abandoned, the public lands withdrawn from entry by the Department of the Interior were not restored to the public domain. This meant that rival schemes—the city especially feared the opposition of private power companies—could not tie up land or water rights in Owens Valley along the aqueduct route.[7]

In cementing this position further, Los Angeles hit on an original if controversial idea: to have additional areas withdrawn from the public domain, citing the necessity of maintaining the purity of the water to be supplied by the aqueduct or claiming the land as forest rather than agricultural land. Chief Forester Gifford Pinchot proved amenable to the idea. Beginning in February, 1907, a series of withdrawals favorable to the aqueduct project were made

[6]"Lippincott's Service," *Graphic* 25 (July 7, 1906), 17.

[7]R. Woodland Gates to Newell, June 29, 1907, file 63-B, OV-GCRW, RBR.

This water wheel was used to raise water from the principal water ditch at the Los Angeles River to a higher elevation; the water was then stored in a brick reservoir in the plaza. The photograph dates from the late 1860's or early 1870's. *Courtesy of Historical Collections, Security Pacific National Bank.*

The Los Angeles River by the north side of what would be established as Griffith Park, 1895. *Courtesy of Historical Collections, Security Pacific National Bank.*

Los Angeles' first reservoir was this brick structure, located in the city's plaza. *Courtesy of Los Angeles Department of Water and Power.*

William Mulholland, chief engineer of the Los Angeles Department of Water and Power from 1902 to 1929. *Courtesy of Los Angeles Department of Water and Power.*

Joseph Barlow Lippincott, the Reclamation Service engineer who played a crucial role in the Owens Valley–Los Angeles water controversy. *Author's collection.*

Los Angeles Plaza, ca. 1868, shortly after the Los Angeles City Water Company received its franchise. The plaza awaits the improvements designed by Fred Eaton. *Courtesy of Los Angeles Department of Water and Power.*

The Los Angeles Plaza in the 1890's, with the Los Angeles City Water Company headquarters immediately to the east of the plaza. *Courtesy of Los Angeles Department of Water and Power.*

Left: Mary Austin supported her husband in complaints against the Reclamation Service. *Courtesy of Huntington Library. Right*: William B. Mathews, DWP attorney. *Courtesy of Los Angeles Department of Water and Power.*

Left: Frederick H. Newell, chief engineer, U.S. Reclamation Service. *Courtesy of Bancroft Library. Right*: Arthur Powell Davis, assistant chief engineer, U.S. Reclamation Service. *Courtesy of Historical Collections, Security Pacific National Bank.*

Left: Harry Chandler, Otis' son-in-law and an investor in the San Fernando Mission Land Company. *Courtesy of Sherman Library*. *Right*: Moses H. Sherman, member of the Board of Water Commissioners in 1905 and an investor in the San Fernando Mission Land Company. *Courtesy of Sherman Library*.

Left: Edwin T. Earl, publisher of the *Los Angeles Evening Express* and an investor in the San Fernando Mission Land Company. *Courtesy of Historical Collections, Security Pacific National Bank*. *Right*: Harrison Gray Otis, publisher of the *Los Angeles Times* and an investor in the San Fernando Mission Land Company. *Courtesy of Sherman Library*.

The Los Angeles Board of Water Commissioners, 1905. *From left*: John J. Fay, John M. Elliott, Moses H. Sherman, William Mead, and Fred L. Baker. *Courtesy of Los Angeles Department of Water and Power.*

J. B. Lippincott, Fred Eaton, and William Mulholland. This photograph appeared in the *Los Angeles Times* on August 6, 1906, less than a week after Lippincott's resignation from the Reclamation Service became effective. *Courtesy of Los Angeles Department of Water and Power.*

Surveying the proposed aqueduct route, ca. late 1906. *From left*: John R. Freeman, James D. Schuyler, Lippincott, Fred P. Stearns, and Mulholland. Freeman, Schuyler, and Stearns were consulting engineers. *Courtesy of Los Angeles Department of Water and Power.*

An aqueduct construction camp. *Courtesy of Historical Collections, Security Pacific National Bank.*

52-mule team hauling steel pipe into position. *Courtesy of Los Angeles Department of Water and Power.*

Aqueduct siphons used to bring water over the hills down to Los Angeles. *Courtesy of Los Angeles Department of Water and Power.*

Workers pose at the portal of the Elizabeth Tunnel, just north of the
San Fernando Valley, where workers set a record for hard-rock drilling.
Courtesy of Los Angeles Department of Water and Power.

Visiting an aqueduct work camp by motor car. Lippincott is second from right. *Courtesy of Los Angeles Department of Water and Power.*

Inspecting the aqueduct intake gates at Owens River, probably February, 1913. *From left:* Lippincott, Mulholland, Roderick McKay of the engineering department, and Board of Public Works member Edward Johnson. *Courtesy of Los Angeles Department of Water and Power.*

One of the many views taken of the Owensmouth Cascades celebration, November 5, 1913. *Courtesy of Los Angeles Department of Water and Power.*

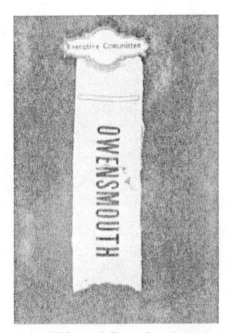

Left: Ribbon of Executive Committee member worn at Owensmouth Cascades celebration, November 5, 1913. *Courtesy of Sherman Library.* *Right*: Souvenir pennant of the Cascades celebration. *Courtesy of Ernest Marquez Collection.*

Engineers turn wheels opening gates of Tunnel No. 108, sending water down the Cascades at the November 5 celebration. *Courtesy of Los Angeles Department of Water and Power.*

William Mulholland, December 27, 1924. *Courtesy of Los Angeles Department of Water and Power.*

The aqueduct after being dynamited, 1927. *Courtesy of Historical Collections, Security Pacific National Bank.*

Repairing the aqueduct after dynamiting, 1927. *Courtesy of Historical Collections, Security Pacific National Bank.*

Left: Andrae B. Nordskog, aqueduct critic and author, who had a major influence on subsequent writers about the water controversy. *Courtesy of Robert Nordskog. Right*: Harvey A. Van Norman, Mulholland's successor as chief engineer of the Los Angeles Department of Water and Power. *Courtesy of Los Angeles Department of Water and Power.*

Saint Francis Dam. The dark triangular stain is normal outflow. *Courtesy of Los Angeles Department of Water and Power.*

Wreckage of the Saint Francis Dam. *Courtesy of Historical Collections, Security Pacific National Bank.*

Devastation caused by the failure of the Saint Francis Dam. *Courtesy of Historical Collections, Security Pacific National Bank.*

At the inquest after the collapse of the Saint Francis Dam. At left is William B. Mathews; Mulholland is second from left. *Courtesy of Los Angeles Department of Water and Power.*

by the Bureau of Forestry. Owens Valley residents soon caught on to the maneuver but found the city's influence impossible to overcome. "During the period of extreme Pinchotism, the Los Angeles water management was the arbiter of settlement in Owens Valley," recalled W. A. Chalfant. For his part, Pinchot considered the issue one of municipal interests against private power companies that were seeking personal gain. "I am impressed by the fact that the chief opposition . . . comes from certain power companies," commented the chief forester, "whose object evidently is for their own pecuniary interest to prevent the municipality from furnishing its own water."[8]

At the National Irrigation Congress meeting at Sacramento in September, 1907, the delegation from Owens Valley confronted Pinchot and Reclamation Service officials and in acrimonious debate accused the government of playing favorites. The Inyoites sought to have resolutions adopted calling for "investigation of alleged official irregularities" and better ways of conducting reclamation work. The delegation also asked the Irrigation Congress to approve its request for proper classification of lands withdrawn by the Bureau of Forestry.

The resolutions were defeated. The city counted too many powerful friends for the decision to have gone otherwise. "Some of the delegates afterward said that Inyo was right," Chalfant bitterly remarked, "but they were not in position to support it." In fact, the Inyo delegation complained so vociferously that it earned the nickname of "kickers from Inyo County."[9]

In September, 1907, Los Angeles asked Pinchot to extend the eastern boundary of the Sierra Forest Reserve to include the portions of Owens Valley that still lacked "protection" from potential

---

[8]W. A. Chalfant, *The Story of Inyo*, p. 368; "To Mr. Smith," *Graphic* 28 (April 25, 1908), 6; *Los Angeles Evening Express*, May 15, 1908; "Owens River Investigation," *Graphic* 24 (March 17, 1906), 18. Department of the Interior withdrawals included one on December 21, 1906, that removed 100,000 acres from the public domain ("Are Government Officials Playing Fair," p. 40).

[9]Chalfant, *Story of Inyo*, pp. 365–366; W. H. Leffingwell to Pardee, February 20, 1908; Newell to Chalfant, March 7, 1908; Newell to P. W. Forbes, March 7, 1908; and Forbes to Newell, March 13, 1908, all in file 63-B, OV-GCRW, RBR.

speculators. Pinchot sent into the valley an investigator, who turned the idea down. A second investigator also reported negatively on the proposal. On the third try, Pinchot received a report favorable to the idea of extending a forest reserve to an area where no trees grew. For this action Congressman Smith severely criticized Pinchot on the floor of the House. Apparently embarrassed by Smith's accusation, California congressmen from the Los Angeles area failed to rise to Pinchot's defense.[10]

Congressman Smith, learning that Pinchot had prepared for Roosevelt's approval a proclamation that would extend the Sierra Forest Reserve's eastern boundary to take in Owens Valley, made an urgent appeal to the president to reject it. He found Roosevelt in the company of Senator Flint and, to Smith's consternation, the president was about to sign the proclamation. Over Smith's protests, Roosevelt signed the document. Los Angeles' water rights remained immune from speculators until the order was withdrawn by President Taft four years later, by which time the aqueduct's construction was almost completed.[11]

Roosevelt has been seen by some writers as someone duped into following the city's wishes, but such a judgment underestimates the president's perceptions and beliefs. He subscribed fully to the utilitarian philosophy of "the greatest good to the greatest number." This can be seen in his speech before the Deep Waterway Convention, given on October 4, 1907, when he was certainly aware of Pinchot's attempts to relocate the Sierra Reserve boundary. In this speech Roosevelt linked water to power production as twin benefits for great numbers of people. "The plan of the city of Los Angeles," he said, "to bring water for its use a distance of nearly two hundred and fifty miles—perhaps the boldest project of its kind in modern times—promises not only to achieve its purpose, but in addition to produce a water-power sufficiently valuable to pay large interest on the investment of over twenty-three million dollars."[12]

[10]Remi Nadeau, *The Water Seekers*, p. 29; Chalfant, *Story of Inyo*, p. 364; Newell to Lippincott, April 2, 1908, and Lippincott to Newell, April 16, 1908, Newell Papers, LC; "Smith," *Graphic* 28 (April 4, 1908), 5–6; U.S. Congress, *Congressional Record*, 60th Cong., 1st sess., 1908, 42, pt. 4, pp. 4120, 4186.

[11]*Los Angeles Times*, April 21, 1908; Nadeau, *Water Seekers*, p. 29.

[12]Theodore Roosevelt, *Works*, 18:152–153.

Clearly, Roosevelt saw not only the benefit to a large population but also the city's intention to pay for the project. As for the wishes of the people living in Owens Valley, Roosevelt regretted their disappointment, but a broader view of distribution and development of the nation's resources required that the valley be sacrificed to the "infinitely greater interest" of the city. And doubts as to how he saw the function of the Reclamation Service were dispelled two months later in his annual message to Congress. "The constant purpose of the government in connection with the Reclamation Service has been to use the water resources of the public lands for the ultimate greatest good of the greatest number."[13]

Another Bond Election

In the spring of 1907 Los Angeles faced the commitment of voting bonds for the construction of the aqueduct. The election campaign in many ways repeated the first bond approval election. There were the exhortations from politicians, newspaper editors, and businessmen that a vote for the bonds was a vote for the city's future. Mulholland's estimate of $23 million, challenged by some critics as unscientific guesswork, had been confirmed by the board of consulting engineers assigned to evaluate the project, and by now Mulholland's status as a water wizard had assumed legendary proportions. Supporters of the bonds campaigned for passage with all the energy active boosters could muster. It was a total effort. The Chamber of Commerce organized the Owens River Campaign Committee, with prominent progressive Republican Meyer Lissner serving as secretary and taking charge of its activities. The Owens River Campaign Committee included representatives from the Chamber of Commerce, the Merchants and Manufacturers Association, the Municipal League, and other important civic and commercial groups.[14]

[13]James D. Richardson, comp., *A Compilation of Messages and Papers of the Presidents, 1789–1908*, 11:1253. For an interesting analysis of Roosevelt's motives, see William L. Kahrl, "The Politics of California Water: Owens Valley and the Los Angeles Aqueduct, 1900–1927, Part I," *California Historical Quarterly* 55 (Spring, 1976), 14.

[14]Vincent Ostrom, *Water and Politics: A Study of Water Policies and Administration in the Development of Los Angeles*, p. 55; J. Gregg Layne, *Water and Power for a Great City: A History of the Department of Water and Power of the City of Los Angeles to December 1950*, p. 105; "The Owens River Report," *Graphic* 26 (December 29, 1906), 10–11.

Committee workers devised any number of ingenious schemes to develop the citizens' water consciousness. Photographic slides of Owens Valley scenes were shown in theaters and at campaign rallies. At one meeting Lippincott's slide presentation was interrupted by a fly's getting on the slide and its shadow projected on the screen. Lippincott took the opportunity to ridicule allegations that Owens River water was impure by saying, "This is a picture of the only microbe in Owens River." People wore lapel buttons with Owens River water attached in tiny vials; stores displayed posters; boys from the Boyle Heights Club fashioned pennants and campaigned for the bond passage; Los Angeles churches designated Sunday, June 9, as "Aqueduct Day"; men drank toasts and women served tea, using Owens River water. Pamphlets were distributed by the thousands. As author Remi Nadeau has observed, "For once Angelenos were taking the same talent for publicity with which they had belabored the East for years and turning it on each other."[15]

Despite the general acceptance of the need for bond passage, a minority remained unconvinced that the city really needed all that water from such a far-off distance. The opposition included such diverse elements as private power companies opposed to municipal power operation, Socialists complaining of the San Fernando Valley speculators, and doubters questioning the water's purity. Foremost among the opposition was Samuel Travers Clover, a newspaperman who had resurrected an old but defunct title, the *News*, to compete with the city's five other dailies. Clover had previously worked for Otis' *Times* and Earl's *Express*, and he approached the bond campaign with a kind of quixotic religious integrity. Ignoring innuendoes that he was being subsidized by the power companies, Clover proceeded to condemn the aqueduct project as financially unworkable, to criticize the water as unnecessary and in fact too alkaline for human consumption, and to proclaim local water resources adequate for the city's needs. Moreover, he boldly took on Otis and the *Times*, charging Otis with creating the aqueduct scheme in order to make a profit out of his San Fernando Valley landholdings.[16]

[15]Nadeau, *Water Seekers*, pp. 32–33; Kahrl, "Politics of California Water," p. 16; *Los Angeles Times*, June 6, 1907.
[16]Anthony Cifarelli, "The Owens River Aqueduct and the Los Angeles *Times*: A Study in Early Twentieth Century Business Ethics and Journalism"

As Otis had done to the *Examiner* in 1905, he now attacked Clover with invective and contempt. He dubbed Clover "Alkali Sammy" and published cruel cartoons, such as the ones depicting Clover as a rather loathsome alligator, or "allegator." Actually, the rivalry between the *News* and the *Times* had gone on for over a year, but the attacks escalated as the June 12 election date neared. Otis had chosen to remain silent on the issue of the San Fernando Mission Land Company. However, Mayor Arthur Harper grew concerned over the effect on the campaign if Clover kept hammering at Otis on the land speculation question. At the urging of Harper, Otis published a lengthy open letter to the mayor in the May 24 issue of the *Times*. "I have no private property interests whatever in the San Fernando Valley," Otis claimed. Furthermore, he had sold out his interest in February, 1905, well before the titanic project was announced and before the Board of Water Commissioners ever approved the concept.[17]

Clover, however, had done his homework—reading back issues of the *Times*—and he reprinted a *Times* editorial from August 23, 1906, wherein Otis had stated that he held "a small interest" in the Porter Ranch property. To be sure, his property interests in the valley had been sold (although he kept his shares in the corporation), and for a generous but not unusual profit. But his dates were wrong. Otis had committed not one but two errors: the statement in the August 23 editorial was a mistake, and his asserted sale in February, 1905, was also untrue. Clover could claim a small victory over Otis on this issue, but he failed totally to convince Los Angeles voters that the project was a plot hatched for the personal aggrandizement of the publisher of the *Times*. Otis simply ignored Clover's accusations and went on to other editorial arguments, such as defending Eaton's role as land buyer and water board agent.[18]

In the closing days of the campaign Clover descended to per-

(Master's thesis, University of California, Los Angeles, 1969), chap. 6, analyzes the Clover-Otis rivalry in the 1907 campaign. See also "Who are the Knockers?" *Graphic* 23 (December 16, 1905), 8–9.

[17]*Los Angeles Times*, May 24 and 25, 1907.

[18]*Los Angeles News*, May 25, 1907; *Los Angeles Times*, May 28, 1907; Richard C. Miller, "Otis and His *Times*: The Career of Harrison Gray Otis" (Ph.D. diss., University of California, Berkeley, 1961), pp. 278–279.

sonal attacks on Mulholland and Lippincott. His insistence on the impurity of Owens River water and his strident dedication to his cause resulted in merchants' withdrawing their advertising and a decline in the *News*'s circulation. Clover could claim a curious kind of integrity when the Pacific Light and Power Company and other private companies ended their opposition to the bonds, since the *Times* could no longer accuse him of serving private power interests. The editor of the *News* overlooked the fact that William Kerckhoff, owner of Pacific Light and Power, was a director of the San Fernando Mission Land Company; he and Henry Huntington, with their diverse business interests, stood to gain in one area even as they lost in another. Before the campaign ended Clover found himself with little more than the support of Job Harriman, an attorney in Socialist politics, and a few others to oppose the bonds.[19]

The outcome was inevitable and probably had been that way all along. "Usually I am not an optimist in such things," observed R. H. Chapman, the editor of the *Graphic*, "but this bond election is such a snap, that the idea of anything like really serious opposition to the issue always has been to me a sort of someone trying to obtain glory or something else, or both, by false pretenses." He predicted a victory margin of seven to one. Otis' major concern was to make the vote as unanimous as possible, and the *Times* ran election-day editorials warning against voter apathy. The Owens River Campaign Committee organized automobiles and carriages to take voters to their polling places. When the votes were counted, the bond supporters could claim a victory margin of ten to one in their favor—21,923 to 2,128. Although the turnout was not large and the margin less than the fourteen to one scored in 1905, it was still an impressive victory. In one precinct the vote was 66 to 1. "The one, poor, misguided, lone voter probably feels lonesome this morning," exulted the *Herald*. "He is reported to be an employee of the *Evening News*."[20]

Samuel Clover accepted the outcome in an editorial entitled

[19]Kahrl, "Politics of California Water," pp. 14–15; Cifarelli, "Owens River Aqueduct and the Los Angeles *Times*," p. 96; *Los Angeles News*, May 28, 1907; Nadeau, *Water Seekers*, pp. 32–33.

[20]*Los Angeles Herald*, June 13, 1907; *Los Angeles Times*, June 12, 1907; "Seven to One," *Graphic* 27 (June 8, 1907), 9.

"Mandate Must Be Obeyed." He conceded his defeat and promised: "There will be no whining by the Evening News, no effort to get a stay of proceedings. The people have taken the responsibility, with all the burdens the enterprise involves, and by their action have relieved us of the duty which we earnestly and conscientiously strove to fulfill, at all times, in the campaign that ended at the polls today." Clover expressed the hope that, with the campaign over, some of his lost advertisers and readers might return to his newspaper. But the damage to the *News* proved fatal, and within a year the newspaper folded.[21]

Clover's campaign against the aqueduct bonds was an uphill struggle with virtually no chance of success. The aqueduct project had captured the imagination of the city, and, when all was said and done, no criticism could detract from the basic realities outlined by Mulholland. The city needed a reliable water supply to ensure growth. Measured against this need, the interests of the land syndicate, which happened to coincide with the interests of the city, made good copy. But the citizens of Los Angeles did not intend to allow such sideshows to divert attention from the main issue: water for maintenance, water for growth. As an added blessing, the electric power that would be generated by the water held the promise of modernizing the city at an inexpensive price and would also be a wholly municipal enterprise. People could envision the aqueduct project as an idea in tune with the progressive spirit of the times, one approved by the president of the United States and, at ten to one, by themselves.[22] Angelenos now waited impatiently for actual construction to begin.

Construction of the Aqueduct

Construction of the aqueduct involved the experimental technology of the new century as well as the proven methods of the past. Automobiles and caterpillar tractors functioned next to mule teams, while electric dredges found use alongside pick and shovel.

[21]*Los Angeles News*, June 12, 1907. Clover became editor of the *Graphic* in September, 1908, and in the 1920's edited *Saturday Night*, a local weekly literary magazine.
[22]"By the Way," *Graphic* 27 (June 15, 1907), 9–10.

Mulholland outlined the broad plan, Lippincott filled in the details, and a host of young engineers, many of whom would make their careers on the grand constructions of the new century, gained valuable experience on the aqueduct project.

The magnitude of the project impressed even Mulholland, who was being prodded by the Los Angeles Board of Public Works, which would be responsible for the aqueduct's construction, to complete the preliminary surveys and plans and get on with the actual work. "The preliminary work necessary to properly enable construction work to begin has been appalling in its magnitude and expense," Mulholland admitted. However, he assured the board "that better and more economic progress could be made with all the accessories in the completed state in which they are now, than to begin in a condition of unpreparedness and run the risk of impeding the work later." By the end of 1908 such preparations had been completed and construction was under way. No less than fourteen divisions were established for apportioning the work of the project, eleven dealing with specific construction locations, plus divisions for railroads, cement works, and power plants.[23]

Although overall the project would send water south on a gravity-flow basis, the aqueduct right-of-way passed through several different types of terrain between the valley and the city. There were several mountain ranges, the Mojave Desert, and numerous hills to consider. Portions of the aqueduct would be lined, other sections unlined, and at key points steel siphons would be needed to bring the water up one side of a mountain and down the other. A series of reservoirs was planned, and a major tunnel had to be bored through the Coast Range to connect the proposed Fairmont Reservoir with a power site in San Francisquito Canyon. The tunnel alone required an estimated five years for completion.

Beyond the details of construction were the problems of hiring thousands of men and handling the payroll, the commissary, housing, supplies, equipment, and maintenance. Supplies were run up in long lists, which included the most miscellaneous items imaginable— $295.90 spent in 1909 for 453 "whips, cushions, etc.," $3.12 spent for 104 glass bottles and corks, $372.67 for over 1,300 pails and

[23]Los Angeles Bureau of the Aqueduct. *Third Annual Report of the Bureau of the Los Angeles Aqueduct to the Board of Public Works.* pp. 7, 9.

buckets, among dozens of other items sorted into nine classifications. The Store Department's supply lists represented just one part of the overall organization. There were an Accounting Department, a Legal Department, and, by far the largest, the Engineering Department with its many divisions. William B. Mathews assumed the leadership of the Legal Department to handle the inevitable lawsuits—in 1908 alone some twenty lawsuits involving the aqueduct were at various stages of litigation in the courts.[24]

Mulholland's secretary, Burt Heinly, advertised the progress of the aqueduct's construction far and wide. A prolific writer, Heinly submitted articles to publications ranging from *National Geographic* to *Scientific American* to *Sunset*, tailoring his style to fit his audience. "Windswept and inhospitable to the tired traveler, the Mojave Desert, with its infrequent water-holes and mile on mile of yellow sand, appears an impossible region in which to quarter an army of five thousand men for four years," he informed readers of *The Outlook*. "And yet this is what a city is doing, under the stalwart leadership of one man." The city was Los Angeles; the stalwart leader, Mulholland. For another popular magazine Heinly exclaimed, "For four years the Owens Valley in name has been to Los Angeles what the El Dorado was to the early California gold seeker." Where the readership was more technically oriented, Heinly toned down his prose and provided facts and figures.[25]

Although Mulholland came to symbolize the motive force behind the aqueduct project, the task of accomplishing the challenge was the work of many men, from Lippincott down through the division engineers to the mule skinners, tunnel borers, and legions of pick-and-shovel laborers. In the course of his work as assistant chief engineer, Lippincott hit on two ideas to reduce costs and increase the rate of construction, goals Mulholland heartily endorsed. One idea was to establish a bonus system for the tunnel crews,

[24]Los Angeles Bureau of the Aqueduct, *Fourth Annual Report of the Bureau of the Los Angeles Aqueduct to the Board of Public Works*, pp. 35–45; *Third Annual Report of the Bureau of the Los Angeles Aqueduct*, pp. 151–152.

[25]Burt A. Heinly, "The Longest Aqueduct in the World," *Outlook* 93 (September 25, 1909), 215; idem, "Los Angeles' Great Aqueduct," *Moody's Magazine* 8 (November, 1909), 339. Other articles by Heinly are listed in the bibliography.

an innovation that spurred the men to reach beyond set goals and
put an element of competition into their labor. If the base footage
of progress was exceeded by the men, they could receive half of the
estimated savings. Everyone benefited from the arrangement: the
men received higher wages, morale was high, and the tunnels—
the most difficult part of the construction project—could be finished
on or before schedule. New records for rapid tunnel construction
were set as different divisions enjoyed a friendly rivalry. The in-
centive factor also contributed to more efficient crews, as loafers
were not tolerated, and a reduction in worker turnover.[26]

Lippincott's second idea called for the use of locally produced
cement for the lining of the channel. To that end a complete cement-
processing plant was established at Monolith, strategically located
halfway down the aqueduct line. Having located local deposits of a
soft volcanic ash known as tufa, Lippincott found it a natural cement
that could be combined with Portland cement. Although the mixture
was slower to harden, it strengthened with age. Use of tufa cement
greatly lowered cement costs, and the Monolith mill eliminated the
high freight charges for transporting cement from distant plants. By
1909 the Monolith mill was in operation, and within two years its
production reached 1,000 barrels a day. Lippincott became so enthusiastic about tufa cement that he publicized its virtues before the
National Association of Cement Users in 1910. Two years later he
presented a major paper on his findings to the American Society of
Civil Engineers. His paper, "Tufa Cement, as Manufactured and
Used on the Los Angeles Aqueduct," was awarded the society's
coveted J. J. R. Croes Medal in 1914.[27]

[26]Kenneth Q. Volk, "Joseph Barlow Lippincott," American Society of
Civil Engineers, Transactions 108 (1943), 1546–47; Los Angeles Department
of Public Service, Complete Report on Construction of the Los Angeles
Aqueduct, pp. 149–156, 199–209. The idea was extended to other areas of
construction, such as the siphon riveting crews.

[27]Volk, "Joseph Barlow Lippincott," p. 1547; Joseph B. Lippincott,
"Experiments with Tufa Concrete," Cement Era 13 (January, 1911), 37–39;
idem, "Tufa Cement, as Manufactured and Used on the Los Angeles Aqueduct," American Society of Civil Engineers. Transactions 76 (December,
1913), 520–581; Los Angeles Board of Public Service Commissioners, Complete Report on Construction of the Los Angeles Aqueduct, pp. 98–110. The
use of tufa cement was not without its critics, however. Several engineers
submitted a pamphlet-form report to the Association of Portland Cement

Although grumblings about his actions as a federal employee could still be heard in Owens Valley, Lippincott preferred not to look back. He served the city that had adopted him as much more than an aqueduct engineer. He was an active member in a number of clubs and professional organizations. Somehow he found time from 1910 to 1917 to serve as a park commissioner. He frequently contributed articles to newspapers and magazines detailing the progress on the aqueduct; on occasion Mrs. Lippincott could persuade him to speak to women's clubs.[28]

Not all of Lippincott's activities concerned tufa cement, bonus systems, or engineering surveys. He often found it necessary to confront some very human problems. Construction work brought tough men to tough places. Lippincott believed the town of Mojave "one of the toughest places in the West, and the officials there have some queer ideas as to the enforcement of the laws." When an aqueduct employee's team of horses was stolen, Lippincott reported, the constable responded to the request for help by stating he was about to get into an important poker game and "would be glad to take up the horse-stealing case, but just then the claims of hospitality would have to be given precedence over those of business."[29]

Manufacturers charging the Monolith and Haiwee cement mills with manufacturing "adulterated" cement (Gervaise Purcell, W. H. Sanders, and Frederick Finkle, *Report on Municipally Manufactured Cements Used on Los Angeles Aqueduct from Owens River to the San Fernando Valley, California*, p. 36).

[28]Typical Lippincott efforts are listed in the bibliography.

Lippincott addressed the Friday Morning Club on May 14, 1909, on "Conservation of Water Power." It is interesting to note that Mrs. Lippincott served as a second vice-president and Mrs. Samuel Clover as the club's corresponding secretary. His speech appeared in the *Los Angeles Herald*, May 15, 1909. Lippincott also attempted to repay Newell for his support during the investigation of 1905–1906. In 1910, at a time when Newell and the Reclamation Service were under attack from critics of Reclamation Service policies, Lippincott wrote Newell offering "to serve you or the Reclamation Service." Newell thanked Lippincott for his concern (Lippincott to Newell, February 5, 1910, and Newell to Lippincott, February 11, 1910, Newell Papers, LC).

[29]*Los Angeles Evening Express*, January 26, 1909. "On Duty at Mojave," *Graphic* 30 (April 10, 1909), 4, also presented this story but with a slight variation: the aqueduct employee had been inside a saloon, while outside his mules (not horses) were being stolen. On another occasion Lippincott's automobile bogged down in the desert. A rancher driving a six-mule team ap-

One persistent irritation plaguing aqueduct officials was the presence of saloons in the small towns and even in the public lands of the desert along the aqueduct route. Saloon owners found the aqueduct employees easy customers for poor-quality whiskey, although Mojave tavern operators refused to allow young Bill Mulholland, the teenaged nephew of the chief engineer, to pay for his drinks. After all, Mulholland and the aqueduct were one and the same, and business had never been so good. Payday incidents occurred all too often. When largely Anglo aqueduct workers ousted Mexican Southern Pacific employees from a Little Lake saloon, the Mexicans soon returned with reinforcements. The aqueduct partisans barricaded the doors and windows of the saloon while the Southern Pacific workers besieged the building for three days and nights. Relieved finally by a combined force of employees from both camps, the aqueduct workers departed from the saloon, leaving it a shambles. "The proprietor of that saloon was so badly frightened," said Lippincott, "that he came to me and begged that I furnish him with a telephone, so that he might call for help in case another outbreak occurred." Lippincott informed the saloon owner that he "was not in the business of providing saloons with telephones at the city's expense," and he refused to do anything to protect the saloon. The owner was compelled to close his saloon at sundown, preferring reduced profits to possible brawls "of the kind that miners and cholos are capable of bringing about when they are full of bad whiskey," as Lippincott put it.[30]

Complaints about the ubiquitous saloons finally resulted in some action being taken against them. On February 5, 1909, the Kern County Board of Supervisors turned down thirteen applications for liquor licenses along the Grapevine Division route, a preventive measure that did nothing about saloons that were already established. Lippincott noted that the saloons were set up on government land

---

peared and, when his mules balked at the sight of the automobile, cursed them so expertly that Lippincott promptly offered him a job. "We need a man who understands mules," said Lippincott, "and you seem to fill the bill." The rancher modestly replied that his vocabulary was actually restricted because he had a copy of *Ladies' Home Journal* with him in the wagon.

[30]*Los Angeles Evening Express,* January 26, 1909; interview with William Mulholland, Van Nuys, California, March 14, 1974.

under Homestead Act provisions, "and there seems to be no way to prevent it."[31]

Help, however, was on the way. The Board of Public Works supported a measure in the state legislature to remedy the problem, and later in the year a bill was passed prohibiting saloons within four miles of the law's intent. The saloon interests challenged the law, and a test case brought the issue to the state supreme court, which upheld the law's constitutionality. Some thirty saloons along the aqueduct route were forced to close by February, 1910.[32]

Mulholland and Lippincott found it necessary from time to time to assure various politicians of the aqueduct's progress. On one such occasion, in April, 1910, six city council members, the city auditor, a representative from the city attorney's office, newspaper reporters, and other notables, accompanied by Mulholland, Lippincott, and the Board of Public Works chairman, General Adna R. Chaffee, journeyed by train from Los Angeles to Mojave "for the purpose of seeing for themselves how the millions of the city's money are being expended on the aqueduct," according to *Examiner* reporter C. A. Hunt. Little could be seen from the windows as the train passed by several work divisions, but Chaffee, Mulholland, and Lippincott had set up a huge map, showing the progress of the aqueduct to date, in the party's private tourist car. From Mojave the group proceeded by automobile some 125 miles to Lone Pine and then on to Independence to see the electric dipper dredges in operation. On such occasions Chaffee proved a genial and informed host, with Mulholland and Lippincott serving as resource persons for the questions asked by the touring VIPs.[33]

To care for the thousands of workers on the aqueduct, the Board of Public Works provided amenities reminiscent of company-town paternalism. Sleeping tents and bunks were provided free, but workers had to supply their own bedding. Married men who had their families with them paid rent for houses or floored frame tents. A hospital department operated field hospitals at nine points along the aqueduct, with medical technicians at each work camp to render

[31]*Los Angeles Evening Express*, January 26, 1909; *Los Angeles Herald*, February 6, 1909.

[32]*Los Angeles Herald*, January 5, 1910.

[33]*Los Angeles Examiner*, April 28, 1910.

first aid for injuries. Employees earning over forty dollars a month paid a monthly fee of one dollar in a crude form of medical insurance; those who earned less than forty dollars paid fifty cents. Laborers' wages began at two dollars per day, but by 1911 few workers earned that low a sum. Individual merit proved of major consideration in promotion and salary increases.[34]

One problem that refused to go away concerned the quality of the food served to the army of workers, as many sometimes as 4,000, strung out in work camps along the aqueduct line. At first the aqueduct project organization included a commissary department, but the difficulties encountered and time consumed in operating it caused a change in policy. On July 3, 1908, the Board of Public Works awarded a contract to D. J. "Joe" Desmond to provide the meals for all the aqueduct workers with the exception of the cement plant, which continued to maintain its own commissary.[35]

Desmond was a thirty-three-year-old businessman, the younger son of the founder of a prominent men's clothing store. He had acquired some degree of fame for his emergency commissary service to the victims of the San Francisco earthquake. Full of energy and enthusiasm, he set about creating an organization that could efficiently feed the workers in the widespread and often remote work camps. Within weeks he established thirty-one cooking camps along the work line, three slaughterhouses, and a series of canteens for the sale of cigars, tobacco, clothing, and other items. By his contract with the Board of Public Works, Desmond was limited to a maximum meal charge of twenty-five cents per meal or five dollars for a twenty-one-meal ticket. To oversee his operation Desmond employed a chauffeur-driven automobile, in which he raced across the desert from one work camp to another. At first the quality of the food could not be faulted: breakfasts of oatmeal, stewed fruit, sirloin steak, bacon and eggs, fried potatoes, biscuits, hot cakes, and coffee; dinners of soup, veal, roast beef, baked beans, mashed potatoes,

[34]Los Angeles Board of Public Service Commissioners, *Complete Report on Construction of the Los Angeles Aqueduct*, pp. 255–256; *Los Angeles Examiner*, May 17, 1912; Nadeau, *Water Seekers*, p. 41.

[35]Los Angeles Board of Public Service Commissioners, *Complete Report on Construction of the Los Angeles Aqueduct*, p. 255; *Los Angeles Times*, undated 1908 clipping, in aqueduct clipping file at Doheny Library, University of Southern California.

salad, pie, and coffee; suppers of meat pie, ham, cold roast beef, spaghetti, stewed prunes, cake, and tea—and this only a partial listing. Observers found the dining tables clean, the kitchens free of flies.[36]

Unfortunately, Desmond found he could not maintain the pace. Meat spoiled in the desert heat, vegetables and other perishables could not be provided, and weevils found their way into the bread. Occasionally food riots erupted in the mess tents. Desmond had not figured an inflation factor into his contract, and increasing food prices soon placed his operation in the red. By 1910 his deficit was in the tens of thousands of dollars and still climbing. He appealed to the Board of Public Works to renegotiate his contract and to raise the meal price to thirty cents, or else take over the operation. After some investigation the board agreed to Desmond's request. As of March 1, 1910, the weekly meal ticket was abandoned, and the thirty-cent price went into effect on November 1.[37]

Reaction from the aqueduct workers was predictable. There had been some grumblings about the quality of the food, particularly after Desmond had begun to cut corners to reduce his deficit. Along with the meal price increase came a reduction in the size of the work force because of a shortage of aqueduct funds. The New York bonding firm, which had been buying bonds ahead of the established rate schedule, decided not to buy additional bonds until the schedule and sale were even again. Mulholland was forced to cut the work force and close down some divisions, laying off workers until money was again available.

The meal price increase and job layoffs provided an opportunity for the Western Federation of Miners (WFM) to begin an active unionizing campaign among those workers still employed on the project. Shortly after the new meal prices went into effect in November, the WFM declared a strike. Tunnel workers, the main work force still employed, left their jobs in protest against the new meal rates, demanding either a wage increase or a return to the old rate.

[36]*Los Angeles Times,* September 8, 1909, and 1908 clipping, Doheny Library; also "Owens River," *Graphic* 29 (July 25, 1908), 5.

[37]Los Angeles Board of Public Service Commissioners, *Complete Report on Construction of the Los Angeles Aqueduct,* p. 256; *Los Angeles Evening Express,* April 1, 1910; *Los Angeles Herald,* March 30, 1912.

Mulholland endured the stoppage, waiting until funds would again be available from the bond sale. The sales resumed in February, 1911, and Mulholland began hiring workers again. Since the project was never a closed shop, the strikers soon gave in, lured by the bonus system and cash advances. By May, 1911, construction all along the aqueduct line had fully resumed, but Mulholland had not heard the last of the unions or their allies, the Socialists, or of the commissary complaints.[38]

Another Land Syndicate

While construction divisions labored in the desert heat on the aqueduct project, a new land syndicate made plans for further development of the San Fernando Valley. The syndicate's membership resembled the San Fernando Mission Land Company, but with some important additions. Involved in this new venture were Harrison Gray Otis, his son-in-law Harry Chandler, and Moses Sherman. Rounding out the "Big Five" who dominated the thirty-man syndicate as a board of control were Otto F. Brant, vice-president and general manager of the Title Insurance and Trust Company, and Hobart J. Whitley, who had achieved some prominence as the developer of Hollywood. In 1909, with Whitley as the main force behind the new syndicate, the Suburban Homes Company was formed. The target of opportunity for the company was the Los Angeles Farm and Milling Company, operated by the Isaac Van Nuys family, which owned 47,500 acres of San Fernando Valley land. J. Benton Van Nuys, representing the family, expressed a willingness to sell; Chandler, acting for the syndicate, obtained an option in September, 1909. The price for the acreage was $2,500,-000, around $53 an acre.[39]

The Suburban Homes Company soon began to ballyhoo its property in a style with which Southern Californians were already long familiar. Otis' *Times* called the valley "the largest single body of fertile, level land in this part of the State, and said to be the

---

[38]Nadeau, *Water Seekers*, pp. 41–43.

[39]W. W. Robinson, *The Story of San Fernando Valley*, p. 37; Remi Nadeau, "The Men Who Opened the Valley," *Westways* 55 (May, 1963), 24; Miller, "Otis and His *Times*," p. 279.

largest single body of land lying so near a big city in the United States"—big enough, indeed, to accommodate perhaps as many as 25,000 people! Plans were carefully made to subdivide the property. The Big Five selected choice portions for their own use. Sherman picked up 1,000 acres around what is now Ventura and Sepulveda boulevards, to be called Sherman Oaks. Otis, further west along Ventura Boulevard, obtained 550 acres that were later sold to Edgar Rice Burroughs and eventually became the heart of Tarzana, named for Burroughs' famous ape-man. Brant took 850 acres at Ventura and Topanga Canyon boulevards and set up a modern dairy ranch there. The developers outlined three new towns—Marion (later renamed Reseda), Owensmouth (later renamed Canoga Park), and Van Nuys. The acreage was subdivided into tracts varying from 5 to 20 acres in size and selling at from $150 to $600 per acre.[40]

Despite their proximity to Los Angeles, the new subdivisions lacked feasible transportation to the city. A Southern Pacific line ran through the valley, but much more was needed. The company proceeded to supply it. A paved road over Cahuenga Pass provided automobile access to the valley. Paralleling the road over the pass went an extension of Pacific Electric streetcar trackage all the way to Owensmouth; the Pacific Electric company received $150,000 and a free right-of-way for building the extension.[41]

Whitley's grand stroke, however, was the creation of a highway twenty-two miles in length, running east-west across the valley. Considering that the road initially was surrounded by nothing but barley fields, its scale was colossal. Two hundred feet wide, with two kinds of pavement—asphalt for automobiles, oil-macadam for horsedrawn vehicles—and with streetcar tracks down its center— the street boasted electric lighting and landscaping that included rosebushes, oleanders, magnolias from the South, acacias from Australia, fan palms from the Canaries, deodars from India, and other exotic trees and shrubs. There was no speed limit. "If there is, anywhere, a highway that exceeds Whitley's twenty-two mile boulevard in width, length, and in the variety and character of its arboreal

[40]*Los Angeles Times*, September 24, 1909; Robinson, *The Story of San Fernando Valley*, p. 38; Nadeau, "Men Who Opened the Valley," pp. 24–25. Marion was the name of Harry Chandler's wife, who was also Otis' daughter.
[41]Nadeau, "Men Who Opened the Valley," p. 25.

ornamentation, it has succeeded effectively in hiding its light under a bushel basket," admired an awed contemporary observer. In naming his showcase boulevard, Whitley used the name of one of the syndicate's members, and Sherman Way was born.[42]

Whitley lost no time in promoting the new subdivisions. To assist in the promotion he brought in William P. Whitsett as sales manager for the Van Nuys subdivision. Whitsett offered a free barbecue, discounted tickets on the Southern Pacific, built ten houses, and staged a grand auction on Washington's birthday, 1911, to open Van Nuys. Thousands came; hundreds bought. A lot was sold every three minutes. Before the year ended, the Pacific Electric connection was completed; within eighteen months the population of Van Nuys was almost 1,000. Whitley followed the Van Nuys success with the Owensmouth opening on March 30, 1912, the auction almost getting lost amid the free barbecue, a race between an airplane and an automobile, and other stunts. The Marion subdivision was launched four months later. Within a three-year period, development of the San Fernando Valley had leaped from its eastern fringe far westward across the valley's barley, bean, and potato fields.[43]

All of this overnight development was performed with the anticipation in mind that the Owens River–Los Angeles aqueduct would shortly become a reality, and with its completion the valley's farms would be able to obtain the water needed to make them function. Considerable argument arose among Los Angeles officials as to how the surplus water—five times as much as was needed in 1913—might be sold. Some officials proposed a consolidation of Los Angeles City and Los Angeles County. Others suggested a complicated plan to charge what the traffic would bear for irrigation use by territories outside the city limits. Mulholland favored the recommendations outlined in a report, submitted to the Public Ser-

[42]Walter V. Woehlke, "The Rejuvenation of San Fernando," *Sunset* 32 (February, 1914), 363; *Los Angeles Examiner*, October 30, 1912. Also to be found in the valley are Chandler Boulevard and a surprisingly modest Otis Avenue.

[43]Nadeau, "Men Who Opened the Valley," pp. 26–27; Merle Armitage, *Success Is No Accident: The Biography of William Paul Whitsett*, pp. 131–133. Whitsett was appointed to the Water and Power Commission in 1924 and later headed the Metropolitan Water District.

vice Commission, that called for annexation of communities desiring to use surplus Owens River water. The city fought its way through several elections before resolving the issue in favor of an annexation policy.[44]

For the San Fernando Valley there was little choice in the matter. On March 29, 1915, residents of some 105,000 valley acres, including areas besides those developed by the Surburban Homes Company, voted to join the City of Los Angeles. On May 4, Los Angeles voters approved the annexation. Together with 4,712 acres in Palms, the annexation more than doubled the size of the City of Los Angeles—from 107.62 to 284.81 square miles. Over the next dozen years further annexations would enlarge the city's boundaries to well over 400 square miles.[45]

Investigating the Project

As the aqueduct neared completion, complaints mounted about its cost, the efficiency of its construction, the profits of private land speculators in the San Fernando Valley, and whether all the water

[44]Ostrom, *Water and Politics*, pp. 149–157; J. H. Quinton et al., *Report upon the Distribution of the Surplus Waters of the Los Angeles Aqueduct*, pp. 19–21; R. F. Goudey, "The Role of Water Supply in the Expansion of the City of Los Angeles through Annexation," typescript, Doheny Library, University of Southern California, Los Angeles. The question of whether Los Angeles had the right in the first place to acquire the water of a geographically distant source has been carefully examined and justified by Gordon R. Miller, "Los Angeles and the Owens River Aqueduct" (Ph.D. diss., Claremont Graduate School, 1978), pp. 124–126, 229, and in Miller's important article, based on chapter 3 of his dissertation, "Shaping California Water Law, 1781 to 1928," *Southern California Quarterly* 55 (Spring, 1973), 9–42.

[45]Ostrom, *Water and Politics*, pp. 157–158; Nadeau, "Men Who Opened the Valley," p. 27; Richard D. Bigger and James D. Kitchen, *How the Cities Grew: A Century of Municipal Independence and Expansionism in Metropolitan Los Angeles*, pp. 166–172; Robinson, *Story of San Fernando Valley*, p. 40. Robinson repeated essentially the same material in a sequence of publications, including several published in numerous editions and revised from time to time, from the 1930's to the 1960's. See his publications: *The San Fernando Valley: A Calendar of Events*, 1938 edition; "The Rancho Story of San Fernando Valley," *Historical Society of Southern California Quarterly* 38 (September, 1956), 225–234; "Myth-Making in the Los Angeles Area," *Southern California Quarterly* 45 (March, 1963), 90–91; and *Los Angeles: A Profile*, pp. 108–109.

was really needed. Many of these issues, already discussed in the
bond campaigns of 1905 and 1907, became a source of debate in
the municipal election of 1911. Generally considered a test between
labor and capital, focusing on the controversial trial of the Mc-
Namara brothers for the bombing of the *Los Angeles Times* on
October 1, 1910, the 1911 election also produced its share of argument over the conduct of aqueduct officials.

The election featured the rather unusual situation of an archconservative *Los Angeles Times* supporting a public water project
(which also included municipal power), while the Socialist candidate, Job Harriman, attacked the aqueduct as a scheme foisted on
the people by the land speculators. Harriman was favored to win
the election because of his position as a defense attorney for the
McNamaras and his endorsement of their innocence. He succinctly
stated the case for the aqueduct's opponents. "Big business, realizing
the wonderful possibilities of profit to be made in exploiting land and
water in the vicinity of Los Angeles, conceives a gigantic plan and
starts to carry it out with official aid," Harriman declared. Key
elements of the plot included buying all available land in and
around the San Fernando Valley, creating a fake water famine that
frightened the citizens of Los Angeles into supporting an aqueduct
construction project, bringing Owens River water to irrigate the
San Fernando Valley, and obtaining a $50,000,000 profit for the
land syndicate "while the city gets none of the aqueduct water."
Harriman accused Leslie C. Brand, Fred Eaton, and William Mulholland of complicity in this plot, each man having done his nefarious duty in defrauding the people of Los Angeles.[46]

The efforts to unionize the aqueduct workers and the complaints about Desmond's commissary service failed to disappear
even after Mulholland was able to resume construction fully. He
now found these complaints merging with the Socialist criticisms of
the very need for the aqueduct. Periodically, he had been compelled
to answer one charge or another about the project, but his focus was
usually a narrow one. Mulholland defined the aqueduct project in

[46]*The Coming Victory*, November 25, 1911, quoted in Ostrom, *Water
and Politics*, pp. 56–57; Edmund Norton, "Politics in Los Angeles," *The
Public* 14 (November 24, 1911), 1191.

engineering terms that excluded the activities of land syndicates or political manipulations. "God Almighty made the topography," he said, "and we had to take reservoir sites where we could find them."[47]

Since the chosen reservoir sites lay in close proximity to the San Fernando Valley, with distribution to the city passing through the valley, questions naturally arose concerning Mulholland's acceptance of divinely ordained topography. At one point enough concern had been expressed about the sites that Mulholland was compelled to present a lengthy communication to the aqueduct's advisory committee. He patiently explained that the aqueduct plans and maps had all along "plainly indicated" that "there were but two reservoir sites in the San Fernando Valley having the proper elevation to serve the purpose of the aqueduct in attaining its fullest advantages." The reasons for the San Fernando location had already been presented in the project's first annual report to the Board of Public Works, but Mulholland repeated the basic problem facing the hydraulic engineer. "It needs little or no engineering knowledge to understand that in the building of such a structure as the aqueduct or its appurtenances it is necessary to rigidly consider and follow the topography of the country, whether for the construction of the canal itself or in the selection of the reservoir sites, wholly disregarding whether the land belongs to Jones, Brown or Robinson," he stated. "The conditions in a mountainous country [such as] in Southern California are arbitrary and the engineering department took no cognizance of land ownership in selecting the route." As it happened, a fair price had been paid for the reservoir sites. "The allegation that a large body of this land was purchased by certain parties following the announcement of the city's purpose to bring the Owens River water here, is not true, as the land in question was in the possession of these parties for quite a long period before the Owens river project was even thought of."

Questions concerning the right-of-way from the San Fernando Valley headworks to the city waterworks were explained by Mulholland, as were points raised on the cost of conveying the water in its last thirteen miles from the end of the aqueduct to the city. How-

[47]Quoted in John R. McCarthy, "Water: The Story of Bill Mulholland," *Saturday Night* 45 (February 12, 1938), 30.

ever, on the last issue presented to Mulholland, the chief engineer
flatly refused to answer any questions:

Regarding the personnel of the board of water commissioners, or any
other board of the city of Los Angeles, . . . it is not an engineering
function, and as to the enhancement of the value of the land it is the
devout wish and hope of the writer that every acre of land, whether
irrigated or not, and every foot of real property within the city will be
enhanced in the manner seemingly deplored in the communication. In
fact it may be said that this was one of the primary purposes of the
aqueduct and it was with the hope of adding to the general prosperity of
the country that the people so nearly unanimously ratified the project.

Then Mulholland concluded, "At the proper time means will no
doubt be devised for properly adjusting the manner of equitably
assessing the direct beneficiaries, but as this is purely a business
matter there is no occasion for its discussion here."[48]

Despite Mulholland's statement and the endorsement of other
engineers,[49] the same arguments surfaced again and again during the
construction period, trying Mulholland's patience. Although the
Socialists lost the 1911 municipal election—the McNamara brothers
changed their plea to guilty just before the December 4 election
day, ruining Harriman's chances—insinuations and, from opponents,
accusations of undue influence by land speculators continued to em-
barrass and harass the chief engineer. To clear the air, Mulholland
asked the city council to establish an aqueduct investigation board
to conduct an impartial investigation that would resolve all complaints concerning the project. Unfortunately for Mulholland's temper, what he received from the city council was a political hot potato.
The council at first appointed five men to the investigation committee. Recognizing the Socialist popular vote in the recent election,
the council assigned two of these positions to Socialists. Then the
council dropped the Socialists from the committee. Outraged, the
Socialists gathered enough signatures in an initiative campaign to
force a special election on May 28, 1912, and won restoration of

[48]*Los Angeles Herald*, April 29, 1909.
  [49]City Engineer Homer Hamlin, along with John H. Quinton and William
H. Code, unanimously concluded "that the San Fernando Valley is the only
place where water can be used in territory contiguous to Los Angeles, which
admits of the economical handling of return water" (*Los Angeles Times*,
August 3, 1911, and see their *Report upon the Distribution of Surplus Waters*).

the Socialist positions. In the meantime, the size of the committee had been reduced from its original five members—attorney Ingle Carpenter, hydraulic engineer Edward Johnson, electrical engineer and aqueduct critic Charles E. Warner, and two Socialists, H. A. Hart and Fred C. Wheeler—to three: Johnson, Warner, and civil engineer Edward S. Cobb. These three conducted an investigation in the spring of 1912. After the May 28 election two Socialists joined the committee but found the non-Socialists reclutant to participate with them, less for ideological reasons than for confusion over the city ordinances that had established and then reconstituted the committee.[50]

An exasperated Mulholland found the political maneuverings maddening. While the Aqueduct Investigation Board, as the committee was called, began its inquiry (minus the Socialists), Mulholland was approached by a reporter who once again brought up the San Fernando Valley land deals. Mulholland blew up. He at last addressed the question of speculative land profits and the aqueduct's creation. "Arable lands which should be selling at about $100 an acre have been seized by a few capitalists who have forced prices to $1,000 an acre," he said. He then angrily divorced what he considered his "duty as an engineer" from the schemes of the land speculators. "Instead of being developed as agricultural lands, the property has been subdivided into town lots and small 'rich men's country estates' at prohibitive values," said Mulholland. "The capitalists have stolen the unearned increment for the next 20 years. The men who have bought up this property have looked forward to the time when the aqueduct would be completed and the plans for distribution of the water through this territory would enhance land values."

Mulholland insisted he had no ulterior motive in his support and work for the aqueduct project. In fact, he did not care whether or not the aqueduct terminated in the San Fernando Valley. His expertise as an engineer, not any involvement with land speculators,

---

[50]*Los Angeles Times*, December 12, 1911; Ostrom, *Water and Politics*, p. 57; Nadeau, *Water Seekers*, pp. 43–44. Nadeau takes a negative view of the Socialist participation, as does Layne, *Water and Power*, pp. 114–115. Layne's interpretation inaccurately describes how the committee came to be constituted, overlooking Mulholland's own request for an investigation.

had determined the terminus of the aqueduct. In any event, the water "must be used somewhere." With the project nearing completion, he could announce that the "strain and the responsibility have shattered my health. Now, under my doctor's advice, I am trying to forget everything connected with the aqueduct. My work is nearly completed, and then I shall take a long rest."[51]

His doctor's advice notwithstanding, Mulholland continued to be very much involved in the final stages of aqueduct construction and the investigation underway concerning the project. Johnson, Cobb, and Warner disagreed on whether to file preliminary reports or to wait until all investigations, including interviews in the field with laborers, foremen, and anyone who had an opinion to offer, could be completed. Warner drafted a preliminary report concerning Desmond's commissary service and asked Johnson and Cobb to sign it. When they refused, Warner filed it anyway, submitting it to the city council on April 2. Warner charged that Desmond had committed such sins as substituting oleomargarine for butter, that inferior food had been provided, that visiting city officials were given free meals, that the men had in effect suffered a wage reduction by having the price of their meals increased, and other sensational claims. Many of Warner's charges, however, were more opinion than substance, such as the claim that Desmond—or any other private contractor—should never have been given the mess contract in the first place, or the view that Desmond had lacked the resources necessary to carry out his contractual obligations.[52]

The City Council received Warner's preliminary report, and a resolution was proposed by one councilman to condemn the Board of Public Works for having awarded the contract to Desmond without first calling for competitive bids. But the council's own investigation produced evidence that the meals were indeed of acceptable quality. One of the foremost defenders of the food was Mulholland. He informed the council, "The first three or four years of the work, I boarded at the same camps with the men and never asked for a specially-prepared meal." He had found that "the average meals were good." Mulholland protested against unjust criticism. "Our

[51]Quoted in McCarthy, "Water," p. 30.
[52]*Los Angeles Herald*, March 30, 1912; *Los Angeles Evening Express*, March 30, 1912.

critics are those who haven't eaten three meals at the camp," he stated. General Chaffee said that the city would have lost money if it had attempted to feed the men. "I never found Mr. Desmond unwilling to improve the mess when I suggested it," he said. In any event, aqueduct personnel were answerable to the Board of Public Works, not the city council, as the aqueduct's legal representative, William Mathews, pointed out. The resolution was turned down, and the commissary system was approved.[53]

The commissary episode indicated that piecemeal revelations would only diffuse whatever influence the Aqueduct Investigation Board might have. When the intitiative to restore the Socialist members to the board was passed on May 28, tensions developed between Johnson and Cobb, on one side, and what had suddenly become an antiaqueduct majority. While Johnson and Cobb considered what their position with the new members should be, plans went ahead for further investigations. Beginning July 9, several weeks of in-depth examination of key aqueduct participants were held. Some five dozen people were called to testify not only on the efficiency of the aqueduct's construction but also on how the city had first come to view the Owens River as its only possible choice for a new water source.

The first people to be called before the Aqueduct Investigation Board were John M. Elliott and John J. Fay, Jr., members of the Board of Water Commissioners when the possibility of an aqueduct from Owens Valley had first been proposed. On the second day of testimony, Wednesday, July 10, Mulholland himself was summoned. He answered one question after another concerning not only the aqueduct's construction, financing, and management, but also how the city had come to select the Owens River as the solution to its water problems. He appeared again on July 11, patiently responding to the board's sometimes repetitive questions.[54]

The line of questioning soon grew tiresome to Johnson and Cobb, who had already spent considerable time investigating various charges and finding them without foundation. They considered much of what was now under discussion to be irrelevant. On Monday,

[53]*Los Angeles Examiner*, May 17, 1912.
[54]Los Angeles Aqueduct Investigation Board, *Report of the Aqueduct Investigation Board to the City Council of Los Angeles*, pp. 40–52.

July 15, Cobb and Johnson tendered their resignations and submitted their own report, "because in our judgment the board is not acting on its own initiative." The engineers felt that "outside influences" were dictating to the Socialist board members. They also objected to the lack of qualifications the Socialists brought to the task. "There is not on the board a sufficient number of members, who, by education or experience, have become familiar with the serious problems incident to the subjects under investigation," Cobb and Johnson informed Mayor George Alexander. Since they, as two-thirds of the investigating board as constituted under the earlier ordinance, had spent some four months doing what the enlarged board now purported to be doing, Cobb and Johnson were submitting their own report, believing "that further service on our part is unnecessary and useless."[55]

Neither Cobb nor Johnson apparently considered their report to be a minority view. Instead, they believed that under the ordinance establishing their board as consisting of three members, theirs was the majority view, and the current investigation a waste of time. Their report generally was favorable to the aqueduct project. Investigation of the various charges had shown them to be specious. "There has not been brought to our attention one particle of evidence that would reflect in any manner whatever upon the integrity of the management of the Aqueduct proposition from its inception to the present time," they declared. This broad conclusion took into account such issues as the purchase of Owens Valley water rights, the city's plans for distribution of the surplus water, pending lawsuits against the city, the activities of the two land syndicates in the San Fernando Valley, the efficiency of construction, and all other complaints. On the basis of their investigation, the two men concluded that "we can assure the citizens of Los Angeles that they have received for their expenditure of money a conduit constructed in a most economical manner, of materials of sufficient adaptability to the purpose for which they were used to make the construction permanent and reliable, showing workmanship as good as should be demanded."[56]

[55]Johnson and Cobb to Alexander, July 15, 1912, reproduced in ibid., p. 29.
[56]*Report of the Aqueduct Investigation Board*, p. 33. The Cobb-Johnson

The remaining board members could hardly have disagreed more with the Cobb-Johnson report. They stood worlds apart on virtually every issue, for understandable reasons. Mayor Alexander afterward criticized them as "men of no experience or qualification fitting them to conduct the proposed investigation." The mayor observed that the two Socialists opposed the investigation "so long as conducted by anybody but the Socialists." The final member, Warner, was "a man who showed by his conduct that he was just as prejudiced as the two Socialists were."[57]

Despite the disapproval of the city's political and business leaders, the remaining board members gamely continued their work. The mayor's criticisms notwithstanding, Warner and the Socialists, E. C. Cady and Henry A. Hart, indicated by their pursuit of controversial points that they had at least done their homework. They put Mulholland through a total of four days of testimony. On Wednesday, July 17, they summoned Lippincott. Occasional acrimony rippled to the surface as questioning brought up Lippincott's past performance with the Reclamation Service. The camping trip to Yosemite, Eaton's plans for the Owens River, when those plans had been made, and Lippincott's service to the city while a federal employee were again reviewed. Lippincott soon became impatient with the line of questioning:

Q. What attitude did Mr. Elliott and other members of the Board [of Water Commissioners] take on this proposition when first presented to them?
A. Do you mean Mr. Eaton's proposition?
Q. Yes.
A. I don't know.
Q. You never discussed that with the Board; I think you said you advised the Board not to engage in that sort of enterprise?
A. I did not say it.
Q. What did you say in that connection?
A. I don't think that this line of investigation is fair. I am perfectly willing to make a statement of facts, but I am not willing to go and say things over and over and over, in the hope that I might make

report was reproduced in the *Report of the Aqueduct Investigation Board* on pp. 32–35 and again on pp. 69–72.

[57]Alexander to George B. Caldwell, October 11, 1912, reproduced in ibid., p. 29.

some slight deviation on cross examination. There is nothing fair about that.

Q. I think you advised the Board not to engage in that enterprise.

A. I did not say it.

Q. You say, that the Reclamation Project was not seriously regarded by the United States Reclamation Service?

A. I do not think it is fair in this cross examination to try to put words into my mouth. I understand that this Board is a Board that is trying to get at the truth and not to try to trap me by miserable statements of that kind.

Q. I am not trying to trap you.

A. I resent it. I claim that was trying to put in my mouth words I did not say.

At one point Lippincott protested against malicious statements that had been made against him during the campaign for the May 28 special election. "I really have a whole lot of pride in this job," he said, "a whole lot of pride in my professional standing and it is a pretty severe thing for a man to spend 25 years in building up a reputation and then to have it destroyed in an unnecessary and ruthless way, and I feel pretty keenly some of these things that have been said about me and would like to have you go into those statements." Even the Socialists conceded Lippincott's point. Hart observed, "I think it was very unwise to say so myself, notwithstanding I am told that it was from a man of my party." To which Lippincott responded, "Well, a professional man has a reputation to make a living out of."[58]

In the days following Lippincott's testimony the board questioned a succession of city officials, businessmen who had various contracts for aqueduct construction supplies, and aqueduct workers from division engineers to foremen and laborers. An odd note was struck when Edward Cobb appeared on July 24. He was asked about the report he and Johnson had submitted on the fifteenth:

Q. That report, I take it, was filed by you—in just what capacity were you acting in filing that report? As members of the old board?

A. I will be hanged if I know myself. I don't know what I was at the

[58]*Report of the Aqueduct Investigation Board*, pp. 53, 56. During the initial investigations Lippincott had written to Newell lamenting that "this Aqueduct Investigation has degenerated into a political affair," and restating his belief that he had done nothing illegal (Lippincott to Newell, April 10, 1912, file 63-B, OV-GCRW, RBR).

time I compiled it and submitted it, except in this way, that I felt that the City Council had a right to such a report from its former appointees, and just what capacity that would put a fellow in you can figure out better than I can.

As questioning continued it became obvious that the current board members were attempting to determine under what authority Cobb and Johnson had written their report. After considerable hair-splitting, Cobb and the board members more or less agreed that the ordinance establishing the new board had replaced the ordinance creating the earlier one. The current board sought this assurance, technical as it might sound, because the mayor had solicited Cobb's and Johnson's views and the current board needed to validate its own authority in the face of a hostile Mayor Alexander.[59]

The final witness—William B. Mathews, who doubted the board had the authority to require that witnesses take an oath, but who took one anyway—appeared on August 16, and Warner, Hart, and Cady then tried to pull all the pieces of testimony together. On August 31 they submitted their own "Report of the Aqueduct Investigation Board" to the city council. Its conclusions differed considerably from the Cobb-Johnson report. In fact, no less than 135 conclusions were presented. They ranged from relatively innocuous statements to severe condemnations of the actions of Otis, Earl, their respective newspapers, the land syndicates, the expertise consulted in surveying possible new water sources for the city, the money paid for water rights, the arrangement with Eaton, the quality of tufa cement, and many, many other criticisms. In some areas the criticisms were not only justifiable but eventually would be justified, as in the city's failure to obtain more than a hundred-foot easement from Eaton at Long Valley for a storage reservoir; not until the late 1930's would this failure be remedied, with the construction of Crowley Lake. The large number of conclusions, however, was soon ridiculed by Mayor Alexander. Unfortunately for the board, in its haste to complete its report it had greatly diminished the effect of the criticisms by failing to pull the conclusions together. To state "that the project also had the support of the Los Angeles *Express*" was not much of a conclusion, since it conveyed nothing that was

[59]*Report of the Aqueduct Investigation Board*, pp. 67–69.

not already known to everyone, but Mayor Alexander counted it
with the same value he gave to the conclusion that Otis, Earl, Sherman, and others benefited from private information to make a killing
on San Fernando Valley property—a conclusion Alexander of
course disputed.

In fairness to the Aqueduct Investigation Board, a question of
semantics enters here, since the board's last fourteen conclusions
were actually recommendations. The board's poor choice of words—
"As a result of our investigation, we present the following conclusions"—enabled Alexander to count each subsequent statement in
the report as a separate conclusion and indict the sum total as "the
veriest rot."[60]

The mayor, as it turned out, had the last word. The board
hoped to publish its findings as an eight-volume series, including its
summary and conclusions along with reports on specific subjects, an
illustrated description by Warner of the aqueduct and the city's
sources of water, and additional reports on water-supply possibilities. The last four volumes would contain the transcript of the
testimony taken between July 9 and August 16. At the "suggestion"
of Alexander, the city council instead authorized the publication of a
single volume—an unwieldly, folio-size book containing not only
the board's report and the transcript of the hearings, but also the
Cobb-Johnson report and a lengthy letter from Alexander to George
Caldwell, president of the Investment Bankers Association of America. Alexander's letter reproduced the entire board report, enumerat-
ing each conclusion and annotating it with remarks that refuted
many of the board's criticisms. Alexander also included other correspondence laudatory of the aqueduct and the city's goals, as well
as letters criticizing the board. All of this material was unattractively
presented in a four-column-to-the-page format. The transcript of
testimony was riddled with inconsistencies in chronology, recording
persons in attendance, and spelling of names. J. Gregg Layne, the
official historian of the Los Angeles Department of Water and
Power, would many years later dismiss the report as "an outstanding

---

[60]Ibid., pp. 30–31; Ostrom, *Water and Politics*, p. 57, accepts the number
135 uncritically.

example of waste of money and effort on the part of a few men to create confusion and distrust."[61]

Mulholland had requested an investigation to clear the air of malodorous implications of corruption. He obtained instead a forum tainted with local politics and polarized by such tragic events as the *Times* bombing and the bitterness of Socialists betrayed by their own potential martyrs, the McNamara brothers. In contrast to the effort by the mayor and the city council to make the report difficult for the average citizen to digest, many people found much of value in it. Such issues as the land syndicates in the San Fernando Valley, the distribution of surplus Owens River water, and the possibility of inefficiency and incompetence in the construction of the aqueduct now played a major part in the 1913 municipal election. Henry H. Rose, with Socialist support, was elected mayor on his promise of dealing with corrupt practices relating to the aqueduct. Following the election, Rose toured the aqueduct line and came back converted to its civic perfection, denying there was faulty construction, incompetence, or any other problem.[62]

[61]Layne, *Water and Power*, p. 114. Much was made of part of the eightieth and eighty-first conclusions: "That no direct evidence of graft has been developed," and "that the Aqueduct system affords opportunities for graft, and that if this Board had had the necessary time to develop all facts along lines suggested by individuals, a knowledge of human nature indicates that men would have to be found who had succumbed to temptation" (*Report of the Aqueduct Investigation Board*, p. 3). In other words, the board smelled smoke but saw no fire. The *Report* did, however, raise many questions concerning financing, record keeping, and the motives of the land syndicates. Although the city council published the board's report in such an inconvenient form, it also separately printed 10,000 copies of the Cobb-Johnson report as *Report on the Los Angeles Aqueduct, after an Investigation Authorized by the City Council of Los Angeles*.

[62]Ostrom, *Water and Politics*, pp. 58–59. W. T. Spilman, *The Conspiracy: An Exposure of the Owens River Water and San Fernando Land Frauds*, reiterated many of the charges of the 1911 election campaign. On Spilman's pamphlet, see Miller, "Los Angeles and the Owens River Aqueduct," pp. 230–232. Another aqueduct critic who over a period of years remained a steadfast opponent of the aqueduct was Frederick C. Finkle. He was coauthor, with Purcell and Sanders, of the *Report on Municipally Manufactured Cements*. Other examples of his work include "Los Angeles Aqueduct Mistakes," *Journal of Electricity, Power and Gas* 34 (January 9, 1915), 25–28, and "Los Angeles' $40,000,000 White Elephant," *Irrigation Age* 30 (May, 1915), 200–202, 216.

Two versions of the aqueduct's history had emerged from the newspaper campaigns of 1905 and 1907 and from the Aqueduct Investigation Board of 1912. There were those who hailed the project as the greatest contribution to the city's development since the arrival of the railroad in 1876, and there were those who condemned the entire effort as a scheme to enrich key local businessmen at the expense of Los Angeles taxpayers. The dual view of the aqueduct would prove most irritatingly enduring.

Dedicating the Aqueduct

As the aqueduct neared completion, plans were formulated for a celebration to greet the arrival of Owens River water, if not in the city proper, then where it would enter the San Fernando Valley. Completion of all construction was estimated for July, 1913, and in February the first Owens River water was turned into the intake, to be stored at the Haiwee Reservoir. Early in May the reservoir gates were opened and the water moved through the conduit across the Mojave Desert. A major setback occurred when the inclined pressure tunnels at Sand Canyon failed, necessitating replacement with steel siphons. Dedication of the aqueduct was put off until November.[63]

Wednesday, November 5, 1913, began as a cool, clear day, ideal for an outing to the northern end of the San Fernando Valley. Four miles north of the city of San Fernando, near what is now Sylmar, a huge trough leading downhill from an aqueduct tunnel would pour Owens River water into storage reservoirs. Between 30,000 and 40,000 people decided to make the outing. Automobiles and horse-drawn carriages shared the dusty roads to the Cascades, as the outlet was called. Since the festivities were scheduled to begin at 11:00 A.M., people planned an early morning start. The official party—Mulholland, Chaffee, Lippincott, civic notables—left the Chamber of Commerce building in Los Angeles at 9:30, leading a parade of vehicles. The city's banks printed free programs listing the schedule of events. Comfort stations were set up to accommodate the

---

[63]Nadeau, *Water Seekers*, pp. 47–48; *Los Angeles Examiner*, October 26, 1912.

crowds. The programs, circulated in the tens of thousands, advised people to take their own drinking cups.

Amid the milling crowds and helter-skelter parking of a wide assortment of vehicles, a grandstand platform had been erected. The celebration commenced with a band concert. Mulholland arrived and took his seat on the platform to the applause of a crowd that was unaware of the latest pressure on the chief engineer. Mulholland's wife was seriously ill, and he had left the hospital only with reluctance. Word of any change in her condition was to be sent to him. The ceremony began with everyone singing "America." Congressman William D. Stephens gave the first address, followed by soprano Ellen Beach Yaw, who sang "Hail the Water":

> Lift your voice in gratitude,
> A river now is here,
> Whose glorious waters flowing free,
> A paradise will rear.
> Here within this land of love,
> May peace forever reign,
> For God has brought us waters pure,
> That Eden we regain.

Another speech, this one given by Chamber of Commerce President Arthur W. Kinney; more music; then it was the turn of former Governor Pardee. After another musical interlude, Mulholland's turn came, to present the aqueduct to the City of Los Angeles. He received a standing ovation complete with hats thrown into the air. Following a short speech—he had made no notes—in which he praised all those who had helped build the aqueduct, Mulholland was given a silver loving cup, as was Lippincott. The time had arrived to open the gates and release the water. By prearranged signal, Mulholland unfurled an American flag. Battery A of the Seventh Regiment, United States Army, fired a salute. At the top of the Cascade, several engineers turned the large wheels that raised the metal gates. Down came the water, slowly at first, then a churning torrent, down to the grandstand and then on to the San Fernando Reservoir.

The formal program was abandoned as thousands of spectators rushed to the sides of the Cascade "so that they could tell their grandchildren that they, by golly, had been right on hand to see water spurt out of the world's greatest pipe," as a biographer of Mulholland later put it. Mulholland turned to Mayor Rose, who was scheduled to accept the water on behalf of the city. Choked with emotion, he said five words: "There it is. Take it." The laconic presentation quickly added to the Mulholland legend. "Those brief words were more eloquent, more symbolic of the grim, dogged persistence that built the aqueduct than any 'silver-tongued' oratory could have been," observed Boyle Workman in his history of Los Angeles. On a personal level, Mulholland was elated to learn a few minutes later that his wife's condition had improved. Along with thousands of others, Mulholland took a drink of Owens River water.[64]

A Friendship Ended

One major figure did not attend the aqueduct dedication. Fred Eaton and William Mulholland were no longer friends. Their relationship had become strained, then finally ruptured over the issue of a storage reservoir at Long Valley. The Water Department wanted a 140-foot dam, which would have a storage capacity that would benefit both city and valley, meeting the future needs of both during dry years. Eaton owned 12,000 acres in Long Valley and wanted at least a million dollars for the property. Mulholland found this an unacceptable figure and also rejected later proposals from Eaton, feeling that his old friend was trying to take advantage of him. Finally, the two men broke over the issue, refusing to see each other.

Because of this personal relationship, the City of Los Angeles postponed construction of a reservoir in Long Valley, although it did have a 100-foot easement there. The lack of such a storage facility meant that Los Angeles, with the aqueduct intake located south of most of the Owens Valley farms and irrigation ditches, could very well not have enough water to run through the aqueduct during a drought period. Attempts by valley and city representatives to reach an agreement on division of the river's stream flow were

[64]Nadeau, *Water Seekers*, pp. 49–51; John McKinney, "Rafting down a River of Schemes," *New West* 4 (January 1, 1979), 72; McCarthy, "Water" (February 26, 1938), 38; Boyle Workman, *The City That Grew*, pp. 315–316. Workman assumed the five-word speech was Mulholland's only statement, overlooking the earlier speech.

at first hopeful for mutual understanding. Negotiations bogged down when H. A. Hart, one of the members of the defunct Aqueduct Investigation Board, obtained an injunction against such a settlement, claiming that the city's best interests were not being served.

While Eaton and Mulholland remained at a standoff, the city soon had second thoughts about guaranteeing water to Owens Valley residents without knowing how much water would be left for the aqueduct in a dry year. Settlement of problems and grievances awaited some development that would spur either side to new action.[65]

[65]Nadeau, *Water Seekers*, pp. 52–53; Ostrom, *Water and Politics*, pp. 58–59; Layne, *Water and Power*, pp. 150–151, 156–157.

6

The Water Wars of the 1920's

"The people of the valley are left in the worst possible condition."—A. H. Swallow, quoted in the *Los Angeles Times*, October 6, 1927

A decade passed. During that time the controversy simmered, never entirely gone from people's minds. With the aqueduct completed and a fact of life, Owens Valley settled in for a period of uneasy coexistence. The general view was that the valley could still enjoy prosperity and development, that there was enough water for everyone if only a proper reclamation project could be constructed or an adequate storage reservoir be made a part of the aqueduct system.

Lippincott's recommendation to abandon the federal reclamation project had not meant the abandonment of valley settlement. The valley north of Independence contained the bulk of Inyo County's population, its lands were more fertile, and its irrigation system was already established through private-enterprise construction of canals and ditches. The city's aqueduct intake, located south of the most settled part of the valley, affected few farmers, and those who had sold their property to the city had made a neat profit.

After losing their hoped-for project, valley residents persisted in attempting to renew the interest of the federal government in an Owens Valley reclamation project. Such efforts, however, proved disappointing. As late as 1919 Owens Valley residents were still appealing to Arthur Powell Davis, who had replaced Newell as director of the Reclamation Service. Davis' response to such appeals was negative. As far as Davis was concerned, any possible Reclamation Service plans had ended with the construction of the aqueduct. "I do not regard the Owens Valley irrigation project as feasible," he stated, "and it certainly is not contemplated for construction by the Reclamation Service."[1]

If the idea of a federally sponsored project thus seemed remote, at least the hope of some sort of major development remained alive. Such hopes, however, were more immediately realized in fiction than shown in fact. In 1914 Peter B. Kyne, a prolific author of western and adventure stories, wrote *The Long Chance*, a tale of intrigue and adventure set in the Mojave Desert, Bakersfield, and Owens Valley, with some side trips to San Francisco and Los Angeles. Kyne's mining-engineer hero envisioned a huge reclamation project in Owens Valley, privately financed, at a time after Los Angeles had announced its aqueduct plans.[2]

Even Mary Austin found hope for the future. Her novel *The Ford*, which appeared in 1917, continued the optimism of *The Long Chance*. Despite the disappointments in her personal life, Austin, who fictionalized the locale of her novel and merged Los Angeles' intentions with San Francisco's ambitions in the Hetch Hetchy Valley of Yosemite, still believed some sort of Owens Valley project was feasible. In her novel she provided roman à clef characterizations of Eaton, Mulholland, Lippincott, and other people involved in the actual events. Lippincott in particular received a negative appraisal as the corrupt government engineer who went along with a scheme to acquire "Arroyo Verde" water rights in the "Tierra Longa" Valley. Although Austin hardly concealed her contempt for the Eaton and Lippincott characters in her novel, in 1917 she believed Tierra Longa, the typification of her Land of Little Rain, the Owens Valley, still had a future. The Owens Valley–Los Angeles aqueduct was an accomplished fact; yet it seemed possible for the valley to retain its promise of potential development.[3]

Willie Chalfant, the Bishop editor who had branded Lippincott as Judas, also found cause for optimism. In 1921 he researched and wrote *The Story of Inyo*, a history of Inyo County. His last chapter

---

[1]Davis to W. B. Mathews, January 27, 1919, file 27-A, OVPM, RBR. In the same file, see also W. W. Watterson to Davis, January 24, 1919, and Davis to Watterson, February 5, 1919.

[2]Peter B. Kyne, *The Long Chance*.

[3]Mary Austin, *The Ford*. These and other novels are discussed in Abraham Hoffman, "Fact and Fiction in the Owens Valley Water Controversy," Los Angeles Westerners Corral, *Brand Book No. 15*, pp. 181–186.

dealt with the aqueduct controversy. After noting the strength of the city and the futile attempts of the valley to oppose Los Angeles, Chalfant observed that discussions between the two factions were progressing toward agreement on such crucial points as a storage reservoir in Long Valley large enough for everyone's needs. In fact, "negotiations for a clear definition of rights and guarantees are in progress—as they have been for long past," noted Chalfant. "A satisfactory agreement should be the final chapter of a long-standing question, and its consummation will be local history of the first importance."[4]

Chalfant was soon disabused of his optimistic expectations. In 1923 Mulholland, with an obvious eye to the publicity his act would generate, hoisted his sleeping bag to his shoulder and announced he was on his way to inspect the Colorado River. Now almost seventy years old, Mulholland actually forsook the rigors of a camping trip along the lines of his 1904 outing with Eaton to Owens Valley. Instead, he and his engineers availed themselves of more modern conveniences (once the photographers had fulfilled their obligations to the Mulholland mystique) as they went to the Colorado River to investigate the possibility of yet more water and power for their growing city.[5]

For Los Angeles was getting thirsty again. The city had indeed grown since the turn of the century, beyond the wildest speculations of the most imaginative booster. The 1920 census revealed a population of more than 576,000 people in the city itself, with adjacent communities similarly sharing in the influx of new citizens. And there was more to come; the 1920's proved to be a boom period for population, real estate, and business development. Southern California's lifestyle was emerging, a dramatic change over the Midwest ethic of earlier immigrants. Los Angeles fell in love with the automobile and designed its newest homes to accommodate the vehicle; the public transit system began its slow decline in the vicious circle of decreasing passengers and increasing fares; the *Times* and the Chamber of Commerce proclaimed to the rest of the nation

---

[4]W. A. Chalfant, *The Story of Inyo*, 1922 ed., pp. 328–329.

[5]Burt I. Twilegar, "Mulholland's 'Pipe' Dream," *Westways* 41 (January, 1949), 16–17.

the blessings of an open-shop city; and the rest of the nation responded with fascination for the movie stars, Aimee Semple McPherson, and the assortment of oddities—cultural, intellectual, political—that earned the city a long-standing reputation for strange behavior.

Whatever their professional and personal proclivities, however, all of the city's citizens needed water to drink, sprinkle on lawns, wash with, or flush down, as well as to provide the power for the many and growing uses of electricity. "Los Angeles is already finding that her municipally owned, almost inexhaustible and cheap water supply, together with unlimited and cheap electric power, is to be the deciding factor," observed local historian John Steven McGroarty, "in making of Los Angeles one of the large manufacturing cities of the United States." The Los Angeles Chamber of Commerce agreed. "An almost inexhaustible supply of water and an abundance of hydro-electric power at low rates have perhaps had more to do with the building up of Los Angeles than have any other mediums."[6]

In the face of the city's growth in population and industry, a new challenge appeared: Southern California in the early 1920's entered a prolonged drought.

From Negotiation to Frustration

No civic leader worthy of the title thought for a moment that Los Angeles' growth had peaked. Projections for future greatness, however, hinged on the same considerations that had caused concern a quarter-century earlier. More water and power were needed—not only for domestic users but for the agricultural producers in such city areas as the San Fernando Valley. The new drought cycle that began in 1921 soon taxed the city's ability to supply water for domestic and irrigation purposes. Mulholland's showmanship in going off to the Colorado River notwithstanding, the city could not wait for the approval, financing, and construction of a water and power

---

[6]John S. McGroarty, *Los Angeles from the Mountains to the Sea*, 1:237; "Water and Power Attract Industries," *Southern California Business* 4 (March, 1925), 12.

link to the Colorado River. By the spring of 1923, the city's water shortage was becoming serious, particularly for local irrigation.[7]

With the Colorado River as a possible new source lying in an indefinite future, Mulholland had to look at what was available in the present. In the construction of the aqueduct system Mulholland, primarily because of his dispute with Eaton, had omitted a crucial element. No dam and storage reservoir existed to control the flow of the Owens River southward through the valley. The choicest spot, Long Valley, remained in Eaton's control. From the aqueduct intake above Independence north to Long Valley, the northern half of Owens Valley contained miles of irrigation canals that diverted the river's waters to farms and ranches. The drought promised to make Owens River water scarce for both city and valley. The aqueduct itself was not the problem, but with the Department of Water and Power (DWP) stalemated at Long Valley, the only recourse was to increase the amount of water available to the city.

This meant tapping underground sources. As groundwater pumping increased, however, the water table fell to lower and lower levels. Farmers around Independence filed injunctions against the city to stop the drain on the groundwater. Mulholland's solution was to buy out such farmers. To acquire additional groundwater rights, the DWP began purchasing properties north of Independence, alarming the northern Owens Valley communities of Bishop and Big Pine.[8]

Owens Valley at first presented a less-than-united front to the city's campaign to buy up property north of the aqueduct intake. Contrary to later remembrances and impressions, a variety of opinions were held concerning what to do about the city's intentions, ranging from eagerness to sell one's farm for a nice profit to stubborn refusal to sell out at any price. One major faction was led by Wilfred and Mark Watterson, the key financial leaders in Inyo County. The Watterson brothers owned the Inyo County Bank, with four offices in valley towns, as well as the National Soda Springs Works, tungsten and vanadium mines, and other business interests. (One brother-in-law was J. C. Clausen, the original surveyor of the

[7]Remi Nadeau, *The Water Seekers*, p. 55.

[8]Ibid.; Marian L. Ryan, "Los Angeles Newspapers Fight the Water War, 1924–1927," *Southern California Quarterly* 50 (June, 1968), 179.

valley for the Reclamation Service back in 1905.) As influential leaders in the valley, the Wattersons urged farmers to establish an irrigation district and turn their water rights over to it, thus creating a consolidated position against future intrusions by the city.

In contrast to the pro-consolidation group, another faction opposed creation of an irrigation district. This group was led by another Watterson, George Watterson, the bankers' uncle, who objected to the surrender of individual water rights and perhaps suspected his nephews of making some sort of power move. When the issue was put to a vote on December 26, 1922, residents of Big Pine and Bishop resoundingly approved creation of the Owens Valley Irrigation District.

In order to head off the problems such a district could create for Los Angeles, the city moved to capture control of the oldest canal on the river before its property owners joined the irrigation district. This was the McNally Ditch, a major canal on the east side of the river, near Bishop. The city enlisted the aid of the president of the McNally Ditch, William Symons, to secure water options on the ditch property for the city. Symons would receive a commission for his work. He obtained the support of Bishop attorney Leicester C. Hall and of George Watterson to obtain the options; both of these men acted out of political motivations. The three men purchased options from virtually every farmer on the river, with Los Angeles' financial support of over a million dollars. Los Angeles now held a key part of northern Owens Valley as well as membership in the irrigation district established to hold off city intrusions.

When news of the option purchases became known, Bishop's citizens were generally outraged. Hall and George Watterson defended their action by insisting they had acted to prevent Wilfred and Mark Watterson from making a personal play for power. Most Bishop citizens, however, sided with the nephews and branded the option-takers as traitors to the valley. "From the purchase of McNally Ditch," observes historian Remi Nadeau, "dates the real beginning of the Owens Valley water war."[9]

Battle lines were soon drawn, if at first only figuratively, as both sides moved closer to a literal confrontation. Farmers illegally

[9]Nadeau, *Water Seekers*, pp. 56–57.

diverted McNally Ditch water into their own ditches, leaving the city in the position of owning a ditch without water. In retaliation, Los Angeles adopted a policy of indiscriminate land and water purchases in the Bishop area, infuriating valley people, who accused the city of "checkerboarding." As tensions mounted and the riverbed below Big Pine ran dry in the summer heat, Wilfred Watterson agreed with Harvey Van Norman and William B. Mathews of the DWP to arrange a meeting in Bishop to settle differences.

On the day of the meeting, August 13, 1923, Big Pine Canal owners discovered city workers attempting to prevent river water from entering their canal by digging a diversion ditch of their own. Under threat of violence from Big Pine citizens, the city men retreated. That evening, angry valley delegations confronted Van Norman and Mathews, viewed Watterson's motives with some suspicion, and refused to endorse a proposal that would give the city a third of the water in return for an end to further city purchases.[10]

Following this stalemate Los Angeles intensified its purchase of valley properties. It bought the Big Pine Canal in October for $1.1 million, only to find that farmers continued diverting the river into private ditches. Farmers and townspeople in the valley felt a way of life was gradually slipping away as the city purchased entire ditches, causing residents to move away, and also made indiscriminate property purchases, leaving farmers uncertain of their neighbors' intentions.

Some valley residents did seem to be in a position to make a profit whichever side won. Involved in the negotiations was the Owens Valley Protective Association, a group led by Fred Eaton, Los Angeles banker W. D. Longyear (whose father, D. M. Longyear, owned a 2,000-acre ranch in the valley), and other Los Angeles bankers with financial interests in the valley. This group had ties to the irrigation district and would benefit from the Wattersons' determination to sell for the highest price possible.[11] Despite some suspicions that the Owens Valley Irrigation District was under the control of Los Angeles financiers who planned to hold up the city for the highest possible price even as district members urged

[10]Ibid., pp. 59–61; Los Angeles Times, August 18, 1923.

[11]Los Angeles Examiner, February 14, 1924; "The Owens Valley Background," Municipal League of Los Angeles Bulletin 2 (August 15, 1924), 10.

the city to buy out the entire district rather than make indiscriminate purchases, valley resistance to city plans helped bring a measure of unity to the struggle.

Generally acknowledged as leaders in the valley were the Watterson brothers, *Owens Valley Herald* editor Harry Glasscock, and rancher Karl Keough. A more militant faction, including members of the Ku Klux Klan, which was experiencing a rise to power nationwide in the mid-1920's, chose the use of force as a possible method of resisting the city. This group threatened irrigation-district opponents such as George Watterson, L. C. Hall, and William Symons. After Hall was kidnapped by a group of vigilantes and almost lynched, he felt compelled to leave the valley, moving to Southern California. Los Angeles city employees, personnel of the DWP, were also threatened.[12]

Sensational publicity over city-valley disagreement appeared in newspapers throughout the state, and extremists reacted violently against a lawsuit filed by the city to recover the McNally and Big Pine canals' water. On May 21, 1924, some forty men dynamited the aqueduct spillway gate near Lone Pine. The damage was minor, but the incident stunned the city. The Los Angeles City Council offered a $10,000 reward for the capture of the guilty parties, newspaper reporters and photographers flocked to the scene, and law enforcement officials from Los Angeles and Inyo County alike joined in the search for clues. Militant valley citizens denied complicity in the incident but showed no remorse about it. Glasscock editorially referred to the dynamiting as "merely the protest of an outraged people."[13]

Inyo County Sheriff Charles A. Collins seemed powerless in the face of widespread valley support of the dynamiters' action. Rumors abounded. So many volunteers, including some prominent citizens, had been available for the dynamiting that no fewer than eleven automobiles had been needed to take them all to the scene. One of the cars, it was said, belonged to Sheriff Collins himself, although it had been used without his knowledge. It was asserted that seventeen of the men had been identified and would shortly be taken into

[12]Nadeau, *Water Seekers*, pp. 63–64.
[13]Quoted in ibid., p. 67.

custody; it was equally rumored that if arrests were made new out-breaks of violence would occur.[14]

While Bishop citizens displayed a militant attitude over the affair, Fred Eaton issued an irenic statement from his Long Valley ranch. "We are a law abiding people," he stated. "We do not ap-prove of violence in any form, nor do we approve, of course, of the aqueduct dynamiting." Enough excitement had been generated by the dynamiting, however, to suggest that Eaton's was a minority view."[15]

Damage to the aqueduct was slight. One immediate benefit from the incident was to bring city and valley people together for new negotiations. By now some city leaders had grown tired of the failure of the Board of Public Service Commissioners to solve the con-troversy and avert the threat of violence. The Los Angeles Cham-ber of Commerce invited valley leaders to come to Los Angeles to state their case, and a chamber committee in return paid a visit to the valley. This chamber committee recommended the creation of an impartial board of arbitrators to set fair prices for valley property. The water board buried this committee report, justifying its action by claiming that the Wattersons, the main valley residents the com-mittee had interviewed, did not represent what a later generation would term a "silent majority" of valley people. Such actions by the water board only taxed the patience of the valley. The Chamber of Commerce chose not to press the issue. "The president of the Cham-ber of Commerce is an old friend and former business associate of mine," said Mulholland. "The chamber will never do anything to hurt me."[16]

Meanwhile, another Los Angeles group paid a visit to the valley. Burton Knisely, editor of the Scripps-Howard chain's *Los Angeles Record*, met with Wilfred Watterson in Bishop. What trans-pired between the two men is not known, but Knisely left the valley committed to its cause. On June 24 the *Record* published a major

[14]*Los Angeles Herald*, May 24, 1924.

[15]*Los Angeles Examiner*, May 25, 1924.

[16]Nadeau, *Water Seekers*, p. 68; *Los Angeles Times*, June 29, 1924; *Los Angeles Record*, August 16, 1924. The Board of Water Commissioners was retitled the Board of Public Service Commissioners in 1911 and in 1925 became the Board of Water and Power Commissioners.

article castigating the DWP's water policies. The paper promised its crusade would be "a constructive work and one that will have a great effect upon the city's water supply in the future—a supply that should be planned to support a city of five million people." The *Record* thus endorsed a curious combination of city boosterism and sympathy with Owens Valley's position. It avoided the contradictions inherent in this editorial view by blaming any and all errors on Mulholland, the water board, and assorted city officials. Succeeding issues endorsed the Chamber of Commerce's mediation efforts, justified the actions of the Big Pine Canal's former owners, and denounced the city for its "policy of nibbling, harrassing [*sic*] and lawsuiting."[17]

Supporters of the DWP quickly discerned the source of the *Record*'s editorial viewpoint. R. E. Chadwick of the Los Angeles Municipal League, a major progressive reform organization, which functioned actively in the 1920's, observed that the *Record*'s articles were "preceded by a similar series in the *San Francisco Call*, written by C. E. Kunze, a brother-in-law of W. W. Waterson [*sic*]; by many perfervid articles in the Bishop [*sic*] Herald, written by the editor, Harry A. Glasscock, who is financially obligated to the Inyo County Bank; and by sporadic attacks on the public service commission appearing in an obscure publication, ownership of which is credited to Volney Craig, of the San Fernando Valley, a persistent enemy of the people's power and water project." The league believed that much of the agitation against the city stemmed from the efforts of private power interests opposed to municipally supplied electric power, as well as from an organized effort in the valley to charge unwarranted sums for land and water rights.[18]

A third group that visited Owens Valley in the summer of 1924 came on instructions from the Public Service Commission to report on the possibility of equitable division of Owens River water between Los Angeles and the valley. One of the members of this three-man engineering board, interestingly enough, was J. B. Lippincott. The Hill-Lippincott-Sonderegger report, submitted on

---

[17]*Los Angeles Record*, June 24 and 25, 1924, and issues following; Ryan, "Los Angeles Newspapers Fight the Water War," pp. 180–181.
[18]"Owens Valley Background," pp. 10, 12.

August 14, claimed that the river could supply enough water to irrigate 30,000 acres in the upper part of the valley, with the remainder sufficient for the city's needs even in a dry year. This meant that purchase of additional valley property, whether wholesale or piecemeal, was not really necessary.[19]

The following month the Public Service Commissioners, Mulholland, DWP personnel, and newspaper reporters met with valley leaders to continue efforts to settle the dispute peacefully. Wilfred Watterson urged the city representatives to buy out Big Pine and Independence and to buy all the remaining lands watered by the Owens River between the Haiwee Reservoir and Bishop. The commission president, Dr. John R. Haynes, agreed with Watterson that the differences could be resolved fairly. "As a matter of fact," said Haynes, "the whole valley should have been bought up in the beginning."

"This should have been done and could have been done cheaply," agreed Watterson. "Now it has became a very complicated situation. . . . If it could be fixed so that we could positively know that there would be no more encroachment it might be best to leave some [unpurchased property], but we must know. The position I have taken lately is to do what the farmers want."

Haynes promised, "I am going to do everything I can to have a definite policy made and made soon."[20]

The policy that emerged shortly afterward was not quite what Watterson expected. On October 14 the commissioners announced a policy that promised to leave 30,000 acres in the Bishop area free of city purchases, this area to receive "an ample and regulated irrigation supply . . . throughout each season as well as every year." Valley residents would retain ownership of the 30,000 acres. The city would lobby for a state highway through the valley "that will make the beautiful mountain country of this region easily accessible to all Southern California, thereby building up a profitable tourist

[19]Nadeau, *Water Seekers*, pp. 68–69; *Los Angeles Times*, September 14, 1924. The other engineers were Louis C. Hill and A. L. Sonderegger.

[20]"Interview with Mr. Wilfred Watterson of Inyo County on Monday, September 22, 1924, Re Owens Valley," typescript, John R. Haynes Papers, Government and Public Affairs Department, University of California, Los Angeles (hereafter cited as GPA).

business for the valley people." A paved road through to Bishop remained seven years in the future, however.[21]

Watterson and the directors of the Owens Valley Irrigation District found the proposal unacceptable, as it omitted compensation to the valley's townspeople and abandoned any thought of buying out the entire valley. The irrigation district refused to compromise: either the city would buy out the entire valley or it would not receive its water from rights already purchased. City and valley had come half-circle. Acting on the Hill-Lippincott-Sonderegger report, the DWP now believed wholesale purchase was no longer necessary for the city's water needs. Watterson's irrigation district, on the other hand, now urged the sale of the entire upper valley.

As negotiations through meetings resumed with little result, Owens Valley men again took matters into their own hands in an effort to arouse publicity about the dispute. On November 16, Mark Watterson, Karl Keough, and a group of men estimated between sixty and one hundred in number took possession of the Alabama Gates, opened the spillway gates, and shut off the aqueduct. The takeover brought national attention to the conflict. *Literary Digest*, a weekly news magazine, featured an article on "California's Little Civil War." Newspapers in New York, Chicago, and other cities editorialized on the problems of growing cities as opposed to the rights of people affected by that growth. While the valley men controlled the spillway gates, public officials and newspaper editors throughout the state called for a solution to the conflict. Sheriff Collins urged Governor Friend W. Richardson to send the state militia to disperse the men at the spillway gates. "Troops are required immediately to end the situation which exists here," he said. "I again appeal for State aid as the only means of handling the situation." Richardson, while offering encouragement to Collins, declined to take such a drastic move, sending instead a special investigator to look into the affair. Valley leader Karl Keough stubbornly proclaimed: "We are here to keep this spillway open. We will stay here until we are driven out or dragged out." Meanwhile, Wilfred Watterson met with the banker members of the influential

[21]"The Los Angeles Aqueduct Seizure—What Really Happened," *Fire and Water Engineering* 22 (December 17, 1924), 1337.

and impartial Los Angeles Clearing House Association to request their support in having the irrigation district purchased by the city. The association refused to consider his request so long as people in the valley conducted themselves in a lawless manner. Watterson returned to the valley and informed a delegation from the spillway gates of the association's position. On November 20 the diversion gates were lowered, and Owens River water again flowed into the aqueduct.[22]

Frustrated with the failure of the water board to develop a plan they could consider equitable, valley leaders pinned their hopes on the Los Angeles Clearing House Association as a potentially influential mediator in the dispute. The bankers offered calm neutrality in a period of high tension. "We know nothing of the merits of this controversy," announced Jackson A. Graves, the association's president and also president of the Farmers and Merchants National Bank. "I have asked Mr. Mulholland of the Water Bureau for a statement of the city's side in the matter, having asked Mr. Watterson, representing the ranchers, for a statement of their side. When we get those statements we will know what each side has to say, and will be in a position to suggest what to do." Graves favored an arbitration board composed of "three of the most eminent judges that can be found in the State" to settle the controversy.[23]

The association invited statements from Watterson and from the water commissioners, who presented their sides of the dispute. For a brief period it seemed as if city and valley might discuss their differences in a moderate manner. The *Los Angeles Times* reprinted the Public Service Commission's October 14 proposal calling for the 30,000-acre zone, no city purchases within the zone, and help for the economy of Inyo County through a paved road to encourage visitation of tourists. In the adjacent column, Wilfred Watterson

[22]"California's Little Civil War," *Literary Digest* 86 (December 6, 1924), 15; *Los Angeles Examiner,* November 18, 1924; Nadeau, *Water Seekers,* pp. 70–76; Ryan, "Los Angeles Newspapers Fight the Water War," pp. 181–182; W. F. McClure, *Report of W. F. McClure, State Engineer, Concerning the Owens Valley–Los Angeles Controversy, to Governor Friend Wm. Richardson,* p. 7.
[23]*Los Angeles Times,* November 21, 1924.

urged equity for the valley.[24] The possibility of a compromise soon proved illusory. When Watterson submitted his formal statement to the Clearing House Association on November 29, he showed little inclination for conciliation. He rejected the city's position and advocated instead three options—the integrity of the 30,000-acre zone plus a reparations payment of $5.3 million to property owners, primarily townspeople, who claimed damages caused by the city; the purchase of the Owens Valley Irrigation District for $12 million; or the purchase of the irrigation district by the city at a price set by a disinterested arbitration board.[25]

In response to Watterson's counterproposals, the Board of Public Service Commissioners presented a severe rebuttal almost one hundred pages long, plus appendices, tearing apart almost every paragraph in Watterson's 125-paragraph statement. The DWP flatly denied any error whatsoever on its part in pursuing a policy for use of Owens River water. "The case presented to the Clearing House of Los Angeles . . . is devoid of a single instance of wrongdoing on the part of Los Angeles, its officials, or agents," the commissioners claimed. They announced their position in a series of "irrefutable statements." Among the "irrefutable statements" were: "The City purchased all of its lands and water rights in Owens Valley from parties who, with but relatively few exceptions, were and still are citizens and residents of that valley. If the City did wrong in buying, they did wrong in selling." Another "irrefutable statement" noted, "In many cases the property was heavily mortgaged, at very high interest rates, to the Watterson Bank . . . and it was generally understood that payment of such mortgages through sale to the City was most welcome to that bank."[26]

The power of the rebuttal was overwhelming, as sentence after sentence of Watterson's statement was picked apart. The commissioners denied that remaining ranch and town properties in the

[24]Ibid., November 26, 1924.

[25]Los Angeles Board of Public Service Commissioners, *Reply of Board of Public Service Commissioners of the City of Los Angeles to the Proposal and Accompanying Documents Dated November 29, 1924, Submitted by W. W. Watterson to Los Angeles Clearing House Association*, pp. 88–89.

[26]Ibid., p. 1.

valley had depreciated as a result of the purchases already made by the city. And they concluded: "even if the City's purchase of lands in the Owens Valley had resulted in the shrinkage of values of remaining ranch and town property, this board would be absolutely without power to expend the public funds entrusted to it in payment of claims on account of such shrinkage or depreciation. Such losses, while very regrettable, are among the hazards which all must take in buying property or establishing a business and cannot be the basis of a legal claim for compensation."[27]

Considering that the valley people had set up their businesses, ranches, and farms before Los Angeles began intruding in the upper valley, the Public Service Commission's statement was rather callous. "This aloof attitude over the plight of the valley townspeople was probably the most ill-considered decision of the water board," observes Remi Nadeau, who concludes that the Public Service Commission distrusted the motives of the Wattersons in speaking for the valley. "Its members seemed to believe that because the city could not legally be made to pay reparations it was justified in disclaiming any interest in the valley whose life it had affected root and branch."[28]

Almost at the same time the Public Service Commission was closing off further possibilities for compromise, Governor Richardson's special investigator submitted his report on the Alabama Gates incident. Richardson had sent State Engineer Wilbur F. McClure to the valley to inquire into the causes of the aqueduct seizure. McClure, whose service as state engineer dated to his appointment in 1912, had lived from about 1897 to 1900 in Owens Valley, during which time he had served as a Methodist minister.[29] Thus his years of public service were linked to an acquaintanceship with Inyo County's people and their problems. Somewhat pressed for time, McClure gathered together affidavits, correspondence, and various reports, along with articles and editorials from newspapers throughout the state, and submitted his findings on January 9, 1925. His

[27]Ibid., p. 91.

[28]Nadeau, *Water Seekers*, p. 76.

[29]Fred Eaton sponsored McClure for membership in the American Society of Civil Engineers in 1886.

report totaled over a hundred pages, of which about half consisted of newspaper editorials, most of them hostile to Los Angeles.

Governor Richardson had asked for a report on conditions in the valley concerning the aqueduct seizure. McClure went beyond these instructions to compile a summary of Owens Valley grievances against the city, specifically against the Public Service Commission. Despite an obvious partiality for the valley's viewpoint, McClure made a sincere effort to meet with DWP officials to get their side of the controversy. When he met on December 24 with the commission members, Mulholland, and other engineers and officials, the Public Service Commission had not yet prepared its report to the Clearing House Association. "I endeavored to convince the commissioners that it would be wise to forget the past and bend our efforts toward a solution of the problem, not only on account of the unrest in Owens Valley, but on account of the good name of Los Angeles," reported McClure. But he found the commissioners unresponsive to suggestions for compromise. "While in Owens Valley I heard some severe criticisms of the chief engineer and Board of Public Service Commissioners," McClure observed, "but none of them exceeded in caustic utterance and bitterness statements made around the table in the Public Service Commissioners room concerning the people of Owens Valley." This position could hardly help the city's image, for "in no instance . . . has a single publication outside of Los Angeles spoken a word in defense of the city's attitude."[30]

The year 1925 had begun with the expectation that some solution to the impasse would be found, but such hopes soon met with disappointment. McClure's report had virtually no political effect on the state level, since Richardson had no desire to pursue the issue, and the Los Angeles Clearing House negotiations with Watterson eventually broke down. The city's aqueduct was operating again, and the valley soon realized its advantageous position had been lost when control of the spillway gates was given back to the city. Los Angeles leaders generously suggested that Owens Valley's future lay in a minimum of agriculture and a maximum of recreational

[30]McClure, *Report*, p. 17.

resort development. "Give Los Angeles a park of greater attraction than the Yellowstone or Yosemite because it is accessible for winter as well as summer sports," William P. Whitsett urged the directors of the Los Angeles Chamber of Commerce, "and make of the Owens Valley towns prosperous and world famous resorts." The "real highway" to make it possible, however, still awaited construction.[31]

Owens Valley leaders could not wait for a proposed road to bring them riches, not while the city was removing their water and leaving the upper valley in terrible uncertainty over its future. "We are having a desperate struggle against the City," Mark Watterson informed Mary Austin, "and the only weapon we have is publicity, and that is about the only thing the City of Los Angeles seems to fear."[32]

Explosive Resistance

Even as Owens Valley leaders despaired of settling the long-standing controversy, the city suddenly completed the circle of frustrated negotiations. The city's immense growth in the 1920's dictated that Los Angeles would not only want all the water that could be obtained from the Owens River but would also establish links to the Colorado River and to Mono Lake. Reversing the stand it had taken after the Hill-Lippincott-Sonderegger report had been submitted in the summer of 1924, the Public Service Commission announced its decision to purchase all lands tributary to the Owens River. While this meant that farmers and ranchers would have an opportunity to sell their property to the city for a good price and then to lease back their lands and continue farming or ranching (minus the water rights), it also meant that the citizens of the valley towns would be left out of the picture. What would happen to their demands for reparations?

An answer soon came from the state legislature, which through adroit Owens Valley lobbying passed a law, effective May 1, 1925, making cities that removed water from a watershed liable for damages to those affected by the loss. Some state legislators expressed

---

[31]W. P. Whitsett, *Straight Ahead for the Owens Valley* (pamphlet).
[32]Watterson to Austin, December 18, 1924, Austin Papers, HL.

the belief that the law might be declared unconstitutional, but valley supporters had won their point. Under the leadership of the Wattersons (who had momentarily shaken the faith of their followers by selling their ranch in the Bishop Creek Ditch to the city), the Owens Valley Reparations Association and the Big Pine Reparations Association were formed. The associations spent months compiling claims, including loss of real estate values in town lots, homes, and buildings, claims of losses of trade by valley mechanics, barbers, electricians, and seventy-six other occupations, and depreciation claims for store fixtures, equipment, and household goods. The sum total of the reparations claims amounted to $2,813,355.43 from 548 claimants.[33]

The controversy was still a long way from settlement. Considerable resentment developed over the DWP's willingness to settle with the Owens Valley Protective Association, paying $260,000 for the Longyear Ranch while refusing to arbitrate with the townspeople.[34] Also, although the DWP continued to buy out farms at about four times their assessed valuation, farmers belonging to the Owens River Canal, better known as the "Keough Pool," objected to the appraised figures offered them. When negotiations bogged down, the Keough Pool farmers and the townspeople joined forces.

While negotiations over purchase of farmlands and the reparations issue dragged on, the feelings of frustration were again punctuated by dynamite blasts. On April 3, 1926, a city water well sustained minor damage, on April 4 a second well was blown up, and there was another blast on April 27. Accompanying the explosions were the editorial blasts of Glasscock's *Owens Valley Herald*, the most militant of the valley papers. "The greatest tragedy that ever happened to a community in the State of California is that which has happened to Owens Valley during the past few years," declared Glasscock. The valley people had been "happy and contented" until "the political monster of Los Angeles—the Los Angeles Water

[33]Vincent Ostrom, *Water and Politics: A Study of Water Policies and Administration in the Development of Los Angeles*, pp. 123–124; Los Angeles Department of Water and Power, *Facts Concerning the Owens Valley Reparation Claims for the Information of the People of California.*

[34]"Is the Water Board Inciting to Riot in Owens Valley?" *Municipal League of Los Angeles Bulletin* 3 (August, 1925), 4.

Board—sent its agent here a few years ago. Since that time the Water Board of Los Angeles has stopped at practically nothing in their work of destruction of this Valley." The water and power commissioners threatened to charge Glasscock with criminal libel, but the editor defied them in an open letter to the commissioners, the Los Angeles newspapers, and the press throughout the state.[35]

Dynamiting occurred again on May 12, but valley representatives negotiating the reparations claims urged the hotheads to stop the acts of violence, which were hurting their cause. Finally, in December, 1926, after months of delay, the city did come to an important decision about the reparations claims. The Department of Water and Power announced that the constitutionality of the state's reparations law would have to be tested in court and upheld before the city could pay out any money. A claimant would sue for damages and, if the law were held to be constitutional, then the city would pay the claims on a class-action basis. Of course, this meant that a long and tedious court process involving trial and inevitable appeal would have to be undertaken before any claims could be paid. The Wattersons protested against this procedure, arguing instead for an arbitration board to determine the fairness of the claims. The city opposed an arbitration board, and stalemate set in again.[36]

In the spring of 1927 the valley's townspeople and the remaining 20 percent or so of farmers and ranchers who had not sold to the city planned one last campaign to arouse public awareness of the city's aggressions. The holdouts had no use for city promises of riches to come from "ever-swelling numbers of yearly visitors—tourists, anglers, campers and lovers of the majestic heights—who will eventually make the Sierra Nevadas the world's premier skyland resort, perhaps winter as well as summer," as the *Los Angeles Times* put it.[37]

To counteract city insistence that times in the valley had never been better, Owens Valley leaders placed a full-page advertisement in the state's major newspapers. "We, the farming com-

[35]*Owens Valley Herald*, April 21 and 28, 1926; Nadeau, *Water Seekers*, pp. 81–82.

[36]Nadeau, *Water Seekers*, pp. 80–82.

[37]*Los Angeles Times*, January 30, 1927.

munities of Owens Valley, being about to die, salute you!" read the gladiatorial battle cry of the farmers. Frederick Faulkner, a reporter for the *Sacramento Union*, was assigned to investigate at first hand affairs in the valley. He interviewed ranchers, farmers, and townspeople, saw where the city had allowed the property it had purchased to return to desert conditions, and returned to Sacramento committed to Inyo County's cause. From March 28 to April 2 the *Union* published Frederick Faulkner's series on "Owens Valley, Where the Trail of the Wrecker Runs," subtitled "the pitiful story of an agricultural paradise, created by California pioneers, condemned to desert waste by water looters."

Faulkner idealized the valley, villainized the city, and omitted no chance to wax sentimental over the grief and hardship suffered by the people of Owens Valley. "Each day brings fresh heartache to the depleted population of this valley," he wrote. "Here's an empty schoolhouse where little children played and studied and learned to love the snow-capped mountains! Here are wrecked homes, dairy barns and stock corrals; the firebrand has not yet come to reduce them to black ash heap [sic] that lies a few miles down the highway!" And so on. Faulkner's purple prose was reprinted in pamphlet form and distributed throughout the state.[38]

One immediate result of the publicity was an unofficial visit to Owens Valley by eight state assemblymen who had been invited to go there by Assemblyman Dan Williams, a supporter of the valley cause though not from Inyo County. Williams had introduced a resolution calling for Los Angeles either to restore the 1923 status quo in the valley or else to compensate valley residents for the damage done to them. The assemblymen spent two days touring the valley, their expenses paid by valley leaders. None of the assemblymen had any engineering background, a fact that did not stop them from drawing conclusions about the Long Valley dam site and other questions involving engineering. They heard only the valley side of the controversy, making no effort to contact city representatives. At one point Assemblyman Van Bernard, while standing on a Bishop street, openly declared his support for the valley. The other assemblymen kept their own opinions silent, lest they be accused of

[38]*Sacramento Union*, March 28–April 2, 1927.

submitting a prejudiced report. This hardly mattered, since the committee of eight's report was roundly condemned by Los Angeles assemblymen anyway for its generous assortment of bias and inaccuracy.[39]

During the hearings on Williams' resolution, DWP representatives requested time to answer the committee of eight's negative report on the city's actions. Wilfred Watterson was also present, along with a valley delegation. William B. Mathews lost his temper in cross-examination, and feelings grew heated as Los Angeles representatives and officials sensed that the assembly intended to condemn the city no matter how eloquent the defense or how accurate its own accusations. Williams consented to an amendment to his resolution, which indicated that deeper political currents were at play. The subject of the resolution as originally worded was "The City of Los Angeles," but the amendment changed the object of criticism to the Bureau of Power and Light within the DWP—not the Bureau of Water Works and Supply. The *Los Angeles Examiner* accused Williams of serving the interests of the Southern Sierras Power Company, which owned a mile of the Owens River gorge. Since the committee of eight urged construction of a 150-foot high dam at Long Valley north of the gorge, the power company could then sell its property to the city for a very high price. Even though the focus of valley grievances was water, not power, the committee of eight, noted the *Examiner*, "willingly switched from blame of Los Angeles to blame of its bureau of power and light."[40]

Los Angeles and Southern California assemblymen angrily protested the one-sidedness of the hearings. Assemblyman Harry Sewell of Whittier reminded the assembly of the possible unconstitutionality of the reparations law, but he failed to convince the legislators from rural areas, who supported the valley's position. The assembly passed the Williams resolution by a vote of 43 to 34.[41]

Dr. John R. Haynes's reaction to the resolution's passage was predictable. "They're a bunch of wild-eyed fools who don't know

[39]*Los Angeles Examiner,* April 25, 1927; *Los Angeles Daily News,* April 25, 1927.
[40]*Los Angeles Examiner,* April 23, 1927.
[41]*Los Angeles Times,* April 23, 1927.

what they are talking about," the water and power commissioner complained. "That assembly resolution is completely silly."[42] Ridiculous or not, on April 25 the resolution went to the state senate and was referred to the Committee on Conservation. Mathews and Van Norman appeared before the committee to argue the case for the DWP. Fortunately for the city, they found a more objective audience this time. The senate committee tabled the resolution, and efforts by valley partisans to restore it to life proved futile. Nevertheless, valley leaders had gained considerable publicity from the assembly-endorsed condemnation, and the city endured growing criticism of its policies.

In an effort to weaken the valley's support of the Wattersons, the city indirectly sponsored the chartering of a new bank for Owens Valley to give the Watterson banks some competition. The Bank of Italy (which would shortly become better known as the Bank of America) approved the idea of a branch in the valley. Edward F. Leahey, the local representative of Los Angeles in the valley, learned that the Wattersons were willing to sell one of their branches. He also learned that the Wattersons might have been engaging in financial irregularities—siphoning bank money into their own private business ventures. The Wattersons grew suspicious and broke off negotiations. Then, with Bank of Italy support, five valley men who opposed the Wattersons applied for a bank charter. The charter was tentatively refused by the state bank superintendent, but Wilfred Watterson grew alarmed at this threat to his financial dominance in Inyo County. He supported a confrontation between valley militants and George Warren, a Big Pine rancher who opposed the Wattersons and who had been one of the applicants for the bank charter. Warren was ordered to leave the county; when he refused, his home was besieged by a mob of Bishop men. Warren had his own hired help armed with rifles. News of the confrontation spread, and alarmed valley supporters backing the Williams resolution in the assembly urged a backing off. The siege was lifted, and violence was for the moment averted.[43]

But not for long. The Board of Water and Power Commission-

[42]*Los Angeles Daily News*, April 23, 1927.
[43]Nadeau, *Water Seekers*, pp. 84–87.

ers gave notice in March that valley landowners had until May 1 to sell their property at the appraisal prices reached by the board of land appraisers, which had included prominent Inyo County officials. The holdouts ignored the announcement. Then, tiring of the prolonged haggling over the reparations claims, the DWP ended negotiations. With all avenues for discussion closed, violence was not long in coming.

On May 27 the siphon at No Name Canyon was dynamited. Water poured from the ruptured pipe into the Mojave Desert. The next night a second early-morning explosion blew up sixty feet of pipe at Big Pine Creek. Cottonwood Canyon was next, as the side walls of an open concrete conduit were wrecked by a 1:30 A.M. explosion on June 6. Despite the DWP's placing of armed guards at strategic points along the aqueduct, valley extremists continued their work with almost monotonous regularity.

By mid-July the aqueduct had been dynamited some ten times. Once again, the Owens Valley–Los Angeles water controversy gained national attention. "The latest dynamitings are believed to be incited by a few of the remaining landowners who are holding out for higher prices together with some of the businessmen of the towns," reported the correspondent for *Outlook*. "The latter apparently fear that the temporary lull in business is but a forerunner of ultimate ruin, and hope to force the payment of reparations by a reign of terror."[44]

Such an appraisal was not exactly the kind of publicity the valley holdouts desired; more appreciated was the series run in the valley's city ally, the *Los Angeles Record*, "The Valley of Broken Hearts," by C. E. Kunze, W. W. Watterson's brother-in-law (a detail not mentioned by the *Record*). In eight articles Kunze outdid Faulkner in reviewing the plight of ranchers and farmers turned out of homes, the perfidy of Lippincott, the meanness of Mulholland, and the DWP's rigid unfairness in refusing reparations to the townspeople.[45]

Not to be outdone by publicists for the valley's cause, the DWP issued its own interpretation of the controversy. In *The Dyna-*

[44]"The Owens Valley Controversy," *Outlook* 146 (July 13, 1927), 343.
[45]*Los Angeles Record*, June 14–22, 1927.

mite Holdup, a pamphlet published at the height of the dynamitings, the DWP listed the motives of "a small group of persons in
Owens valley, aided and abetted by certain outside interests," who
wanted the city to pay exorbitant prices for the remaining private
ranchland and for reparations "for alleged injury" to valley business interests. "Every legitimate effort has been made by the responsible officials of the city to support and increase the material
prosperity of the valley and to establish a system of water development and conservation mutually beneficial to the valley and the
city," the DWP argued. "But the board is convinced that the people
of Los Angeles are unwilling to buy peace with the lawless element
of the valley at the price this band of desperadoes is demanding."[46]

A belief that the perpetrators of the dynamitings were friends
of Inyo County officials prompted the city to pressure state officials
to intervene, either by sending in the militia or by deputizing members of the attorney general's staff. No arrests had been made. "Obviously, the reason is that the sheriff and the district attorney of
Inyo county are friends and neighbors of the men responsible for the
damages," argued one editorial. Water and Power Commissioner
John R. Richards noted that the city's desire to test the reparations
law was based on the suggestion of Governor Clement C. Young,
and protests about length and expense of trying a court case were
no excuse for lawlessness.[47]

An elusive kernel of truth lay somewhere between, on the one
hand, the city's insistence that valley landowners had received
generous prices for their property, that the city planned to develop
the area's recreational potential, and that few people had suffered,
and, on the other hand, the valley extremists' argument that the
valley had been devastated physically and economically. The fact
of the matter was that most valley landowners had indeed received
fair prices for their farms and ranches. It was also true that the
city, in its aggressive pursuit of water, had made serious errors in
its valley policy, from its failure to construct a reservoir at Long
Valley to its overlooking the effect of its water policy on the valley

[46]*The Dynamite Holdup* (pamphlet).
[47]"Obligation of Attorney-General," *Saturday Night* 7 (June 25, 1927),
4; John R. Richards, "Why Not Settle the Owens Valley Trouble?" *Municipal
League of Los Angeles Bulletin* 4 (July 30, 1927), 1.

towns. At the same time, it should be noted, the Wattersons did not speak for all valley residents, or even a large part of them. Their followers consisted mainly of townspeople, particularly Bishop residents, the holdout property owners of the Owens Valley Irrigation District, and "outside interests," such as absentee landholders who benefited from the stand taken by the Wattersons. The city repeatedly claimed the valley was being represented by the "wrong leaders," a term the city used almost synonymously with the Watterson brothers. But the Wattersons, wielding their political and financial power, were the only leaders of note the townspeople and remaining landholders could claim. Then, at the peak of the dynamite violence, while city officials urged the governor to take action against lawlessness, the people of the valley learned their leaders were vulnerable in a quite unexpected way.

Fall of the Wattersons

At noon on August 4, 1927, directors in the five Inyo County banks affixed notices to their doors and closed them, leaving gatherings crowds to read the brief but shocking announcement: "We find it necessary to close our banks in the Owens Valley. This result has been brought about by the past four years of destructive work carried on by the city of Los Angeles."[48]

In the days and weeks that followed there would grow an uneasy suspicion that Los Angeles was not the reason for the failure of the Watterson banks. At first Inyo County citizens rose to the defense of the Watterson brothers, pledging almost a million dollars to make up the money shortages. After this initial vote of confidence, increasing doubts arose over what Wilfred and Mark Watterson were saying and what State Bank Superintendent Will C. Wood was finding in the bank records.

On August 10 Wood announced more than $800,000 was missing from the Watterson banks in the form of cash, bonds, and notes and as statistical discrepancies. The Watterson financial and commercial empire—banks, mining companies, various subsidiary

[48]Nadeau, *Water Seekers*, p. 93. A slightly variant version is in Graydon Oliver, "Prosperous Condition of Owens Valley District Is Revealed by Many Vital Statistics," *Modern Irrigation* 3 (August, 1927), 25.

corporations—was bankrupt. Wood gave the brothers a week to come up with the missing funds. When their efforts to do so proved unsuccessful, the initial pledges notwithstanding, Wood charged them with embezzlement and had them arrested. Friends put up bail—$25,000 per brother—and the Wattersons began a campaign in Inyo to justify their actions. They claimed it had been necessary, following the city's invasion in 1923, to channel bank funds into other Watterson businesses as a way of maintaining a local economy hurt by the decline of agriculture. Blaming the city for their actions, however, soon seemed a hollow excuse. The brothers had falsified banking reports to the state, had never canceled loans and mortgages paid off by Inyo County farmers, had sold securities without authorization, and in all of these acts had betrayed the trust of the community in which they had been born and had lived all their lives.

The people betrayed included hundreds of Inyo County citizens, many of whom had placed their life savings in the banks. Many had deposited the money obtained from sale of their properties to the City of Los Angeles. *Owens Valley Herald* editor Harry Glasscock was so disillusioned by the Wattersons' actions—his newspaper presses and equipment were held by Watterson notes, and for all intents and purposes his paper would soon be dead—that several months after the trial, he committed suicide.[49]

The fall of the Wattersons had occurred after Edward L. Leahey, the city's representative in the valley, had grown suspicious of Watterson support for militant valley leaders. He obtained a financial statement that indicated money had been provided by the Wattersons to Glasscock and other aqueduct opponents. Armed with evidence of possible financial misdealings, Leahey and DWP counsel William B. Mathews requested that an investigation be made. Wood's investigator showed up at the Inyo County Bank to make an audit, surprising Wilfred Watterson by the two-months' premature visit. The shortages were quickly detected; eventually thirty-six counts of embezzlement were made against the banker brothers.[50]

Los Angeles reported sympathetically on the plight of the valley people. The city promised relief in the form of construction projects,

[49]Nadeau, *Water Seekers*, pp. 94–95; *Los Angeles Times*, November 12, 1927.

[50]*Los Angeles Times*, August 11 and November 12, 1927.

road building, and development of new industry based on tourism and the area's scenic attractions—what it had been calling for all along. Clarence A. Dykstra, a former water and power commissioner, echoed the hopes of Commissioner William P. Whitsett for "a great American Switzerland" with "good roads, good taverns, well stocked streams, and capable hosts" to transform the valley's economy from its present straits to future prosperity. "It is an alluring prospect," observed Dykstra.[51]

The residents of Owens Valley could only respond numbly to such optimistic predictions for their future. It was the present that was their time of trouble. "The people of the valley are left in the worst possible condition," attorney A. H. Swallow declared in petitioning for involuntary bankruptcy for the Wattersons. "They have absolutely nothing in which to live. Their every penny, in one form or another, went into the Watterson coffers and the collapse of the Wattersons has left them penniless."[52]

In the fight with the city the people of Owens Valley had presented somewhat less than a united front. A wide gap existed between the farmer who willingly sold his property to the city for a fair price and the stubborn militants who expressed their opposition by resorting to dynamite. Whatever their differences, the Owens Valley residents had one thing in common. They did their banking at the only available bank—which for Inyo County was the chain operated by the Wattersons. The nearest competitor was at Lancaster, 150 miles away. A. P. Giannini had plans in the works to open a branch of his Bank of Italy, but valley citizens in 1927 found no alternative but to deal with the Watterson banks. In doing so, they placed their savings in the care of the leaders of one of the most extreme factions of valley resistance to the city's plans and policies. Under the circumstances, the valley view of the Wattersons on trial became one of betrayal rather than martyrdom.

On November 1 the trial began at Independence. There was some surprise at the speed with which the jury was selected with approval by the Watterson defense counsel. The court clerk read the thirty-six counts of embezzlement; the most recent audit had

[51]*Los Angeles Times*, October 19, 1927; C. A. Dykstra, "Owens Valley, a Problem in Regional Planning," *Community Builder* 1 (February, 1928), 11.
[52]*Los Angeles Times*, October 6, 1927.

found the amount of the theft to be almost $450,000. District Attorney Jess Hession made his opening statement without resorting to oratory. The jury and courtroom audience listened in stunned silence as Hession developed his case. "It was the first time many of them had heard in detail," observed a Los Angeles reporter, "just what the Wattersons are accused of doing."[53]

. The trial's outcome was a foregone conclusion, considering the weight of the evidence. It took the jury six hours to reach a verdict of guilty on all counts. Valley people who had known the brothers all their lives were torn between emotions of sympathy and bitterness. One man who had believed in the innocence of the Wattersons until the trial began and who had lost his life savings in a Watterson bank summed up the general feeling. "Well, if the jury of twelve men and women from this county sat there and heard all the evidence that was put in and voted guilty against them, I guess there's no doubt about it," he said. "Don't hardly seem possible to me. It isn't the money I lost so much as the faith in men that I have lost. Why, I trusted those men like they were brothers of mine." A Los Angeles opinion offered harsher judgment. "There is no doubt that these men were the chief instigators of all the unreasonable agitation against Los Angeles," observed veteran newspaperman William A. Spalding, "and morally responsible for the acts of outlawry that had been perpetrated."[54]

As the brothers went off to serve a one-to-ten-year sentence in San Quentin—they would be paroled in 1933—few valley people could be found who disapproved of the verdict. Even in pro-Watterson Bishop there was general acceptance that the brothers were convicted felons, not martyrs. Los Angeles applauded the fairness of the trial, painful as it was for all concerned. But where to go from here? Later in November, Perry Sexton, a valley resident, confessed to being one of the aqueduct dynamiters. A Bishop justice of the peace heard Sexton's confession, refused to believe it, and released him, along with six other suspects. No other effort was made to arrest anyone.[55]

[53]Ibid., November 2, 1927.

[54]Ibid., November 12, 1927; William A. Spalding, *History and Reminiscences, Los Angeles City and County, California*, 1:458.

[55]"Nemesis for the Wattersons," *Saturday Night* 8 (November 19, 1927), 3; Nadeau, *Water Seekers*, p. 96.

As the Wattersons fell, so fell the spirit of resistance against the city. To many breadwinners, too proud to accept charity but penniless after the bank debacle, employment with the city was preferable to continuing a fight that had gone stale. The DWP sponsored a program to construct new DWP buildings, repair existing ones, and drill wells. For some valley people this must have been like fighting thirst by drinking one's own blood. But short of leaving the valley, which many did, there was no other choice if one wanted work.[56]

Not all bitterness toward the DWP came from lifelong residents of Owens Valley. City and valley had forged an economic link dating back to the 1870's, and there were people who had business interests in both areas. Charles C. Chapman, a wealthy orange grower who helped develop the city of Fullerton and who was involved in real estate development in Southern California, also owned the Tinnemaha Ranch in Owens Valley. A generous and kindly man, Chapman reserved uncharacteristically bitter words for William Mulholland, whom he blamed for the ruin of agriculture in the valley. "A devastating military campaign would have done no more damage to the property and homes of a happy people than was done under the leadership of this man," he remarked. When the value of his ranch declined, Chapman found the only customer for it was the DWP. In his recollection of the negotiations he left a most unflattering portrait of the DWP's chief engineer. "I called upon Mr. Mulholland to discuss the Water Company buying the ranch as it had other properties in the valley," he recalled. "He would not even talk with me, simply saying, in his rough, German dictatorial manner, that the city had no use for it. Not until the purchase of the property was put into the hands of a commission, was there an opportunity for me to sell to the city, my only prospect." Chapman took a $50,000 loss in selling his ranch to the city.[57]

For the city, the end to resistance marked a moment of triumph. "Owens Valley has passed its crisis," editorialized the *Los Angeles Examiner.*

[56]Ostrom, *Water and Politics*, p. 125.

[57]Charles C. Chapman, *Charles C. Chapman: The Career of a Constructive Californian,* ed. Donald H. Pflueger, p. 142.

The Wattersons, supposed champions of right and promoters of progress, proved to be the valley's incubus. With the brothers in San Quentin, the evil influence is removed. There's no one now to pay dynamiting bills, and no one, so far as anyone can imagine, who wants to blow up the aqueduct.

The spirit in the valley is willingness to cooperate with the city in working out problems so that the people there shall prosper. And the spirit here is the desire to cooperate with the valley.[58]

Despite such editorial optimism, many more obstacles remained in the path of a settlement of the issues confronting city and valley. After some five years of negotiation, violence, and controversy over the DWP's policies in the valley, Mulholland and the city had yet to face their greatest challenge and most horrible tragedy. Following on the collapse of valley resistance, the challenge and tragedy came all too soon.

Failure of the Saint Francis Dam

Los Angeles' triumph over the valley proved permanent, but the spirit of the victory ended abruptly on the night of March 12, 1928, barely three months after the Wattersons were packed off to prison. On that date, just before midnight, the Saint Francis Dam in San Francisquito Canyon north of Los Angeles collapsed. More than four hundred people were killed—the exact number will never be known—as a wall of water raged down the Santa Clara Valley fifty-four miles to the Pacific Ocean. Completed only in 1926, the dam had been unknown to most of the residents of the area. Those few who knew about it probably resented what they felt was another encroachment by the City of Los Angeles on a rural region's water rights. Los Angeles had bid unsuccessfully for the surplus waters of Francisquito Creek, then built the dam to provide storage for surplus Owens River water in case of drought in Southern California.

On March 12, 1928, all Los Angeles city-owned reservoirs, including the Saint Francis, were filled to capacity. During the day Mulholland and his assistant, Harvey Van Norman, were called to the dam by the damkeeper, who had noticed a new leak in the

---

[58]*Los Angeles Examiner*, November 17, 1927.

dam. Concrete dams frequently have cracks and small leaks, and Mulholland found nothing unusual about this one. Various workmen and employees in the dam area had made remarks about the dam's possible failure, more out of mordant humor than serious concern. Mulholland inspected the leak and declared it of no consequence. At 11:57 P.M. the dam failed.

Released by the failure of the dam, the reservoir's water coursed down the Santa Clara Valley, its initial depth more than one hundred feet, washing huge pieces of the concrete dam down with it, uprooting trees, obliterating farm homes. Highway bridges, orange groves, automobiles, everything in the path of the flood was swept away. As word spread of the dam's failure—first noticed in Los Angeles by a flicker of lights, followed by blackout—people performed heroically in alerting the valley's residents. The Union Oil refinery near Santa Paula sounded its shrill whistle; at Fillmore the fire bell was rung. Telephone switchboard operators stayed at their posts, calling residents. Thousands were evacuated and saved. Hundreds of people, however, perished, their tragic fate possibly determined for them by delays between the time utility officials learned there was a problem and when they spread the warning.

The next morning survivors surveyed the horrible disaster and demanded answers. Mindful of its dismal record with Owens Valley—some people suspected the dam might have been dynamited—Los Angeles joined with Ventura County in setting up relief and restoration committees. All claims were paid, and everyone was spared the expense of court settlements, defeating the hopes of ambulance-chasing lawyers who had flocked to the valley from as far away as Stockton.

Various agencies appointed committees to investigate possible causes of the dam's failure. Governor Young appointed a commission; Los Angeles County District Attorney Asa Keyes retained a group, while the Los Angeles City Council obtained the services of Bureau of Reclamation Commissioner Elwood Mead. The DWP conducted its own inquiry, and the Los Angeles County Board of Supervisors hired J. B. Lippincott to make a report. Other investigating groups also submitted their findings. Most of the investigating committees concluded that the dam had first failed on the west side, where the leak had been detected and then inspected by Mulholland. More modern research has yielded another explanation. Charles F. Outland, who has examined the Saint Francis Dam tragedy exhaustively and, in all probability, definitively, argues that the dam failed first on the east side, where the geological formations had been unstable.[59]

Ultimately, blame fell on William Mulholland. He had taken entirely too much responsibility on his own authority and had paid too little attention to critics who vainly complained of faulty rock on the east canyon wall. Engineer Frederick Finkle, for example, had argued against the location of the dam in 1924.[60]

On arriving at the site of the tragedy on March 13, Mulholland almost collapsed with shock. The Board of Water and Power Commissioners debated whether to fire him or simply grant his request for a leave of absence while the DWP was under investigation. The board chose to grant his request and urged Mulholland "to remain on the job he has so faithfully filled for half a century."[61]

The Los Angeles County Coroner began an inquest on March 21. Mulholland testified before the coroner's jury that he alone should be blamed for the tragedy. He may have suspected sabotage in the destruction of the dam, and he hinted at the possibility, but in the end he assumed sole responsibility. In this the coroner's jury concurred. Its verdict states, "The construction and operation of a great dam should never be left to the sole judgment of one man, no matter how eminent."[62]

Above all, the survivors of the tragedy needed help in putting their lives together. While relief committees provided immediate

[59]Charles F. Outland, *Man-Made Disaster: The Story of St. Francis Dam—Its Place in Southern California's Water System, Its Failure and the Tragedy of March 12 and 13, 1928, in the Santa Clara River Valley*, pp. 197–198.

[60]Finkle to John R. Haynes, August 12, 1931, Haynes Papers, GPA. Finkle enclosed a clipping of an undated newspaper that printed his report of September 8, 1924, predicting that the Saint Francis Dam "if kept full for any length of time . . . will unquestionably fail." The report was made at the request of the Santa Monica Anti-Annexation Committee.

[61]*Los Angeles Times*, March 20, 1928.

[62]Los Angeles County Coroner, "Transcript of Testimony and Verdict of the Coroner's Jury in the Inquest Over Victims of St. Francis Dam Disaster," Book 26902, March 21, 1928, p. 3, quoted in Robert William Matson, *William Mulholland: A Forgotten Forefather*, p. 64.

assistance, Los Angeles and Ventura counties' officials assured the payment of fair compensation for the loss of life and property. "History will view the total picture and record that the settlements were just and paid in a relatively short period of time," observed Charles Outland in his study of the disaster. The beneficiaries received "more money at less cost to Los Angeles than would have been the case if the matter had been dragged through the courts; and the friendly adjudication of thousands of individual losses without recourse to the courts stands as a unique achievement in California history."[63]

The Saint Francis Dam disaster was the second-worst catastrophe in the modern history of California, exceeded in loss of life and property by only the 1906 San Francisco earthquake and fire. In contrast to the San Francisco tragedy, though, the Saint Francis Dam failure is remembered mainly by its survivors. Outland has complained, "San Franciscans have long worshipped at the pagan shrine of their "damndest, finest ruins' and the accumulated printed material on the subject is endless. But Saint Francis Dam has been allowed to decay into historical wreckage as shattered as the ill-fated dam itself."[64] Ironically, even the attempt to commemorate the fiftieth anniversary of the tragedy was prevented. Because of mudslides and rock slides on the access road, the Santa Clarita Valley Historical Society was forced to postpone indefinitely its placing of a historical marker at the dam site.[65]

However imperfectly later generations would remember the Saint Francis Dam disaster, in the late 1920's California residents were vividly aware of the water controversy and the tragedies it produced. But as the events became part of the historical record, the way in which those events would be remembered took a new turn. The manner by which the city had come to its pinnacles of power and influence was being evaluated by an obscure civic reformer whose influence on later historians would far exceed their memory of him. The civic reformer's name was Andrae B. Nordskog.

---

[63]Outland, *Man-Made Disaster*, p. 168.
[64]Ibid., p. 9. The site is now almost unrecognizable.
[65]*Los Angeles Times*, March 12, 1978.

His weapon was the pen; his enemies were everyone who had ever been connected with the creation of the Owens Valley–Los Angeles aqueduct.

7

Andrae Nordskog and the Persistence of Conspiracy History

"I have championed the people of Owens Valley in my paper, on the platform and over the radio. It is my conviction that many of their claims are just."—Andrae B. Nordskog, quoted in the *Los Angeles Times*, November 2, 1929

THE arrest and conviction of the Watterson brothers on charges of embezzlement marked the end of active resistance from the people of Inyo County. Although the triumph of the city was almost immediately marred by the tragedy of the Saint Francis Dam disaster, Los Angeles could now look forward to consolidating its position in Owens Valley. Resistance, however, did continue, in another form— one that defined not how the struggle would end but how it would be recorded as history.

During the three-year water war Owens Valley residents were not without defenders in Los Angeles. The *Los Angeles Record*, a major metropolitan newspaper, ran numerous articles demanding that city officials deal fairly with valley residents. A second newspaper went much further than the *Record* in asserting Owens Valley rights and accusing the city of wrongdoing. This paper was the curiously titled Los Angeles *Gridiron*, published weekly by a self-styled civic reformer named Andrae B. Nordskog.

Nordskog earned his credentials as a reformer while living an astonishingly full life, combining several careers into one personality. Born in 1885 in Story City, Iowa, of Norwegian parentage, Nordskog (at first named Arne Andreas, which was later changed to Andrae

B.) attended Des Moines College, where he studied voice. A talented tenor with interests in electronic gadgetry, Nordskog went on concert tours around the country, while developing electrical devices in his spare time. At age nineteen he married and soon had a growing family. He became interested in the manufacture of phonograph records and in 1921, after settling in Santa Monica, California, he established Nordskog Records. Having also acquired a reputation as a concert tenor, Nordskog gave voice lessons, appeared in musical recitals, and served briefly as manager of the newly created Hollywood Bowl. His record company produced New Orleans jazz records, which have since become collectors' items. A business reversal some time around 1923, in which a banker cheated Nordskog, resulted in a move to Los Angeles and an interest in reform.[1]

At first Nordskog wrote articles for community newspapers, while still deriving income from giving voice lessons. His main targets in the 1920's were telephone companies, which, in the absence of rate regulation, were charging unfair rates. In late 1926 he began publication of the Los Angeles *Gridiron*, a small weekly newspaper with ambiguous claims as to circulation. The first issues focused on such reform efforts as reduction of telephone rates, paving of streets, installation of storm drains, and development of city parks. Before very long, however, Nordskog's newspaper concentrated on the fight between Inyo County and the City of Los Angeles over not only Owens River water but the very land of the Owens Valley, as Los Angeles accelerated its policy of buying out valley farmers and ranchers.

The reasons for Nordskog's focus on water problems are not entirely clear. By his own account, Nordskog drove up to Owens Valley some time in June, 1927, "and visited with its citizens whose souls were dwarfed and shrunk because of the terrible warfare carried on by crooked politicians of a great and wealthy city." He

---

[1]Biographical information on Nordskog is from *Who's Who on the Pacific Coast*, pp. 483–484; John Bently and Ralph W. Miller, "Andrae Nordskog," *Jazz Monthly* (May, 1959), 8–10; *Record and Show Mirror* (London), April 16, 1960, p. 6; Nordskog Papers prospectus, Minnesota Historical Society, Minneapolis, Minnesota (hereafter cited as MHS); and materials provided by Mr. Robert Nordskog.

went there "to learn first-hand the source of the trouble then exist-ing."[2] Nordskog met Willie Chalfant, publisher of the *Inyo Register*, and other Owens Valley residents, including Mark and Wilfred Watterson. Convinced of the injustice done to the valley, Nordskog offered the Wattersons the services of his newspaper and a promise to appear on public forums on behalf of the valley's cause. However, some financial support would be needed. The Wattersons agreed to provide Nordskog with between $3,500 and $4,000, payable in cash installments, to subsidize Nordskog's work. The funds would be passed to Nordskog through the Wattersons' brother-in-law, Jacob C. Clausen.[3]

The Watterson subsidy deserves investigation on a number of counts. Why would the Inyo bankers pay for the support of a small weekly newspaper in Los Angeles when the Owens Valley people already had the editorial backing of a major metropolitan daily, the *Los Angeles Record*? Did the Wattersons believe Nordskog's claims for his newspaper's influence and his contacts with important offi-cials? "A busy week I have had," Nordskog wrote to Wilfred Watter-son on June 27. "Have already arranged for several lectures to be given to the best clubs in the city at the Biltmore Hotel, Ambassador Hotel and other places and have been able to stir up the proper sentiment." Conferences had been held with Mayor George Cryer, Governor Clement Young, and State Attorney General U. S. Webb. On July 2 he stated, "I am positive that we can win. We will win this fight. So positive of it am I that I have given hours of time to it when I should have been resting. . . . I am doing everything in my power to bring this matter to a climax, spending three to four times more energy than I thought would be necessary."[4]

In one typical example of spending energy, Nordskog addressed the Women's City Club at the Morosco Theater on July 11. Accord-ing to the *Los Angeles Times* (which could always be counted on to treat Nordskog's appearances with sarcasm), Nordskog was accom-

[2]Andrae B. Nordskog, "Water is Plentiful," pp. 8, 9, Andrae B. Nords-kog Collection, MHS.
[3]"Out of Their Own Mouths," *Municipal League of Los Angeles Bulletin* 5 (October 31, 1927), 3. This article contains important and controversial excerpts of correspondence between Nordskog and the Wattersons.
[4]Ibid.

panied by two bodyguards because of alleged threats on his life. "No physical violence was offered Nordskog by the assembled women," observed the *Times*, although the discussion did become heated. Nordskog called for arbitration between the city and those valley residents who had been unfairly treated. He agreed that the dynamiters of the aqueduct should be arrested, but he predicted "even greater violence" if the city would not agree to arbitration.

Municipal League spokesman John R. Richards refused to appear at the same meeting with Nordskog, preferring to reserve his own presentation on the issues for the group's following meeting. A rebuttal was given by Dr. Laura Locke, who criticized Nordskog for making unsupported statements. She argued that, like Nordskog, she had visited Owens Valley but had found the region prospering from tourist traffic.[5]

Nordskog apparently resented the *Times* statement about his need for protection, for the next day the newspaper printed a clarification. Robert G. Vans said he and a friend had appeared with Nordskog out of support for his reform efforts. He also denied reports that Nordskog's life had been threatened. Despite Vans's disclaimer, the impression given was that Nordskog did indeed have two bodyguards. As *Saturday Night*, a Los Angeles weekly literary magazine published by Samuel Clover in the 1920's, put it, the presence of the bodyguards "explains why the speaker was not molested when he made statements that he could not substantiate." The magazine also referred to Nordskog as the "missionary from Inyo County." Nordskog's view of the Morosco meeting, communicated to Wilfred Watterson, was that it had been a "big success" and that Richards, with "cold feet, stayed away." He boasted, "I was tipped off that he would fail to appear, but really I didn't think he was that big a coward." As to his reception: "The women got the drift. I spoke one hour."[6]

Nordskog delivered other lectures in Los Angeles, and he distributed 100,000 copies of July issues of the *Gridiron*. For this work

[5]*Los Angeles Times*, July 12, 1927.

[6]Ibid., July 13, 1927; "Inyo County's Missionary Pleader," *Saturday Night* 7 (July 16, 1927), 3–4; "Andrae B. Nordskog in the Light of the Watterson Verdict," *Municipal League of Los Angeles Bulletin* 5 (November 30, 1927), 1–2.

Wilfred Watterson sent $2,000, funneled through Clausen and given to Nordskog as a cash payment "as he does not want it known that he is working directly for the property owners' assn. here." The *Gridiron* headlines, carrying Nordskog's byline and photograph, placed him firmly in support of the valley: "L.A. Refuses to Arbitate [*sic*]"; "Owens Valley Suffers Loss"; "Citizens Demanding Truth"; "Water Board Quizzed"; "$31,000,000 Water Waste." *Gridiron* editorials were reprinted in Owens Valley papers, and valley editorial cartoons appeared in the *Gridiron*.[7]

Then, on August 4, 1927, the five Watterson banks closed their doors. Over the next few months valley resistance crumbled as the truth about the Wattersons' embezzlement emerged during their indictment, trial, conviction, and sentencing. Although Nordskog never received the remaining amount of the promised subsidy, he vowed to continue the fight. Beginning in September he obtained free radio time on KGEF, a church-operated station owned by the Reverend Robert Shuler, himself a controversial supporter of civic reform. For eighteen weeks Nordskog baited water department officials through press and radio. He sent copies of the *Gridiron*—his photograph now showing him holding a radio microphone—to every member of the Board of Water and Power Commissioners each week. Mulholland and the commissioners, who had long ignored Nordskog's attacks, now found him getting under their skin. Dr. John R. Haynes, prominent civic leader and a member of the Water and Power Commission, approached Reverend Shuler and asked for equal time. On several occasions, because of extreme statements he made, Nordskog lost the privilege of using the radio station—a circumstance he blamed on coercion from city water officials. Nordskog also claimed the DWP pressured *Gridiron* advertisers to take their business elsewhere. In one instance, when Nordskog had planned to use a front-page article declaring the Hollywood Dam unsafe, his printer refused to print the story, claiming it would alarm the community and raise insurance rates. Nordskog relented but kept the galley sheet, a prophetic souvenir of the disaster that

---

[7]"Out of Their Own Mouths," p. 3; Los Angeles *Gridiron*, July 1, 8, 15, 22, and 29, 1927; *Owens Valley Herald*, July 13, 1927.

occurred a few months later with the failure of the Saint Francis Dam.[8]

Haynes, Mulholland, and other water officials endured Nordskog's editorial barrage as best they could. The Department of Water and Power and the City of Los Angeles already had a dubious political image, however, and Nordskog's simplified accusations could not be as simply answered.

Then the city had a lucky break. In a move of dubious legality, water board representatives gained access to private files in the Wattersons' Inyo County Bank. The bank had been taken over by the state superintendent of banks, Will C. Wood. One of Wood's subordinates, acting without authority and under the impression that the city men were investigating a question concerning an irrigation district, allowed them to remove a quantity of letters from the files. When he found out, Wood demanded that the letters—originals and any copies made—be returned to the bank. But Wood did not learn of the removal of the documents until late November, and long before then Haynes, Richards, and other friends of the DWP had made good use of them. The Municipal League of Los Angeles published excerpts from the correspondence in their bulletin on October 31, implicating certain Los Angeles critics of their city's water policy in acts ranging from cooperation to collusion. Among the revelations were letters between Nordskog and the Wattersons concerning the subsidy.[9]

Nordskog's editorial cries of outrage could not mask the bald fact that he had served as "a civic crusader for pay." He denied the charges emphatically. "True, I have championed the people of Owens Valley in my paper, on the platform and over the radio," he stated. "It is my conviction that many of their claims are just." While he admitted receiving "some expense money," he saw "nothing criminal in that." He claimed that thousands of extra copies of the *Gridiron*

[8]Andrae Nordskog, "Boulder Dam in the Light of the Owens Valley Fraud," pp. 3, 15–16, and idem, "Testimony of Andrae Nordskog," pp. 24–26, both in Andrae B. Nordskog Collection, MHS.

[9]"Out of Their Own Mouths," p. 3; Nordskog, "Water is Plentiful," pp. 229–230.

had been sold to Owens Valley readers. "That is the only revenue I have received."[10]

The *Times* delighted in seeing some of its critics caught in a compromising situation. The correspondence indicated "that a small clique in Owens Valley, with the paid assistance of some Los Angeles journalists, was playing a game which had for its object the squeezing of Los Angeles taxpayers and water users out of every cent obtainable, largely for the benefit of the Wattersons, whose financial condition, due to speculation, was becoming desperate and who were driven to correspondingly desperate measures." After the Wattersons were found guilty on November 11, the Municipal League's bulletin published additional correspondence between the bankers and Nordskog.[11]

In their acrimonious exchange, the *Bulletin* and the *Gridiron* ironically ignored their own gray areas. Nordskog attacked the Municipal League and the Department of Water and Power for illegally taking private letters but did not once mention the incriminating subsidy agreement. The Municipal League, on the other hand, criticized Nordskog's acceptance of Watterson money without enlightening *Bulletin* readers as to how the letters had been obtained. Months later Nordskog found the published correspondence still being used against him, as in one instance when he tried to address the city council during a hearing on storm drain construction. He also lost the use of Reverend Shuler's radio station.[12]

Nordskog's participation in the water-wars episode might have ended at this point, with Nordskog remaining a peripheral figure in the controversy. Indeed, he has received little more than passing notice in standard accounts of the water controversy and virtually no mention at all in general histories of California. Where he is

[10]*Los Angeles Times*, November 2, 1927.

[11]Ibid., November 4, 1927; "Nordskog in the Light of the Watterson Verdict," pp. 1–2. *Los Angeles Record* owners, while not receiving money from the Wattersons, communicated to them the prices the Department of Water and Power was willing to offer for certain ranches ("Out of Their Own Mouths," p. 1).

[12]Los Angeles *Gridiron*, January 26, 1928; *Los Angeles Times*, September 21, 1928; "Out of Their Own Mouths," p. 3; "Nordskog in the Light of the Watterson Verdict," pp. 1–2; Nordskog, "Water is Plentiful," pp. 229–230; John R. Haynes to Franklin Hichborn, December 1, 1927, Haynes Papers, GPA.

mentioned, the authors have disparaged his role. Vincent Ostrom in his study *Water and Politics* pegged Nordskog as a publicist hired by the Wattersons "to press their demands in Los Angeles through the medium of the *Gridiron*." Remi Nadeau in *The Water Seekers* called Nordskog a "self-appointed Los Angeles reformer" in the 1950 edition of his book, then dropped the "self-appointed" comment in the 1974 edition. Like Ostrom, Nadeau noted that Nordskog's interest in championing the valley was based upon payment from the Watterson brothers to carry on an anticity crusade. In actuality Nordskog did most of his crusading after the Wattersons were exposed as embezzlers, despite his not receiving any further funds, and his personal crusade was to have a lasting effect on the water dispute.[13]

It might be expected that, having been exposed as a paid supporter of the valley's cause, Nordskog would at the very least adopt a low profile about the controversy. However, the opposite occurred. Nordskog may have accepted Watterson money, but he also believed in the integrity of the valley's position—and in the evildoing of the city. Instead of giving up on the valley, Nordskog intensified his concern.

A New Crusade

Early in 1928 Nordskog made plans to go to Washington, D.C., to examine Bureau of Reclamation records dealing with the original involvement of the Reclamation Service in the aborted Owens Valley reclamation project. He also intended to speak to congressional representatives concerning the Swing-Johnson Boulder Dam bill, which he opposed. Nordskog brought along copies of the front page of a *Gridiron* issue with an "Open Letter to Congress" containing arguments against the construction of Boulder Dam. The letter was specifically concerned with salt intrusion, pumping costs, and the expense of developing power plants. Haynes, Anthony Pratt, and other members of the Municipal League were aware of Nordskog's presence in Washington, and they contacted the lobbyists who

[13]Vincent Ostrom, *Water and Politics: A Study of Water Policies and Administration in the Development of Los Angeles*, p. 129; Remi Nadeau, *The Water Seekers*, 1950 ed., p. 109 (cf. 1974 edition, p. 91).

favored the bill. These lobbyists defused Nordskog's open letter by publicizing the Watterson embezzlement and Nordskog's connection with the banker brothers.[14]

If his attempt to impress the Seventieth Congress met with disappointing results, Nordskog was far more successful in his search of Bureau of Reclamation records. On arriving at the bureau offices, he presented his request to inspect back files. The request was apparently given routine acceptance, although Nordskog elevated the permission granted to something far more grand. He claimed, "I was given the most unusual privilege ever given to a private citizen by being permitted to read some 4,000 secret letters and official documents in the files of the United States Reclamation Service in the Department of the Interior relating to the fraudulent operation of the Owens River Reclamation Project which was killed by collusion with Los Angeles real estate speculators, bankers and certain newspaper publishers who made millions upon millions on the deal and who are continuing to make money at the expense of the ratepayers and taxpayers of this city."[15]

Soon after his arrival in Washington, Nordskog contacted Jacob Clausen asking for "information relating to the promises which allegedly had been made by the Reclamation Service to the Owens Valley ranchers." Nordskog wrote to Clausen on March 9; the former Reclamation Service engineer replied on March 20. On March 12 the Saint Francis Dam failed, giving a special urgency to Nordskog's search in the records. Clausen answered regretfully that he no longer had his old records, which had been lost or loaned out over the years. He did recall that private initiative had been discouraged because of government activities in the valley and a general expectation that the federal reclamation project would become a reality. When Los Angeles developed its aqueduct plans, applications for projects such as reservoirs met with the city's opposition, and the bureau acceded to the city's wishes. "In this way the City was given everything, and the private parties nothing," stated Clausen.

[14]"Congress Warned of Andrae Nordskog," *Municipal League of Los Angeles Bulletin* 5 (April 1, 1928), 5. For Nordskog's version see Nordskog, "Boulder Dam in the Light of the Owens Valley Fraud," pp. 3–4. His "An Open Letter to Congress" is in Los Angeles *Gridiron*, February 3, 1928.

[15]Nordskog, "Testimony," p. 2.

"And, of course, all pending applications, even if filed before, were held up and disapproved. This all amounted to a forced relinquishment."[16]

Nordskog, to be sure, was not a professional historian. The National Archives, where Bureau of Reclamation records would eventually be stored, did not exist in 1928, and apparently the Bureau of Reclamation clerks who brought out the records for Nordskog's inspection were not professional archivists. In 1928 there was no way of photocopying important documents inexpensively. There were three choices as to research methodology: copy by hand, use a typewriter, or steal the letters. Nordskog used all three methods. He began by summarizing, in longhand, the contents of the letters. Then he started copying the letters verbatim, some of them on a borrowed typewriter. Finally, possibly frustrated by the sheer volume of documents, he either stole some letters or else was given extra copies by a nondedicated clerk. Multiple copies of many of the letters probably made it easier for Nordskog to persuade the clerk to part with them.[17]

And what letters! There before his eyes were Austin's letter of August 4, 1905, to Theodore Roosevelt and the president's letter of June 25, 1906, to Secretary of the Interior Hitchcock. There were the reports of Sanders, Henny, and Taylor of July 28 and 31, 1905, to Newell, Arthur Powell Davis' letter of July 28, 1905, inquiring about Eaton's alleged masquerade, and dozens of letters concerning right-of-way applications that conflicted with the city's aqueduct plans. Nordskog took notes on hundreds of letters in the bureau's general files pertaining to the Owens Valley reclamation project.

From the correspondence he examined, Nordskog began to formulate an outline detailing Reclamation Service malfeasance and incompetence, plus collusion with Los Angeles so that, at the same time the greatest good came to the greatest number, a few select

[16]Nordskog. "Water is Plentiful," pp. 18–20. Clausen's letter is reproduced on pp. 19–20.

[17]Andrae B. Nordskog Papers, Water Resources Center Archives, University of California, Berkeley (hereafter cited as WRCA). The Nordskog materials at Berkeley include a key, in longhand, to the "Boulder Dam in the Light of the Owens Valley Fraud" manuscript, a copy of which is at the Minnesota Historical Society.

members of the greatest number would profit by the city's triumph and could enrich themselves considerably. Although Los Angeles had acted to protect its own interests, Nordskog chose to interpret the city's actions in the most sinister light possible. The letters he examined clearly indicated the Reclamation Service had made serious errors of judgment. Nordskog took the errors a step further and evolved a thesis that incorporated the failure of the Reclamation Service to develop an Owens Valley reclamation project, the aggression and misrepresentation of Los Angeles in securing water rights and an aqueduct route, deviousness by Los Angeles civic and business leaders in making millions in San Fernando Valley real estate, and incompetence and tragedy in wasting taxpayers' money and constructing the Saint Francis Dam and other potentially unsafe reservoirs. As his research progressed, Nordskog added a final, current element to the story: the supporters of the Boulder Dam project on the Colorado River were the same people who had supported, financed, and even constructed the Owens Valley–Los Angeles aqueduct.

To Nordskog the bureau letters appeared as a sign from heaven, perhaps on a scale comparable in more recent times to Daniel Ellsberg's discovery of the Pentagon Papers. "While in Washington I worked day and night pouring [sic] over the records and it was seldom that I got any sleep until from two to four o'clock A.M.," he recalled. "I spent four weeks at the Capital City and I came away with more material than I could use in many volumes, so I will have to abbreviate many of the facts I will quote." Rebuffs from Secretary of the Interior Hubert Work and U.S. Senator Lawrence C. Phipps, chairman of the Committee on Irrigation and Reclamation, to the effect that the events with which Nordskog was concerned were twenty-five years old and had already been reviewed, failed to dissuade Nordskog. Notes in hand, he returned to Los Angeles fired with the conviction that he had indeed experienced a revelation, that he had seen "secretly guarded" and "dusty" files to which none before him had been given access.[18]

[18]"Boulder Dam in the Light of the Owens Valley Fraud," pp. 16, 492–497. See also Andrae B. Nordskog, *Spiking the Gold, Or, Who Caused the Depression . . . and the Way Out*, p. 4.

On returning to Los Angeles, Nordskog assumed a heavy work load. The tasks of putting out the *Gridiron*, presenting lectures, doing radio programs, and appearing at public hearings all competed with the time needed to complete a manuscript based on his research. There were also trips to Nevada, Arizona, and various places in California to locate other documents and to speak with people. Meanwhile, another issue caused growing concern for Nordskog. Los Angeles laid plans for a $38,800,000 bond issue in 1930 for construction of an aqueduct from the Colorado River to Los Angeles as a part of the Metropolitan Water District. Harvey Van Norman, a name only slightly less scandalous to Nordskog's thinking than Mulholland's, and the old Chief's successor as head of the DWP, led the campaign for the bonds. This only reinforced Nordskog's conviction that the "Mulholland political crowd" was promoting the project with the intention of amassing even greater wealth and once again cheating the taxpayers.[19]

Nordskog's Manuscript

By the summer of 1929 Nordskog had written most of his manuscript, which he titled "Boulder Dam in the Light of the Owens Valley Fraud." It reproduced in part or entirely many of the Reclamation Service letters he had uncovered. The task of publishing a manuscript of its size—in finished typescript it came to 540 double-spaced pages—seemed beyond the resources of his Gridiron Publishing Company, so Nordskog began to check around for someone who might lead him to a publisher. One likely prospect, Nordskog decided, was a local writer named Carey McWilliams.

At this time McWilliams had achieved a measure of local literary fame through his columns in the *Los Angeles Times*, the literary weekly *Saturday Night*, and articles in a number of magazines. In addition, McWilliams had just published his first book, a

---

[19]H. A. Van Norman and E. A. Bayley, "Colorado River–Los Angeles Aqueduct Project," *Engineering News-Record* 100 (May 31, 1928), 850–854; H. A. Van Norman, "Then, There Is the Great Aqueduct to Build," *Southern California Business* 8 (September, 1929), 16–17; Nordskog, "Boulder Dam in the Light of the Owens Valley Fraud," pp. 459–461.

biography of Ambrose Bierce, and he was in communication with some prominent literary figures, including Mary Austin, who was then living in New Mexico.[20]

On August 6, 1929, McWilliams informed Austin of a visit Nordskog had made to him. He reported that Nordskog was "finishing a manuscript about the Owens Valley—a technical, detailed, voluminous record of the entire situation. He has devoted years to the task and is something of an engineer." Nordskog had clearly made a positive impression on the young writer. "It occurred to me that if you want any verification of facts about the Valley, he could give you expert opinion," McWilliams suggested.[21]

At McWilliams' suggestion Nordskog wrote to Mary Austin, and for a time Nordskog found both authors entranced with his research. "He has a vast amount of material about Owens Valley and his book should be a sensation," McWilliams predicted to Austin. The information Nordskog had gathered continued to impress McWilliams. He reported on Nordskog's finding the Austin-Fysh letters of protest buried in Department of the Interior files. "He said that one of the letters was one of the most passionate and moving documents he had ever read. He has copies of all this material."[22]

By the end of the year, with the manuscript almost completed, Nordskog at last brought McWilliams a portion of it. McWilliams admired the work but expressed some reservations to Austin about Nordskog's prose style. He credited Nordskog with having done an amazing piece of research, proving "conclusively, by correspondence which he copies from the files of the Sec. of Interior that the govt. officials in the Reclamation Service were hand and glove with the water board of Los Angeles. Moreover that they deliberately deceived the settlers of Owens Valley; moreover that the same officials and engineers are responsible for the St. Francis dam disaster, and the fall of the dam at Oakland; moreover that the same crowd

[20]Carey McWilliams, *Southern California: An Island on the Land*, pp. xvi–xvii (a reprint of the 1946 text with a new introduction); idem, "Writers of the Western Shore," *Westways* 70 (November, 1978), 16–20.

[21]McWilliams to Austin, August 6, 1929, Austin Papers, HL.

[22]McWilliams to Austin, [late 1929?], ibid.; Austin to McWilliams, December 22, 1929, McWilliams Papers, SCD.

is spending millions of dollars, about thirty! at San Gabriel; MORE-
OVER that this self same crowd propose to build BOULDER DAM!"
McWilliams, utterly convinced of the veracity of Nordskog's findings, pronounced it as the "most sickening yarn I have ever read,"
a story that kept him awake at night thinking of the "conspiracy,
double-dealing, rotten politics, greed, avarice, amusing chicanery,
etc." Yet with all of this research, Nordskog wrote "like a bond
salesman touched with a yen to be a poet."[23]

Nordskog promised to send a copy of his manuscript to Austin,
and it appears he did mail her about two-thirds of it. His method of
presenting his information to McWilliams, however, was no longer
as tantalizing as it had been at first and was getting somewhat tiresome. Nordskog proved reluctant to let McWilliams handle the
manuscript, preferring to read portions of it aloud. A strain soon
developed in their relationship. McWilliams believed Nordskog had
"done a fine bit of investigation," with commendable industry. But
the manuscript clearly suffered from amateurish writing. There was
"a lot of extraneous matter and he waves the flag at intervals."
Nordskog was "very vain and has tried to induce me to write a
long and pompous 'Foreword' which I have declined to do," Mc-
Williams informed Austin. He suggested that she might be the one
to write an introduction. "My name would mean nothing in an introduction," declared McWilliams, "and I refuse to write a foreword
about N. as I see no necessity for so doing." He also suggested that
author Louis Adamic might be of assistance in finding a publisher for
Nordskog's manuscript.[24]

Mary Austin agreed with McWilliams on the manuscript's faults
and virtues. She also expressed some irritation over Nordskog's
urgings that she contact possible New York publishers for him.

[23]McWilliams to Austin, [December?] 1929, Austin Papers, HL.

[24]McWilliams to Austin, January 27, 1930, Austin Papers, HL. Louis
Adamic was at this time preparing for *New Leader* an article on the Mooney
case, which also mentioned Los Angeles' aggressive water policies. Its anticity
bias prompted John R. Haynes to write a letter of complaint to Norman
Thomas, whose League for Industrial Democracy published *New Leader*
(Haynes to Thomas, April 14, 1930, and Thomas to Haynes, April 21, 1930,
Haynes Papers, GPA). Adamic also published an article critical of Los
Angeles later that year in *Outlook*: "Los Angeles! There She Blows!" *Out-
look* 155 (August 13, 1930), 563–565, 594–597.

Nordskog's failure to accept her advice and suggestions eventually brought her to exasperation. "Nordskog is evidently incapable of handling his material successfully," she concluded.[25]

Although the exchange of correspondence between Nordskog and Austin is not available, it seems clear that Austin rejected Nordskog's invitation to write a foreword. Her unfavorable impression of Nordskog's insistent attitude was echoed by McWilliams who by March, 1930, was quite tired of Nordskog's pomposity and refusal to accept literary criticism. "N. is quite all that you say and more. A more pestiferous fellow you could scarcely imagine," he wrote to Austin. "Too much energy is, I believe, a dubious gift. . . . The man has little or no idea of how to handle his material and it would be an act of arrogance to attempt a few words of advice." On April 2, in their last discussion of Nordskog, Austin informed McWilliams that publisher Alfred A. Knopf had rejected Nordskog's manuscript. "They think, as we do, that the material is very badly handled."[26]

Nordskog now faced a dilemma only partly of his own making. The Great Depression had become a fact of life, making it all the more difficult for an author to find a publisher willing to accept a large manuscript. Nordskog's own press could not handle the task, although he did publish several small books in the early depression years.

Any possibility that a major book publisher would consider the Boulder Dam manuscript was prevented by Nordskog himself. He stubbornly refused to allow any editing. McWilliams' assessment of

[25] Austin to McWilliams, March 3 [1930], McWilliams Papers, SCD.

[26] McWilliams to Austin, March 22, 1930, Austin Papers, HL; Austin to McWilliams, April 2, 1930, McWilliams Papers, SCD. In 1971 McWilliams recalled his encounters with Nordskog for me. "I came to have a distinctly unpleasant impression of Nordskog," he stated. "I don't remember why he came to see me. He may have read something I had written or some one may have suggested that he see me. In any case he wanted help with the manuscript, not editorial help, but help in getting it published or in securing financing for publication. Over a period of time he became quite insistent about all this, disagreeably so. When I wrote Mrs. Austin that he had 'too much energy' I was probably referring to his attempts to pressure me. I also remember that he did not respond very well to comments and suggestions about the manscript" (McWilliams to the author, April 19, 1971, author's files).

the manuscript was a correct one. Jam-packed with quotations, lengthy excerpts, and reproductions of entire letters, the manuscript offered considerable ammunition to critics of Los Angeles water policy and the Boulder Dam project. But its organization was chaotic: frequent leaps forward and backward in time, an over-burdening personal bias, and a continuing air of the author's in-credulity at looking over "dusty" files combined to make the manu-script unpublishable without the sharp blue pencil of a professional editor. Nordskog seemed unaware of the contradiction between his claims for "secretly guarded" files containing material long "sup-pressed" and the fact that he had experienced no difficulty in in-vestigating the files himself and indeed had with ease carried off some of those very same letters. Passages dealing with Nordskog's own difficulties with the Board of Water and Power Commissioners, his programs on KGEF, and his trip to Washington seemed extrane-ous, more appropriate for an autobiography than for a serious study linking the Boulder Dam project with events of a quarter-century earlier.

Overall, the manuscript lacked objectivity. An impartial editor would have immediately noted Nordskog's chthonian descriptions of Mulholland, Lippincott, Van Norman, Otis, Chandler, and other figures involved in the water controversy. First inspection gives the impression of a massively researched exposé. A second look reveals problems McWilliams may have noted and conveyed unsuccessfully to Nordskog. The chief shortcoming of Nordskog's work was his single-mindedness, his conclusions reached before his research was begun. He included only those letters which seemed incriminating. Other letters, which modified or contradicted his views, were ignored. The possibility that additional documentation might be found else-where was not even considered.

No professional historian could afford to make this kind of argument without suffering the severest criticism from his colleagues. But Nordskog was not a professional historian. He was a journalist committed to reform, and he had no interest in presenting evidence that might contradict his thesis. As a result, the Reclamation Service investigation into Lippincott's conduct was deemphasized and dubbed a "whitewash"; the estrangement between Arthur Powell Davis and Lippincott was made permanent rather than temporary, and personal as well as professional; statistics were given that misled rather than informed. Stafford Austin's own land speculations were ignored, as was Jacob Clausen's marriage into the Watterson family.

Nordskog placed everyone in two camps, the noble defenders of Owens Valley and the villainous supporters of obtaining water and power for an ambitious and aggressive Los Angeles. Where some people proved hard to categorize, he explained away contradictory conduct with a superficial excuse. This was necessary, since for Nordskog to do otherwise would have been to defame people whose reputations were unblemished by accusations of corruption.

Nordskog was also blind to the fact that others might sincerely subscribe to principles different from his own. For example, he wrote to Gifford Pinchot inquiring as to why Owens Valley acreage had been withdrawn from "forest" land. Pinchot, who had survived the famous controversy with Richard Ballinger in the Taft years to go on to a political career that included the governorship of Pennsylvania, responded forthrightly: the land "was withdrawn because the effort was being made to file upon that land in advance of the creation of the Aqueduct in order to hold up the city. I believed then, and I believe now, just as President Roosevelt believed, that the greatest good of the greatest number was subserved by the construction of the Aqueduct, and I did what I could do to forward the project and prevent any persons from holding it up. Indeed, I am convinced that I did well."[27]

To Nordskog's mind, however, the "greatest good of the greatest number" was merely an excuse for robbing Owens Valley of its water, not a tenet of Progressive-Era philosophy. Hence, in Nordskog's view Theodore Roosevelt was "duped" into approving legislation favorable to Los Angeles. If Roosevelt had not been fooled, then he too would have to be considered one of the villains.

The Southwest Water League

With the manuscript at last completed, Nordskog could turn his mind to other problems, at least when he was not busy seeking

[27]Pinchot to Nordskog, January 14, 1930, in Nordskog, "Water is Plentiful," p. 199.

a publisher for his book. He spent the early months of 1930 campaigning against the $38.8 million bond issue that, if passed, would result in the construction of the Owens Valley–Los Angeles aqueduct up to the Mono Basin. Given the projected Colorado River aqueduct of the Metropolitan district, which called for $200 million from eleven Southern California cities, Nordskog saw the Mono extension as an unnecessary waste of taxpayers' money. The voters saw otherwise, approving the bonds by a margin of nine to one.[28]

The bond election marked a battle lost, not a war. To safeguard the interests of cities not a part of the Metropolitan Water District, 113 representatives from forty-eight Southern California cities met in Lynwood on October 18, 1930, to found the Southwest Water League. The opinions of the delegates varied from tentative support of the Metropolitan Water District to outright opposition. Some delegates viewed the new organization as simply a data-gathering study group, while others saw it as a means for safeguarding their water rights. Nordskog was named temporary chairman, a position that shortly afterward was changed to president. Nordskog subsequently used this position to continue his efforts to awaken the public to the dominance of the Los Angeles "water crowd."[29]

Nordskog soon found the Southwest Water League provided a convenient device not only for policing the Metropolitan Water District, but also for publicizing his research into the Owens Valley

[28]H. A. Van Norman, *Statement Concerning the $38,800,000 Bond Issue of the Bureau of Water Works and Supply*; idem, "Why Los Angeles Voted $38,800,000 for Water and How it will be Spent," *Western City* 6 (June, 1930), 17–19; Nordskog to Williamson Summers, May 11, 1930, Nordskog Papers, WRCA.

[29]*Los Angeles Times*, October 19 and December 1, 1930. Suspicions concerning Nordskog's leadership soon surfaced. Dr. George P. Clements, manager of the agricultural department of the Los Angeles Chamber of Commerce, reported that he had been invited to serve on a committee under Nordskog "to investigate the waters of the state of California. This committee has among its members some real outstanding men, but I doubt if they really know who their leader is." Clements declined the invitation (Clements to General Manager Arthur G. Arnoll, December 15, 1930, Clements Papers, Lettercase 1, SCD). Walter E. Hellinger, who had been appointed the league's secretary, soon resigned, claiming the league was "working contrary to its stated first intentions," and became an active supporter of the Metropolitan Water District ("Synopsis of the Meeting of the Southwest Water League," February 7, 1931, Haynes Papers, GPA).

controversy and Bureau of Reclamation incompetence. At least one league member, Samuel C. Evans of Riverside, the executive director of the Boulder Dam Association, took exception to Nordskog's statistical methodology. At Evans' request Nordskog submitted a list of twenty Bureau of Reclamation projects on which, Nordskog said, the eventual costs ran much higher than the original estimates, totaling as much as a 50 percent cost overrun. Evans objected to Nordskog's figures, noting that many projects had been sizably enlarged. As a case in point, he cited the Salt River project in Arizona, where the original estimate was for the dam alone and did not include diversion canal systems, pumping plants, road construction, or other improvements. Evans protested, "Your figures applied in an endeavor to show that probably the same excess of costs of estimates, as you quote them, would apply to the building of the proposed Metropolitan Water District Aqueduct from the Colorado River are very misleading, and we would respectfully request that you make reference to this correction." Nordskog acknowledged the criticism without comment at the next league meeting.[30]

A new opportunity for Nordskog to alert the public to Los Angeles' water aggressions came in early 1931 when the state senate adopted a resolution creating a special committee to investigate the city's actions in Owens Valley. The resolution had been introduced by Senate Senator Joe Riley of Bishop, whose constituency included Inyo and Mono counties. Five state senators were appointed, four of them from Northern California, and empowered to hold hearings and gather records. Nordskog was asked to testify before the committee in Sacramento on April 1. Determined to make the most of his appearance, Nordskog boiled down his 540-page "Boulder Dam" manuscript to 28 typewritten pages, which he read to the committee. He then printed his testimony in the April 7 issue of the *Gridiron*. On April 18, at the monthly meeting of the Southwest Water League, he secured the approval of the league membership to send the testimony to the state legislature as a league resolution. The resolution apparently made a positive impression on Speaker of the Assem-

[30]Nordskog to Evans, February 3, 1931; Evans to Nordskog, February 13, 1931; "Synopsis of a Meeting of the Southwest Water League," February 21, 1931, all in Haynes Papers, GPA.

bly Edgar C. Levey of San Francisco. He ordered that Nordskog's communication be printed in the *Assembly Journal*. Fifteen hundred reprints of the communication were then run off by the State Printing Office, with far-reaching consequences for California's history and historians.[31]

At first glance Nordskog's *Communication to the California Legislature Relating to the Owens Valley Water Situation* appears to be an official state document, which in one sense it is, having been printed by the state. On the cover there appears the State Seal of California; within its pages there is a letter of transmittal. The *Communication* is in three parts. The first part, pages 3–4, reprints the Southwest Water League's April 18 resolution; the second, pages 5–8, reprints Nordskog's letter of transmittal from the April 21 *Gridiron*, which he sent as a cover to the investigating committee. It lists twenty-five charges against the Reclamation Service, the City of Los Angeles, and various officials, particularly J. B. Lippincott. The third part, pages 9–28, contains the core of the "Boulder Dam in the Light of the Owens Valley Fraud" manuscript. Key letters were reproduced that appeared to incriminate Los Angeles water officials and businessmen acting in collusion with Reclamation Service officials. The events of 1903 to 1906, considered long dead by the secretary of the interior when Nordskog corresponded with him in 1928, were laid open and linked to the Boulder Dam project. Lippincott, Mulholland, Senator Frank Flint, Newell, Eaton, Chandler, and various Los Angeles businessmen and officials were accused of conspiring to defraud Owens Valley residents of their water and to make a killing in San Fernando Valley real estate at the same time. The failure of the Saint Francis Dam, the scandal connected

[31]California, Senate, *Journal*, March 9, 1931, pp. 797–798; March 19, 1931, pp. 1075–80, March 23, 1931, pp. 1157; *Los Angeles Times*, April 2, 1931; Los Angeles *Gridiron*, April 7 and 21 and May 5, 1931; Andrae B. Nordskog, *Communication to the California Legislature Relating to the Owens Valley Water Situation*. California, Assembly, *Journal*, April 27, 1931, pp. 2712–26, was the first legislative printing of Nordskog's communication. Earlier, on March 21, the Southwest Water League had submitted a petition to the assembly opposing Assembly Bill No. 1882, which would have excluded San Diego and other municipalities from Colorado River benefits because they were not members of the Metropolitan Water District. The petition was ordered printed (*Assembly Journal*, April 10, 1931, pp. 2153–54).

with the location of the San Gabriel Dam, and other dam failures were laid to Mulholland and the Bureau of Reclamation, and Nordskog accused the same people of trying the same nefarious dealings with the proposed Boulder Dam. "The Mulholland political crowd that has been in control of such gross mismanagement as heretofore cited," Nordskog concluded, "is in control of the Boulder Dam situation."[32]

During the years of the water wars there had been, to be sure, plenty of name-calling, but nothing like Nordskog's accusations. He brought a dizzying array of statistical figures and quotations from Reclamation Service records to support his argument. There had obviously been disapproval and discontent over the events of 1903 to 1906, and anger over the aqueduct had escalated in the 1920's into violence. Now, in the 1930's, critics of the actions of Los Angeles had what appeared to be a state-sponsored document supporting the view that it had all been a giant conspiracy.

Given its impact on subsequent writers of California history, the third section of the *Communication* deserves closer notice. Its title reads: "Statement of Facts Prepared for the Special Investigating Committee of the State Senate of California, Relating to the Operations of the Los Angeles Water-Power Board, in its Attempts to Obtain a Domestic Water Supply from Owens Valley in California, as Presented by Andrae B. Nordskog, at Sacramento, California, April 1, 1931." The authoritative title, "Statement of Facts," combined with the state seal on the reprint's cover, has led some historians to believe it is an official report. In actuality it is nothing more than the distillation of an unpublished, and probably unpublishable, manuscript by an amateur historian dedicated in his belief that the Owens Valley had been cheated of its rights by the City of Los Angeles. Its failure to indicate the source of the letters other than to mention "dusty" or "secret" files, however, meant that readers had to take the authenticity of the letters on faith, as well as the interpretation Nordskog gave them.[33]

On May 7 the State Senate Special Investigating Committee released its findings on Inyo and Mono counties' water difficulties.

[32]Nordskog, *Communication*, p. 28 and throughout.
[33]Ibid., p. 9.

The committee's report criticized Los Angeles for inconsistent appraisals in its program of purchasing valley properties, particularly urban businesses in such towns as Bishop and Independence. The city came in for hard raps for its insensitivity to valley business losses that resulted from the exclusion of such items as store fixtures and equipment from the appraisals. The committee recommended that instead of the city's using a blanket option form, greater flexibility and good will should have been shown to the valley people, who were selling not only their businesses, homes, and lands, but their way of life. Mainly concerned with current problems, the committee ignored the historical questions raised by Nordskog's *Communication.*[34]

Nordskog, who still had hopes for publication of his full-scale manuscript as late as 1932, had to settle for the *Communication* pamphlet. As a consolation prize, the windfall of 1,500 copies printed at state expense proved most agreeable to Nordskog. He urged his *Gridiron* readers to write to Sacramento for their copies. Every major library in the state received a copy, as did many minor ones. Carey McWilliams, dissatisfied with Nordskog personally, still thought highly of the *Communication.* He obtained a copy, as well as a copy of the committee's report, and urged Mary Austin to send for them too.[35]

[34]California, Senate, Special Investigating Committee, *Report of Senate Special Investigating Committee on Water Situation in Inyo and Mono Counties,* pp. 9–10; *Senate Journal,* May 7, 1931, pp. 2447–52, and May 11, 1931, p. 2549.

[35]McWilliams to Austin, June 22, 1931, Austin Papers, HL. In 1932, having turned his attention to depression problems, Nordskog wrote *Spiking the Gold; Or Who Caused the Depression and . . . the Way Out,* a small book he himself published. In his foreword he stated: "The author of this book has recently completed a book entitled '*Boulder Dam in the Light of the Owens Valley Frauds*' [sic] containing 540 pages in manuscript form. This is one of the most astounding exposes of Municipal and Governmental mismanagement on record in the United States. Mr. Nordskog has spent the better part of five years compiling facts and data in connection with this heart-gripping story revealing how thousands of hard working farmers were driven from their homes by city-wise politicians who stole millions upon millions of dollars worth of water and water rights belonging to these farmers who have since been driven to the four corners of the earth to start life anew. . . . Those desiring to place orders for '*Boulder Dam in the Light of the Owens Valley Frauds*' will be given preference in delivery when the book is

The *Communication* pamphlet soon had surprising repercussions for some people. "When this report was circulated throughout California," Nordskog recalled, "the City of Long Beach, for whom J. B. Lippincott was working, publicly stated that he might be fired, because of his ugly record in the Owens Valley."[36]

Lippincott's Reaction

By 1931 Joseph Barlow Lippincott, at age 67, could look back on a long and successful engineering career. Although he had left public service after the completion of the aqueduct in 1913, he periodically returned to government work on a consulting basis. Besides participating in the regular work of his firm, Lippincott served as consulting engineer for waterworks and flood-control projects in Santa Barbara, San Francisco, Denver, Honolulu, and many other cities. His work included not only hydraulic engineering but also advising the Automobile Club of Southern California on road-route surveys and the testing of concrete for highway construction. As a public-minded citizen, Lippincott had served on several Los Angeles city commissions, including the Parks and the Civil Service commissions. His professional career was highlighted by a long and active membership in the American Society of Civil Engineers, attending meetings, serving on committees, and giving papers; in 1931 he was chairman of the society's Irrigation Division committee on a national reclamation policy.[37]

---

published" (*Spiking the Gold*, pp. 3–4). The manuscript was never published. In 1955 Nordskog updated and revised it, but its content and tone remained essentially the same. The revised manuscript, titled "Water is Plentiful," was never published either.

[36]Nordskog, "Testimony," p. 24.

[37]Kenneth Q. Volk, "Joseph Barlow Lippincott," American Society of Civil Engineers, *Transactions* 108 (1943), 1547–49; Gerald J. Giefer and Anelle McCarty Kloski, comps., *Water Resources Reports and Papers in the J. B. Lippincott Collection*, Archives Series Report No. 21; J. B. Lippincott, "From Orange Blossoms to 'Conifers' Included in Project for Angeles Reserve Road," *Touring Topics* 11 (July, 1919), 12–15; Abraham Hoffman, "Angeles Crest: The Creation of a Forest Highway System in the San Gabriel Mountains," *Southern California Quarterly* 50 (September, 1968), 311–317; J. B. Lippincott et al., "Report of the Committee of the Irrigation Division on 'A National Reclamation Policy,'" American Society of Civil Engineers, *Proceedings (Papers and Discussions)* 57 (January, 1931), 129–133.

Lippincott firmly believed that Los Angeles had done the proper thing in its negotiated purchase of Owens Valley property. Thus it must have come as a shock to Lippincott to learn that the controversial events of a quarter-century earlier, which he assumed had been long ago investigated and settled, were suddenly in the public eye again. Some time after the committee report and Nordskog's *Communication* were printed, copies came into his possession. His reaction can only be imagined. The very first charge in the letter of transmittal stated: "Mr. J. B. Lippincott, supervising engineer of the Reclamation Service, in collusion with Los Angeles politicians and financiers, conspired to destroy the Owens Valley project in favor of a big land promotion scheme in San Fernando Valley, 250 miles to the south to which the waters from the Owens River were to be taken by an aqueduct to be paid for by the taxpayers of Los Angeles."[38]

Stung by the accusations that stained his personal and professional integrity, Lippincott turned to his old friend and colleague, Frederick Newell, for advice. "You will remember at one time we had some conversation about the relation of the Reclamation Service in Owens Valley and my connection with it in particular," he wrote to Newell on July 14, 1931. "I was criticized at the time for what I did, but, looking back at it I think that I was perfectly open and above board in doing what I thought was to the best public interest." He reminded Newell of his private practice while in Reclamation Service employ, admitting it had been a source of irritation for Newell at the time. Then he came to the heart of his problem. Recent agitation, "backed up by some unknown influence opposed to the proposed Colorado river aqueduct of the city, has been stirring up this old situation and have had some legislative investigations, etc.," stated Lippincott. "One of these reports was published recently as a communication to the California Legislature. There are some things in this that I never heard of before, among others, a letter from Davis dated Aug. 24, 1905, as shown on page 22. I thought that you might be interested in looking over this communication."[39]

The Davis letter referred to by Lippincott had been written to

[38]Nordskog, *Communication*, p. 5.
[39]Lippincott to Newell, July 14, 1931, Newell Papers, LC.

Newell shortly after Stafford Austin made his accusations against the Reclamation Service. It strongly suggested that Lippincott might have committed financial irregularities in assigning Owens Valley expenditures to other reclamation projects, possibly to decrease the amount Los Angeles would have to pay to the government for project expenses. Obviously writing in anger, Davis withdrew an earlier endorsement of a salary increase for Lippincott. "I am convinced that Mr. Lippincott is so blind to the public interest and so biased by private and selfish considerations that it will be impossible to secure loyal services from him," Davis had written so long ago.[40]

Lippincott could only conclude his letter to Newell by once again, after all these years, pleading his case: "Looking back at the whole situation I think we did what was absolutely right in favoring the necessities of the City of Los Angeles instead of trying to irrigate the farm lands in the Owens Valley with a federal project. If after reading this letter you care to write to me I would be pleased to have you do so."[41]

Newell's response was somewhat less than Lippincott had hoped for. Now seventy years of age, Newell pleaded the need to refresh his memory of events long past. He did recall that Lippincott "did a highly commendable thing in securing the excess waters for Los Angeles." In order to prepare a statement for Lippincott, however, Newell would have to go through his voluminous files. "I shall want to take a day off, or more nearly a month off, to dig through these and back to the attitude of my mind of that time." But he did promise to respond with a more knowledgeable answer.[42]

A week later Newell sent his promised statement. Unfortunately for Lippincott, its contents were less than satisfying. Once again, Newell reminded Lippincott of all the letters that had been written in 1905, in which matters were "explained by you so often that I do not know of anything which may be added." Newell did believe the *Communication* distorted its evidence. "The people who prepared the pamphlet seem to have a very curious notion regarding

[40]Nordskog, *Communication*, pp. 22–23. The original document is Davis to Newell, August 24, 1905, file 63-B, OV-GCRW, RBR.

[41]Lippincott to Newell, July 14, 1931, enclosing committee report and *Communication*, Newell Papers, LC.

[42]Newell to Lippincott, July 23, 1931, ibid.

the authority or responsibility of the field men employed by the U.S. Geological Survey, and grouped in the Reclamation Service," he said. "The most that any of us could do was to conduct research, make reports and recommendations." Financial responsibility lay ultimately with the secretary of the interior, then Ethan Allen Hitchcock. Also the secretary had the final word on approval or disapproval of proposed projects. Newell recalled that Hitchcock seldom changed his mind after making a decision. Various factors had no doubt contributed to the rejection of the Owens Valley project—the financial status of the reclamation fund, uncertain titles—and as Newell remembered it, Hitchcock was relieved to have the city "take the project off" his hands. "The points to be emphasized in these matters is [*sic*] that the Secretary of the Interior was not an automaton acting according to reports of individuals or boards, but was a man who did his own thinking and drew his conclusions from many sources of which we know little," Newell informed Lippincott. "The principal actors have died and the material on file available for inspection is by no means representative of the information or advice upon which the Secretary acted."[43]

Lippincott's hopes for historical justification from Newell thus met with disappointment. The *Communication* distorted the facts by placing them in an incomplete and biased context, while Newell could only place ultimate responsibility on a long-dead secretary of the interior, since his own best recollections were corroded with the rust of time.

Nordskog's *Communication* marked the apogee of Andrae B. Nordskog's involvement in the Owens Valley–Los Angeles water controversy. The Southwest Water League continued to claim his time. In July, 1931, he went to Washington, D.C., again and created a minor scene when he called for the cessation of work on Boulder Dam until voters approved or disapproved the $200 million aqueduct bond issue. His argument was that the bond issue would fail, a prediction that proved wrong. The league also supported Senator James Allen's resolution of April 28, 1933, demanding Los Angeles honor its obligations and spend the bond money voted in 1930. The state senate adopted this resolution unanimously. Nordskog prepared

[43]Newell to Lippincott, July 29, 1931, ibid.

a league report that again stressed the historical connections between the first moves of the Reclamation Service in 1903 and current Los Angeles policies. Senator Allen ordered the report printed
in the *Senate Journal,* and extra copies were again made of a Nordskog indictment.[44]

Although Nordskog would in the future be involved in water
issues from time to time, current events required he give his attention to newer and more immediate challenges. One of these challenges was the Great Depression itself. Shortly after his meeting
with Interior Department officials on the Boulder Dam issue, Nordskog was in Monte Ne, Arkansas, helping to form a new political
party, the Liberty party. The ostensible leader of the party, William
H. "Coin" Harvey, had won fame for his role in the free-silver
debates in the 1890's. Now eighty years old, Harvey agreed to serve
as the party's leader until a later convention could formally nominate
a presidential candidate. Nordskog won a place as a leading con-
tender for the vice-presidential candidacy. Eleven months later, in
July, 1932, a formal party convention meeting in San Francisco
nominated Frank E. Webb for president and Andrae B. Nordskog
for vice-president on the Liberty party ticket, a coalition that at one
point or another took in Harvey, Norman Thomas, and Jacob S.
Coxey. By the end of the year, with Franklin Roosevelt elected
president, Nordskog was folding the *Gridiron* and organizing The
New American, Incorporated, a "National Secret Order" inviting the
membership of "natural born citizens and those who have taken out
their first papers two or three years ago."[45]

The Effects of Nordskog's Research

With Nordskog's attention diverted to esoteric political fringes,
there remained the influence of his publications, which far outlasted
the Liberty party or The New America, Incorporated. His *Communication* came to have an important influence on generations of

[44]*Los Angeles Times,* July 11, 1931; T. H. Watkins, *The Grand Colorado: The Story of a River and Its Canyons,* p. 171; *Senate Journal,* April
28, 1933, pp. 2053–54, May 11, 1933, pp. 2742–56; Andrae B. Nordskog,
Report of the Southwest Water League Concerning Owens Valley.

[45]*Los Angeles Times,* August 27, 1931, and July 5, 1932; Los Angeles
Gridiron, December 16, 1932.

writers who never heard of Andrae B. Nordskog. Those who did know him, such as McWilliams, overlooked his personal idiosyncracies and accepted the research at face value. Among the first persons to utilize the *Communication* were men with newspaper backgrounds. Other writers soon joined them.

In 1933 Morrow Mayo, a former staff editor for the Associated Press, wrote a book about Los Angeles, titled simply *Los Angeles*, published by a major New York publisher, Alfred A. Knopf. More than a series of episodes yet less than a history, the book generally presented an unfair view of the city. The unfriendliest view came in the chapter titled "The Rape of Owens Valley." Much of his account paraphrased Nordskog's *Communication*, from which he also directly quoted. Like Nordskog, Mayo had written to Gifford Pinchot; unlike Nordskog, he had received a less than satisfactory answer. Mayo went further stylistically than Nordskog, building on Nordskog's information to reach a dramatic and negative conclusion:

In conclusion, it may be said that Los Angeles gets its water by reason of one of the costliest, crookedest, most unscrupulous deals ever perpetrated, plus one of the greatest pieces of engineering folly ever heard of. Owens Valley is there for anybody to see. The City of the Angels moved through this valley like a devastating plague. It was ruthless, stupid, cruel, and crooked. It deliberately ruined Owens Valley. It stole the waters of the Owens River. It drove the people of Owens Valley from their home, a home which they had built from the desert. It turned a rich, reclaimed, agricultural section of a thousand square miles back into primitive desert. For no sound reason, for no sane reason, it destroyed a helpless agricultural section and a dozen towns. It was an obscene enterprise from beginning to end. Today there is a saying in California about this funeral ground, which may well remain as its epitaph: *"The Federal Government of the United States held Owens Valley while Los Angeles raped it."*[46]

Reviewers generally liked Mayo's book. R. L. Duffus in the *New York Times Book Review* said, "Mr. Mayo's book sets down some lively impressions of that strange West Coast phenomenon." Herbert Asbury in *Nation* was particularly impressed, finding it "a volume which the student of American phenomena will find invaluable. . . . So far as my knowledge extends, it is the first honest and unbiased history of the weirdest municipality on earth." Said the

---

[46]Morrow Mayo, *Los Angeles*, pp. 245–246 (emphasis in the original).

Boston Transcript's reviewer, "the book is not only an excellent history but a strong and vital picture of the real city."[47]

Despite the enthusiastic reviews, Mayo's book did not wear well over time. Historians read the chapter on Owens Valley and found it subjective, inaccurate, and unhistorical. Remi Nadeau was especially critical. "To refute his statements one by one would seem unnecessary if they had not been believed and repeated by later writers," he stated. "Unfortunately Mr. Mayo's book was unchallenged for many years and stood as the prime source on the Owens Valley story for other writers. The distorted claims were tacitly accepted as fact. Many Angelenos believed that their city 'robbed' Owens Valley of its water and used it for nothing else than to fatten San Fernando Valley."[48]

Leading professional historians of the state's history have generally dismissed Mayo's version of the water wars, while being much less critical of Nordskog's *Communication*, and for the most part overlooking the link between the two. Walton Bean condemned the Mayo version as "extremely unreliable," while Andrew Rolle declared Mayo had "exaggerated the facts in dramatizing the plight of of the valley residents." On the other hand, Julian Nava and Bob Barger still find Mayo quotable, and John Caughey, along with Warren Beck and David Williams, still recommend it in their bibliographies, though they do not comment on its reliability. Ultimately, Leonard Pitt found the Mayo account durable enough to cite against the official DWP version by Don Kinsey (written in 1928) in his collection, *California Controversies*. If the assumption is that by reading such polarized views the reader can discern where lies the truth, then for this particular controversy wisdom must be prayed for.[49]

[47]*New York Times Book Review*, March 12, 1933, p. 5; *Nation* 136 (May 10, 1933), 536; *Boston Transcript*, March 4, 1933.

[48]Remi Nadeau, *The Water Seekers*, p. 107. For a pro–Los Angeles view on the city's search for water published at this time, see John S. Mc-Groarty, *California of the South: A History*, 1:225–256.

[49]Walton Bean, *California: An Interpretive History*, p. 353; Andrew F. Rolle, *California: A History*, p. 503; Julian Nava and Bob Barger, *California: Five Centuries of Cultural Contrasts*, p. 296; John W. Caughey, *California: A Remarkable State's Life History*, p. 451; Warren A. Beck and

Second only to Mayo's book in lasting impact was the revised edition of W. A. Chalfant's *Story of Inyo*. Chalfant, as had his father before him, published the *Inyo Register*; the family roots in the valley dated back to gold-rush days. In *Story of Inyo*'s first edition, published in 1922, Chalfant delivered a critical yet unpolemical account of the city's dealings in the valley. He condemned the federal government—Lippincott and Newell in particular—for acting in the city's interests; but he also listed a number of deeds performed by Los Angeles that were done in a spirit of equity. He wryly observed, "In phrasing more accurately descriptive than elegant, 'the government held Owens Valley while Los Angeles skinned it' "—a phrase revised to a far harsher symbolism by Mayo eleven years later.[50]

When the time came to prepare a second edition of his book, Chalfant completely revised the aqueduct chapter. Much had happened in the intervening years: the intensified purchasing of valley lands, the dynamitings, the Watterson embezzlements, the abandonment of homes. Moreover, Chalfant had new ammunition. He, too, had a copy of Nordskog's *Communication*. He indicated his plans for the revised chapter to Mary Austin. "What was done and what has happened in Inyo will be set forth in the next edition of 'The Story of Inyo,' to come out some time in 1933," said Chalfant. "In the first book of that name, there was hope that a solution of the trouble might be possible, and the pacific chapter on the subject is one of which I have never been proud. The next time it will be covered, from the conception of Fred Eaton's idea in 1892 to the last development before final proof sheets are read."[51]

Chalfant more than kept his word; the single chapter in the 1922 edition was expanded to seven chapters, almost a fifth of the book, in the revised edition. He clearly acknowledged his debt to the *Communication*: "Reliance for the official correspondence quoted in this chapter is principally on findings by Mr. Andrae B. Nordskog,

---

David A. Williams, *California: A History of the Golden State*, p. 531; Leonard Pitt, ed., *California Controversies: Major Issues in the History of the State*, pp. 144–168.

    [50]W. A. Chalfant, *The Story of Inyo*, 1922 ed., p. 329.
    [51]Chalfant to Austin, November 8, 1932, Austin Papers, HL.

of Los Angeles, in reluctant departmental files in Washington, for the use of which obligation to Mr. Nordskog is acknowledged. He widely disseminated these matters, in communications to the California State Senate and subsequent publication, and without challenge." In the pages that followed, Chalfant reproduced many of the letters Nordskog had included in his *Communication*.[52]

Like Mayo, Chalfant received a mixed reaction for his version of the controversy. Remi Nadeau labeled it a "terrific diatribe" but found its background information useful for his own historical account. Of the Mayo and Chalfant books, Chalfant's was better grounded in research, while Mayo's was more dramatically written. Both books spawned a geometric succession of sympathetic writers much less critical of subjectivity and hearsay evidence than professional historians. Far too many books and articles have appeared dealing with the water controversy to discuss here, but a brief historiographical survey may illustrate the endurance of Nordskog's interpretation of events and the passive acceptance of inaccurate secondary sources which themselves became historical evidence.

In 1946 Carey McWilliams wrote *Southern California Country*, now considered a classic critical study of the development of the Southern California region. One chapter, "Water! Water! Water!" traced, among other themes, the Owens Valley controversy. McWilliams freely acknowledged his debt to Morrow Mayo, who in turn had utilized the work of Nordskog. Three years later Ralph Hancock's *Fabulous Boulevard* appeared, a history of Los Angeles' Wilshire Boulevard and its environs. In referring to the sources for the history of the city's search for water, Hancock declared, "It is told best in Carey McWilliams' *Southern California Country* and Morrow Mayo's *Los Angeles*." He quoted Mayo's sentence on the city's rape of the valley and, in an observation of current water demands, noted that Arizona was the next "prospect for ravishment." In 1951, in *The Water and the Power*, Albert N. Williams presented a badly distorted version of the first years of the controversy, generously derived from Mayo. Also derived from Mayo was the version given by William G. Bonelli in 1954, in *Billion Dollar Blackjack*, a polemical tract against the *Los Angeles Times*

---

[52]Chalfant, *The Story of Inyo*, pp. 348 ff.

and the Otis-Chandler dynasty. Bonelli acknowledged his debt to Mayo but suggested that the rape quotation be modified because "it ignores the men who planned the rapine."[53]

Popular histories by definition retell other people's stories rather than try original research. When the magazine *Electrical West* ran an article, "Rivers of the West," that borrowed heavily from Williams' *The Water and the Power*, the copycatting proved too much for Charles H. Lee, a prominent San Francisco civil engineer. During his long career Lee had worked on the Los Angeles aqueduct and had known Lippincott personally. "In reading the section . . . I was astonished to find statements of slanderous untruths regarding a man, long dead, who participated in early water development of Southern California, namely J. B. Lippincott, a well known engineer of Los Angeles and a prominent member of the American Society of Civil Engineers," Lee wrote. "I knew Mr. Lippincott as an honorable man, an honest and dedicated public servant and one who acted from the highest motives in the public interest. . . . Mr. Lippincott was the unfortunate victim of a situation over which he had no control. Although his personal judgment may have been poor in exposing himself to accusations of bad faith by accepting employment with the City after leaving the Reclamation Bureau, yet his personal motives were of the highest and his ethics unimpeachable."[54] Such corrective statements, however, were made all too rarely as new generations of writers continued to rely on the same few sources.

Two studies were published in the 1950's which attempted to put some objectivity into the controversy. Both Remi Nadeau's *The Water Seekers* and Vincent Ostrom's *Water and Politics*, although not exclusively concerned with the Owens Valley–Los Angeles dispute, did provide important information based on contemporary

[53]Carey McWilliams, *Southern California Country: An Island on the Land*, chap. 10; Ralph Hancock, *Fabulous Boulevard*, pp. 227–228; Albert N. Williams, *The Water and the Power: Development of the Five Great Rivers of the West*, pp. 80–81; William G. Bonelli, *Billion Dollar Blackjack*, pp. 117–125.

[54]Charles H. Lee to John R. Callahan, September 7, 1962, California Section, California State Library. I am grateful to Allan R. Ottley for calling attention to this letter. Cf. "The Rivers of the West," *Electrical West* 75 (August, 1962), 354.

newspapers, published records, personal interviews, and, judging from their bibliographies, Nordskog's *Communication*. As noted above, neither Nadeau nor Ostrom thought much of Nordskog as a reformer, but they did not question his performance as a researcher.[55]

By the 1960's the controversy's historiography had become so badly encrusted with mythical barnacles that one California historian at last felt it necessary to take some corrective measures. W. W. Robinson, while not an academic historian (he was an executive with Title Insurance and Trust Company), had written a respectable number of books and articles on local history, including a series of pamphlets on Southern California cities. In an article entitled "Myth-Making in the Los Angeles Area," Robinson addressed one part of the Owens Valley conspiracy story. He traced the conspiracy viewpoint back to McWilliams and Mayo, though he did not pursue its origins beyond these writers. Robinson correctly noted that there were two syndicates rather than one. "Both syndicates were speculative ventures by speculative-minded men," observed Robinson, who noted that land profits were long-range rather than immediate and, in the case of the Suburban Homes Company, did "not seem overwhelmingly large." In any event, Robinson dismissed the conspiracy theory as the result of poor research. "My account of the 'conspiracy' is based on a personal examination of the minutes of the board of directors of San Fernando Mission Land Company, and of the mountainous files of the Los Angeles Suburban Homes Company, discussions with some of the principals, and a close study of public records and of newspaper stories," he claimed. "Historians and writers continue to stub their toes in the San Fernando Valley when dealing with questionable source material."[56]

[55]In his bibliography Ostrom listed the *Communication* under the heading "Government Publications and Documents." Nadeau recognized Nordskog's authorship but accepted Nordskog's use of Reclamation Service correspondence without question. Ostrom, unaware of the contact between McWilliams and Nordskog, assumed that McWilliams derived his interpretation from the editorial campaigning of Samuel T. Clover in 1907. Inasmuch as Clover lacked access to Reclamation Service correspondence in 1907, and from examination of McWilliams' presentation, my study argues for the influence of Nordskog on subsequent writers.

[56]W. W. Robinson, "Myth-Making in the Los Angeles Area," *Southern California Quarterly* 45 (March, 1963), 90–91. With a few minor differences, the same account appears in Robinson's *Los Angeles: A Profile*, pp. 108–109.

Unfortunately Robinson's demolition of the conspiracy version required readers to take his word on faith rather than on hard evidence. To claim there was no conspiracy because of his "personal examination" of "mountainous files" put Robinson in much the same category as Nordskog. Meanwhile, the barnacles continued to grow. Charles Outland, author of the definitive study of the Saint Francis Dam disaster, accepted Chalfant uncritically in his article on Ventura County water-diversion proposals. "Chalfant presents an almost unimpeachable case, quoting from letters and documents to prove his point" that Lippincott "sold out the people of the valley for the city of Los Angeles." The letters and documents, as we have seen, came to Chalfant from Nordskog.[57]

With the Owens Valley controversy remaining very much alive in the late 1960's and 1970's, articles and books appeared with frequency. Again, the research for these studies was narrowly based on limited sources, with Morrow Mayo's work still found usable.[58] When the Pacific Center for Western Historical Studies at the University of the Pacific inaugurated a monograph series, it chose for its first selection a 1934 master's thesis which, except for the addition of an epilogue and the changing of verb forms from present to past tense, remained the same as originally written. More than half of

---

For documentation of his claims to debunk the conspiracy myth, Robinson cited his own *The Story of San Fernando Valley*, pp. 37–38, 40. Neither this book nor other editions and versions (see above, chap. 5, n. 45) address the questions of whether Moses Sherman leaked word of the aqueduct plans to the first land syndicate or to those who would make up the second syndicate, the relationship of Reclamation Service officials to Los Angeles water officials, Otis' conflict of interest in editorially supporting the aqueduct while owning land that would benefit from it, or problems that developed between Los Angeles and Inyo County. Robinson himself was open to accusations of bias, since Otto F. Brant, a member of the second land syndicate, was a major executive with the Title Insurance and Trust Company.

[57]Charles F. Outland, "Historic Water Diversion Proposals," *Ventura County Historical Society Quarterly* 5 (August, 1960), 5.

[58]Frank E. Moss, *The Water Crisis*, pp. 157–158, is so full of errors as to be useless. Glenn A. Vent and Herbert J. Vent, "Owens Valley, Case Study in Historical Geography and Sequent Occupance," *Pacific Historian* 16 (Spring, 1972), 61–73, relies heavily on Mayo. Note also the version given by Stephen Longstreet in *All Star Cast: An Anecdotal History of Los Angeles*, pp. 149–151, 355, and the one by David Halberstam, *The Powers That Be*, pp. 113–116, which gives new life to old errors.

242   VISION OR VILLAINY

the small volume's forty-eight notes cited just three works—Mayo,
Chalfant, and the 1933 Nordskog–Southwest Water League report.[59]

More recent studies have also come out, all based on previously
published sources or at best on contemporary published records.
William Kahrl produced an interesting analysis on the controversy
in a two-part article for *California Historical Quarterly* in 1976,
but he made almost no use of unpublished letters. Kahrl's interpretation was severely criticized by Gordon Miller, who in his Ph.D.
dissertation on the aqueduct project effectively demolished Kahrl's
attempt to establish the artificiality of the 1904–1905 water famine.
Kahrl, who noted Mayo's influence and rightly labeled the book a
"sensationalist tract," nonetheless wrote with a proconspiracy bias
himself. William K. Jones, in a 1977 *Journal of the West* article
based on his master's thesis, relied on contemporary and secondary
published works, with no research at all in unpublished sources.
Jones found Mayo useful for two citations, one of which turns out
to be incorrect.[60]

During one of the periodic episodes of tension between the Los
Angeles Department of Water and Power and Owens Valley residents in the 1970's, a newspaper reporter interviewed some Inyo
people, including one Bishop resident who said: "The whole story's
been told. Just read *The Story of Inyo* or *The Water Seekers*—
though I doubt you can find them now. I think they were suppressed.
But it's all there, how the Chandler-Mulholland combine deliberately

[59]Richard Coke Wood, *The Owens Valley and the Los Angeles Water
Controversy: Owens Valley as I Knew It*; see my review of this book in
Arizona and the West 16 (Spring, 1974), 70–72.

[60]William Kahrl, "The Politics of California Water: Owens Valley and
the Los Angeles Aqueduct, 1900–1927," *California Historical Quarterly* 55
(1976), 2–25, 98–120; Gordon R. Miller, "Los Angeles and the Owens River
Aqueduct" (Ph.D. diss., Claremont Graduate School, 1978), pp. 254–260;
William K. Jones, "Los Angeles Aqueduct: A Search for Water," *Journal of
the West* 16 (July 1977), 5–21. The best discussions of the historiography
behind the controversy are Anthony Cifarelli, "The Owens River Aqueduct
and the Los Angeles *Times*: A Study in Early Twentieth Century Business
Ethics and Journalism" (Master's thesis, University of California, Los Angeles,
1969), pp. 116–122, and Miller, "Los Angeles and the Owens River Aqueduct," chap. 5. Cifarelli's analysis is limited to the conspiracy-viewpoint writings, whereas Miller presents a more comprehensive discussion. Miller dis-
cusses Nordskog on pp. 237–239 but does not clearly trace his effect on later
writers.

raped this valley and made millions of dollars doing it."[61] Myths do die hard; such is the state of the Owens Valley–Los Angeles water controversy and its history as people remember it—or want it to be remembered.

Andrae B. Nordskog was a polemical journalist who dedicated himself to exposing what he saw as the facts behind the Owens Valley–Los Angeles water controversy. He was the only person who ever attempted to locate unpublished source material, hard evidence that revealed what the participants themselves said about the events in which they were involved, not just what others said they said or what later writers would write about them. Whatever its shortcomings—and there were many shortcomings—the legacy of Nordskog's research is very much with us today.[62]

[61]*Los Angeles Times*, December 1, 1974. For the record, *Story of Inyo* has gone through at least five printings, and *Water Seekers* was published in a revised edition in 1974.

[62]This claim is made with all due apologies to Remi Nadeau, whose *Water Seekers* is based in part on personal interviews. But he could not interview Mulholland, Eaton, Lippincott, Newell, Otis, or Chandler, who were all dead, and the correspondence of the principal people involved at the time of the events would seem far more reliable than testimony given twenty to fifty years afterward. Nadeau credits Samuel Clover as the direct antecedent of the conspiracy viewpoint, but no evidence has surfaced to indicate that Nordskog in the late 1920's was familiar with Clover's 1907 editorial efforts. It is interesting to note that Clover, who in the late 1920's was publishing a weekly Los Angeles literary magazine, was a good friend of Carey McWilliams.

The other major study of the topic, Vincent Ostrom's *Water and Politics*, focuses on governmental administration of water policies rather than tracing the history of the people who made those policies. It is hoped that one virtue of this book will be to indicate where original materials can be found and another that the entire controversy can be given proper historical perspective.

8

Dominance of the
· Department of Water and Power

"Forget it, Jake—it's Chinatown."—Walsh to Jake Gittes, *Chinatown* (1974)

In later life the men involved in the creation of the aqueduct experienced a mixture of professional successes, controversies, and failures, as well as personal tragedies.

Frederick Haynes Newell, after serving as chief engineer and director of the Reclamation Service for its first decade, stepped down from the directorship in 1914—a casualty of complaints from reclamation-project water users over bureau policies on repayment of money into the reclamation fund.[1] Subsequent years brought appointments and honors that helped compensate for the sacrifices made in government service. He headed the Department of Civil Engineering at the University of Illinois for five years, served on numerous commissions, wrote and edited books, and was a cofounder of The Research Service, a consulting organization. Newell also helped establish the American Association of Engineers in hopes of promoting a more humanistic view among engineers.

The recipient of an honorary doctorate from the Case School of Applied Sciences, Newell also found other honors coming his way. The American Geographical Society awarded him its Cullum Gold Medal in 1918. Inscribed on its reverse side was the statement, "He carried water from a mountain wilderness to turn the waste places of the desert into homes for freedom." On July 5, 1932,

[1]Samuel P. Hays, *Conservation and the Gospel of Efficiency: The Progressive Conservation Movement, 1890–1920*, pp. 247–248.

shortly after his seventieth birthday and about a year following his last correspondence with Lippincott, Newell died of heart failure at his home in Washington, D.C.[2]

Following Newell's departure from the Reclamation Service, Arthur Powell Davis assumed the post of director for a decade. During that time the Reclamation Service grew in operation and scope, with Davis personally supervising the construction of more than one hundred dams and thousands of miles of canals in sixteen states. His government service came to an abrupt end in 1923, however, when Secretary of the Interior Hubert Work removed Davis and reorganized the service into the Bureau of Reclamation, to be headed by a "businessman," in keeping with the integration of business and politics in the 1920's. The scandal that followed proved embarrassing to all concerned. Although Elwood Mead, an internationally known engineer, assumed the new position of commissioner of reclamation following the businessman's brief tenure, the controversy surrounding Davis' dismissal highlighted the inescapable fact that the once idealistic goals of reclamation could not be, and indeed never had been, divorced from the realm of politics.[3]

After his dismissal from federal-government service, Davis became the chief engineer and general manager of the East Bay Municipal Utility District in California, which consisted of nine cities on the eastern shore of San Francisco Bay. He later worked on irrigation projects as a consulting engineer in the Soviet Union and in his last years served as a consulting engineer for various projects in the United States, including the Colorado River aqueduct. His differences with Lippincott had only temporarily disturbed their long friendship, which continued through correspondence and occasional meetings until Davis' death at age 72 in 1933.[4]

Like Newell and Davis, the Los Angeles men who brought

[2]*Dictionary of American Biography*, 7:456–457; Allen B. McDaniel, "Frederick Haynes Newell," American Society of Civil Engineers, *Transactions* 98 (1933), 1597–1600; Edwin T. Layton, "Frederick Haynes Newell and the Revolt of the Engineers," *Midcontinent American Studies Journal* 3 (Fall, 1962), 17–26.

[3]Gene M. Gressley, "Arthur Powell Davis, Reclamation, and the West," *Agricultural History* 42 (July, 1968), 242–244.

[4]*Dictionary of American Biography*, 11 (Supp. One), 224–226; Charles A. Bissell and F. E. Weymouth, "Arthur Powell Davis," American Society of Civil Engineers, *Transactions* 100 (1935), 1582–91.

about the aqueduct linking the Owens River to Los Angeles found their later fortunes to contain mixed blessings. Fred Eaton, who had done so much to popularize the idea of the aqueduct, had broken with Mulholland over the proposed sale of the Long Valley dam site. Their friendship ruptured, Eaton retreated to his Long Valley ranch. He boycotted the dedication of the aqueduct in 1913, and during the water wars of the 1920's he consistently refused to compromise on his million-dollar asking price for his property.

Then a business reversal caused by an ironic twist of fate brought Eaton's opposition to an end. Unknown to Eaton, some of the officers of his Eaton Ranch Company had borrowed $200,000 and had taken a mortgage on the ranch—from the Watterson brothers. The Wattersons sold the paper to another bank, with the $200,000 on deposit in their own bank. When the Watterson banks closed, the money disappeared, and Eaton was left with a mortgage he had not signed and no money with which to pay it off. He fought the holder of the mortgage in the courts for five years, but in 1932 finally lost the contest, as the mortgage was foreclosed. The City of Los Angeles then bought the property for $650,000—$100,000 less than it had offered to Eaton directly. After various debts had been settled, Eaton possessed only a fraction of the million dollars he had originally and stubbornly demanded.[5] Eaton's health failed. Bitter and broken by the foreclosure experience and with little time left, Eaton summoned Mulholland, his friend of earlier days.

William Mulholland had lived through triumph and tragedy in his long career. Under his guidance the DWP had become one of the most powerful local agencies in the country. Mulholland's salary was higher than the mayor's. His DWP brought water and power to the city from as far away as Mono Lake and, before long, from the Colorado River. His DWP had built tunnels, aqueducts, and storage reservoirs. His DWP had built the Saint Francis Dam.

[5] J. Gregg Layne, *Water and Power for a Great City: A History of the Department of Water and Power of the City of Los Angeles to December, 1950*, pp. 212–213; *Hollywood Citizen-News*, December 6, 1932. Eaton's ex-wife wrote a poignant if somewhat rambling letter to Water and Power Commissioner John B. Haynes detailing the family's grievances. Haynes expressed sympathy but could offer no consolation over the disposition of the property (Helen Lucretia Eaton to Haynes, July 16, 1932, and Haynes to Mrs. Eaton, July 25, 1932, Haynes Papers, SCD).

There had been many honors for Mulholland. The University of California conferred an honorary Doctor of Laws degree on him in 1914. He belonged to numerous engineering societies and organizations, served as consultant to the projects of other cities, was called on to serve as a member of the Engineering Advisory Board on Water Resources and Development for the State of California. He was known as the first engineer in the United States to make major use of electric power on large projects and the first in the world to use caterpillar tractors. The honors and titles meant little after March 13, 1928. "I envy the dead," he said. "Don't blame anybody else, you just fasten it on me. If there is an error of human judgment, I was the human."[6] While investigations proceeded into the cause of the Saint Francis Dam disaster, Mulholland became remote and dispirited. In November, 1928, at age 72 and after fifty-one years of service to Los Angeles, he resigned his position and went into retirement.

When Eaton summoned Mulholland to his home after almost thirty years of silence, Mulholland responded promptly to the request. The two men, now grown old and humbled by circumstance, made their peace with each other. A few months later, on March 11, 1934, Eaton died. Mulholland reported to his daughter that he had dreamed of Eaton. "The two of us were walking along—young and virile like we used to be. Yet I knew we were both dead." Mulholland died fifteen months later, on July 22, 1935.[7]

The eulogies for Mulholland were numerous, mainly recognizing his accomplishments while forgiving his mistakes. As the years passed, the superhuman role Mulholland had played in the city's history came to overshadow his humanity. Legend obscured the man, and later generations of Angelenos came to think of him in terms of the monuments named for him: the highway, the dam

[6]Remi Nadeau, *The Water Seekers*, rev. ed., pp. 102–103; Charles F. Outland, *Man-Made Disaster: The Story of St. Francis Dam—Its Place in Southern California's Water System, Its Failure and the Tragedy of March 12 and 13, 1928, in the Santa Clara River Valley*, p. 211; Robert William Matson, *William Mulholland: A Forgotten Forefather*, pp. 64–65; Richard Dillon, *Humbugs and Heroes: A Gallery of California Pioneers*, p. 264.

[7]Nadeau, *Water Seekers*, pp. 11, 110. Nadeau poetically but erroneously linked Eaton and Mulholland's birthdays by claiming they were born but a day apart, but they were actually born two weeks apart.

opposite the Hollywood Bowl, the junior high school in the San Fernando Valley, and the memorial fountain at Los Feliz Boulevard and Riverside Drive, on the site of the shack where he had once lived as a ditch tender, overlooking the Los Angeles River. One biographer went so far as to refer to him as a "forgotten forefather." In truth, Mulholland left remarkably little evidence beyond official records for any historian who might hope to understand the man. Mulholland, a symbol of the growth and influence of Los Angeles, ended his career a tragic figure who had mistakenly believed in his own infallibility.[8]

Newell, Davis, Eaton, Mulholland—by 1935 all the key figures in the creation of the aqueduct had passed from the scene, save one. Joseph Barlow Lippincott had left government service for good after completion of the aqueduct in 1913, excepting the inevitable calls for consultation work that seem the badges of successful engineers. His Los Angeles–based engineering firm achieved a high reputation for competence, and Lippincott himself enjoyed considerable fame within the engineering profession.[9]

Lippincott's career had not been without controversy, and his role in the Owens Valley dispute was but one of a number of heated issues during his professional life. Lippincott recognized the unavoidable problem faced by every engineer who plotted a road or planned a sewage system or other public works: for every group that favors the work, another opposes it. His goal was to get the job

[8]Matson, *William Mulholland.* Lippincott wrote a two-part biographical essay commissioned by the Mulholland Memoir Committee of the Los Angeles Section of the American Society of Civil Engineers ("William Mulholland— Engineer, Pioneer, Raconteur," *Civil Engineering* 11 [February, 1941], 105– 107, and [March, 1941] 161–164). Van Norman wrote the memoir for the American Society of Civil Engineers, *Transactions* 101 (1936), 1604–08. In 1962 Gordon S. Fay, an engineering professor at Los Angeles Valley College, in an open letter to the *Los Angeles Times,* urged greater recognition for Mulholland's part in construction of the Colorado River aqueduct, the Panama Canal, the Hoover Dam, and the Oakland Bay Bridge, a claim that perhaps Mulholland himself would find excessive (*Los Angeles Times,* February 20, 1962).

[9]Gerald J. Giefer and Anelle McCarty Kloski, comps., *Water Resources Reports and Papers in the J. B. Lippincott Collection,* Archives Series Report No. 21, indexes the business records of Lippincott's firm held by the Water Resources Center Archives, University of California, Berkeley. The collection also includes scrapbooks containing newspaper clippings and photographs.

done and let the politicians do the arguing. Professionally, this philosophy served Lippincott well. Engineers thought highly of him, and younger engineers found him helpful and generous in sharing his knowledge. "He was the type of person that, once you entered the room with him, you [immediately recognized] his knowledge of water and his authority in dealing with it," recalled Harold Hedger, a Los Angeles flood control engineer. "I think he was a great person to help other engineers, too." An engineer who worked for the Lippincott firm recalled Lippincott's informality when, meeting prospective job applicants in a hot Arizona hotel room, he conducted the interviews in his underwear.[10]

During World War I Lippincott's company received a contract for construction of Camp Kearny and improvements at Forts Mac-Arthur and Rosecrans and an airfield near San Diego. For many years he served as a consulting engineer to the Automobile Club of Southern California. He traveled to Hawaii, Mexico, Japan, and numerous western states on engineering matters, wrote many technical papers for the American Society of Civil Engineers, dabbled in politics (he actively supported Hoover in 1932), and was at worst bruised rather than battered by Nordskog's accusations in 1931. The American Society of Civil Engineers voted him an honorary membership in 1936. At the beginning of World War II Lippincott, who had been born during the Civil War, found himself at age 78 involved in plans for the construction of firing ranges, military camps, and airfields, requiring him to put off giving time to his avocation, raising citrus fruits on his four groves in the San Fernando Valley.[11]

Lippincott entered the work of the new war with his customary enthusiasm, but unfortunate personal circumstances brought a tragic finish to his life. His daughter Rose had perished in the 1918 in-

[10]Harold Hedger, "Harold Hedger, Flood Control Engineer," Oral History Program, University of California, Los Angeles, typescript, p. 62; interview with Paul F. Gemperle, March 28, 1971.

[11]"Joseph Barlow Lippincott," *Civil Engineering* 7 (January, 1937), 76–77; Kenneth Q. Volk, "Joseph Barlow Lippincott," American Society of Civil Engineers, *Transactions* 108 (1943), 1543–50; J. B. Lippincott to "fellow engineers," September 28, 1932, and Lippincott to J. D. Galloway, October 20, 1932, J. D. Galloway Papers, BL. Lippincott was president of the Engineers' Hoover Committee of Southern California. See also Lippincott to Catherine Edson, September 25, 1933, Edson Papers, Box 3, Folder 14, SCD.

fluenza epidemic, and World War II now claimed his son Joseph, a naval lieutenant at Corregidor in the Philippines. The months following the fall of Corregidor brought no word as to whether his son was living or dead. Belief that his son had been killed contributed to a decline in his health. On November 4, 1942, Lippincott suddenly passed away, not knowing that his son had been taken prisoner—but spared the harsh news that his son would not survive the war.[12]

There remained the secondary figures in the drama, people destined to carve out various niches of importance in engineering history and now, like Mulholland, mainly remembered as public monuments rather than human beings. Harvey Van Norman succeeded Mulholland as general manager of the DWP, but he never offered himself as the stuff from which legends are made.[13] He did his job and he did it well, and the city remembered his contribution by renaming the San Fernando Reservoir in his honor. When the dam cracked in the 1971 Sylmar earthquake, requiring evacuation of thousands of San Fernando Valley residents, few people remembered the man; it was the dam that dramatically brought Van Norman's name to their attention.

Another San Fernando Valley dam was named for A. C. Hansen, who had headed the Jawbone-Mojave section of the aqueduct project and had gone on to other service in the region. Hamlin Street recalls City Engineer Homer Hamlin who once worked in Lippincott's firm. Haynes Street and the DWP's Haynes Steam Power Plant recognize Dr. John R. Haynes and his services as a water and power commissioner and in other civic activities. Similar honors

[12]The exact date of Joseph Reading Lippincott's death is not known. From Corregidor's surrender in May, 1942, until October, 1944, he was at the Cabanatuan prison camp on Luzon; following a move to Bilibid prison, Lieutenant Lippincott was among 1,619 men taken aboard the *Oryoku Maru* for transfer to Japan. On December 15, 1944, the prison ship, which carried no markings identifying it as carrying prisoners of war, was bombed by American planes. Survivors were transferred to two other ships and taken to Japan. Only about 400 of the original 1,619 reached Japan alive. Joseph Reading Lippincott was not among them. The Bureau of Naval Personnel arbitrarily selected December 15, 1944, as the date of death of all prisoners who perished on the trip (D. C. Allard, Head, Operational Archives Branch, Naval History Division, Department of the Navy, to the author, September 5, 1972, author's files).

[13]Orlando Northcutt, "Van Norman Heads Los Angeles Water-Power Unified Department," *Pacific Municipalities* 43 (April, 1929), 169.

have been given to other pioneers who helped make the region's public works a modern reality: there is the Ezra F. Scattergood Steam Power Plant near Playa del Rey, honoring the chief of the old Bureau of Power and Light; Lake Mathews for William B. Mathews, DWP attorney and, later, general counsel for the Metropolitan Water District; and Morris Dam above Pasadena for Samuel Morris, who succeeded Van Norman as general manager of the DWP.

From the Arizona border to the Pacific Ocean, from Owens Valley to San Diego, along the conduits of the Los Angeles aqueduct and the Colorado aqueduct, the reservoirs, steam power plants, pumping stations, streets, and other landmarks pay tribute to men who dedicated their careers to promoting the greatest good for the greatest number—to be sure, for their particular greatest number.

The critics, on the other hand, must be found at best in whatever mention is given them by historians; at worst they are simply forgotten by later generations who fail to realize the debt owed to the gadflies. The Austins, Clovers, Finkles, Nordskogs, and the Chalfants, varying in their criticism from constructive alternatives to bitter condemnation, helped keep the city's public projects free of graft even while exaggerating the possibility of such graft. In many ways their activism was ahead of its time—they would have been quite at home in an era of environmental consciousness—but in the context of their own period they presented an alternative to the speculative growth that characterized Los Angeles in the twentieth century. Unfortunately, too few people appreciated these Cassandras; it is in our own time that the value of their suggestions can be measured and the untaken options considered.

The City Is Censured

Mulholland's retirement signaled the end of an era for Los Angeles and the beginning of a new image for the DWP. There was, in truth, much to live down. The city had a badly tarnished image, and no amount of self-justification or explanation could rationalize the negative publicity. From Owens Valley came bitter comments from those who blamed Los Angeles for all the misfortune that had come to them. "In all history there was never a more flagrant example of one part of a country, politically and financially powerful, destroying a weaker section, and doing it without regard to obligations, moral or financial," wrote Elsie Watterson, sister of Mark and Wilfred, to Mary Austin. To her the calamity was much more than the failure of the banks and the valley's economic problems. "There is a story of injustices stretching over a period of years," she stated, "of ruthless methods on the part of one group to crush another, smaller and more helpless; the story of an oppressed people and of stricken leaders."[14]

Beyond the bitter complaints there was ridicule. Humorist Will Rogers, who was, after all, a resident of Los Angeles, having bought a large estate in Pacific Palisades, visited Bishop in August, 1932. He put his observations about the aqueduct controversy into his syndicated newspaper column:

Ten years ago this was a wonderful valley with one-quarter of a million acres of fruit and alfalfa. But Los Angeles had to have more water for the Chamber of Commerce to drink more toasts to its growth, more water to dilute its orange juice and more water for its geraniums to delight the tourists, while the giant cottonwoods here died. So now this is a valley of desolation.[15]

Rogers' column appeared in such papers as the *New York Times*, the *Tulsa Daily World*, and the *Kansas City Star*. Such widespread publicity hardly helped improve the city's image. The *Los Angeles Times*, nevertheless, boldly carried the column on its front page.

The City of Los Angeles and Owens Valley were by the early 1930's attempting to reach a final settlement that would put an end to the protracted negotiations. In April, 1929, Van Norman headed a special committee appointed by the Board of Water and Power Commissioners to appraise all properties in the valley that were not yet in the city's possession. The task took four months and resulted in 8,500 typewritten pages and more than 2,500 photographs. The report covered 847 properties. While a three-man arbitration committee appointed by the mayor negotiated the purchase of remaining ranch properties, Judge Harlan J. Palmer, president of the Board of Water and Power Commissioners, led a committee of city officials to

[14]Watterson to Austin, April 4, 1928, Austin Papers, HL.
[15]*New York Times*, August 26, 1932. There are minor variations, mainly in punctuation, in the newspapers carrying the column.

Independence to meet with valley representatives. The goal of this group was nothing less than the purchase of all the property in Bishop, Laws, Big Pine, Independence, and Lone Pine, the five towns in Owens Valley, at peak prices.[16]

To provide the funds necessary for this last massive purchase of valley property, Los Angeles voters approved a $38,800,000 bond issue in May, 1930, endorsing their DWP by an overwhelming margin. The bond issue was the largest one voted by the city up to that time. Armed with this huge treasury (which also provided for an eleven-point program, recommended by Van Norman, that included construction of new dams, extension of the aqueduct to Mono Lake, purchase of properties from private power companies, and enlarging the capacity of existing reservoirs), Los Angeles offered generous prices for the properties.[17] "At the present time we have voted in Los Angeles some eight or ten million dollars in bonds to buy out all the town lots, grocery stores, blacksmith shops, churches, laundries, and everything else of Owens Valley so that even those who indirectly may have been injured by the purchase by the city of the farm lands will be compensated," observed Lippincott. "This has been done in order to try to remove the last valid complaint that can be made against the city and its operations."[18]

Unfortunately, the purchase of the properties bogged down in red tape and nitpicking. Judge Palmer had served on the board for one year—July, 1929, to June, 1930—and found in meeting with valley representatives that they were willing to negotiate in an equitable manner. A schedule of purchase prices was worked out, with the price to include store fixtures and equipment in the town properties. Also, the transactions were to proceed directly to escrow rather than through an option arrangement that would delay receipt of the full purchase price. However, not long after Palmer left the board, the other water and power commissioners balked at Palmer's negotiated prices, returned to the use of options, and refused to

[16]Layne, *Water and Power*, pp. 207–208.

[17]Ibid., p. 211; H. A. Van Norman, "Why Los Angeles Voted $38,800,-800 for Water and How It will be Spent," *Western City* 6 (June, 1930), 17–19; idem, *Statement Concerning the $38,800,000 Bond Issue of the Bureau of Water Works and Supply.*

[18]Lippincott to Newell, July 14, 1931, Newell Papers, LC.

consider certain adjustments recommended by Palmer. Commissioner Frank Brooks won no friends in the valley when he asserted that Palmer "came up here arbitrarily and without authority and raised those prices and we had to accept them. He was the cause of all this trouble. He was the fly in the ointment. He didn't have any business doing a stunt like this."[19]

Months dragged by, yet final settlement of the long-standing dispute still seemed remote. Valley residents also found the city wanted sellers to agree to an insulting paragraph placed in the sale options. The paragraph contained a waiver by which the signer agreed to give up all claims for any damages or liabilities, present or future, against the city. While town merchants raised little objection to releasing the city from litigation over water diversion—the purpose of the purchase program in the first place—they felt that injuries to their businesses were quite another matter and wanted some sort of reparations payment beyond the sale of the property. D. E. Lutz, a Bishop grocer, illustrated the argument. He reported that his business had declined from $110,000 in 1924 to $40,000 in 1930, with almost a fourth of his current business on credit. Moreover, he would not be able to settle his credit accounts until the city paid the people who owed him money.[20]

The city's slow pace in concluding the settlements exasperated W. A. Chalfant, who had concluded his history of Inyo County in 1922 on the optimistic note that the differences could be amicably settled. "We are done for," he said in March, 1931. "And if they had let us alone we would have had as prosperous a community as any that borders the city of Los Angeles. I have talked water until I've had water on the brain." Chalfant observed that former Owens Valley residents now gathered together at various places in the state, from Pomona to Merced, to hold annual picnics "just to keep alive the memories of the old days. . . . One of the big questions

---

[19]*Los Angeles Record*, February 20, 1931. At this time the *Record* was running another multipart series, this time criticizing the Department of Water and Power for its handling of the negotiations as well as reminding readers of the origins of the controversy.

[20]Ibid., February 28, 1931.

with those of us still remaining is where to go from here. It's not an easy question to answer."[21]

Nevertheless, Owens Valley gave it a try. Bishop residents sought an injunction against Los Angeles to stop pumping of underground water supplies from the north end of the valley. At Lone Pine, the residents formed a property holders' protective association and fired off a telegram to the water and power commissioners. "We distinctly desire to correct the impressions gained that your Lone Pine appraisals were satisfactory," it read. The association condemned the optioning of properties rather than direct escrow and promised to take legal action to prevent further withdrawal of surface and underground waters "until such time as you feel it conducive to Los Angeles' interests to deal promptly with Lone Pine on a fair and equitable basis."[22]

Meanwhile, complaints against the city had found an audience in the political arena. Although Governor James Rolph, Jr., declared he had no intention of investigating the controversy, assuring Los Angeles Mayor John C. Porter that he merely had "asked to familiarize myself with the project, with no intention whatever of injecting myself into it,"[23] Owens Valley partisans did have a champion who displayed the enthusiasm the governor lacked. As noted earlier, State Senator Joe Riley, representing Inyo and Mono counties, introduced a resolution on March 9, 1931, calling for a five-man state senate special investigating committee to examine accusations against the city as the result of its water diversions from Inyo and Mono counties.[24]

The resolution, as discussed earlier, touched off a hot dispute as arguments were heard in the senate's conservation committee. People from the Owens Valley and Mono Basin areas complained to the state senators of the city's failure to live up to its agreements, while Van Norman and other Los Angeles representatives defended

[21]Ibid., March 5, 1931; see also Chalfant to Austin, November 8, 1932, Austin Papers, HL.

[22]*Los Angeles Record*, March 10, 1931.

[23]*Los Angeles Examiner*, February 1, 1931.

[24]California, Senate, *Journal*, March 9, 1931, pp. 797–798.

their position.[25] On March 19, State Senator J. W. McKinley of Los Angeles County submitted a substitute resolution that, while almost identical to Riley's resolution, did differ in asking that the special investigating committee be made a joint legislative committee with three members each from the senate and assembly. A slight increase in the committee's expenses was also asked for, with each legislative house paying half. Preferring to keep the investigation in senate hands, the state senators rejected the substitute resolution by a roll-call vote of 27–6. They then adopted Riley's resolution on a roll-call vote of 27–8, with five Los Angeles–area senators dissenting. Several days later the president of the senate appointed the five members of the committee. Of the five, only one, Nelson Edwards, was from south of the Tehachapi Mountains, and his district included Riverside, Imperial, and Orange counties. No state senator from Los Angeles County served on the committee.[26]

The committee members proceeded to conduct hearings exclusively in Inyo and Mono counties and in Sacramento, ignoring complaints of water-and-power officials that no hearings were scheduled to be held in Los Angeles. Arthur Strasburger, a department store executive who had accepted an appointment to the Board of Water and Power Commissioners in October, 1930, and was now serving as the board's president, sent an open letter to all the investigating committee members, Governor Rolph, and Lieutenant Governor Frank Merriam. He protested against the one-sided testimony being taken by the committee. "Criticism is easy," he said. "It is human to err." Strasburger conceded that "some mistakes have been made" by the city in its twenty-five years of dealing with the valley. "On the other hand, people of Owens Valley, likewise, have made mistakes." He denounced "avaricious leaders, influential, unscrupulous citizens and politicians," who "promoted lawless conduct and resorted to all sorts of schemes, not for the preservation of the valley as they pretended, but in order to create a great real

[25]*Los Angeles Examiner*, March 10, 1931. Dr. Haynes wrote a long letter to the governor as a supplement to the statements of the water and power officials.

[26]*Senate Journal*, March 19, 1931, pp. 1075–78, and March 23, 1931, p. 1157.

estate promotion out of the situation to their own financial gain."

Strasburger reminded the committee that much of the hardship in the valley was because of the failure of the Watterson banks in 1927 rather than any city schemes. By buying the town properties as well as the ranches and farms, Los Angeles was acting in a fair and generous manner. "Everyone knows that in purchasing these towns we actually will receive no appreciable amount of water," he stated. "The real underlying reason back of this program is the honest, honorable, and laudable effort to try to satisfy the people of Owens Valley and forever clean up the situation."[27]

Los Angeles representatives found it necessary to travel to Sacramento to present their views. While there, they endured Andrae Nordskog's criticisms. In addition to presenting his *Communication to the California Legislature*, Nordskog testified in person, taking the opportunity to condemn Los Angeles officials for their "gross mismanagement" and blaming "self-seeking politicians" for abusing the trust of Los Angeles voters.[28]

Los Angeles found few friends in the state senate's special investigation. On May 7, after five weeks, the committee submitted its report to the state senate. In examining the dispute, the committee had decided to consider the situations in Inyo and Mono counties separately. Most of its report dealt with the complaints of the Inyoites. It described the valley's economy, the city's diversion of surface water and drilling of wells, the drying up of Owens Lake. "The damage wrought by the taking of these waters is apparent," the committee declared.

The farm lands purchased by the city of Los Angeles are reverting to desert. The lands not yet purchased are suffering from the shortage of water due to the exhaustion of the subsurface water by the pumping and drainage carried on by the city of Los Angeles. The former occupants of these lands have migrated to other portions of the State and the west. The few remaining landowners find themselves confronted with a condition of isolation. Their neighbors are gone. Their local markets are gone, and most of their ranches are being surrounded by complete desolation.

[27]*Los Angeles Times*, April 16, 1931.
[28]Ibid., April 2, 1931.

The remaining landowners now realize that they can not hold their lands and farms, and that they can not prosper without cooperative neighbors.[29]

The committee recognized that Los Angeles understood the changing environment of the valley and that the recent $38.8 million bond issue had been voted "for the purpose of 'cleaning up the situation in Owens Valley.' "[30] Indeed, the city acknowledged that without the region's agricultural base, the small towns could not survive. Following the passage of the Reparations Act of 1925, the city had begun appraisal of town properties. However, the city had proved inconstant in accepting town business losses and in including store fixtures in the appraisals. In its recommendations the committee made seven basic points. Los Angeles should complete its program of purchasing all the water and lands in Owens Valley and should do so without further delay. Business property owners should be compensated not only for their property but for economic loss, store fixtures, and equipment. Where disputes existed between offers and asking prices, and where the difference was minimal, quick settlement should be made. The objectionable option form, with the seller required to waive all damage claims, should be abandoned. For the Mono Basin, where the city had promised fair dealing but had subsequently pressed eminent-domain condemnation suits, the committee urged rapid settlement through negotiation. Failing that, the condemnation suits should be resolved as soon as possible. Legislation should be adopted that would in the future protect the rights of rural communities while recognizing the needs of growing municipalities. Finally, Mono Basin owners under existing law had to travel out of their county to defend their cases in the condemnation suits, since the plaintiff—Los Angeles—easily obtained changes of venue. The committee recommended that, at the very least, the city should advance defendant costs where such venue changes were granted.[31]

Overall, the committee found Los Angeles guilty not so much of wrongdoing as of political bungling and bureaucratic incompetence. It pointedly ignored Nordskog's efforts to raise the issue of collusion

[29]*Senate Journal*, May 7, 1931, p. 2449.
[30]Ibid.
[31]Ibid., pp. 2450–52.

between the Reclamation Service and the city, of the speculation in San Fernando Valley land, or of the many other specters from the past Nordskog had included in his *Communication*. Instead, the committee simply urged the city to do what it was supposed to be doing, what it had said it would do: achieve a final settlement. "Your committee heard testimony to show that the long-continued delay has resulted in very greatly increased expense to the city of Los Angeles," the report stated, "and that speedy adjustment would thereby effect a great saving to the city of Los Angeles, not only in prices to be paid for property and business losses, but in pay rolls, legal expenses, and other miscellaneous expenses almost or quite sufficient to cover the increases asked, to say nothing of the determinate loss in good will."[32]

The committee's findings could have been harsher; its final report gives the impression that it was written by hostile people trying to be fair. Four days later, on May 11, the state senate adopted the report, and 2,500 separate copies were printed to make it available to interested parties.[33]

The Special Investigating Committee had in effect censured the City of Los Angeles for its conduct. All the city could do at this point was to follow the committee's recommendations, which, after all, were the city's own stated goals anyway. The city, through the DWP, attempted to deal as fairly as it believed it could with the remaining farmers, ranchers, and townsmen of the valley, as it pursued its policy of purchasing as much acreage as possible and eliminating the problem of sharing water with ranchers who held superior rights to upstream Owens River water. Eventually the city would purchase more than 300,000 acres in the valley, about 98 percent of all privately owned property there.[34]

One last echo of the bitter dispute, a postscript to the violence of the 1920's, occurred later that year, on November 1. Two sections of the aqueduct's Grapevine Siphon were dynamited, closing down the aqueduct for three days until the break was repaired.

[32]Ibid., p. 2451.

[33]Ibid., May 11, 1931. p. 2549. The report was printed as *Report of Senate Special Investigating Committee on Water Situation in Inyo and Mono Counties*.

[34]Gordon R. Miller, "Los Angeles and the Owens River Aqueduct" (Ph.D. diss., Claremont Graduate School, 1978), p. 162.

Van Norman, claiming inside knowledge, absolved Owens Valley men of any complicity in the bombings. The dynamitings were blamed on labor agitators in Los Angeles. Everyone hoped that such actions would not occur again.[35]

A Hope for Reconciliation

Chalfant's remark about "water on the brain" could well apply to many others in 1931 and in the years that followed. While the city tried to settle the last of the negotiations in the valley, other water issues also demanded attention.

Foremost in the mind of the public at this time were the Boulder Dam project, on which construction had begun on March 11, 1931, and the Metropolitan Water District's Colorado River aqueduct, a 240-mile conduit scheduled for creation after voters approved a $220,000,000 bond issue in September. The voters gave their consent by a five-to-one margin, insuring enough water, it was asserted, to supply the needs of water district member cities until 1980.[36] Also, the Mono Basin Extension Project, which extended the aqueduct from Owens River north to Mono Lake for a total aqueduct length of 338 miles, was part of the plan approved by voters in the May, 1930, $38.8 million bond election. Construction on this project began in 1934 and took six years to complete.[37]

During the 1930's the DWP constructed three new reservoirs on the aqueduct system. The Bouquet Reservoir was built to replace the ill-fated Saint Francis Dam; construction began in 1932, and by March, 1934, aqueduct water began to fill it. A second reservoir,

[35]*Los Angeles Evening Express*, November 7, 1931; Layne, *Water and Power*, p. 211.

[36]"World's Greatest Municipal Water Project Nears Construction," *Western City* 7 (January, 1931), 31. The charter member cities were Anaheim, Beverly Hills, Burbank, Colton, Glendale, Los Angeles, Pasadena, San Bernardino, San Marino, Santa Ana, and Santa Monica.

[37]Layne, *Water and Power*, pp. 218–231 passim; Raymond F. Goudey, "Engineering Outlook for Southern California," *Civil Engineering* 5 (September, 1935), 545; "Progress Report on the Mono Project by the Board of Consultants, February 1935," typescript, WB-358, Los Angeles Department of Water and Power Archives, Los Angeles; Wayne W. Wyckoff, "Progress on Thirty-Million Dollar Mono Basin Project is Reviewed." *Southwest Builder and Contractor* 94 (August 4, 1939), 18–22.

at Grant Lake in Mono County, was built to store aqueduct water on the Mono Extension.[38]

The DWP's third reservoir of the 1930's did much to remedy the long-standing controversy over water storage in Owens Valley itself. In 1935 work commenced on a 181-foot dam at the Long Valley site, the location long recognized as the key point above Owens Valley that could provide enough water for both city and valley needs. During the quarter of a century it had remained under Fred Eaton's control, the Long Valley site had become far more than the source of the feud between Eaton and Mulholland. Its construction came late—too late for Eaton and Mulholland, too late for the thousands of Owens Valley ranchers and farmers who, along with the growing city of Los Angeles, might have benefited from its strategic location.

At the time of its completion, the dam—its lake at seven miles long by three miles wide the largest reservoir in the aqueduct system—was looked to as an expression of final reconciliation between city and valley. Although the property had been under Eaton's control for almost as long as the city-valley conflict, his name was passed over when the Board of Water Commissioners considered the naming of the lake. To name the lake for Eaton would only have perpetually reminded valley residents of what might have been. Instead, the lake was dedicated to the memory of Father John J. Crowley, a Catholic priest who had devoted years to reconciling city and valley. Crowley had helped found the Inyo-Mono Associates, which encouraged the rebuilding of the valley's economy by advertising its scenic attractions to tourists, a policy also highly favored by the DWP. To promote the area's attractions, Father Crowley held such publicized activities as saying Mass atop Mount Whitney and a special 3 A.M. Mass for Catholic fishermen. Thousands of tourists came to Inyo County, breathing new life into the towns. In the spirit of reconciliation, Los Angeles in 1939 approved resale of the municipal properties (minus the water rights) back to the townspeople, disposing of almost 50 percent of its townholdings

[38]Layne, *Water and Power*, pp. 213–215, 228; Charles T. Leeds et al. to Van Norman, August 31, 1934, WB-347, Los Angeles Department of Water and Power Archives.

within five years. Tourists and visitors from Los Angeles could finally visit the valley without feeling they had to endure the hostility of the natives.[39]

Unfortunately, Crowley did not live to see his efforts realized, for in March, 1940, he was killed in an automobile accident. On October 19, 1941, the lake and dam were formally dedicated, with a bronze plaque set in a granite boulder memorializing the contributions of Father Crowley. Among the speakers at the ceremony were Van Norman, who made a few introductory remarks, and Chalfant, the newspaper publisher and author who had long fought the city. Chalfant paid tribute to the work of Father Crowley. He also recognized the completion of the dam as a possible beginning of harmonious relations at last between city and valley. "It is a promise of the end of dissensions and we welcome its implied pledge that hereafter City and eastern Sierra shall work hand in hand for upbuilding," he said. "We cannot but regret that this enterprise was not constructed long ago; there would have been less of history to forget . . . but we congratulate the builders and rejoice with them."[40]

By the end of the decade, Los Angeles citizens could with some accuracy believe that their city had indeed done much to restore amicable relations with Owens Valley and improve its municipal image. The decade had also seen significant changes for the city. To provide for its ever-increasing population—1,238,000 in 1930, up to 1,504,000 by 1940—the city had supported construction projects requiring millions upon millions of dollars in bonds. The projects on their completion provided electricity and water from distances of hundreds of miles and helped generate expansion and improvement of sewage disposal plants, storm drains, highways, and other public works. The city's industrial base likewise expanded, with new industries taking advantage of Southern California's climate and resources.

There were, as many critics were quick to point out, some

[39]Layne, *Water and Power*, p. 229; Miller, "Los Angeles and the Owens River Aqueduct," pp. 180–186; Irving Stone, "Desert Padre," *Saturday Evening Post* 216 (May 20, 1941), 9–11, 105–107; Vincent Ostrom, *Water and Politics: A Study of Water Politics and Administration in the Development of Los Angeles*, p. 136.

[40]Quoted in Layne, *Water and Power*, p. 230, and Nadeau, *Water Seekers*, p. 113, from *Inyo Register*, October 23, 1941.

shortcomings. The city's rapid transit system seemed in irreversible decline, the highways needed more planning and coordination as more and more automobiles clogged city arteries and, considering the growth of the aviation industry, the city sadly lacked a first-class airport. For most of the 1930's, the city endured a corrupt political machine, until an aroused citizenry at last voted in a reform administration.

Still, the urban growth was .impressive. "It is apparent that engineering projects are being shaped to provide a safe foundation on which to base a great expansion of industries, agricultural development, commercial enterprises, and residential areas," observed a staff member of the DWP. "Under these favorable conditions, Southern California should continue to be a very good place to live."[41] And Harvey Van Norman, firmly at the helm yielded by his famous predecessor, humbly conceded "that without the vision and foresight shown in the development of an aqueduct water supply, Los Angeles would still be a sleepy village situated in a semi-arid country, on the edge of a desert—but now transformed by the magic of water and its by-product, electricity, to the interesting metropolitan city you see before you today."[42]

Growth of Two Regions

If the controversy had truly ended at this point, on the eve of World War II, one might agree that fairy tales did have verifiable happy endings. But the controversy was no fairy tale, and reality has the disturbing but inevitable habit of moving on to newer complications. So it was that city and valley did not, as they would in a fairy tale, live happily ever after. New developments occurred, times changed. Southern California reaped the benefits of a wartime economy; the aircraft industry mushroomed out of all proportion, and servicemen visiting the city on leave mentally noted the moderate climate and open space. With the wartime boom came some unwelcome developments as well: air pollution, lack of housing, and

[41]Goudey, "Engineering Outlook for Southern California," p. 548.
[42]H. A. Van Norman, "Romance in the Development of the Los Angeles Water Supply," *Journal of the American Water Works Association* 28 (September, 1936), 1210.

strains on every public service from education to sanitation. Despite the problems, the city and its environs continued to grow, though the pace slackened as the open spaces filled up with new suburban tracts, shopping centers, apartment buildings, and, finally, condominiums. The rail transit system died, and by the 1960's the freeways governed the Angeleno life-style.

Inyo County, by contrast, did not at first reap the benefits of a hoped-for revitalization of its economy through tourism. During World War II about the only visitors Inyo County received in quantity were the Japanese and Japanese-Americans incarcerated at the Manzanar Detention Center. But in the years following the end of the war, the Inyo-Mono region's attractions soon brought visitors by the tens of thousands. Lakes were artificially stocked with fish by Los Angeles and state hatcheries, with Crowley Lake the favorite spot for anglers—up to 80,000 fishermen annually. The region also attracted hunters, hikers, sightseers, glider pilots, sky divers, devotees of ghost towns, horseback riders, boaters, water skiers, snow skiers, photographers, and many others. Construction of ski resorts, chair lifts, all-weather roads, and campgrounds boomed. The town of Bishop found 90 percent of its business generated by the recreation industry. Highway 395, completed from Los Angeles to Bishop only in 1931, by the 1960's had penetrated Mono County, sprouting dozens of motels, restaurants, gasoline stations, and other service facilities to accommodate the needs of the growing number of visitors, two-thirds of whom came from Southern California. Inyo County's population grew from a low point of 7,625 in 1940 to almost double that number in 1975, mainly in response to the growth of the recreation industry.[43]

Without question, Inyo and Mono counties prospered in many ways far beyond the hopes of the ranchers and farmers who had once dominated the region's economy. Moreover, the area—apart from the cluster of service facilities in the towns along Highway 395—escaped the smog that plagues Los Angeles almost as a curse for its urban expansion. Yet when all is said and done—when the statistics citing roads built, wages earned, and ski resorts constructed are put aside, when comparisons of revenue from service stations

[43]Miller, "Los Angeles and the Owens River Aqueduct," pp. 188–207.

as against cattle raising are not made—the fact remains that Inyo and Mono counties are economic vassals of the city of Los Angeles. Since the time when the city made its massive purchases of Owens Valley real estate, the people who called the valley their home and who remained there have found their fortunes inextricably linked with the DWP. As author Remi Nadeau has observed, the valley "is no longer the home of frontier farmers breathing the exhilarating air of self-reliance. It is a tributary province of the city it helped to build."[44]

The Dispute Continues

The city-valley relationship has been a somewhat tempestuous one since the 1940's. With the dominant personalities gone from the scene, the DWP assumed an impersonal, faceless image that minimized the dramatic conflicts of the past and replaced them with the efforts of professional bureaucrats who carried out city directives. Inyo and Mono counties' residents found the DWP and its guiding light, the Board of Water and Power Commissioners, patronizing in attitude and making policy unilaterally. Indeed, the city seemed capable of enacting new irritations whenever it seemed that long-standing grievances might at last be forgotten, or at least put aside. For example, in 1944 the Board of Water and Power Commissioners ended a policy of preference to leaseholders who wished to buy valley property, moved to a system of sealed bids, and then suspended the sales program entirely when valley residents protested the changes. This was followed by an increase in rental fees, notice of which was rather tactlessly given during Christmas week of 1944—at a point in time when the federal government was enforcing wartime rent controls. Valley protests against these actions led to a state law providing equity in questions of sales, leases, and rentals to leaseholders of city-owned property.[45]

If Owens Valley residents hoped the aqueduct and its extension to the Mono Basin would quench the city's thirst for water and power, they were disabused of such thoughts in the 1960's when the DWP built a second aqueduct to the valley. Unlike the first aque-

[44]Nadeau, *Water Seekers*, p. 113.
[45]Ostrom, *Water and Politics*, pp. 136–137.

duct, the second one was built with a minimum of publicity. DWP officials presented a logical argument for the necessity of what it called the "second barrel." California had lost a major court decision with Arizona in 1963 over the apportionment of Colorado River water; the city had to use Mono Basin waters or else risk losing its permit; Owens River–Mono Basin water would in the long run cost less; the quality of this water was higher than that of alternative sources. The Board of Water and Power Commissioners authorized the project, and in August, 1964, the DWP began construction of the second aqueduct. It was completed in 1969 at a cost of some $90 million, enriching the city's water supply by about 25 percent.[46]

For Owens Valley, the second aqueduct and the increased amount of water going to Los Angeles was the last straw. Inyo and Mono counties' residents may have found their local economy successfully transformed from agriculture to recreation, but many resented their status as an economic servant of the city. It had been the intention of the DWP to secure the additional water supplies by pumping groundwater from the northern end of Owens Valley, as it had done in the 1920's. The valley soon protested this latest expropriation of the river. Curiously, many protests against city policy were directed to the lost way of life rather than current realities. The appeals to the past carried a powerful emotional argument, which the DWP found difficult to counter. "The Owens Valley has had most of its water diverted to Los Angeles, its farmlands have shrunk, its once-bright future dimmed to an uncertain and certainly unhappy prospect," lamented Congressman Jerome Waldie in 1971, overlooking the fact that the region now derived its prime revenues from recreation.[47]

In a similar vein, T. H. Watkins, an Owens Valley partisan and at one time owner of the Chalfant Press, flatly stated in 1971 that after the completion of Crowley Lake, "Owens Valley was now a suburb of Los Angeles." Two attorneys writing in a law review

[46]Los Angeles Department of Water and Power, *The Second Los Angeles Aqueduct*.

[47]U.S. Congress, *Congressional Record—Extension of Remarks*, 92nd Cong., 1st sess., May 12, 1971, pp. E4297–98. Waldie presented an article on "The Owens Valley Transformation" sent to him by the Concerned Citizens of Owens Valley Organization.

in early 1978 considered the controversy a "tragedy," blamed the city for "improper dealings," which "are still carried on by the city," and criticized recent court decisions for capitulating "to the city's relentless pursuit of its manifest destiny." A *New West* writer in 1977 went so far as to title his article "How Green Was My Valley," reviving the conspiracy version (with an added plug for the motion picture *Chinatown*). "Writers of this persuasion represented the valley as an agricultural Garden of Eden," observes Gordon Miller, one of the few recent writers who has approached the topic with two virtues notably lacking in most accounts—willingness to do some research and some effort at objectivity. He noted that because of recreation "the valley's economic prospects were brighter than they ever could have been had it remained strictly a farming community."[48]

Owens Valley resentment over the latest intrusion led to new struggles in the 1970's, as yearnings for what might have been gave way to alarm over what was happening in the here and now. Passage of the California Environmental Quality Act in 1970 brought new complexities to the Owens Valley–Los Angeles water controversy. The Inyo County Board of Supervisors filed a lawsuit in 1973 to prevent the DWP from pumping water beyond specified limits. In order to withdraw additional water from the Owens River and Mono Basin, the DWP would have to justify the need through an environmental impact report. Its first effort was rejected as inadequate in September, 1973, by the Sacramento County Superior Court. The DWP then tried again, spending half a million dollars and three years to justify its increase in water withdrawals. Soon both sides were claiming victories as well as suffering setbacks, as injunctions, appeals, and still more injunctions were sought by the Inyoites to limit the withdrawal of water and by the DWP to permit the continuance of its operations without hindrance. "Those bastards 'bout picked this valley to bones by now, so now they're going after the marrow," complained a longtime valley resident in 1974. "Been

[48]T. H. Watkins, "The New Romans," in Robert H. Boyle, John Graves, and T. H. Watkins, *The Water Hustlers*, p. 144; David Blake Chatfield and Bruce M. Bertram, "Water Rights of the City of Los Angeles: Power-Politics and the Courts," *San Fernando Valley Law Review* 6 (Spring, 1978), 151; Ehud Yonay, "How Green Was My Valley," *New West* 2 (March 28, 1977), 21–25; Miller, "Los Angeles and the Owens River Aqueduct," pp. 266, 268.

that way all my life, bleeding this valley dry. And it's the same way now. They just never give up."[49]

The valley found new allies in an era of environmental consciousness. By the end of the 1970's the DWP again was playing the part of the villain as its policy of pumping groundwater lowered the valley's water table and its diversion of tributary streams caused the lowering of the level of Mono Lake. Valley forces derided the attitude of "neocolonialism" practiced by the city, referring to the DWP as the "Kingdom of Water and Power." They called attention to the growing list of species endangered by the gradual drying up of the valley and lake, from butterflies to bighorn sheep. In 1976 Inyo County's grand jury condemned the DWP's approach to the valley's environment. "The grand jury considers this threat a major turning point in the history of the valley," it stated, "a point so critical that the county must be willing to go all the way toward protecting the future of Owens Valley."[50]

As if to punctuate the grand jury's remarks, the diversion spillgates on the aqueduct near Lone Pine were blown up early on the morning of September 15, 1976. It was the first time in almost half a century that such violence had occurred; as in the water wars of the 1920's, law-enforcement authorities unsuccessfully searched for possible suspects.[51]

Meanwhile, the state's third district court of appeals rejected the DWP's second environmental impact report, causing the DWP to increase its use of California Water Project water at an increased cost of some $2 million yearly. The state itself was into one of the worst droughts in its history, making water scarce in all parts of the state. In taking its action, the court found it could please neither side. City and valley remained far apart on the amount of water, measured in cubic feet per second, that could be withdrawn without harming the area's environment. "Neither party can have what it

[49]*Los Angeles Times*, December 1, 1974; Tom Gorton, "Californians Are Foaming over Owens Valley Water," *Planning* 43 (June, 1977), 22.

[50]Judith Morgan and Neil Morgan, "California's Parched Oasis," *National Geographic* 149 (January, 1976), 106; *Los Angeles Times*, August 30, 1976.

[51]*Los Angeles Times*, September 16, 1976.

wants or needs," stated the court. "The needs of both must be recognized and balanced."[52]

The DWP tried again, reworking its statement in an effort to make it acceptable to the court. In November, 1978, public hearings were held in Bishop and Los Angeles on the DWP's Draft Environmental Report. Valley witnesses spent the evening in Bishop criticizing almost all the DWP points; DWP representatives, for their part, said most of the criticisms were based on distorted interpretations of the environmental report. By now the controversy had passed beyond the realm of public understanding. Both sides hired scientific consultants to interpret the impact of DWP policies in the valley, and the *Los Angeles Times*, in reporting on the dispute, found it necessary to provide readers with a glossary of technical terms.[53]

Beyond the removal of groundwater from the valley floor, there was the issue of Mono Lake. The lake, to the alarm of environmentalists, was drying up under the annual withdrawal of 300 million gallons of water from the streams that feed the lake. The drop in the water level threatened to harm the lake's brine shrimp—with adverse consequences for the migrating birds that feed on the shrimp. Los Angeles' demands on the lake, however, continued to exceed the ability of the lake to retain its level, much less allow the lake to be restored to previous natural levels. Yet how to reconcile the differing priorities?[54]

By the spring of 1979 the time seemed ripe for compromise, as anything would be preferable to the stubborn impasse. Los Angeles and Inyo County representatives labored over a compromise plan that would be acceptable to both sides. Among its provisions,

[52]Ibid., August 19, 1976. In contrast to the attitude of the *Times* in 1905, the *Times* of the 1970's periodically presented in-depth reports covering both sides of the argument, and its letters-to-the-editor section printed some severe criticisms from bitter Inyoites. See, for example, *Los Angeles Times* articles in January 23, 1973, December 1, 1974, August 30, 1976, June 26, 1977, and December 17, 1978, and letters-to-the-editor in December 30, 1974, January 22, 1975, September 23, 1976, and November 5, 1976, issues. Editorial articles of interest include William L. Kahrl, "Owens Valley Water: The Long, Bitter Fight," October 4, 1976, and "The Rape That's Not," October 26, 1976, by Louis H. Winnard, DWP general manager and chief engineer.

[53]*Los Angeles Times*, December 17, 1978.

[54]*Valley News* (Van Nuys, Calif.), June 15, 1979.

the plan offered a five-year study of water supply in Owens Valley, after which a mutually agreeable plan for future water use would be worked out. The DWP would store water obtained in wetter years for use in case of a drought period. In return, Inyo County would drop its lawsuit against the city. The amount of water to be pumped by the DWP from the underground reserves was pegged at 155 cubic feet per second (c.f.s.).

The negotiating committee released the proposal on June 22, without endorsement from itself, the city, or county governments. DWP General Manager Louis Winnard expressed cautious optimism about the proposal's chances, while Inyo County Supervisor Richard Engle confessed mixed emotions over the plan. On June 28 the Los Angeles Board of Water and Power Commissioners approved the compromise agreement. Inyo County residents, however, protested against the plan, insisting that the average rate of groundwater pumping be limited to 120 c.f.s., and even this amount met considerable dissent. In turn, the Board of Water and Power Commissioners rejected the 120 c.f.s. figure, and the truce plan collapsed.[55]

The Mono Lake controversy was no nearer solution than the groundwater dispute. The National Audubon Society, the Sierra Club, and the Mono Lake Committee, along with five other plaintiffs, sued the DWP to compel a reduction in the siphoning of water from the lake's tributary streams, charging violation of state and federal laws. With the lawsuit pending, a supervisor of Inyo National Forest, a state Department of Water Resources official, a Mono County supervisor, and officials from the state Department of Fish and Game, the U.S. Fish and Wildlife Service, and the Bureau of Land Management, tried to create a report that could recommend stabilization of the lake level. The DWP representative dissented from the task force's call for cutting back on the city's use of Mono Lake water—a position not unexpected, since the cost to the city for replacement water from the Metropolitan Water District could run at least $18 million a year.[56]

[55]*Los Angeles Times*, June 23 and 29, 1979; *Valley News*, July 20, 1979.
[56]*Valley News*, May 22 and August 10, 1979. A very active Mono Lake Committee continues to oppose DWP removal of water from the lake's tributary streams.

Summary

More than seventy-five years have passed since the beginning of the controversy, and the 1980's hold little hope for untangling the philosophical or the legal differences. The heroes and villains of an earlier age have given way to governmental agencies, the courts, and ongoing arguments over the degree of environmental impact a given area can stand.

On July 1, 1977, the citizens of the City of Los Angeles for the first time experienced government-mandated water rationing, in the face of the prolonged drought and the court-imposed limitations on water withdrawals from the aqueduct system. Angelenos found themselves taking a crash course in water conservation. The DWP provided free kits containing test materials for toilet-tank leaks, shower-head water savers, and a plastic bag for displacing water in the tank so that households would flush away fewer gallons People were urged to operate their air conditioners at higher settings and to use their dishwashers only with full loads. "Captain Hydro, Hero of Water Conservation," appeared in DWP posters and comic books to alert children to the need for conserving water. The citizens of the city cooperated in reducing per capita consumption of water; the customary glass of water disappeared from restaurant tables, to be served upon request only, accompanied by disapproving looks. Mercy was granted when the court of appeal lifted the restriction on pumping until the end of March, 1978, recognizing the city's sincere effort to practice water conservation. As it happened, in early 1978 the state again entered a wet cycle, and people could breathe a bit easier (while still being urged to retain the conservation habits acquired during the drought).[57]

The DWP could take credit for educating the public about the limitations of the natural resource most essential for the city's survival, but many citizens questioned some of the contradictions and inconsistencies that arose during the drought crisis. People conserved on water and power use, but as consumption declined so did revenue, and the DWP had to charge more to those who used less. Those

---

[57]Richard G. Lillard, *A Bridge over Troubled Waters: A Report on Four All-Day Meetings*, pp. 6–7.

who had consumed water and power prodigiously in the past found it easier to meet cutback levels than people who had long practiced conservation and had little room for reductions. There were other inequities and annoyances, too, most of them forgotten once the drought ended. However, the public view of the DWP was never again so unqualified as in earlier times of reputed efficiency and dedication.

The performance record of the DWP in operating its dozens of dams, hundreds of miles of aqueducts, and numerous distributing stations for water and power was not without its darker moments over the years. The Saint Francis Dam disaster was only an extreme worst example; occasional breakdowns on the aqueduct line, power outages, and other problems have occurred almost since the completion of the aqueduct in 1913. From time to time breaks in the aqueduct have required the efforts of large numbers of men to plug the leak. For example, a break in the covered conduit section in the rugged terrain north of Mojave, on January 7, 1950, resulted in the spillage of millions of gallons of water into the desert. The aqueduct was closed down while work crews labored to close a 100-foot gash in the conduit's side wall. The aqueduct was out of commission for almost two weeks, and over 228 million gallons of water irrigated the desert before the flow could be stopped.[58]

Then there was the Baldwin Hills Reservoir, completed in 1951 at a cost of $11 million, built to supply residents of southwestern Los Angeles. The reservoir performed its duty for a dozen years, until its sensational failure in December, 1963, when the dam crumbled, sending millions of gallons of water into a residential area and killing several people. Fortunately, advance warning helped in evacuation of the area below the reservoir after the leak was spotted. A local television station, KTLA, had the rare opportunity from its helicopter to televise the disaster-in-progress, down to the very moment the dam collapsed. After the disaster, remarkably few people could be found who had even been aware of the reservoir's existence.[59] A similar evacuation was made necessary in Feb-

[58]Layne, *Water and Power*, pp. 308–310.
[59]Russ Leadabrand, "The Day the Dam Broke." *American Forests* 70 (February, 1964), 30–33.

ruary, 1971, following the Sylmar earthquake, although in this instance the DWP could claim a higher authority was more directly responsible for the crack in the Van Norman Dam.

With the DWP's modern image somewhat tarnished by current environmental controversies, it is regrettable that so little of its actual history is known to the general public. Apart from the relatively few old-timers who date back to the early years of the century, citizens of Los Angeles have little historical understanding of how things got the way they are. Books that deal with the history of the city's water-resource development and the sacrifice of Owens Valley and that attempt some degree of historical objectivity are depressingly few in number, far exceeded by the torrent of polemical books and articles that perpetuate myths and distortions. Since the release of the motion picture *Chinatown* in 1974, a disturbingly large segment of the public has come to accept a movie version of its history, which bears little resemblance to the truth.

This book has attempted to reconstruct the truth of the Owens Valley–Los Angeles water controversy's origins in terms of the men who lived through the era. Central to the controversy was the role played by Joseph Barlow Lippincott, seen even now as a corrupt government official.[60] As has been shown in this book, Lippincott was the unwitting victim of later historiographical distortions that ignored or omitted the actual progress of events. In fact Lippincott was answerable to his superior for his decision to recommend termination of the proposed Owens Valley reclamation project. Far from whitewashing the Reclamation Service, the Department of the Interior ordered an investigation into Lippincott's conduct in the Owens Valley affair, largely on the accusations of a self-interested

[60]Yonay, "How Green Was My Valley," p. 25, included a remarkable capsule history version of the controversy containing numerous factual errors and a sarcastic interpretation based on Mayo's writings. Yonay called Mulholland a water commissioner, had Eaton as mayor of Los Angeles in 1904, and depicted Lippincott as deliberately deceiving his superiors in the Reclamation Service. Unfortunately, the distortions and errors of this account, not to mention its endorsement of the historical veracity of the motion picture *Chinatown*, received wide circulation in a popular magazine. Thus, more than seven decades after the origins of the water controversy, the issues continue to be as muddy as ever.

minor government official, Stafford Austin. This investigation included taking depositions from all parties concerned. It recommended Lippincott's dismissal from government service on charges of conflict of interest. Lippincott himself maintained that the "conflict" had perhaps occurred from poor judgment but insisted he had committed no illegal acts.

Despite the investigating officer's negative recommendation and other pressures for the engineer's dismissal, Lippincott was not fired, suspended, or otherwise compelled to resign. Secretary of the Interior Ethan A. Hitchcock, not involved politically in California affairs, took no action against Lippincott after hearing his personal appeal. Lippincott promised to end all outside work at once—in fact, had already taken measures to do so—and he agreed not to repeat the practice as long as he continued as a federal employee. His departure from government service was based partly on the attractive opportunity to work on a major project as Mulholland's chief assistant, the financial advantages of the position, and the Reclamation Service's plans to relocate its far-west headquarters. Lippincott was certainly aware of the public criticism that might occur from his taking the position, but he was also convinced that in his actions his conscience, with concessions to errors in judgment, was clear.

Accusations of conspiracy involving—to greater or lesser extent—Lippincott, Eaton, Mulholland, and the Otis-Sherman-Chandler land syndicates stem from separate and successive sources. The first of these came from Stafford Austin, a discontented federal employee who was himself involved in various land speculations. Then came Henry Lowenthal's opposition in the *Los Angeles Examiner*'s editorial pages. Lowenthal questioned the secrecy behind the obtaining of the water rights and the rapidity with which the first bond campaign was conducted; he was also unhappy over the *Times*'s breaking the pact of secrecy concerning the purchases of water options by the city. Two years later, in 1907, Samuel T. Clover's *News* revealed the connection of Otis to San Fernando Valley land, a detail Los Angeles citizens were willing to overlook in their approval of the aqueduct construction bonds. With the aqueduct almost completed, the issues were again aired before the public, this time by the Aqueduct Investigation Board in 1912, but when the smoke cleared from this latest action no evidence of illegal activities could be found. Eaton, Mulholland, and Lippincott had no part in San Fernando Valley land speculations; the evidence against Moses Sherman, the connecting link between the water board and the first land syndicate, remains circumstantial. Certainly in 1905 the San Fernando Mission Land Company did not buy the entire San Fernando Valley or any major part of it.

Remarkable as was the effort that resulted in the construction of the aqueduct, the city's vision was tragically blurred by an economic myopia where Owens Valley was concerned. Although the city needed water, it by no means needed the amount that would be coming down the aqueduct once it was finished. Mulholland argued that the city's water rights were at stake in the matter; to obtain less than what was allowed might set undesirable precedents. At the same time, not needing a storage reservoir at Long Valley in the immediate future, Mulholland ignored Owens Valley needs while ending a friendship with Eaton over the issue of how much money that reservoir site was worth.

Following ten years of relative peace, the controversy surfaced again, literally exploding in the 1920's. The city continued to link prosperity with growth and in doing so increased its control over Owens Valley land and water. Frustrated by their failure to withstand the pressures of the city, some Owens Valley residents repeatedly dynamited the aqueduct. Others sold their ranches and farms but unfortunately deposited their money in the Watterson banks. The arrest and conviction of the Watterson brothers ended valley resistance for a time, but the defeat only spurred the determination of Andrae Nordskog, the first person to examine Reclamation Service records, to expose what he believed were political manipulators who gained from the city's water policies. Nordskog concluded that a massive fraud had taken place and that the "Mulholland political crowd" planned to do it again with the proposed Boulder Dam. Although his book-length manuscript "Boulder Dam in the Light of the Owens Valley Fraud" never saw print, Nordskog's distillation of it, in the form of a communication to the state legislature, came to influence the writings of Morrow Mayo, W. A. Chalfant, and generations of subsequent historians and journalists.

As has been shown, few writers on the controversy have ever bothered to trace the course of the dispute beyond Nordskog's interpretation. The emphasis has been a backward look, from the present megalopolis position of Los Angeles; conclusions about how the city acquired this status have in effect preceded exploration of the question of which other ways the city might have developed. For all their influence and power, the master architects of the city's destiny could at best plan, scheme, and speculate on the development of Los Angeles as it existed in the year 1905. They could not predict the future, but they could envision what might be accomplished within speculative parameters. It is one of the ironies of the long period encompassing the persistence of the controversy that reality came to make their visions seem modest, and their alleged villainy so large.

Bibliography

Bibliographical Note

A number of articles cited in the bibliography are from the *Graphic*, a Los Angeles weekly magazine published in the first decades of this century. So far as I know, the only complete run of this magazine is at the Los Angeles Public Library. Another rare item, the Los Angeles *Gridiron*, has been microfilmed by the Los Angeles Public Library. Although its file is incomplete, the library has the best run of the *Gridiron*. A few scattered copies are in the Haynes Collection at the University of California, Los Angeles.

The published books and articles cited in the bibliography include contemporary published writings as well as secondary studies. While many published items were utilized as documentation, as shown in the notes, other items, as described in the narrative and notes, were deficient in accuracy and objectivity. Such items are included in the bibliography to indicate the scope of the research; inclusion does not constitute an endorsement of their research value.

Unpublished Material

ARCHIVES

American Society of Civil Engineers. Personnel records. American Society of Civil Engineers, New York City.

Aqueduct clipping file. Doheny Library, University of Southern California, Los Angeles.

Austin, Mary Hunter. Austin Papers. Huntington Library, San Marino, California.

Clements, George P. Clements Papers. Special Collections Department, University of California, Los Angeles.

Haynes, John R. Haynes Papers. Government and Public Affairs Department, University of California, Los Angeles.

Knight, William H. Knight Papers. Special Collections Department, University of California, Los Angeles.

Lippincott, Joseph B. Lippincott Papers. Water Resources Center Archives, University of California, Berkeley.

————. Status of Employees, Joseph Barlow Lippincott, National Personnel Records Center (Civilian Personnel Records), St. Louis, Missouri.

Los Angeles Department of Water and Power. Archives. Los Angeles, California.

Los Angeles Public Library. California Biography File. Los Angeles, California.

Lungren, Fernand. Lungren Papers. Huntington Library, San Marino, California.

McWilliams, Carey. McWilliams Papers. Special Collections Department, University of California, Los Angeles.

Newell, Frederick H. Newell Papers. Library of Congress, Washington, D.C.

Nordskog, Andrae B. Nordskog Papers. Minnesota Historical Society, Minneapolis.

————. Nordskog Papers. Water Resources Center Archives, University of California, Berkeley.

Pardee, George C. Pardee Papers. Bancroft Library, University of California, Berkeley.

Sheffield, W. R. Correspondence. Santa Barbara City Water Department, Santa Barbara, California.

U.S. Department of the Interior. Bureau of Reclamation Papers. Record Group 115. National Archives, Washington, D.C.

MANUSCRIPTS, THESES, AND DISSERTATIONS

Brown, Leahmae. "The Development of National Policy with Respect to Water Resources." Ph.D. dissertation, University of Illinois, 1937.

Cifarelli, Anthony. "The Owens River Aqueduct and the Los Angeles Times: A Study in Early Twentieth Century Business Ethics and Journalism." Master's thesis, University of California, Los Angeles, 1969.

Davison, Stanley R. "The Leadership of the Reclamation Movement, 1875–1902." Ph.D. dissertation, University of California, Berkeley, 1951.

Eckman, James W. "The Search for Water in the South Coastal Area of Santa Barbara County." Master's thesis, University of California, Los Angeles, 1967.

Goudey, R. F. "The Role of Water Supply in the Expansion of the City of Los Angeles through Annexation." Typescript. Doheny Library, University of Southern California, Los Angeles.

Jones, William K. "The History of the Los Angeles Aqueduct." Master's thesis, University of Oklahoma, 1967.

Judge, Anna F. "Reclamation of Lands in California." Master's thesis, University of California, Berkeley, 1924.

Kleinman, Betty Mae. "Organization of the United States Bureau of Reclamation." Master's thesis, University of California, Berkeley, 1946.

Mellon, Knox, Jr. "Job Harriman: The Early and Middle Years, 1861–1912." Ph.D. dissertation, Claremont Graduate School, 1972.

Miller, Gordon R. "Los Angeles and the Owens River Aqueduct." Ph.D. dissertation, Claremont Graduate School, 1978.

Miller, Richard C. "Otis and His *Times*: The Career of Harrison Gray Otis of Los Angeles." Ph.D. dissertation, University of California, Berkeley, 1961.

Milliman, Jerome W. "The History, Organization, and Economic Problems of the Metropolitan Water District of Southern California." Ph.D. dissertation, University of California, Los Angeles, 1956.

Spriggs, Elisabeth Mathieu. "The History of the Domestic Water Supply of Los Angeles." Master's thesis, University of Southern California, 1931.

Thomas, Eleanor Pyle. "The History and Settlement of the Owens River Valley Region." Master's thesis, University of Southern California, 1934.

Wood, Richard C. "The History of the Owens Valley and the Los Angeles Water Controversy." Master's thesis, College of the Pacific, 1934.

INTERVIEWS AND ORAL HISTORY

Gemperle, Paul F. Interview. Pasadena, California, March 28, 1971.

Hedger, Harold. "Harold Hedger: Flood Control Engineer." Oral History Program, University of California, Los Angeles, 1968. Typescript.

Killion, Robert H. Interview. Reseda, California, December 28, 1972.

Mulholland, William. Interview. Van Nuys, California, March 14, 1974.

Nordskog, Mrs. Gertrude. Interview. Los Angeles, California, March 30, 1971.

Published Materials

GOVERNMENT PUBLICATIONS

Boggs, Edward M. "A Study of Water Rights on the Los Angeles River, California." In Elwood Mead, Director, *Report of Irrigation In-*

vestigations in California. U.S. Department of Agriculture, *Bulletin No. 100*, pp. 327–351. Washington, D.C.: Government Printing Office, 1901.

California. Assembly. *Journal.*

California. Joint Committee of Senate and Assembly. "Report of the Joint Committee of the Senate and Assembly Dealing with the Water Problems of the State, Submitted to the Legislature of the State of California, March 23, 1931." *Appendix to Journal of the Senate.* Sacramento: State Printing Office, 1931.

California. Senate. *Journal.*

——. Special Investigating Committee. *Report of Senate Special Investigating Committee on Water Situation in Inyo and Mono Counties.* Sacramento: State Printing Office, 1931.

Hutchins, Wells A. *The California Law of Water Rights.* Sacramento: State of California Printing Division, 1956.

Johnson, Edward, and Edward S. Cobb. *Report on the Los Angeles Aqueduct, After an Investigation Authorized by the City Council of Los Angeles.* Los Angeles: Municipal Newspaper Department, 1912.

Layne, J. Gregg. *Water and Power for a Great City: A History of the Department of Water and Power of the City of Los Angeles to December, 1950.* Los Angeles: Los Angeles Department of Water and Power, 1952.

Lee, Willis T. "Geology and Water Resources of Owens Valley, California." U.S. Department of the Interior, Geological Survey, *Water-Supply and Irrigation Paper No. 181.* Washington, D.C.: Government Printing Office, 1906.

Lippincott, Joseph B. "California Hydrography." U.S. Department of the Interior, Geological Survey, *Water-Supply and Irrigation Paper No. 81.* Washington, D.C.: Government Printing Office, 1903.

Los Angeles Aqueduct Investigation Board. *Report of the Aqueduct Investigation Board to the City Council of Los Angeles.* Los Angeles: n.p., 1912.

Los Angeles Board of Public Service Commissioners. *Complete Report on Construction of the Los Angeles Aqueduct.* Los Angeles: Department of Public Service, 1916.

——. *Reply of Board of Public Service Commissioners to the Proposal and Accompanying Documents Dated November 29, 1924, Submitted by W. W. Watterson to Los Angeles Clearing House Association.* Los Angeles: n.p., n.d.

Los Angeles Bureau of the Aqueduct. *Annual Reports to the Bureau of the Los Angeles Aqueduct to the Board of Public Works.* 7 vols. Los Angeles: Department of Public Works, 1907–1912.

Los Angeles Municipal Arts Department. *Mayors of Los Angeles.* Los Angeles: n.p., 1968.

McClure, W. F. *Report of W. F. McClure, State Engineer, Concerning the Owens Valley–Los Angeles Controversy, to Governor Friend Wm. Richardson.* Sacramento: State Printing Office, 1925.

Newell, F. H., comp. "Proceedings of the First Conference of Engineers of the Reclamation Service." U.S. Department of the Interior, Geological Survey, *Water-Supply and Irrigation Paper No. 93.* Washington, D.C.: Government Printing Office, 1904.

————. "Proceedings of Second Conference of Engineers of the Reclamation Service." U.S. Department of the Interior, Geological Survey, *Water-Supply and Irrigation Paper No. 146.* Washington, D.C.: Government Printing Office, 1905.

Quinton, J. H.; W. H. Code; and Homer Hamlin. *Report upon the Distribution of the Surplus Waters of the Los Angeles Aqueduct.* Los Angeles: Board of Water Commissioners, 1911.

U.S. *Statutes at Large.*

U.S. Congress. *Congressional Record.*

U.S. Department of the Interior. Geological Survey. *First Annual Report of the Reclamation Service.* Washington, D.C.: Government Printing Office, 1903.

————. *Second Annual Report of the Reclamation Service, 1902–3.* Washington, D.C.: Government Printing Office, 1904.

————. *Third Annual Report of the Reclamation Service, 1903–4.* Washington, D.C.: Government Printing Office, 1905.

————. *Fourth Annual Report of the Reclamation Service, 1904–5.* Washington, D.C.: Government Printing Office, 1906.

————. *Fifth Annual Report of the Reclamation Service, 1906.* Washington, D.C.: Government Printing Office, 1907.

NEWSPAPERS

Los Angeles Daily News.

Los Angeles Evening Express.

Los Angeles Examiner.

The Gridiron (Los Angeles, Calif.).

Los Angeles Herald.

Los Angeles Record.

Los Angeles Times.

Inyo Independent (Independence, Calif.).

Inyo Register (Bishop, Calif.).

Owens Valley Herald (Bishop, Calif.).

San Francisco Chronicle.

San Francisco Examiner.

Valley News (Van Nuys, Calif.).

BOOKS

Armitage, Merle. *Success Is No Accident: The Biography of William*

Paul Whitsett. Yucca Valley, Calif.: Manzanita Press, 1959.

Austin, Mary. *Earth Horizon: Autobiography*. New York: Literary Guild, 1932.

————. *The Ford*. Boston: Houghton Mifflin Company, 1917.

Ayers, James J. *Gold and Sunshine: Reminiscences of Early California*. Boston: Gorham Press, 1922.

Bean, Walton. *California: An Interpretive History*. New York: McGraw Hill, 1968.

Beck, Warren A., and David A. Williams. *California: A History of the Golden State*. Garden City, N.Y.: Doubleday, 1972.

Berger, John A. *Fernand Lungren: A Biography*. Santa Barbara: Schauer Press, 1936.

Bigger, Richard D., and James D. Kitchen. *How the Cities Grew: A Century of Municipal Independence and Expansionism in Metropolitan Los Angeles*. Los Angeles: UCLA Bureau of Governmental Research, 1952.

Bonelli, William G. *Billion Dollar Blackjack*. Beverly Hills: Civic Research Press, 1954.

Bowman, Lynn. *Los Angeles: Epic of a City*. Berkeley: Howell-North Books, 1974.

Boyle, Robert H.; John Graves; and T. H. Watkins. *The Water Hustlers*. San Francisco: Sierra Club, 1971.

Burdette, Robert J. *American Biography and Genealogy, California Edition*. 2 vols. Chicago: S. J. Lewis Publishing Company, n.d. [19–].

Caughey, John W. *California: A Remarkable State's Life History*. Englewood Cliffs, N.J.: Prentice Hall, 1970.

Chalfant, W. A. *The Story of Inyo*. Bishop, Calif.: privately printed, 1922. Rev. ed., 1933.

Chapman, Charles C. *Charles C. Chapman: The Career of a Constructive Californian*. Edited by Donald H. Pflueger. Los Angeles: Anderson, Ritchie, & Simon, 1976.

Cleland, Robert Glass. *The Cattle on a Thousand Hills: Southern California, 1850–1880*. San Marino, Calif.: Huntington Library, 1951.

Clover, Samuel T. *Constructive Californians: Men of Outstanding Ability Who Have Added Greatly to the Golden State's Prestige*. Los Angeles: Saturday Night Publishing Company, 1926.

Cooper, Edwin. *Aqueduct Empire: A Guide to Water in California, Its Turbulent History, and Its Management Today*. Glendale: Arthur H. Clark Company, 1968.

Crump, Spencer. *Ride the Big Red Cars: How Trolleys Helped Build Southern California*. Los Angeles: Crest Publications, 1962.

Cutright, Paul R. *Theodore Roosevelt: The Naturalist*. New York: Harper and Brothers, 1956.

Dictionary of American Biography. New York: Charles Scribner's Sons, 1934. *Supplement One,* 1944.

Dillon, Richard. *Humbugs and Heroes: A Gallery of California Pioneers.* Garden City, N.Y.: Doubleday, 1970.

Doyle, Helen McKnight. *Mary Austin: Woman of Genius.* New York: Gotham House, 1939.

Dumke, Glenn S. *The Boom of the Eighties in Southern California.* San Marino, Calif.: Huntington Library, 1944.

Freeman, Vernon M. *People—Land—Water: The Santa Clara Valley and Oxnard Plain, Ventura County, California.* Los Angeles: Lorrin L. Morrison, 1968.

Fremont, John C. *Memoirs of My Life.* 2 vols. New York: Belford Clarke, 1887.

Giefer, Gerald J., and Anelle McCarty Kloski, comps. *Water Resources Reports and Papers in the J. B. Lippincott Collection.* Archives Series Report No. 21. Berkeley: Water Resources Center Archives, University of California, 1970.

Gottleib, Robert, and Irene Wolt. *Thinking Big: The Story of the Los Angeles Times, Its Publishers, and Their Influence on Southern California.* New York: G. P. Putnam's Sons, 1977.

Guinn, J. M. *Historical and Biographical Record of Southern California.* Chicago: Chapman Publishing Company, 1902.

Halberstam, David. *The Powers That Be.* New York: Alfred A. Knopf, 1979.

Hancock, Ralph. *Fabulous Boulevard.* New York: Funk and Wagnalls, 1949.

Hays, Samuel P. *Conservation and the Gospel of Efficiency: The Progressive Conservation Movement, 1890–1920.* Cambridge: Harvard University Press, 1959.

Illustrated History of Los Angeles County, California. Chicago: S. J. Lewis Publishing Company, 1889.

James, George Wharton. *Reclaiming the Arid West: The Story of the United States Reclamation Service.* New York: Dodd, Mead and Company, 1917.

Kyne, Peter B. *The Long Chance.* New York: Grosset and Dunlap, 1914.

Lee, W. Storrs. *The Great California Deserts.* New York: Alfred A. Knopf, 1963.

Lillard, Richard G. *A Bridge over Troubled Waters: A Report on Four All-Day Meetings.* Los Angeles: Victor Gruen Center for Environmental Planning, 1978.

———. *Eden in Jeopardy—Man's Prodigal Meddling with His Environment: The Southern California Experience.* New York: Alfred A. Knopf, 1966.

Longstreet, Stephen. *All Star Cast: An Anecdotal History of Los Angeles.* New York: Crowell, 1977.

McGeary, M. Nelson. *Gifford Pinchot: Forester-Politician.* Princeton, N.J.: Princeton University Press, 1960.

McGroarty, John S. *California of the South: A History.* Chicago: S. J. Clarke, 1930–1935. 5 vols.

———. *Los Angeles from the Mountains to the Sea.* Chicago: American Historical Society, 1921. 3 vols.

———, ed. *History of Los Angeles County.* Chicago: American Historical Society, 1923. 3 vols.

McWilliams, Carey. *Southern California Country: An Island on the Land.* New York: Duell, Sloan & Pearce, 1946.

———. *Southern California: An Island on the Land.* Reprint ed. Salt Lake City: Peregrine Smith, 1973.

Matson, Robert William. *William Mulholland: A Forgotten Forefather.* Monograph No. 6. Stockton: Pacific Center for Western Studies, 1976.

Mayo, Morrow. *Los Angeles.* New York: Alfred A. Knopf, 1933.

Men of Achievement in the Great Southwest: A Story of Pioneer Struggles during Early Days in Los Angeles and Southern California. Los Angeles: Los Angeles Times, 1904.

Morison, Elting E., ed. *The Letters of Theodore Roosevelt.* Cambridge: Harvard University Press, 1962. 5 vols.

Moss, Frank E. *The Water Crisis.* New York: Frederick A. Praeger, Publishers, 1967.

Nadeau, Remi. *City-Makers: The Story of Southern California's First Boom, 1868–76.* 3rd ed. rev. Costa Mesa, Calif.: Trans-Anglo Books, 1965.

———. *Los Angeles: From Mission to Modern City.* New York: Longmans, Green, & Co., 1960.

———. *The Water Seekers.* Garden City, N.Y.: Doubleday, 1950. Rev. ed., Salt Lake City: Peregrine Smith, 1974.

National Cyclopaedia of American Biography. New York: James T. White & Company, 1906–.

Nava, Julian, and Bob Barger. *California: Five Centuries of Cultural Contrasts.* Beverly Hills: Glencoe Press, 1976.

Newmark, Harris. *Sixty Years in Southern California, 1853–1913.* 4th ed. rev. Los Angeles: Zeitlin and Ver Brugge, 1970.

Nordskog, Andrae B. *Spiking the Gold; Or, Who Caused the Depression . . . and the Way Out.* Los Angeles: Gridiron Publishing Company, 1932.

O'Flaherty, Joseph S. *Those Powerful Years: The South Coast and Los Angeles, 1887–1917.* Hicksville, N.Y.: Exposition Press, 1978.

O'Neill, Owen H., ed. *History of Santa Barbara County, State of Cali-*

fornia: Its People and Its Resources. Santa Barbara: Harold McLean Meier, 1939.

Ostrom, Vincent. *Water and Politics: A Study of Water Policies and Administration in the Development of Los Angeles.* Los Angeles: Haynes Foundation, 1953.

Outland, Charles F. *Man-Made Disaster: The Story of St. Francis Dam—Its Place in Southern California's Water System, Its Failure and the Tragedy of March 12 and 13, 1928, in the Santa Clara River Valley.* Glendale: Arthur H. Clark Company, 1963.

Parcher, Marie Louise, and Will C. Parcher. *Dry Ditches.* Bishop, Calif.: privately printed, 1934.

Pearce, T. M. *The Beloved House.* Caldwell: Caxton Printers, 1940.

―――. *Mary Hunter Austin.* New York: Twayne Publishers, Inc., 1965.

Pinchot, Gifford. *The Fight for Conservation.* Americana Library ed. Seattle: University of Washington Press, 1967.

Pitt, Leonard, ed. *California Controversies: Major Issues in the History of the State.* Glenview, Ill.: Scott, Foresman and Company, 1968.

―――. *The Decline of the Californios: A Social History of the Spanish-Speaking Californians, 1846–1890.* Berkeley and Los Angeles: University of California Press, 1966.

Richardson, James D., comp. *A Compilation of the Messages and Papers of the Presidents, 1789–1908.* 11 vols. Washington, D.C.: Bureau of National Literature and Art, 1909.

Robinson, John W. *Trails of the Angeles: 100 Hikes in the San Gabriels.* Berkeley: Wilderness Press, 1971.

Robinson, W. W. *Los Angeles: A Profile.* Norman: University of Oklahoma Press, 1968.

―――. *The San Fernando Valley: A Calendar of Events.* Los Angeles: Title Insurance and Trust Company, 1938.

―――. *The Story of San Fernando Valley.* Los Angeles: Title Insurance and Trust Company, 1961.

Rolle, Andrew F. *California: A History.* 3rd ed. Arlington Heights, Ill.: AHM Publishing Corporation, 1978.

Roosevelt, Theodore. *Works.* Memorial ed. 24 vols. New York: Charles Scribner's Sons, 1923–1926.

Schumacher, Genny, ed. *Deepest Valley: Guide to Owens Valley and Its Mountain Lakes, Roadsides, and Trails.* San Francisco: Sierra Club, 1962.

Smythe, William E. *The Conquest of Arid America.* Rev. ed. New York: Macmillan, 1905.

Spalding, William A. *History and Reminiscences, Los Angeles City and County, California,* 3 vols. Los Angeles: J. R. Finnell & Sons Publishing Company, 1931.

Streeter, Clarence R., ed. *Saga of Inyo County.* Bishop, Calif.: Southern Inyo American Association of Retired Persons, 1977.

Walker, Franklin. *A Literary History of Southern California.* Berkeley and Los Angeles: University of California Press, 1950.

Warne, William E. *The Bureau of Reclamation.* New York: Praeger, 1973.

Watkins, T. H. *The Grand Colorado: The Story of a River and Its Canyons.* Palo Alto: American West Publishing Company, 1969.

Weaver, John D. *El Pueblo Grande: A Nonfiction Book about Los Angeles.* Los Angeles: Ward Ritchie Press, 1973.

Wheelock, Walt. *Southern California Peaks.* Glendale: La Siesta Press, 1973.

Who's Who in California: A Biographical Directory, 1928–1929. San Francisco: Who's Who Publishing Company, 1929.

Who's Who on the Pacific Coast. Chicago: A. N. Marquis Co., 1951.

Willard, Charles Dwight. *The Herald's History of Los Angeles City.* Los Angeles: Los Angeles Herald, 1901.

Williams, Albert N. *The Water and the Power: Development of the Five Great Rivers of the West.* New York: Duell, Sloan and Pearce, 1951.

Wood, Richard Coke. *The Owens Valley and the Los Angeles Water Controversy: Owens Valley as I Knew It.* Monograph No. 1. Stockton: Pacific Center for Western Historical Studies, 1973.

Workman, Boyle. *The City That Grew.* Los Angeles: Southland Publishing Company, 1936.

PAMPHLETS

The Dynamite Holdup. Los Angeles: Department of Water and Power, n.d.

Facts Concerning the Owens Valley Reparations Claims for the Information of the People of California. Los Angeles: Department of Water and Power, n.d.

Faulkner, Frederick. *Owens Valley: Where the Trail of the Wrecker Runs.* Reprinted from *Sacramento Union* of March 28–April 2, 1927.

Kinsey, Don J. *The Romance of Water and Power.* Rev. ed. Los Angeles: Department of Water and Power, 1932.

———. *The Water Trail: The Story of Owens Valley and the Controversy Surrounding the Efforts of a Great City to Secure the Water Required to Meet the Needs of an Ever-Growing Population.* Los Angeles: Department of Water and Power, 1928.

Mono Lake and the Billion Dollar Threat to California's Water Supply. Los Angeles: Department of Water and Power, 1979.

Nordskog, Andrae B. *Communication to the California Legislature*

Relating to the Owens Valley Water Situation. Sacramento: State
Printing Office, 1931.
———. *Report of the Southwest Water League Concerning Owens
Valley.* Sacramento: State Printing Office, 1933.
Owens Valley and the Los Angeles Aqueduct. Los Angeles: Department
of Public Service, 1925.
Purcell, Gervaise; W. H. Sanders; and Frederick Finkle. *Report on
Municipally Manufactured Cements Used on Los Angeles Aqueduct
from Owens River to the San Fernando Valley, California.* Phila-
delphia: Association of American Portland Cement Manufacturers,
1912.
The Second Los Angeles Aqueduct. Los Angeles: Department of Water
and Power, 1970.
Spilman, W. T. *The Conspiracy: An Exposure of the Owens River
Water and San Fernando Land Frauds.* Los Angeles: Alembic
Club, 1912.
Van Norman, H. A. *Statement Concerning the $38,800,000 Bond Issue
of the Bureau of Water Works and Supply.* Los Angeles, 1930.
*William Mulholland, Father of the Los Angeles Municipal Water Sys-
tem.* Los Angeles: Department of Water and Power, 1939.
Whitsett, W. P. *Straight Ahead for the Owens Valley.* Van Nuys: Bank
of Van Nuys, 1924.

ARTICLES

Adamic, Louis. "Los Angeles! There She Blows!" *Outlook* 155 (August
13, 1930), 563–565.
"Andrae B. Nordskog in the Light of the Watterson Verdict." *Municipal
League of Los Angeles Bulletin* 5 (November 30, 1927), 1–2.
"Another Use for Owens River." *Graphic* 23 (September 9, 1905), 9.
"Are Government Officials Playing Fair? Some Facts about the Owens
River Valley Condition." *Irrigation Age* 24 (December, 1908), 40–
41.
"The Bad Record of the L.A. Record." *Municipal League of Los An-
geles Bulletin* 5 (April 1, 1928), 4.
Barrows, H. D. "Water for Domestic Purposes vs. Water for Irrigation."
Historical Society of Southern California. *Annual Publications* 8
(1911), 208–210.
Bates, J. Leonard. "Fulfilling American Democracy: The Conservation
Movement, 1907 to 1921." *Mississippi Valley Historical Review* 44
(June, 1957), 29–57.
Baugh, Ruth E. "Land Use Changes in the Bishop Area of Owens Valley,
California." *Economic Geography* 13 (January, 1937), 17–34.
Bently, John, and Ralph W. Miller. "Andrae Nordskog." *Jazz Monthly*
(May, 1959), 8–10.

"Better Prospects for Settlement of Owens Valley Dispute." *Engineering News-Record* 94 (May 7, 1925), 767–768.

Bies, Frank. "Glendale's Brand." *Westways* 70 (May, 1978), 40–41.

Bissell, Charles A., and F. E. Weymouth. "Arthur Powell Davis." American Society of Civil Engineers. *Transactions* 100 (1935), 1582–91.

Blanchard, C. J. "National Reclamation of Arid Lands." *Annual Report of the Smithsonian Institution, 1906* (Washington, D.C.: Government Printing Office, 1907), pp. 469–484.

———. "Redeeming the West." *Sunset* 17 (September, 1906), 207–214.

———. "Winning the West: An Account of the Marvelous Progress of Our Reclamation Service in Reclaiming the Desert." *National Geographic* 17 (February, 1906), 82–89.

Bossemeyer, George L. "The Desert Mining Region of Southern Nevada Today." *Pacific Monthly* 15 (May, 1906), 455–458.

Breed, L. C. "The Los Angeles Aqueduct." *Pacific Municipalities* 18 (July, 1908), 103–105.

Brennecke, Olga. "How Los Angeles Built the Greatest Aqueduct in the World: A Story of Interesting Municipal Activity." *Craftsman* 23 (November, 1912), 188–196.

Brown, Mora M. "Meet—Chalfant of Inyo." *Desert* 6 (April, 1943), 9–12.

"By the Way." *Graphic* 27 (June 15, 1907), 9–10.

"California's Little Civil War." *Literary Digest* 83 (December 6, 1924), 15.

Carlson, Martin E. "William E. Smythe: Irrigation Crusader." *Journal of the West* 7 (January, 1968), 41–47.

Chadwick, R. E. "The Owens Valley 'Background.'" *Municipal League of Los Angeles Bulletin* 2 (August 15, 1924), 9–10.

Chalfant, W. A. "Cerro Gordo." *Historical Society of Southern California Quarterly* 22 (June, 1940), 55–61.

———. "Charley's Butte." *Irrigation Age* 24 (December, 1908), 46–47.

Chatfield, David Blake, and Bruce M. Bertram. "Water Rights of the City of Los Angeles: Power-Politics and the Courts." *San Fernando Valley Law Review* 6 (Spring, 1978), 151–194.

"City's Dealings with Owens Valley." *Municipal League of Los Angeles Bulletin* 3 (April 30, 1926), 5–7.

"A Community that Exploits Itself." *World's Work* 7 (November, 1903), 4152–53.

"Confidence in Mulholland." *Graphic* 25 (September 29, 1906), 12.

"Congress Warned of Andrae Nordskog." *Municipal League of Los Angeles Bulletin* 5 (April 1, 1928), 5.

Criswell, Ralph L. "Water and Power Projects of the City of Los Angeles." *Pacific Municipalities* 42 (March, 1928), 77–80.

Cross, Frederick C. "My Days on the Jawbone." *Westways* 60 (May, 1968), 3–8.

Davis, Arthur Powell. "The American Desert and Its New Water Works." American Water Works Association. *Proceedings* 28 (1908), 459–469.

Dole, Arthur MacDonald. "How Los Angeles Grows." *Sunset* 16 (December, 1905), 176–188.

Dorland, C. P. "The Los Angeles River—Its History and Ownership." Historical Society of Southern California. *Annual Publications* 3 (1893), 31–35.

Douglas, Clara E. "Those Nevada Bonanzas." *Sunset* 17 (September, 1906), 258–265.

Dykstra, C. A. "Owens Valley, a Problem in Regional Planning." *Community Builder* 1 (February, 1928), 8–12.

Eaton, Fred. "The Water Controversy at Los Angeles." *California Municipalities* 1 (November, 1899), 99–106.

Eckman, James W. "The Search for Water in the South Coastal Area of Santa Barbara County." *Noticias* 13 (Summer, 1967), 1–16.

Elliott, John M. "Why Bonds Must Be Voted Speedily." *Graphic* 23 (August 19, 1905), 5–6.

Finkle, F. C. "Los Angeles Aqueduct Mistakes." *Journal of Electricity, Power and Gas* 34 (January 9, 1915), 25–28.

———. "Los Angeles' $40,000,000 White Elephant." *Irrigation Age* 30 (May, 1915), 200–202, 216.

Freeman, L. R. "Desert Irrigation in the Far West." *American Review of Reviews* 29 (March, 1904), 305–310.

Frost, Stanley. "Politics Gets the Reclamation Service." *Outlook* 134 (August 29, 1923), 666–668.

Ganoe, John T. "The Beginnings of Irrigation in the United States." *Mississippi Valley Historical Review* 25 (June, 1938), 59–78.

———. "The Origin of a National Reclamation Policy." *Mississippi Valley Historical Review* 18 (June, 1931), 34–52.

Glass, Mary Ellen. "The Newlands Reclamation Project: Years of Innocence, 1903–1907." *Journal of the West* 7 (January, 1968), 55–63.

Gorton, Tom. "Californians Are Foaming over Owens Valley Water." *Planning* 43 (June, 1977), 21–22.

Goudey, Raymond F. "Engineering Outlook for Southern California." *Civil Engineering* 5 (September, 1935), 545–548.

Gressley, Gene M. "Arthur Powell Davis, Reclamation, and the West." *Agricultural History* 42 (July, 1968), 241–257.

Guinn, J. M. "Some Early History of Owens River Valley." Historical Society of Southern California. *Annual Publications* 10 (1917), 41–47.

Hampton, Edgar Lloyd. "An Irishman Moves West." *Success* 7 (August, 1923), 28–31.

Heinly, Burt A. "The Aladdin of the Aqueduct." *Sunset* 28 (April, 1912), 465–467.

———. "An Aqueduct Two Hundred and Forty Miles Long." *Scientific American* 106 (May 25, 1912), 476.

———. "Carrying Water Through a Desert: The Story of the Los Angeles Aqueduct." *National Geographic* 21 (July, 1910), 568–596.

———. "A Combined Water-Supply, Irrigation, and Power Project." *Engineering Magazine* 38 (November, 1909), 161–174.

———. "Construction and Completion of the Los Angeles Aqueduct." *Engineering Magazine* 45 (April, 1913), 1–17.

———. "The Longest Aqueduct in the World." *Outlook* 93 (September 25, 1909), 215–220.

———. "The Los Angeles Aqueduct: Causes of Low Cost and Rapidity of Construction." *Municipal Engineering* 37 (November, 1909), 289–296.

———. "Los Angeles—A City in Business." *National Municipal Review* 3 (January, 1914), 97–102.

———. "Los Angeles' Great Aqueduct." *Moody's Magazine* 8 (November, 1909), 339–345.

———. "Municipal Progressiveness and the Los Angeles Aqueduct." *American City* 6 (April, 1912), 662–664.

———. "Restoring the Los Angeles Siphon." *Municipal Journal* 36 (May 7, 1914), 633–635.

———. "Sanitary Features of Los Angeles Aqueduct." *Municipal Journal* 40 (January 13, 1916), 35–37.

———. "Water for Millions." *Sunset* 23 (December, 1909), 631–638.

Hitchcock, Ethan A. "A New National Policy." *Independent* 54 (January 9, 1902), 71–73.

"Ho! For Owens River." *Graphic* 23 (August 19, 1905), 3, and 24 (May 5, 1906), 12–13.

Hoffman, Abraham. "Angeles Crest: The Creation of a Forest Highway System in the San Gabriel Mountains." *Southern California Quarterly* 50 (September, 1968), 309–345.

———. "Fact and Fiction in the Owens Valley Water Controversy." Los Angeles Westerners Corral, *Brand Book No. 15* (Los Angeles: The Westerners, 1978), 179–191.

———. "Joseph Barlow Lippincott and the Owens Valley Controversy: Time for Revision." *Southern California Quarterly* 54 (Fall, 1972), 239–254.

———. " 'My Father Owns Stock': Private vs. Public Control of the Los Angeles River." *Western States Jewish Historical Quarterly* 12 (January, 1980), 124–133.

———. "Origins of a Controversy: The U.S. Reclamation Service and the Owens Valley–Los Angeles Water Dispute." *Arizona and the West* 19 (Winter, 1977), 333–346.

————. Review of *The Owens Valley and the Los Angeles Water Controversy: Owens Valley as I Knew It*, by R. Coke Wood. *Arizona and the West* 16 (Spring, 1971), 70–72.

————. Review of *William Mulholland: A Forgotten Forefather*, by Robert William Matson. *Southern California Quarterly* 59 (Spring, 1977), 119–120.

Holt, L. M. "How the Reclamation Service is Robbing the Settler." *Overland Monthly*, 2nd series 50, (November, 1907), 510–512.

Hoyt, Franklyn. "The Los Angeles and Independence Railroad." *Historical Society of Southern California Quarterly* 32 (December, 1950), 293–308.

Hudanick, Andrew, Jr. "George Hebard Maxwell: Reclamation's Militant Evangelist." *Journal of the West* 14 (July, 1975), 108–121.

"Inyo County's Gesture." *Saturday Night* 7 (July 9, 1927), 3.

"Inyo County's Missionary Pleader." *Saturday Night* 7 (July 16, 1927), 3–4.

"Is the Water Board Inciting to Riot in Owens Valley?" *Municipal League of Los Angeles Bulletin* 3 (August, 1925), 4–5.

Jones, William K. "Los Angeles Aqueduct: A Search for Water." *Journal of the West* 16 (July, 1977), 5–21.

"Justice to Lippincott." *Graphic* 23 (September 23, 1905), 10–13.

Kahrl, William L. "The Politics of California Water: Owens Valley and the Los Angeles Aqueduct, 1900–1927." *California Historical Quarterly* 55 (Spring, 1976), 2–25, and (Summer, 1976), 98–120.

Layton, Edwin T. "Frederick Haynes Newell and the Revolt of the Engineers." *Midcontinent American Studies Journal* 3 (Fall, 1962), 17–26.

Leadabrand, Russ. "The Day the Dam Broke." *American Forests* 70 (February, 1964), 30–33.

————. "Dry Lake, Dry Land." *Westways* 63 (February, 1971), 14–16.

Lee, Lawrence B. "Environmental Implications of Governmental Reclamation in California." *Agricultural History* 49 (January, 1975), 223–229.

————. "William Ellsworth Smythe and the Irrigation Movement: A Reconsideration." *Pacific Historical Review* 41 (August, 1972), 289–311.

Lilley, William, and Lewis L. Gould. "The Western Irrigation Movement, 1878–1902: A Reappraisal." In *The American West: A Reorientation*. Edited by Gene M. Gressley, pp. 57–74. Laramie: University of Wyoming Publications, 1966.

Lippincott, Joseph B. "Experiments with Tufa Concrete." *Cement Era* 13 (January, 1911), 37–39.

————. "Frederick Eaton." American Society of Civil Engineers. *Transactions* 100 (1935), 1645–47.

———. "From Orange Blossoms to 'Conifers' Included in Project for Angeles Reserve Road." *Touring Topics* 11 (July, 1919), 12–15.

———. "General Outlook for Reclamation Work in California." *Forestry and Irrigation* 11 (August, 1905), 349–353.

———. "The Los Angeles Aqueduct." *American Review of Reviews* 42 (July, 1912), 65–73.

———. "Los Angeles Aqueduct." Utah Society of Engineers. *Monthly Journal* 3 (April, 1917), 89–124.

———. "Mountain Stream Characteristics of Southern California." *Out West* 23 (July, 1905), 75–82.

———. "Mulholland's Memory." *Civil Engineering* 9 (March, 1939), 199.

———. "Operations of the Reclamation Service in California." *Pacific Monthly* 16 (September, 1906), 384–391.

———. "Park Methods and Results: A Comparison of Los Angeles and Other Western Cities." *California Outlook Supplement* 11 (November 18, 1911), 3–5.

———. "The Reclamation Service in California." *Forestry and Irrigation* 10 (April, 1904), 162–169.

———. "The South Haiwee Earth Dam and Reservoir of the Los Angeles Aqueduct." *Engineering Record* 65 (February 3, 1912), 116–118.

———. "Spend Millions to Give Away Our Costly Water?" *Los Angeles Times*, April 14, 1913.

———. "Tufa Cement, as Manufactured and Used on the Los Angeles Aqueduct." American Society of Civil Engineers. *Transactions* 76 (December, 1913), 520–581.

———. "William Mulholland—Engineer, Pioneer, Raconteur." *Civil Engineering* 11 (February, 1941), 105–107, and (March, 1941), 161–164.

———. "The Yuma Project," *Out West* 20 (June, 1904), 505–518.

Lippincott, J. B., et al. "Report of the Committee of the Irrigation Division on 'A National Reclamation Policy.'" American Society of Civil Engineers. *Proceedings (Papers and Discussions)* 57 (January, 1931), 129–133.

"Lippincott's Service." *Graphic* 25 (July 7, 1906), 17.

"The Los Angeles Aqueduct Seizure—What Really Happened." *Fire and Water Engineering* 22 (December 17, 1924), 1312–13.

"Los Angeles Water Supply Question." *Municipal Engineering* 13 (September, 1897), 150–152.

Lummis, Charles F. "In the Lion's Den." *Out West* 23 (September, 1905), 279–280.

McCarthy, John R. "Water: The Story of Bill Mulholland." *Saturday Night* 45 (1937–1938). Published in 16 installments.

McDaniel, Allen B. "Frederick Haynes Newell." American Society of Civil Engineers. *Transactions* 98 (1933), 1597–1600.

McKinney, John. "Rafting down a River of Schemes." *New West* 4 (January 1, 1979), 72–74.

McWilliams, Carey. "Writers of the Western Shore." *Westways* 70 (November, 1978), 16–20.

Miller, Gordon R. "Shaping California Water Law, 1781 to 1928." *Southern California Quarterly* 55 (Spring, 1973), 9–42.

Moody, Charles Amadon. "Los Angeles and the Owens River." *Out West* 23 (October, 1905), 417–442.

Morgan, Judith, and Neil Morgan. "California's Parched Oasis." *National Geographic* 149 (January, 1976), 98–127.

Mulholland, C. "The Owens Valley Earthquake of 1872." Historical Society of Southern California. *Annual Publications* 3 (1894), 27–32.

Mulholland, William. "A Brief Historical Sketch of the Growth of the Los Angeles Water Department." *Public Service* 4 (June, 1920), 1–7.

———. "Earthquakes in Their Relation to the Los Angeles Aqueduct." *Bulletin of the Seismological Society of America* 8 (March, 1918), 13–19.

———. "History of Water Supply Development for the Metropolitan Area of Los Angeles." *Hydraulic Engineering* 4 (July, 1928), 432–433.

———. "The Municipal Water Supply of Los Angeles." *Pacific Municipalities* 32 (November, 1915), 539–544.

———. "The Proposed Aqueduct from the Colorado River." *Journal of the American Water Works Association* 17 (April, 1927), 409–416.

———. "The Straight of the Owens River Deal." *Graphic* 23 (August 5, 1905), 4–5.

———. "Water Supply of Los Angeles." *Journal of the American Water Works Association* 20 (October, 1928), 463–466.

———. "The Water Supply of Southern California." Engineers and Architects Association of Southern California. *Proceedings* 2 (1907), 113–123.

"Must Have Owens River Water." *Graphic* 26 (May 25, 1907), 4–6.

Nadeau, Remi. "The Men Who Opened the Valley." *Westways* 55 (May, 1963), 24–27.

"Nemesis for the Wattersons." *Saturday Night* 8 (November 19, 1927), 3.

Newell, F. H. "Reclamation of the Arid Public Lands." *Independent* 54 (May 22, 1902), 1243–44.

————. "The Reclamation Service." *Popular Science Monthly* 66 (December, 1904), 107–116.

————. "The Reclamation Service and the Owens Valley." *Out West* 23 (October, 1905), 454–461.

————. "The Reclamation of the West." *Annual Report of the Smithsonian Institution, 1903.* Washington, D.C.: Government Printing Office, 1904.

————. "The United States Reclamation Service in the Arid West." *Engineering News* 50 (November 26, 1903), 485–486.

————. "The Work of the Reclamation Service." *Annual Report of the Smithsonian Institution, 1904.* Washington, D.C.: Government Printing Office, 1905.

————. "Work of the Reclamation Service in California." *Forestry and Irrigation* 11 (August, 1905), 346–347.

"No Longer Headquarters." *Graphic* 25 (November 3, 1906), 21–22.

Northcutt, Orlando. "Van Norman Heads Los Angeles Water-Power Unified Department." *Pacific Municipalities* 43 (April, 1929), 169–170.

Norton, Edmund. "Politics in Los Angeles." *The Public* 14 (November 24, 1911), 1190–92.

Nowinson, David. "The Water Wizards." *Westways* 72 (March, 1980), 53–56.

"Obligation of Attorney-General." *Saturday Night* 7 (June 25, 1927), 3–4.

Oliver, Graydon. "Prosperous Condition of Owens Valley District Is Revealed by Many Vital Statistics." *Modern Irrigation* 3 (August, 1927), 25–27.

"On Duty at Mojave." *Graphic* 30 (April 10, 1909), 4.

"Out of Their Own Mouths." *Municipal League of Los Angeles Bulletin* 5 (October 31, 1927), 1–3.

Outland, Charles F. "Historic Water Division Proposals." *Ventura County Historical Society Quarterly* 5 (August, 1960), 2–17.

"Owens River." *Graphic* 29 (July 25, 1908), 5.

"Owens River Champions." *Graphic* 25 (July 7, 1906), 17.

"Owens River Investigation." *Graphic* 24 (March 17, 1906), 18–19.

"Owens River Pilgrims." *Graphic* 26 (May 4, 1907), 14–15.

"Owens River Project." *Graphic* 24 (April 21, 1906), 13–14.

"The Owens River Report." *Graphic* 26 (December 29, 1906), 10–11.

"The Owens Valley Background." *Municipal League of Los Angeles Bulletin* 2 (August 15, 1924), 10.

"The Owens Valley Controversy." *Outlook* 146 (July 13, 1927), 341–343.

"Owens Valley: Fact and Fable of a Water War." *Aqueduct* 44 (Winter/Spring, 1977), 4–9.

"The Owens Valley Situation." *Municipal League of Los Angeles Bulletin* 5 (March 1, 1928), 8.

"Position on Water Situation." *Municipal League of Los Angeles Bulletin* 2 (August 15, 1924), 12.

"Progress on Thirty-Million Dollar Mono Basin Project is Reviewed." *Southwest Builder and Contractor* 94 (August 4, 1939), 18–22.

Randau, John A. "Bringing Rivers to the People." *Westways* 60 (May, 1968), 3–8.

Richards, John R. "Owens Valley." *Municipal League of Los Angeles Bulletin* 5 (September 30, 1927), 1–2.

————. "Why Not Settle the Owens Valley Trouble?" *Municipal League of Los Angeles Bulletin* 4 (July 30, 1927), 1–2.

Ridgeway, Rick. "In Earth's Way." *Westways* 69 (May, 1977), 56–59.

"The Rivers of the West." *Electrical West* 75 (August, 1962), 344–371.

Robinson, W. W. "Myth-Making in the Los Angeles Area." *Southern California Quarterly* 45 (March, 1963), 83–94.

————. "The Rancho Story of San Fernando Valley." *Historical Society of Southern California Quarterly* 38 (September, 1956), 225–234.

Ryan, Marian L. "Los Angeles Newspapers Fight the Water War, 1924–1927." *Southern California Quarterly* 50 (June, 1968), 177–190.

"The San Fernando Valley." *Pacific Monthly* 15 (May, 1906), 583–590.

"Seven to One." *Graphic* 27 (June 8, 1907), 9.

Sherwin, Louis. "The Walrus of Moron-Land." *American Mercury* 13 (February, 1928), 190–197.

"Smith." *Graphic* 28 (April 4, 1908), 5–6.

Smith, Bertha H. "The Making of Los Angeles." *Sunset* 19 (July, 1907), 237–254.

Smith, Mary Timpe. "Growing Up with the City." *Los Angeles Times Sunday Magazine* (October 19, 1930), 5, 16.

Smythe, William E. "The Social Significance of the Owens River Project." *Out West* 23 (October, 1905), 443–453.

Socha, Max K. "Second Owens River Aqueduct Planned for Los Angeles." *Western City* 41 (June, 1965), 35–38.

"State Wins National Judgment Against Los Angeles in Owens River Valley Case." *Engineering News-Record* 143 (September 22, 1949), 12.

Stewart, William R. "A Desert City's Far Reach for Water." *World's Work* 15 (November, 1907), 9538–40.

Stone, C. H., and F. M. Eaton. "A New Analysis of the Water of Owens Lake, California." *Journal of the American Chemical Society* 28 (September, 1906), 1164–70.

Stone, Irving. "Desert Padre." *Saturday Evening Post* 216 (May 20, 1941), 9–11, 105–107.

Swift, Morrison I. "Public Purchase of the Los Angeles Water System."

Public Ownership Review 2 (August–September, 1898), 50–59.

"The Technical Staff in the Employ of the United States Government." *Engineering Record* 50 (July 9, 1904), 37.

"Three Great Projects." *Graphic* 23 (September 16, 1905), 4–6.

"To Mr. Smith." *Graphic* 28 (April 25, 1908), 6.

Twilegar, Burt I. "Mulholland's 'Pipe' Dream." *Westways* 41 (January, 1949), 16–17.

Van Norman, H. A. 'Romance in the Development of the Los Angeles Water Supply." *Journal of the American Water Works Association* 28 (September, 1936), 1205–10.

———. "Then, There Is the Great Aqueduct to Build." *Southern California Business* 8 (September, 1929), 16–17.

———. "Why Los Angeles Voted $38,800,000 for Water and How It will be Spent." *Western City* 6 (June, 1930), 17–19.

———. "William Mulholland." American Society of Civil Engineers. *Transactions* 101 (1936), 1604–08.

Van Norman, H. A., and E. A. Bayley. "Colorado River–Los Angeles Aqueduct Project." *Engineering News-Record* 100 (May 31, 1928), 850–854.

Van Valen, Nelson. "A Neglected Aspect of the Owens River Aqueduct Story: The Inception of the Los Angeles Municipal Electrical System." *Southern California Quarterly* 59 (Spring, 1977), 85–109.

Vent, Glenn A., and Herbert J. Vent. "Owens Valley, Case Study in Historical Geography and Sequent Occupance." *Pacific Historian* 16 (Spring, 1972), 61–73.

Volk, Kenneth Q. "Joseph Barlow Lippincott." American Society of Civil Engineers. *Transactions* 108 (1943), 1543–50.

"Vote for the Owens River Bonds!" *Graphic* 27 (June 8, 1907), 3–4.

W. S. B. "The Record of the Owens River Project." *Out West* 30 (April, 1909), 258–276.

"Water and Power Attract Industries." *Southern California Business* 4 (March, 1925), 12–13.

"Water Board." *Graphic* 26 (May 25, 1907), 12.

"Water under the Bridge." *Los Angeles* 20 (January, 1975), 34–35.

"Western Water Fight." *Newsweek* 91 (June 12, 1978), 49–55.

Wetmore, Charles A. "Owens River Water." *Graphic* 27 (June 8, 1907), 9.

"Who are the Knockers?" *Graphic* 23 (December 16, 1905), 8–9.

Winther, Oscar O. "The Rise of Metropolitan Los Angeles, 1870–1900." *Huntington Library Quarterly* 10 (August, 1947), 391–405.

Woehlke, Walter V. "The Rejuvenation of San Fernando." *Sunset* 32 (February, 1914), 357–366.

Wollaber, A. B. "The Owens Valley and the Los Angeles Aqueduct." *Monthly Weather Review* 38 (January, 1910), 129–132.

"Workers for the West." *Land of Sunshine* 15 (August–September, 1901), 185–187.

"World's Greatest Municipal Water Project Nears Construction." *Western City* 7 (January, 1931), 31.

Wyckoff, Wayne W. "Progress on Thirty-Million Dollar Mono Basin Project is Reviewed." *Southwest Builder and Contractor* 94 (August 4, 1939), 18–22.

Yonay, Ehud. "How Green Was My Valley." *New West* 2 (March 28, 1977), 21–25.

Index

Printed in the United States
724700003B